SILVERSTONE

The home of British motor racing

SILVERSTONE

The home of British motor racing

Chas Parker

Foreword by David Coulthard

To JP and Will, the best of companions
– for all the special memories

First published in May 2013

A catalogue record for this book is
available from the British Library

ISBN 978 085733 072 7

Library of Congress catalog card no 2012955430

Published by Haynes Publishing, Sparkford,
Yeovil, Somerset BA22 7JJ, UK
Tel: 01963 442030 Fax: 01963 440001
Int. tel: +44 1963 442030 Int. fax: +44 1963 440001
E-mail: sales@haynes.co.uk
Website: www.haynes.co.uk

Haynes North America Inc.,
861 Lawrence Drive, Newbury Park,
California 91320, USA

Printed and bound in the USA by Odcombe Press LP,
1299 Bridgestone Parkway, La Vergne, TN 37086

Jacket illustrations
Front: Ronnie Peterson (Lotus-Ford 72E) leads away at the re-start
of the 1973 British Grand Prix (*Michael Hewett*)
Rear, clockwise from top left: Jack Brabham (Brabham-Repco
BT19) leads at the 1966 *Daily Express* International Trophy race
(*LAT*); Nigel Mansell on his wasy to victory in the 1987 British
Grand Prix (*LAT*); Alberto Ascari leads Luigi Villoresi (both Maserati
4CLT/48s) in the 1948 RAC Grand Prix (*LAT*); The start of the 1983
Grand Prix International 1000km (*Author*); A 2006 aerial view of
Silverstone circuit (*LAT*)

ACKNOWLEDGEMENTS

One of the great joys about researching and writing a book of
this sort is the people you meet along the way.

Special thanks must go to Ian Titchmarsh, long-time
commentator at Silverstone, who gave up so much of his time
to assist and encourage me with the project, easing the way
from the word go and reading through the final copy for me.
Thanks must also go to Stuart Pringle and Stephanie Sykes at
the British Racing Drivers' Club for their assistance, patience
and hospitality, even allowing me to stay at the BRDC Farm
while I was rummaging through the archives – all above and
beyond the call of duty.

Mention must also be made of the *Motor Sport* digital
archive, which proved to be an invaluable research tool, a
complete set of which was kindly donated by the magazine's
editor Damien Smith. Also to Volkswagen UK for the loan of a
Passat Saloon SE 1.6 TDI 105PS to attend the 2012 Goodwood
Festival of Speed and British Grand Prix when my own car
lunched its engine.

Those others who gave freely of their time or who helped
facilitate interviews or source material include: Jim Bamber,
Derek Bell, Gordon Blackwell, Martin Brundle, Janet Cesar
(Silverstone Racing Club), David Coulthard, Norman Dewis,
Nicki Finlayson (Volkswagen UK), Emerson Fittipaldi, Wayne
Gardner, Stuart Graham, Alex Goodfellow, Mika Häkkinen,
Neville Hay, Johnny Herbert, Syd Herbert, Lord Alexander
Hesketh, Michael Hewett, Nigel Mansell, Jochen Mass, Sir
Stirling Moss, Tim Parnell, Win Percy, Richard Phillips, Barbara
Proske (Red Bull Racing), Alain Prost, Duncan Rabagliati,
Chelsea Reay, Ingo Roersch (Volkswagen Motorsport), Sir Jack
Sears, Sir Jackie Stewart, John Surtees, Katie Tyler, Ian Wagstaff,
John Watson, Mark Webber, Martin Whitmarsh, Desiré Wilson,
Kevin Wood (LAT), Gabrielle Zajacka and Liz Zettl.

And thanks also to Mark Hughes and Steve Rendle at Haynes,
for their patience when the project was running late, and their
confidence that it was worth pursuing in the first place.

Contents

Foreword

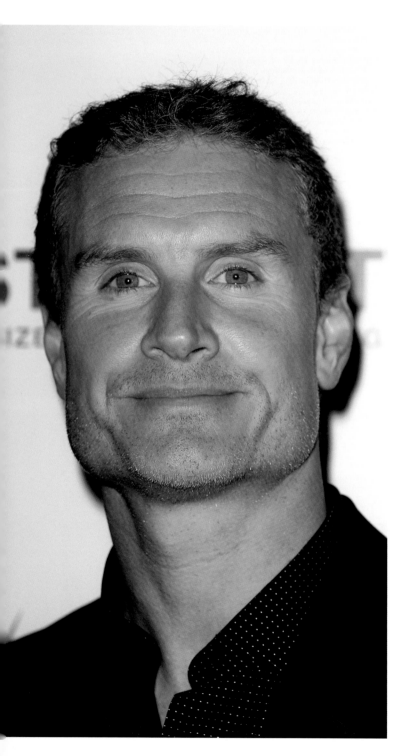

I was delighted to be asked to write the Foreword for this book because not only does Silverstone rank among my top four circuits in the world, alongside Monaco, Spa and Suzuka, but it also holds special memories for me, having twice won the British Grand Prix there.

As a Formula One driver, you always want to win your home Grand Prix, so those races were something pretty special and, as a result, Silverstone is close to my heart. Winning there was definitely one of the highlights of my career and something I know I will look back on with tremendous pride.

The circuit has a long and distinguished history: the very first race meeting held there in 1948 was a Grand Prix, and it continues today with its latest state-of-the-art facilities and the fact that it has secured the long-term future of the British Grand Prix.

Silverstone has changed a lot since I first raced there, and it still presents a great challenge for a driver, but the thing that sets it apart from other tracks to my mind is the atmosphere. Even as a young boy I could pick up on the atmosphere and the buzz that there was around the British drivers. British fans are very supportive of the home drivers, and when you see all the flags and know that they are for you, it's fantastic. To be honest though, British spectators are always really knowledgeable and appreciative of the sport, regardless of the nationality of the drivers.

I always loved the atmosphere at Silverstone and made a point of staying in my motorhome on the campsite at Grand Prix time. There's a real festival feeling about the place, because once the race has finished everyone hangs around and, if it's a fine summer's day, you can sit out on the grass having a beer and a burger and it's a great way to round off the weekend.

Silverstone and the British Racing Drivers' Club don't always get enough credit for the levels of investment they put back into the circuit, not only to improve the actual track layout, but also the facilities for the fans.

This book has been written by carefully researching the archives of the BRDC, and talking to people who have worked and raced at Silverstone over the years. It covers every significant event in the circuit's history, from its early days as a disused World War Two airfield, right up to its latest incarnation as a world-class circuit.

Silverstone certainly deserves the title 'the home of British motor racing' and I think that this book shows just why that is.

DAVID COULTHARD

Introduction

ABOVE *The BRDC Farm, which houses the Club's library and archive. (Author)*

In 2012 I attended my 42nd British Grand Prix, and if Silverstone operated a loyalty scheme of any sort then I should at least be due a free burger by now. Admittedly, only 33 of those home Grands Prix were held at the Northamptonshire track, the other nine dating back to the days when the race alternated between there and Brands Hatch in Kent.

When I first visited Silverstone in 1973, it was one of the fastest tracks on the Grand Prix calendar, second only to Monza in Italy, and that was Silverstone's trademark – a fast, swooping circuit. Woodcote was the corner which sorted the men out from the boys, and one of the iconic images of the track is of the late Ronnie Peterson sliding through the corner on the absolute limit of adhesion in his JPS Lotus-Ford 72E during qualifying for the 1973 British Grand Prix.

In those days it was still very easy to see the track's origins as a Second World War airfield (from which Wellington bombers used to operate), the huge runways remaining visible and easily identified for what they were. It was flat, largely featureless, and the wind blew across it mercilessly at times. Look at Silverstone today and it is less easy to picture its origins. The line of those runways is largely still there, but they have become camouflaged by the myriad track configurations and infrastructure that have sprung up, particularly in recent years. That wind still blows across it, though!

In 2010, the track layout was modified considerably, and grandstands and spectator banks were raised to improve the view. The following year, the new Wing pits and paddock complex was completed, and the start line was moved to its new home between Club and Abbey. With this, Silverstone had completed its transformation from wartime airfield to 21st century state-of-the-art facility, but a nice link with the past was retained in the naming of part of the new section of track – the Wellington Straight commemorating the previous incumbents of this piece of Northamptonshire.

Whilst researching this book I spent many hours – no, make that days, which became weeks – immersed in the archives of the British Racing Drivers' Club, which is housed in the old farmhouse, once occupied by legendary track manager and later chairman of Silverstone Circuits, Jimmy Brown and his family, on the inside of the circuit near Abbey Corner. Sitting in the conservatory or the library there, it was very easy to be distracted each day by the sound of racing engines as test or track days took place on the circuit. The BRDC kindly made the accommodation at the farmhouse available to me, and the Pat Fairfield room, overlooking Abbey Corner, became almost a second home.

It was partway through my research, though, that my heart sank. I came across an article in the October 1957 issue of *Motor Sport* magazine entitled 'Pity the unhappy historian'. It detailed different accounts from unnamed publications of the same event, all with differing reasons why, for example, a driver had retired, or contradicting reports of the race order at the end of the first lap. A similar column in the August 1968 issue, bemoaning the misreporting in five journals of the grid for that year's French Grand Prix, only increased my concerns. I mention this by way of apologising for any errors that may have crept into the accounts of events in this book – memories can be unreliable, but so too can contemporary reports.

There is so much history – both on and off track – associated with Silverstone that it has been difficult to fit it all in, but I can honestly say that it has been a privilege and an education to write the story of the home of British motor racing.

CHAS PARKER

ABOVE *Aerial view of the circuit taken in 2006. (LAT)*

Early Days

"After the war, knowing that people you were fond of had come back, that you weren't going to be bombed anymore, I think we rather did go over the top with relief. One had no feeling of responsibility. The worst was over, nothing else could happen. It was time to party without having at the back of one's mind what was happening on the other side of the channel."
Liz Zettl – Race Telephones

RIGHT *Oil drums mark the perimeter of the course on the wide runways, as winner Luigi Villoresi leads team-mate Alberto Ascari in their Maserati 4CLT/48s in the 1948 RAC Grand Prix. (LAT)*

Those words pretty much sum up the post-war mood of the country in the late 1940s – a sense of relief, and the feeling that life could get back to something resembling normality. Yet, there was also a desire for excitement, for thrills and spills. It was time for going motor racing again.

And it was that devil-may-care attitude which probably prompted a group of enthusiasts, led by one Maurice Geoghegan, to organise what has gone down in folklore as the first motor sporting event to be held on an old airfield at Silverstone in September 1947 – the Mutton Grand Prix.

The site had already been abandoned by the military. Indeed, its life as an operational airfield was brief, having opened in March 1943 and closed in 1946. The airfield was a base for No.17 Operational Training Unit, using the Vickers Wellington bomber and, at its peak, some 2,000 personnel were stationed there.

When the war ended, the Rootes Group leased the five hangars at the airfield for storing thousands of Hillman Minx, Sunbeam Talbot and Humber Snipe cars (together with assorted spares) intended for export. Geoghegan, who lived at 'The Quarries' in nearby Silverstone village, had obtained permission from the local manager, a Mr A. Mitchell, to use the perimeter road and runways in 1946 to test a Frazer Nash he had built.

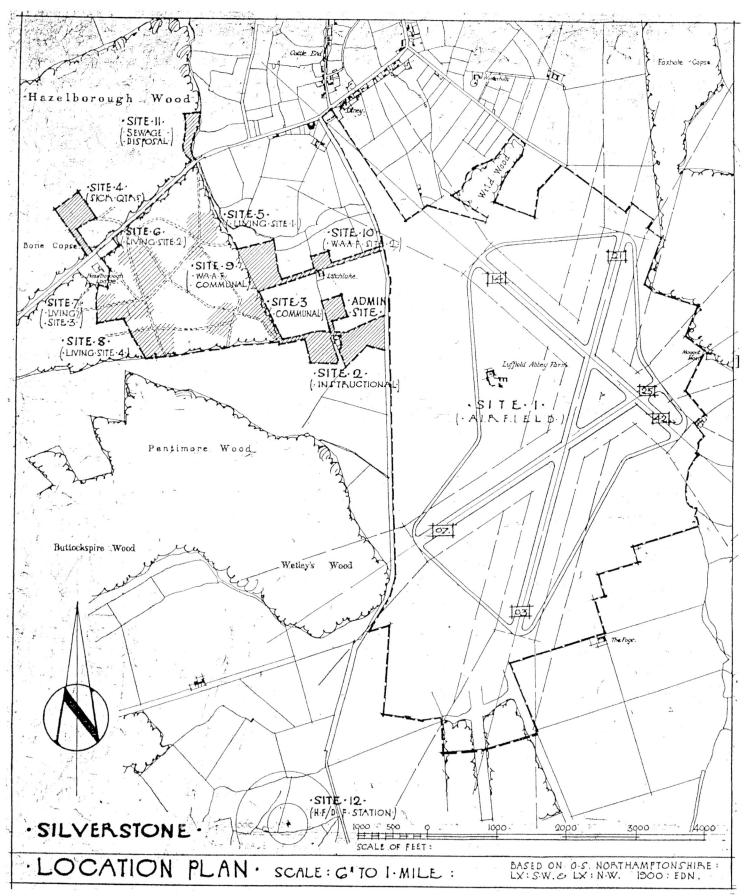

ABOVE *Map of Silverstone airfield, 1943. (BRDC)*

He devised a two-mile, roughly triangular, course running from where Club Corner now is, anticlockwise down the perimeter road to Stowe, up to Becketts and then down one of the runways to Club.

A year later, following the September 1947 Shelsley Walsh hill climb, a Frazer Nash gathering was held at the Mitre Oak at Ombersley, and an impromptu race meeting was organised for the following day at Silverstone. On the Sunday morning, some 11 cars arrived and a depot was established on the dispersal point at Maggots. According to an account in the *Chain-Gang Gazette* (the journal of the Frazer Nash Car Club) the turn from Becketts on to the runway to Club, without any markers to give a line, required "putting on sufficient steering lock and praying until some long tufts of grass appeared on the skyline to port. When negotiated satisfactorily this brought one nicely back on to the runway."

Some "considerable lappery was indulged in" and all apparently went well until Geoghegan and another driver, Peter Douglas Osborn, rounded Club quite rapidly and were confronted by a sheep. The impact was "sufficient to remove the front axle from one car" and the poor sheep ended up some way down the road, obviously dead. The event was henceforth known as the 'Mutton Grand Prix'.

Who won the race and how long it lasted is not recorded, but apparently "friendly negotiations with the sheep-owning farmer were satisfactorily concluded with the changing hands of folding money, and the party proceeded to the Saracen's Head in Towcester to refuel."

Another illicit race meeting at the airfield was attempted a month later, on 25 October 1947, when a group of racers from the 500 Club turned up at the gates of the airfield en masse, but were sent packing by the caretaker, as this account from the 500 Club's magazine *Iota* of November 1947 relates: "One of the members… said he knew the farmer who owned the land on which Silverstone airfield had been created. The farmer was sympathetic to clubs using the perimeter track and several, including the BDC (Bentley Drivers' Club) were already doing so. A date was fixed (25 October) and we set off, with cars on makeshift trailers, in convoy one Saturday morning."

What is interesting is that, according to this account, other clubs were already using the perimeter roads for impromptu meetings as well. It continues: "We arrived about 11am, dismounted the cars, started them and prepared to do a few practice laps. Before long a large chap riding a bicycle came up to us, panting somewhat, and demanded to know what we were doing. We gave the obvious explanation, emphasising that we had the farmer's permission to be there. He countered that the airfield still belonged to the Ministry. He was the caretaker and the farmer had no right to give us permission to be there; we must leave at once.

"We stood our ground until the man said he would call the police to evict us and pedalled off. We took no notice and carried on with what we were doing, but the police, a sergeant and constable, duly arrived in what was then the traditional police car, a black Wolseley resplendent with a chromed bell on the front, accompanied by the caretaker furiously pedalling alongside. The sergeant, give him his due, seeing we were a reasonably respectable bunch, listened to what we had to say and virtually pleaded with the caretaker to stretch a point and let us stay, even emphasising that we had saved our petrol rations to come all the way from Bristol and we would do no harm by driving a few laps around the airfield. But the caretaker was unmoved; we must go. Then he looked at his watch, jumped on his bike and pedalled off. It was noon.

"The sergeant then said: 'What a pity you didn't leave it a bit later to arrive, the caretaker always finishes at noon sharp on Saturdays. The other clubs come here in the afternoons and we,' indicating the constable and a space near the gate, 'often park over there and watch, thoroughly enjoying it!' He went on to say, however, that as the caretaker had asked them to evict us they had no alternative but to do so."

ABOVE *Nissen huts on the old airfield. (BRDC)*

The group then retired to the Saracen's Head, where the landlord suggested they called on Lord Hesketh (father of the current Lord who founded the Hesketh F1 team) at his nearby Easton Neston estate.

"Three of us, committee members, went to the Hall and rang the bell expecting a butler to answer it. Imagine our surprise when Lord Hesketh himself opened the door, having on several leads yapping French poodles. We explained the situation and he said: 'Come in dear boys, let's have some sherry and talk about it.'"

He then apparently produced a map of his estate and traced out a likely course, but this had to be abandoned when it was found that it crossed Watling Street. "Well, I suppose we can't close that!" he remarked. Instead, a short sprint inside Towcester horse racing course was decided upon, and a good time was had by all.

Prior to all this, another group of would-be racers had been more successful at driving round the old airfield. The road cars stored in the hangars by Rootes had caught the attention of a group of schoolboys at nearby Stowe School. As Liz Zettl, who was then assistant bursar at the school, recalled: "There was a little gang of boys at Stowe School and they were car mad, and the big hangars were all occupied by brand new cars before they went on to forecourts, and these boys knew they were there.

"The fellow on the gate happened to be the Mayor of Brackley, and these boys went up there, tipped him, and asked if they could borrow a car and try to drive round in it. 'Oh, yes of course you can, you're welcome to,' was the reply. So they took these cars out, which were supposed to be being stored, and belted round. It didn't matter if they bashed one, they just put it back and took another one.

"All was going well. They used to cycle up from Stowe and cycle back and they were enjoying themselves so much that on a Sunday they suddenly realised they were going to be late for Chapel. So they said to this fellow, 'Look, can we take one of the cars, we'll park it outside the school where it can't be seen, and we'll bring it back after Chapel?' 'Oh yes, you can do that.'

"They drove out, but Silverstone had just got a new policeman, and he took one look at the boy driving, who was obviously not 16, stopped him and asked to see his driving licence. Well, of course, the fat was in the fire then.

"Fortunately, the headmaster, Roxburgh, had a great reputation – wonderful man and headmaster – and he managed to keep it all under wraps, so it didn't get out."

Liz, together with her husband Ewald, who taught modern languages at the school, was already a car enthusiast herself, having, as she put it, "sneaked myself into Brooklands aged about 14", but the pair were in a minority at the school.

"Most of Stowe School," she said, "except for some of the boys, were very anti-Silverstone and thought it a nasty, noisy, thing. Just like my father was horrified when he found out I was going to Brooklands. He said: 'You don't want to get muddled up with that. That's a nasty, smelly sport.'"

Nasty and smelly it might have been in some people's eyes, but there were plenty of enthusiasts at the time eager to find a venue for casual motor sport in the absence of a permanent facility, since Brooklands and Donington Park, Britain's two major pre-war venues, had both fallen victim to wartime occupation.

Donington, scene of the last pre-war Grand Prix, had been requisitioned by the military and used as a vehicle depot. An approach had been made to Castle Donington Parish Council to support the early release of the circuit from the military, but at a meeting on 18 March 1948, the Parish Council decided unanimously to support proposals to make Donington a permanent vehicle depot instead.

Brooklands was in large part usable but a section had been cut out of the famous banking at Byfleet and buildings erected on the track itself. The Vickers Armstrong Company had stated that it would not only be necessary to restore the racing surface, which had deteriorated, but would involve substantial rebuilding of the track which had been destroyed by buildings. The company also said that it would not, at that time, be able to face the disorganisation of its works that would result from the removal of several substantial buildings from the track itself.

Motor racing had already returned on the Continent, where the closure of public roads for such events was not a problem. A French Grand Prix was held at Lyon as early as 21 September 1947, with another at Reims on 18 July 1948.

Britain wasn't without motor sport entirely, though, and the various clubs and enthusiasts had been quick to get things underway, organising speed trials, hill climbs and rallies. Venues such as Prescott and Shelsley Walsh had been pressed back into service for hill climbs, as had Stanmer Park in Brighton, which also hosted its annual Speed Trial along the sea front. Other speed trials took place at Poole and Bo'ness in Scotland, the 500 Club staged a series of races for its members on a 0.65-mile circuit laid out at the Blackburn Aircraft Company's aerodrome at Brough, and even Jersey had held a Junior Car Club meeting.

What was lacking was circuit racing, even though a number of motoring clubs had approached the Air Ministry for permission to use redundant airfields for this purpose. Anticipating that casual use of such airfields for motor and motorcycle racing could not be continued indefinitely, the RAC began negotiations with the Air Ministry in 1946 with the object of regularising the position before any official ban might be considered.

At that time the Ministry had already received 15 applications from motoring clubs for the use of aerodromes, and the proposal envisaged the handing over of one or more airfields to the RAC, which would be responsible, in consultation with the Ministry, for allocating these to the clubs concerned.

Progress was slow, however, and in 1947 it was reported at a meeting of the British Racing Drivers' Club (BRDC) that "prospects for racing in this country are not good as no circuit is yet available, which is more unfortunate because of the offer of the *Daily Graphic* to sponsor on a very generous scale the first post-war international race to be held in England." In April 1948 *The Autocar* reported that hundreds of propositions for racing circuits had been examined, with at least five showing promise. The perimeter track of one airfield seemed probable until opposition was expressed because of the proximity of a mental home. Another was cancelled owing to "the violent reaction" of a local landowner.

The RAC eventually narrowed the choice down to two possible airfield sites – one at Snitterfield, near Stratford-upon-Avon, and the other at Silverstone in Northamptonshire. The latter was accessible by main roads from the south and midlands alike, lying 65.5 miles from Hyde Park Corner and 5.25 miles from the nearest large town, Towcester.

On 30 June 1948, Wilfred Andrews, chairman of the RAC, announced at a meeting in London that, after months of intricate negotiations with many different departments, it had secured a one-year lease on the Silverstone site and hoped to hold an International Grand Prix there on 2 October.

The mammoth task of clearing and preparing the airfield, which was rather bleak, with many Nissen huts and pieces of aircraft and barbed wire lying around, fell to a man whose name was to become synonymous with the track for the next 40 years – Jimmy Brown. Brown was not unfamiliar with airfields, having flown as a

British Racing Drivers' Club

The British Racing Drivers' Club (BRDC) was originally conceived as a dining club by Dr Joseph Dudley Benjafield, who won Le Mans in 1927 along with S.C.H. 'Sammy' Davies in a Bentley 3-litre. It was customary for him to host regular dinners for those of his friends who were also racing drivers, the majority of whom also belonged to the Bentley team for which he drove, hence them being known as the Bentley Boys.

The club was officially formed in 1928 with the objects of promoting the interests of motor sport in general and furthering the interests of British drivers in particular, whilst at the same time extending hospitality to those from overseas.

wartime pilot with the RAF, but the task now facing him was something new. He had only two months in which to transform a redundant airfield, the centre of which was still being used for growing crops, into a suitable venue for an international motor race.

Drawing on a workforce from the local village, Brown organised the placing of 170 tons of straw bales, 250 marker tubs, 10 miles of signal wiring and 620 marshals. Uprights for the temporary bridge across the circuit only went into concrete on the Tuesday before the race, and the grandstands were still being completed on the Friday. The pits were described as rudimentary and the gents' toilet in the paddock consisted of a tent under which a hole had been dug for the men to stand around.

Tim Parnell, later a director of the BRDC but then aged just 16, was helping his father Reg, who was racing a 4CLT/48 Maserati in the main event, and he particularly remembers the pits: "They were built of scaffold tubing," he explained, "and the one thing I remember about the pits is that my father's transporter drew up alongside, and Alan Smith, who was at that time my father's mechanic but went on to become a famous engine tuner, drove the transporter into the side of the them. He caught one of the poles sticking out the side and knocked that part of the pits down. And, of course, Earl Howe (BRDC president) came up to my father and gave him such a bollocking for trying to destroy the pits."

Because the budget for the race was not sufficient to tempt the Alfa Romeo team, who were the big stars of the day, the FIA (Fédération Internationale de l'Automobile), the governing body of motor sport, wouldn't grant the title 'British Grand Prix', so it was called the RAC Grand Prix. Even so, by race day Silverstone had

Programme notes from the 1948 RAC Grand Prix

"The course has been chosen with two main aspects in view. Firstly, that the maximum possible frontage should be available to spectators, with freedom of movement to change their view at will. Secondly, that it should simulate a true road circuit in reproducing corners of varying severity and of right and left type. It is interesting to note that the perimeter track is 55ft wide at all points, and where the cars turn into a runway the width is no less than 150ft. The corners have therefore been marked or defined with the aid of straw bales and marker tubs, in order to reduce these extreme widths, which are not to be found upon normal highways, and there is no doubt that this method has given the course a true road atmosphere.

"By studying the aerial photograph of the course, it will be apparent that a number of optional circuits can be laid out at any time in the future at Silverstone, and to followers of motor sport it will also be apparent that the famous corners on many European circuits can be reproduced on this RAC Silverstone circuit.

"The present Grand Prix circuit measures 3 miles, 1,180 yards."

RIGHT *Circuit map from the 1948 RAC Grand Prix programme. (BRDC)*

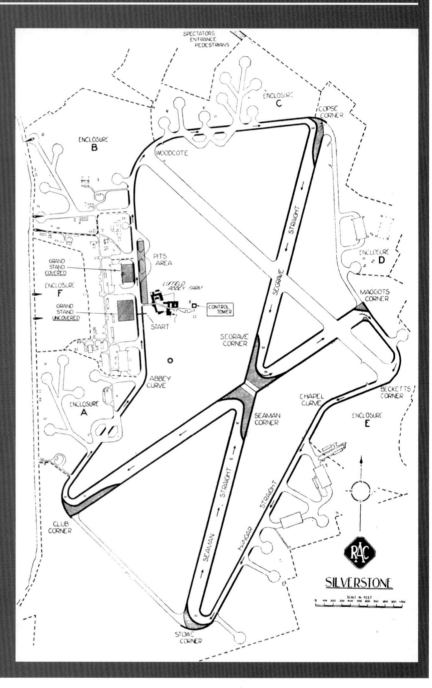

taken on all the atmosphere of a big Continental Grand Prix and, according to *Motor Sport* magazine: "A perfect sunset on the Friday evening gave way to a beautiful day on 2 October and at an early hour streams of vehicles flowed along the admirably policed and signposted routes to the new course."

The start and finish point and pit area lay between Abbey Curve and Woodcote amongst the buildings of Luffield Abbey Farm. Opposite the pits were two small structures, one of which was uncovered, serving as grandstands, while a pedestrian bridge, bearing advertisements for *The Motor*, was located over the track at the beginning of the pits, with the start line just behind it. Parking arrangements and spectator facilities were rudimentary. There was a lot of mud, but twice as many people attended as had ever turned up for a race meeting in this country before, with spectators sitting on the grass close to the track, and kept back only by a single rope. Two commentary points were in place, one at the pit area and the other at the intersection of Segrave and Seaman corners.

At 11.45am, John Cobb, the holder of the World Land Speed Record, officially opened the new circuit by driving around in a Healy Sportsmobile escorted by the three motorcycle Tourist Trophy winners of that year – Artie Bell, Freddie Frith and Maurice Cann.

The first event to be held on the circuit was the 500cc National race, 50 miles around the new track. Apparently only 19-year-old Stirling Moss and Colin Strang saw Earl Howe drop the flag, and so raced away ahead of the rest of the pack. Some of the drivers were not even in their cars, and mechanics were still on the grid. Strang led Moss at the start, but by the end of the first lap Moss in his Cooper-JAP T5 was in front. After three laps, Spike Rhiando was up to second, and when Moss retired with a loose engine drive sprocket, Rhiando in his golden Cooper-JAP T5 assumed the lead. Rhiando was actually suffering a fuel leak and being badly burned, but pressed on to win at an average speed of 60.68mph from John Cooper in his Cooper-JAP T5, with Sir Francis Samuelson, also in a JAP-powered T5, in third. Silverstone had held its first official motor race.

And so to the Grand Prix. Practice had taken place on the Thursday and Friday beforehand, and pole position had been taken by the Talbot-Lago of Louis Chiron, with Emmanuel de Graffenried's 4CL Maserati, Philippe Étançelin's Talbot, Bob Gerard's ERA R14B and Leslie Johnson's ERA E-Type joining him on the front row. Despite RAC patrols having met the Maserati team and having escorted them from the docks to the circuit, the cars of Luigi Villoresi and Alberto Ascari arrived late and missed the official practice session. They therefore had to start from the back of the grid.

Chiron led initially from Johnson's ERA, Parnell's Maserati, Étançelin and Gianfranco Comotti's Talbot but, despite starting from the back, the two Maserati 4CLT/48s of Villoresi and Ascari quickly carved their way through the field. After three laps Villoresi led from his team-mate, with Chiron a long way back in third and later to retire with gearbox problems. Villoresi eventually took the flag 14sec ahead of Ascari in an impressive one-two for Maserati, averaging 72.28mph and setting a lap record for the new circuit of 76.82mph. A popular third was the pre-war ERA of Bob Gerard.

Comparing it to a number of the Continental circuits, some described the airfield track as "flat

Description of a lap from the 1948 RAC Grand Prix programme

"The start takes place opposite Luffield Abbey Farm and below the Grandstand area, running past the two groups of pits on the right-hand side, and in about 400yds, the Woodcote Curve to the right has to be negotiated. This is a fast, gentle right-hand bend, which should produce some fine examples of high speed cornering. A fast straight follows for more than a quarter of a mile, when the sharp right-hand Copse Corner turns the driver from the perimeter track onto the main runway, entering the Segrave Straight (in honour of the late Sir Henry Segrave of motor racing fame). At the end of this straight, a sharp left-hand turn (Segrave Corner) takes the driver into another straight formed by a secondary runway, and in approximately a quarter of a mile there are two very interesting right-hand corners in close succession, viz. Maggots Corner and Becketts Corner; the first name, though a little odd sounding, is derived from a local moor bearing the name Maggots' Moor, and the second from the fact that it is very near to the site of Sir [sic] Thomas à Beckett's Chapel. Continuing, the course runs through the left-hand Chapel Curve and ahead through Hangar Straight where high speeds can be obtained prior to negotiating the difficult right-hand Stowe Corner (the nearest point to Stowe School). The driver is now on the main runway again, facing in the opposite direction and has a fast and slightly uphill run on Seaman Straight (in honour of the late Dick Seaman), where the course turns left at Seaman Corner and runs slightly downhill to the very difficult right-hand Club Corner, past the Club enclosure on a fast straight stretch, at the end of which the very deceptive left-hand Abbey Curve takes us back to the starting line."

and dull". It was also bumpy, and some of the drivers wore stomach belts. Reg Parnell was one of those caught out by the hazards of an airfield circuit. "The runway surface was pretty rough, and my father spun and hit a landing light that knocked the bottom of the petrol tank, and that's what put him out of the race," said his son Tim.

One of the other competitors was John Bolster, who went on to become a commentator and technical editor of *Autosport* magazine. Bolster drove his ERA to an impressive sixth place, and writing in 1978 on the occasion of the track's 30th anniversary, recalled one problem concerning the two opposing hairpin bends in the centre of the track. "Seaman, the left-hand hairpin, was so close to Segrave that you could see chaps coming the other way, over the straw bales," he wrote. In fact, as a result of competitors' concerns about the unsettling sight of another car hurtling towards them in the opposite direction, a canvas sheet was erected at the intersection of the two straights prior to the race.

A spectator at that very first Silverstone Grand Prix
was future British saloon car champion and British
Racing Drivers' Club president, Jack Sears. "I was
living in Sussex at the time," he recalled, "and I
went up there with some friends and we stood
just after Club Corner and watched Villoresi win in
his 4CLT/48 Maserati; and his pupil, Alberto Ascari,
finished second.

"There was a massive crowd and it took ages
to get out, but in those days we never seemed to
worry about things like that."

Attendance at that inaugural Grand Prix was
estimated at 100,000, and at the end of the event
the massive crowd invaded the track, making it
impossible to hold the prize-giving. Later, the

RAC placed on record its appreciation of those
spectators who got into the circuit without being
asked to pay but who then sportingly sent the
money to the organisers.

Motor Sport asked in its subsequent report:
"Did you encounter the Silverstone Spiders?" The
BBC did not cover itself in glory in its coverage
of the Grand Prix, the commentator apparently at
one point having stated that a Ferrari was in the
lead, when none was entered.

Less than a month after this hugely successful
inaugural meeting, the competitions committee of
the RAC decided to hold another Grand Prix the
following year, and scheduled it for 14 May 1949.
In the meantime, the various motoring clubs

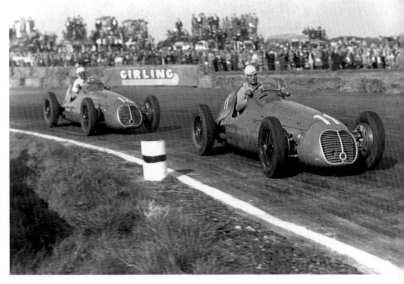

were clamouring for a chance to use the new circuit themselves. On 9 December, at the RAC's annual meeting with club delegates, Earl Howe announced that Silverstone would be available to clubs that wished to hold meetings on Saturdays, and to individuals for daily testing from Mondays to Thursdays. Clubs would have to provide all equipment but would get the services of a track manager.

The Bugatti Owners' Club was the first to hire the facilities by booking the track for a meeting to be held on 18 June. However, it was the Vintage Sports Car Club that organised the first Silverstone club meeting by holding a one-kilometre speed trial there along the main

runway on 23 April, plus a race meeting on 2 July. The Bentley Drivers' Club booked a meeting for 23 July, and the Midland Motoring Enthusiasts' Club (MMEC) hired the track for speed trials on 30 July.

Club events would be run along a 2.4-mile circuit starting on the main runway, turning right at Copse, through Maggots and Becketts to Stowe, where a sharp right hairpin took the cars back on to the main runway again. Speed trials would be run up the kilometre-long runway. With the circuit unfenced, it was decided by the RAC that the public could not be admitted to these events.

Despite all the enthusiasm for the new venue, it has to be remembered that Silverstone was in

ABOVE LEFT *The ERA R9B of Geoffrey Ansell rolled at Maggots on lap 23 of the 1948 RAC Grand Prix, throwing the driver out. Ansell escaped with only cuts and bruises. (Michael Hewett collection)*

ABOVE *Alberto Ascari leads his team-mate and eventual winner Luigi Villoresi in their Maserati 4CLT/48s in the 1948 RAC Grand Prix. (LAT)*

those days only ever regarded as a temporary measure, and at a meeting of the BRDC on 21 March 1949, the secretary reported: "Whilst by no means ideal, Silverstone provides a valuable stopgap until either Donington becomes available or some other circuit is built to replace it."

For the 1949 Grand Prix, a new course layout, using only the perimeter track and not the runways, was used, but with a second-gear chicane at Club Corner to slow the cars. The start line remained between Abbey and Woodcote but was repositioned just forward of the *Motor* pedestrian bridge and not behind it, as it had been the previous year. The circuit map from the event programme also shows that an additional South Grandstand had been constructed on the exit of Stowe, together with an East stand at the exit of Becketts Corner. No fewer than nine refreshment tents are also marked.

On 14 May, for the second time in seven months, Silverstone took on "all the atmosphere that characterises a really important international motor race", and garlands of flowers decorated the refreshment tent behind the pits. Once again, the 500cc cars opened the proceedings, with victory going to Stirling Moss in his Cooper-JAP T9 from the Norton-powered Cooper T7 of Ron 'Curly' Dryden. According to reports, everyone then had a picnic lunch before the Grand Prix itself.

TOP *Winner of the 1948 RAC Grand Prix, Luigi Villoresi in his Maserati 4CLT/48. (LAT)*

ABOVE *Villoresi takes the chequered flag to win the first-ever Grand Prix to be held at Silverstone. (LAT)*

RIGHT *Villoresi is all smiles as he wears the winner's laurels after the 1948 RAC Grand Prix. (LAT)*

The front row consisted of the previous year's winner, Luigi Villoresi, on pole in a Maserati, with Prince B. Bira's Maserati, Peter Walker's ERA, the Swiss driver Baron Emmanuel 'Toulo' de Graffenried in another Maserati and Bob Gerard's ERA, alongside him. Victory went to de Graffenried, and Gerard took a magnificent second place ahead of the 4.5-litre Talbot-Lago of Louis Rosier.

At the end, de Graffenried insisted that Gerard shared the winner's wreath with him, and many years later admitted in an interview that Silverstone was his favourite circuit. "I suppose I shouldn't say that, but I liked it because there were no trees to fly into if you went off the track," he said.

At one point, the Thin Wall Ferrari of Ken Richardson, who had taken over from Raymond Mays, hit a bump at Abbey and the car spun off the track into the spectator enclosure at Abbey Curve, injuring five people, but fortunately none of them seriously.

Another casualty of the race was John Bolster, who was again competing in his ERA and who crashed at Stowe Corner, overturned and was taken to hospital. The crash put an end to Bolster's competitive career, and writing in *Autosport* many years later he recounted: "I was driving a car which had been fitted experimentally with two-stage supercharging. The performance was immense but the extra weight up front ruined

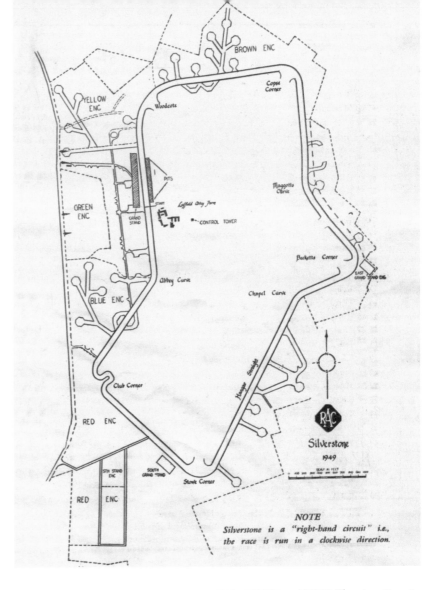

ABOVE *The circuit map from the 1949 British Grand Prix programme. (BRDC Archive)*

LEFT *The Talbot-Lago T26C of Johnny Claes leads eventual second-place finisher Bob Gerard in his ERA B-Type at the 1949 British Grand Prix. (LAT)*

ABOVE *Prince Bira and Luigi Villoresi, in their Maserati 4CLT/48s, battled hard for the lead in the early stages of the 1949 British Grand Prix before both retired. (LAT)*

RIGHT *Having retired from the 1949 British Grand Prix, Ecurie France Talbot-Lago driver Louis Chiron assumes pit-board duty. (LAT)*

the handling. I was able to retain some sort of control until just before half distance, when the emptying of the rear tank aggravated the nose-heavy condition and I brushed a straw bale at Stowe. Instantly, the car overturned, rolling on me the first time and chucking me out on the second roll. As I skated along the road, the ERA went end-over-end and pinned me to the ground. It was a very bloody accident, and as the ambulance went to the wrong corner I was left writhing in agony for 20 minutes or more, which nearly proved fatal – luckily I have always been tough."

The BBC covered the race on the radio, with Max Robertson and Murray Walker providing the commentary. Press photographers from the daily newspapers nearly went on strike as they were not allowed access to the course during the race, but were placated by being allowed into the winner's enclosure.

Meanwhile the BRDC was keen to organise an event of its own at the circuit and had been negotiating with the RAC for a proposed race on 20 August 1949. The RAC wanted 33per cent of the net receipts as its charge for the use of Silverstone, which for the type of event envisaged would amount to about £3,000. Around the same time, Tom Blackburn, general manager of Beaverbrook Newspapers, which owned the *Daily Express* and *Sunday Express*, had heard about the 100,000-strong crowd at the Grand Prix, some of whom had queued for up to six hours to get in, and decided that any sport that could draw that number of people to a disused airfield in the middle of the country was worth supporting. Basil Cardew, motoring correspondent at the *Express*, therefore arranged a meeting between Blackburn and BRDC secretary Desmond Scannell, at which it was agreed that the newspaper would underwrite the costs of a special meeting at Silverstone. The agreement was concluded with nothing more than a handshake, and thus the first *Daily Express* International Trophy, an event that was to become synonymous with Silverstone, was initiated.

The newspaper also paid for a bridge to be built across the circuit just before Woodcote Corner, enabling vehicles to gain access to the centre of the track, and on 20 August, for the second time that year, a six-figure crowd turned up for an international race meeting at the circuit, but this time with a different format from the two previous international meetings.

The programme notes read: "For the International Trophy race the Continental practice of running a race in two heats and a final has been adopted, thus providing three thrilling starts and finishes. The heats will be run over 20 laps

Press facilities

Press facilities were different in those days, as the 'Instructions for the press concerning the issue of news bulletins from Race Control' from the 1949 *Daily Express* International Trophy meeting illustrate: "Please bear in mind that the speed with which bulletins are issued depends on how fast the timekeepers can sift their data; Race Control Office, furthermore, is on the far side of the pit area, so that the sheets have to be delivered by hand.

"Long before you have your Roneo'd confirmation, the p.a. announcer, Mr Rodney Walkerley of The Motor will, of course, have given the placings and figures over the loudspeakers.

"Mr Walkerley will run through each string of names and figures twice. If passing cars drown his words both times, you can get a further recap by yelling 'REPEAT' to an official stationed at the foot of the Press section of the pit grandstand. He will instantly signal Mr Walkerley.

"Throughout the meeting, Mr Dennis May will be on your side of the track, hither-and-yonning between the open-air Press enclosure and the Press section of the stand. Please take your troubles to him."

of the 3-mile Silverstone circuit; the final being contested over 30 laps, equivalent to 90 miles."

Overall victory in the race went to the Ferrari of Alberto Ascari ahead of the Maseratis of Giuseppe Farina and Baron Emmanuel de Graffenried. The difference between racing regulations then and today is illustrated by the following incident note from heat two of the main race. "Car No.38 L Chiron (Talbot) lost his radiator cap at Maggots Curve. After retrieving the filler cap he proceeded back to his pit, refitted cap with packing, filled up radiator with water and carried on with the race." Imagine looking around on the track for a missing radiator cap while the race is in progress. Meanwhile, during the final it was reported that at 4.20pm, a marshal at Hangar Straight had found one Dachshund dog.

Another incident report, this time from the final, was of an event that marred the otherwise successful meeting: "We very much regret to announce that St JOHN HORSFALL of Dulwich, Suffolk, was fatally injured when his ERA Car No.4 crashed at Stowe Corner during the International Trophy race at Silverstone this afternoon."

The race programme for the International Trophy shows no fewer than 11 entrances into the circuit, all on the west side from Club up to Woodcote, with the exception of a single one on the north between Woodcote and Copse. Enclosures are divided into 'Red' at the south end,

The bulletin from the RAC's competitions department in July 1949, stating its case on the use of redundant airfields

"In anticipation that casual use of redundant airfields for motor and motorcycle racing could not be continued indefinitely, the Royal Automobile Club commenced negotiations with the Air Ministry in 1946 with the object of regularising the position before an official ban became a possibility.

"Whereas, at the end of the war, Ministries were prepared to view applicants for the use of airfields with sympathy, remembering that it had been Service requirements which had deprived motorists of Brooklands and Donington Park both for sport and testing purposes, it was correctly foreseen by the RAC that this state of affairs could only be a temporary one.

"Change of general conditions, the pressing of the claims of agriculture and landowners, observance of the convenience and legal rights of local residents; such difficulties alone threatened to approach the point where it became almost impossible to make an airfield available to a casual applicant such as a motor club, whilst any taxpayer had the right to ask why a profit-making event should be organised on government-owned roadways for which only a nominal rental was being charged.

"Facing this situation, the RAC asked the Air Ministry to state terms on which suitable airfields could be made permanently available for motoring sport, and expert drivers examined a large number of prospective airfield courses before Silverstone, near Towcester, was selected as the best compromise with which to test long-term use of airfields for motor racing.

"Whilst these negotiations were proceeding, the RAC did its best to encourage the Air Ministry to release various airfields for casual use by motoring clubs, but a condition of the terms upon which Silverstone was obtained was that in future no other airfields would be released except on a full-term lease to a body of adequate standing, controlled only by the RAC in order to obtain proper representation of the sport throughout Great Britain. On this basis various negotiations are still open in respect of Scotland and the North of England, and take on increasing importance as no effective advance has been made in efforts to free Donington Park.

"The RAC reluctantly decided that it was itself not able to accept the responsibility for more than one airfield until at least the success of such a circuit could be proven over a reasonable period.

"Subsequent experience has shown that airfields, where by the very nature of the layout no facilities already exist, demand the expenditure of very large sums of money to obtain a minimum standard of spectator safety and amenities and adequate control of a meeting to which the paying public is to be admitted.

"The burden of informing motor clubs that they would no longer be permitted casual use of an airfield by the Air Ministry was placed upon the RAC and, in general, clubs have appreciated and honoured this decision, which was conveyed to all interested parties in a letter dated 9 August 1948."

'Blue' between Club and Abbey, 'Green' between Abbey and Woodcote, 'Yellow' around Woodcote and 'Brown' at the north of the circuit between Woodcote and Copse. The start line was still between Abbey and Woodcote, with the pits on the inside of the circuit and a pits grandstand opposite. Two other grandstands are indicated at the south of the circuit around Stowe Corner, though the one at Becketts at the Grand Prix is not marked.

On race day, over 1,000 people were on duty and the 14 doctors and 120 St John Ambulance Brigade personnel, manning 11 first aid posts and a tented hospital, dealt with over 600 cases.

The financial breakdown for the meeting shows that, of a total gate of just £24,000, over 33per cent (amounting to £8,500) was paid in Entertainment Tax. By way of illustration, of the 25s (£1.25) paid for a pit grandstand seat, 11s 10d (59p) went in tax. Of the remaining 13s 2d (66p), an average of 6s (30p) was paid to the contractor for erecting the stand, leaving a balance of 7s 2d (36p) of the original 25s (£1.25). Despite the record crowd and the sponsorship from the *Daily Express* it meant that there was virtually nothing left when all the expenses had been met.

In August 1949 the chairman of the RAC, Wilfred Andrews, reported that, with regard to a possible long-term lease of Silverstone, the Air Ministry was to relinquish control of the land, and that it was probable that a further 12-month lease could be obtained. In December the Air Ministry agreed that the rental for 1950 for Silverstone should be £900, plus rates estimated to be around £450.

One of the last meetings to be held in 1949 was organised by SUNBAC – the Sutton Coldfield

Wellingtons at Silverstone

The Air Ministry acquired Luffield Abbey Farm, together with some adjacent farmland, in 1942 and the airstrip was constructed by John Mowlem and Co. Ltd at a cost of £1,112,565, with three runways in the standard Second World War triangle format. Each runway was 150ft wide, with the longest, at 6,000ft, running roughly north-south from where Copse Corner now is down to Stowe. Two shorter runways bisected this: one, at 3,900ft, running from Woodcote to Becketts and the other, at 4,200ft, from Becketts down to where Club Corner would be. A perimeter road, which would eventually form the layout of the circuit, ran around the outside of the runway complex.

Five large hangars were located at the airfield. Two Type T2 hangars were located on the east side of what is now the Hangar Straight, and another two on the west side of the straight between what became Abbey and Woodcote corners, opposite Luffield Abbey Farm. A third, Type B1 Hangar, was located by the perimeter road to the west of the straight between Copse and Maggots.

The airfield was opened in March 1943 as a base for No.17 Operational Training Unit, operating the Vickers Wellington bomber. The unit's role was to take airmen who had completed their basic training as pilots, navigators, bomb aimers, wireless operators and gunners to 'crew up' over a 12-week residential course and receive further training in night flying and bomb aiming exercises before joining an operational squadron and flying raids into occupied Europe. At its peak, some 2,000 personnel were stationed with the unit, and in total around 8,600 aircrew were trained at Silverstone and its satellite airfield Turweston, a few miles to the south-west.

The base was extensive and not just bounded by the perimeter roads around the runways. Hundreds of Nissen huts for administration and accommodation were located in the woods the other side of the Dadford Road, on the north-west corner of the airfield itself in an area known as the Straights. This woodland still exists, although the A43 dual carriageway cuts across its north-west corner, bisecting it from the adjacent Hazleborough Wood, where the sick quarters were housed.

Within the Straights were five living sites and one command area, plus a separate WAAF living and communal area. Outside the woods, alongside the Dadford Road, were buildings for administration and training. In total there were 41 huts housing officers' quarters, 30 sergeants' quarters and 61 airmen's barracks. All this, plus huts for training, showers, latrines, mess rooms – even tailor's, barber's and shoemaker's shops are located on the plan of the site.

The control tower was located next to Luffield Abbey Farm buildings within the perimeter road, and now houses the shower block for the BRDC (British Racing Drivers' Club) campsite.

In June 1943, 54 Wellington bombers, also known as 'Wimpies', were stationed at Silverstone. The Wellington was a twin-engine long-range aircraft, and for many years was one of the RAF's main strike bombers. It was designed by Barnes Wallis and built at Brooklands in Surrey, giving a motor sport connection to the aircraft which first flew in June 1936. Apart from the Spitfire and the Hurricane, more Wellingtons were built during the Second World War than any other British aircraft.

The Wellington, which had a wingspan of 26.26m, stood 5.31m high and was 18.54m in length, was unusual in that its geodetic design, constructed of light alloy and covered with fabric, allowed bullets to pass right through it without causing significant damage. Because of this, and the way the design distributed weight and stress in a number of directions, significant portions of it could be shot away and the aircraft would still be able to fly, unlike an aircraft with a monocoque construction.

Wellington MkICs, IIIs and Xs were stationed at Silverstone and, although used extensively by Bomber Command during the war, by 1943 they had been superseded by the Halifax and Lancaster four-engined bombers and were used predominantly for training purposes. Only two Wellingtons remain in existence; one of them, which was recovered from the bottom of Loch Ness, is at Brooklands Museum.

RAF Silverstone closed in November 1946 and was declared a 'surplus inactive station' in October 1947. On 23 September 1989, a memorial was dedicated at the old entrance to the circuit in memory of all those who had served and trained with No.17 OTU at RAF Silverstone and RAF Turweston.

Early history

If Silverstone had adopted the principle of naming parts of the circuit after significant individuals, then perhaps Malger the Monk would have featured among these.

Malger (or Mauger) was the first prior of the small Benedictine priory of Luffield, dedicated to the Virgin Mary, and built during the reign of Henry I around 1116. It was founded by Robert Bossu, Earl of Leicester, who "for the souls of William, King of England, and Queen Matilda, and Roger de Bellamont and Adeliza his wife and Robert his father, and for the health of the souls of himself and Waleran his brother, gave in alms to Malger the Monk, the servant of God, a small land".

A royal hunting lodge, eventually abandoned during the reign of Edward I, already existed in Whittlebury forest, and Henry I commanded that all the foresters of 'Whittlewode' permit the prior and monks to have "all convenient accommodation in the forest, without waste and to protect them from all injury and contumely so long as they were under his patronage".

The nearby settlement of Silson was mentioned in the Domesday book of 1086 as 'The Hamlet in the Wood' and the name Silverstone is said to be a derivation of Silvatone, or 'wood town'. Luffield is thought to mean 'lovely field', or possibly Lufa's field, and the priory's chapel of St Thomas the Martyr, dedicated to Thomas Becket, was located close to the present Chapel Corner. It is from this ecclesiastical past that the corner names of Abbey, Chapel, Becketts and Luffield originate.

The priory was acquired by Westminster Abbey in 1503, being subsequently referred to as Luffield Abbey. After the dissolution of the monasteries, ownership passed to the crown and then to various titled owners. In 1914 the Whittlebury Estate, of which Luffield Abbey Farm was part, was sold at auction. During the Second World War it was selected as the site for an airfield for Bomber Command.

and North Birmingham Automobile Club – on 3 September. One of the people taking part that day was Norman Dewis, who went on to become test driver for Jaguar. "I came here in 1949 when I built my own 500 car," he explained. "Of course, it was just a disused aerodrome and they'd made up a circuit from the main runway and the perimeter track by just putting out straw bales, and they were the markers for the corners. I've got a wonderful photograph of me coming down into Copse Corner, and there's this guy in a mac, just standing right on the apex smoking his pipe.

"In those days, we didn't bother about safety. There were no safety aspects. But that was after the war – they were good days. 500 racing was cheap because after the war we hadn't got a lot of money to spend, so we built our own race cars. On the starting line, there was myself with a Rudd engine, there was Jack Moor with a Wasp, he had a Norton engine, Wing Commander Aikens, he had his 500 with a Triumph, another one with a BSA, another one with a Scott water-cooled, and Stirling Moss in his Kieft – different cars, different makes. We built them ourselves, but it was great fun and there was good racing, very keen racing.

"The club circuit developed pretty quickly, about 18 months after the main circuit, because it suited the small cars better.

"The other interesting thing was, at the start and finish line there was just a bus, a double-decker bus. The timekeepers were in the top part of the bus, and we used to line up in front of the bus and then they would start us off by dropping the flag. That was from the word go.

"The sporting side was good because we used the centre runway as a collecting place for the cars. We used to park the cars there, like open-air pits, and if you were stuck for something – a spark plug or something else on the car – you'd walk along and a guy would say, 'Can I help you?' And you'd help each other out to make sure you were all on the start line. Sharing plugs and everything. No charge, just 'Pay me back next time or do me a favour.' That's how it was – a very good atmosphere. It was a good sport."

So, with three successful international meetings under its belt, the clubs making regular use of the facility and a further year's lease secured, prospects for Silverstone in the new decade of the 1950s looked decidedly promising.

1948

ABOVE *The grid lines up for the first-ever race at Silverstone, for 500cc cars, on 2 October 1948. Nearest the camera is the Cowlan 500 of R.L. Coward (21) alongside the Cooper-Jap T5s of race-winner Spike Rhiando (11) and Stirling Moss (5). (BRDC Archive)*

RIGHT *Villoresi (left) and Ascari celebrate their one-two finish in the 1948 RAC Grand Prix. (LAT)*

■ The first-ever race held at Silverstone circuit was the 500cc support race to the 1948 RAC Grand Prix on 2 October. The race was won by Spike Rhiando in a Cooper-JAP T5 after early leader Stirling Moss, in a similar car, retired with a loose engine drive sprocket.

■ The RAC Grand Prix produced a one-two for Maserati with Luigi Villoresi leading home his team-mate Alberto Ascari in their pair of 4CLT/48 models, despite both cars having started from the back of the grid after arriving too late for practice. Bob Gerard brought his ERA B-Type home in third place.

1949

■ Fastest time of the day at the VSCC's speed trial on 23 April was set by J.B. Norris's Alta at a time of 28.43sec.

■ The first post-war race to be awarded the title 'British Grand Prix' was held on 14 May, this time using a circuit laid out around the perimeter roads and with a chicane at Club Corner. It was won by Baron Emmanuel de Graffenried driving a 1.5-litre Maserati 4CLT/48. Bob Gerard in his 1.5 ERA B-Type was second, ahead of the 4.5 Talbot-Lago of Louis Rosier.

■ The supporting 500cc F3 race was won by Stirling Moss in his Cooper-JAP T9.

■ The first-ever club meeting at the circuit took place on 18 June, organised by the Bugatti Owners' Club. Five races were held and the 48-mile final over 20 laps was won by Ronnie Symondson in his Bugatti Type 57S. The 2.3-mile Club circuit turned right up the runway at Stowe to rejoin the full circuit at Copse Corner, and quickly became popular with club racers.

■ The Maidstone and Mid-Kent Motor Club held a meeting of nine races for racing and sports cars on 25 June.

■ The VSCC's Members' Day races on 2 July consisted of four-lap scratch races for a variety of classes, and an eight-lap '1908 GP Itala' Trophy scratch race for vintage cars, won by the Delage of Dick Habershon. A one-hour high-speed trial attracted 40 entries, although 14 non-started. The fastest average time was set by W.A.L. Cook in his 4.5-litre Bentley.

■ On 9 July the 500 Club held a series of races for its members. The 100-mile race was won by Peter Collins in his Cooper MkIII at 66.5mph, and *Motor Sport* commented: "What a godsend Silverstone is to the clubs!"

BELOW *Baron Emmanuel de Graffenried takes his Maserati 4CLT/48 to victory in the 1949 British Grand Prix. (LAT)*

ABOVE *Stirling Moss finished second in his Cooper-JAP in the 500cc event at the 1949 International Trophy meeting in August. (LAT)*

■ The Bentley Drivers' Club held a meeting on 23 July, while on 30 July the Midland Motoring Enthusiasts' Club held a meeting with both scratch and handicap races for a variety of classes.

■ The first *Daily Express* International Trophy race was held on 20 August and was run as two 20-lap heats and a 30-lap final, using the same course layout as the Grand Prix earlier in the year but omitting the unpopular chicane at Club. The first heat of the main race was won by Prince Birabongse in his Maserati 4CLT/48, with Alberto Ascari's Ferrari 125 second and the Maserati of Reg Parnell third. The second heat produced a one-two-three for Maserati with Giuseppe 'Nino' Farina winning in his 4CLT/48 ahead of Luigi Villoresi and Baron Emmanuel de Graffenried. Ferrari took the victory in the final, though, thanks to Alberto Ascari, with Farina second and de Graffenried third. The meeting was marred by the death of St John Horsfall, whose ERA crashed and flipped over the straw bales at Stowe Corner on lap 13 of the final.

■ Eric Brandon won the 500cc race in a Cooper-Norton T7 ahead of Stirling Moss's Cooper-JAP T9.

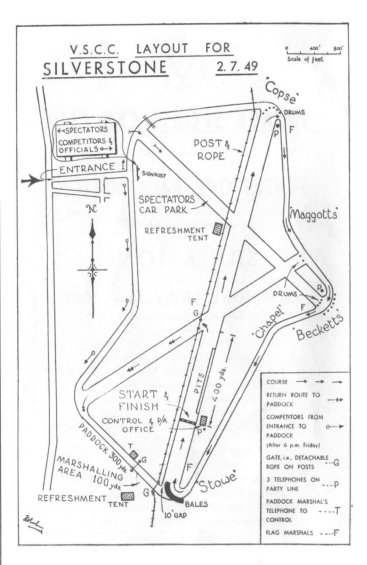

ABOVE *A map showing the layout of the Club circuit as used at the VSCC meeting in July 1949.*

■ The supporting hour-long production car race, where the cars lined up for a Le Mans-style start, was regarded by many as the race of the day. It produced a victory for Leslie Johnson in the new XK120 3.5-litre Jaguar, ahead of his team-mate Peter Walker.

■ The event included demonstrations by British record holders John Cobb, 'Goldie' Gardner and Bob Berry (bike), plus a parade of high-performance cars.

■ On 3 September, SUNBAC (Sutton Coldfield and North Birmingham Automobile Club) held a meeting comprising five races. Victory in the 500cc race went to the Cooper of Ken Carter, who also won the over 1000cc supercharged and over 1300cc unsupercharged sports car event in his Alfa Romeo.

■ The first motorcycle races at the circuit, organised by the British Motorcycle Racing Club (BMCRC), were held on 8 October.

1950s

"There was nothing approaching those early days at Silverstone... These were the days when the timekeepers occupied an old bus, and race control, helped on its way by Boy Scout volunteers, was located in an old cowshed."
Desmond Scannell, BRDC secretary

The start of the new decade heralded the creation by the sport's governing body, the FIA, of a world championship for drivers, to be contested over seven events during the year. Silverstone, having established its credentials as a suitable venue, was not only awarded the honour of hosting the inaugural race in the championship, but the event was also given the title 'Grand Prix d'Europe'. If that wasn't enough, the King and Queen accepted an invitation from the RAC to be present, the first time that a reigning monarch had attended a motor race in this country.

Fine weather greeted the record crowd, which began arriving in the car parks at 6.00am on race day, 13 May 1950. Those arriving in sports cars such as MGs, Jaguars and Rileys, were directed to exclusive car parks.

Watching archive film of that event, Silverstone looks impressive. To the right of the main straight is a long line of pit buildings, with a painted white line demarcating the pit lane. A scoreboard stands on the infield behind the pits, above which Union flags are fluttering in a stiff easterly breeze. The track is wide, its border opposite the pits marked by white painted oil drums, behind which lie two rows of straw bales, a few metres apart, and beyond those the temporary grandstands. At the

RIGHT *José Froilán González leads away in his Ferrari at the start of the 1954 British Grand Prix ahead of the Maserati 250F of Stirling Moss and the two Mercedes-Benz 196 streamliners of Juan Manuel Fangio and Karl Kling. González led the event from start to finish. (LAT)*

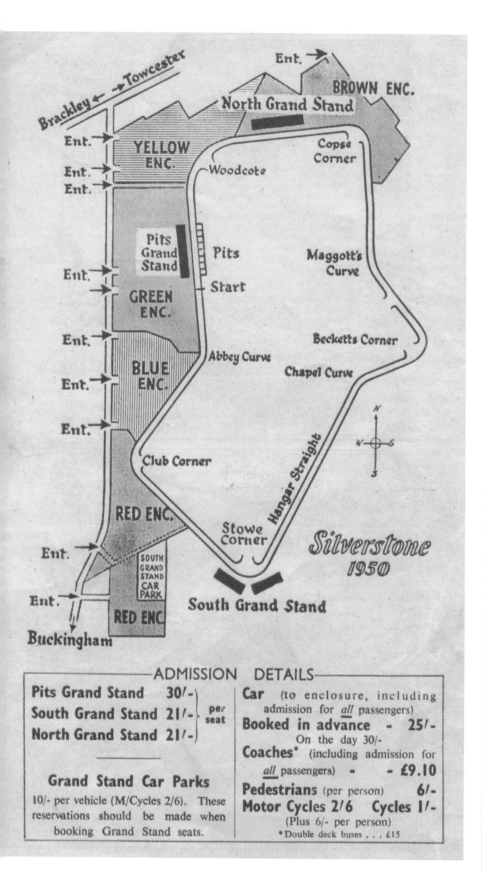

ADMISSION DETAILS

Pits Grand Stand	30/-	} per seat	
South Grand Stand	21/-		
North Grand Stand	21/-		

Grand Stand Car Parks

10/- per vehicle (M/Cycles 2/6). These reservations should be made when booking Grand Stand seats.

Car (to enclosure, including admission for *all* passengers)

Booked in advance - 25/-
On the day 30/-

Coaches* (including admission for *all* passengers) - - £9.10

Pedestrians (per person) 6/-

Motor Cycles 2/6 **Cycles** 1/-
(Plus 6/- per person)
* Double deck buses . . . £15

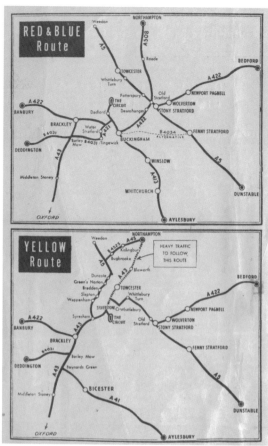

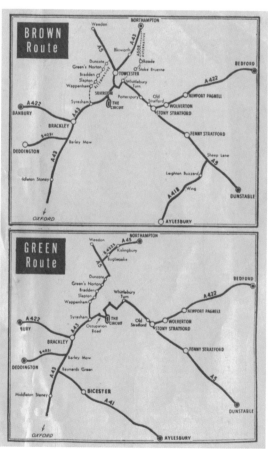

ABOVE AND RIGHT *Silverstone operated a series of colour-coded advisory routes for spectators to take, depending on which part of the country they were travelling from, taking them into specified car parks. (BRDC Archive)*

beginning of the row of pits is the pedestrian footbridge carrying sponsorship from *The Motor*, beneath which lies the start-finish line.

A wide variety of support vehicles and transporters from the likes of Alfa Romeo, Talbot-Lago, and Dunlop Racing Services fill the paddock while the four Alfa Romeo 158s, which headed the entry, sit side-by-side on the grass. All around the track are various large canvas marquees, crowds of spectators line the track and the buildings of Luffield Abbey Farm can be seen on the infield.

The track layout remained as it had for the 1949 races, except that the chicane at Club Corner had been removed and the radius of Woodcote eased. This, together with an increase in performance of the cars, resulted in a reduction in lap times of some 20sec.

The royal party, comprising King George VI and Queen Elizabeth, HRH Princess Margaret, Earl Mountbatten (in his capacity as president of the RAC) and Lady Mountbatten, had travelled in the royal train to nearby Brackley station. At 2.00pm the royal party arrived at the circuit by car and completed a tour of the track before being introduced to the drivers by Earl Howe. They then took their places in the royal box, which had been erected opposite the pits between the two grandstands, and was suitably decorated with bunting and roses and furnished with gilded chairs. From here they watched the start, before moving on to a specially constructed viewing platform, which afforded them a closer view of the racing.

TOP *The royal cars parade down the main straight prior to the 1950 Grand Prix d'Europe. (LAT)*

ABOVE *King George VI is introduced to the drivers prior to the 1950 Grand Prix d'Europe. (LAT)*

LEFT *The royal party moved from a special grandstand opposite the pits to a trackside vantage point for a closer view of the action. (LAT)*

The cars, resplendent in their national colours, were pushed from the paddock by the mechanics into the pit area, where they were lined up in echelon formation prior to setting out on the warm-up lap and then forming up on the grid. The quartet of Alfa Romeo 158s of Giuseppe 'Nino' Farina, Luigi Fagioli, Juan Manuel Fangio and Reg Parnell were on the front row, ahead of a mix of Talbot-Lagos, Maseratis, ERAs and Altas. The Union flag was raised and dropped and the field accelerated towards Woodcote Corner.

Motor Sport reported: "Earl Howe sat between the King and Queen, and as the flag was about to fall the King looked up from his programme and eagerly down towards the starting grid. As the cars roared away he appeared to be heavily interested, but the noise and the smoke took the Queen a trifle unawares as the mass start of a race does to those close to the course…"

At the end of the first lap the Alfas were already pulling away from the rest of the field in the first four places, with Farina at the front. Such was their superiority that Farina, Fagioli and Fangio took turns to lead throughout the race, before Fangio retired with a broken con-rod, and Farina led home Fagioli and Parnell.

LEFT *Juan Manuel Fangio hit a straw bale and later retired from the 1950 Grand Prix d'Europe with a broken con-rod in his Alfa Romeo 158. (LAT)*

BELOW *Fangio makes a pit stop in his Alfa Romeo 158 during the 1950 Grand Prix. The Argentinian would later retire with a broken con-rod. (LAT)*

LEFT *After 56 of the 70 laps, the scoreboard shows that the Alfa Romeos were running one-two-three-four in the 1950 Grand Prix. (LAT)*

LEFT *Giuseppe Farina takes the flag to become the first winner of a world championship Grand Prix at the 1950 Grand Prix d'Europe. (LAT)*

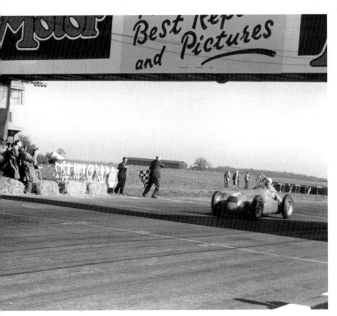

RIGHT *Farina receives the laurels after winning the first-ever world championship Grand Prix. (LAT)*

One of the perennial problems to face Silverstone over the years raised its head at that event. *Motor Sport* recorded that the congestion into and out of the circuit had caused much bad feeling, and feared it might have set back the popularity of the sport just when it had reached a new peak. The magazine stated: "The roads leading to and from the RAC's circuit are unsuited to the traffic a major race meeting now attracts. The selfishness of some users of the car parks, lack of internal organisation and poor cooperation on the part of the Buckinghamshire constabulary, added up to the unpleasant experiences of which so many racegoers still speak."

The next major meeting to take place at the circuit was the International Trophy race on 26 August, organised by the BRDC and again supported by the *Daily Express*, which put up a prize fund of £2,000. The Duke of Edinburgh attended the event and later expressed his thanks for a "most exciting and thrilling day" at Silverstone.

In *Silverstone: The Story of Britain's Fastest Circuit* by Peter Carrick, Desmond Scannell, secretary of the BRDC, recalled: "There was nothing approaching those early days at Silverstone. The public, starved of motor racing for so many years, used to arrive the night before, coming from as far as the west country and from the far north of Scotland. Gates opened at 6.00am. It was all enormous work and there were no precedents to work to, but the small corps of officials was supplemented by a mass of volunteers. These were the days when the timekeepers occupied an old bus, and race control, helped on its way by Boy Scout volunteers, was located in an old cowshed. A doctor in Towcester was co-opted to run the medical services. Straw bales were the only protective measures we had. All installations had to be temporary as there was no permanent tenancy, and for the same reason no major investment could be allocated to lavatories and similar amenities which, to be admitted, were a

BELOW *The exposed nature of the Silverstone pits can clearly be seen at the start of the one-hour International Production Car race at the 1951* Daily Express International Trophy *meeting. Earl Howe looks on as the drivers sprint towards their cars. (LAT)*

little rugged in the early days. While there appears to have been little opposition to Silverstone developing as a race circuit from the people in the village, cooperation from other sides was not always forthcoming."

One of the people working behind the scenes on the race telephones in those early days was Liz Zettl. "We were stationed originally in Jimmy Brown's chicken house, which he had had moved into the centre of the circuit for Race Control," she explained. "And we had four telephones that had been the old RAF telephones. They had a big switchboard and if anything happened, the corners came through to the switchboard and the switchboard to us, and vice versa.

"On each corner you had a little gang of people, overseen by the observer. You usually had at least two flags, at the big corners an ambulance, first aid people, crowd controllers, and there was a little hut on each corner, which was for the observer and was connected in those days to the switchboard. And if somebody spun off or anything, he would ring up and say 'race telephones', and they would put him through to us, and he would say 'number 22 spun and continued'. So, whoever took the call would write a little note and pass it down the line to whoever was doing the logbook." This logbook then formed an accurate account of every incident in the race and when it had occurred.

By the end of 1950, Silverstone was hosting many club events as well as its two big international meetings, but at the RAC's Annual Meeting of the Clubs at Pall Mall on 12 January 1951, chairman Wilfred Andrews dismissed reports that crowds for the previous year's two big meetings had been 150,000 as stated in the press, nor even 100,000. He claimed that the figure was closer to 80,000 and said that he deplored such exaggeration since the government wouldn't climb down as regards taxation whilst it thought that large paying crowds attended race meetings, so perhaps it was in his interests to keep the published figures low.

Not long afterwards, the RAC decided that it was not within its remit as the governing body of motor sport to operate a motor racing circuit and so announced that it would not be seeking to renew its lease on Silverstone when it ran out at the end of the year. Wilfred Andrews explained: "It is obviously undesirable for a governing body itself to own a course and there is the question as to whether, in the present circumstances, it is wise to organise events that might be run by other specialist clubs with greater advantage to the sport as a whole."

At the BRDC board meeting of 4 July that year, club secretary Desmond Scannell suggested that the club should endeavour to take over the circuit with some backing from the *Daily Express*. He said that it was desirable that the circuit should be leased for a minimum period of three to four years, during which time it would be possible to recoup the capital which would have to be spent on the provision of amenities.

The club pursued its new venture with enthusiasm. In August, the following proposals were agreed: to move the pits to a site around Woodcote Corner; to confine repairs or resurfacing of the track to a width of 40 feet; to erect earth banks on the corners; and to make the corners more like those to be found on a road circuit.

One of the problems that hadn't been foreseen was that of the farm, which still existed on the inside of the circuit, and of the tenant farmer, Mr G.W. Graham. At the September 1951 meeting, the secretary reported on the progress of negotiations and referred to a request from the Ministry of Agriculture that the club should agree to the tenant farmer ploughing up the Green car park. Earl Howe suggested that the Buckinghamshire police be consulted as they would not be in favour, which would strengthen the club's hand when refusing. According to the minutes of the meeting, the secretary also commented on difficulties that the RAC had experienced in dealing with the farm tenant.

Despite this, on 29 October it was announced that the club had taken over the lease from the RAC to run Silverstone. A statement read: "The Ministry of Agriculture has now agreed to re-lease to the British Racing Drivers' Club the motor racing circuit at Silverstone for a period of four years from January 1st next. The first major car event there in 1952 will be the fourth international *Daily Express* Trophy meeting scheduled for May 10th." The statement went on to say how Silverstone had become synonymous with motor racing to the British public and how it had played a big part in the development of the British sports cars that had been so outstandingly successful that year. Since it opened, Silverstone had held an average of 12 club meetings each year in which young drivers had been able to gain valuable experience.

However, negotiations with the Ministry over the details of the lease continued into early the following year, and although all outstanding problems had been cleared up, Mr Graham, the tenant farmer, had raised various matters with the Ministry regarding his own lease, which was

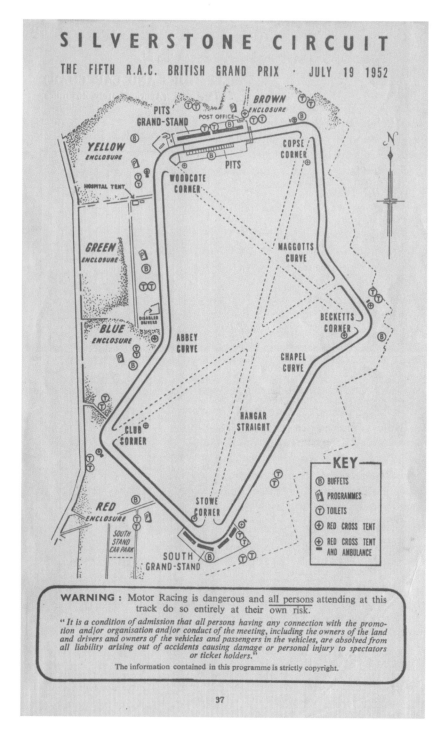

37

ABOVE *A map of the circuit taken from the programme for the 1952 British Grand Prix, showing the repositioned start-finish line. (BRDC Archive)*

and the club also agreed to engage a Mr Rose as gateman, provided he could become proficient in first aid. It was also decided that it would be desirable to obtain a suitable vehicle for use as a Fire Tender and Emergency Ambulance.

In February 1952, arrangements had been made with Mills Scaffolding to provide the race control building on a hire rental basis, but despite exhaustive enquiries it was reported that "no feasible scheme with regard to lavatories had been revealed". The cost of providing the necessary number of units was prohibitive, but it was proposed to install semi-permanent units in the pits and South Grandstand areas, at Becketts and in the paddock. It was also proposed that the pits be built in concrete with a promenade on top.

In the meantime, an invitation had been received from the RAC to organise the fifth British Grand Prix on 19 July. It was agreed to accept the invitation along with an offer of sponsorship from the *Daily Express*.

Work on improving the facilities at the circuit continued apace with the construction of spectator protection in the form of a ditch about three feet deep, one side of which would slope gently up towards the road while the other side would be vertical and surmounted by a two foot bank. By the end of April, though, construction of the lavatories and pits was behind schedule and the value of the building licence had been nearly expended. As a result, orders for the construction of the control office and two blocks of lavatories had to be cancelled, and the revised target was just to complete the work now in progress.

The banks and ditches were dug from Woodcote to Becketts, and at Stowe and Club corners. The approach into Stowe and the corner itself had been resurfaced, and while no protective barriers were being provided at Abbey, spectators were being moved back at this point.

To help fund all the work required at the circuit, Desmond Scannell had written to between 200 and 300 club members requesting an interest-free loan, the response to which had been positive. By the middle of 1952 the target figure of £5,000 in the form of loans had been reached. In addition, the expected receipts from permanent advertising had been exceeded, the total being £3,700 against an estimated £2,000.

The *Daily Express* Trophy race on 10 May was the first to utilise the permanent pits and new start-finish line, and despite poor weather it was deemed to be a success, especially since the traffic had flowed much more easily following the provision of wider access gates. It was noted, though, that the finishing line was too close to

delaying matters, as the Ministry would not grant the lease to the club until it had granted the lease to Mr Graham.

On a brighter note, it had been agreed with the *Daily Express* that the newspaper would sponsor a meeting at Silverstone in each of the next four years, and applications had been received from 15 different clubs that wanted to hold meetings on the Club circuit.

With the handover of the lease to the BRDC, Jimmy Brown was appointed track manager,

Woodcote, which was now 'blind' because of the erection of an inner bank. As a result, it was decided to move the bank back and consider moving the timekeepers and the finishing line further east. As it happened, there was insufficient time to achieve the latter before the Grand Prix in July, but the earth bank was moved back and visibility into the corner was greatly improved as a result.

By the time of the British Grand Prix on 19 July, the infrastructure had improved considerably. A map of the circuit shows the pits between Woodcote and Copse and a line of two pits grandstands located opposite. There are now four south stands at Stowe and a number of buffet outlets, Red Cross tents and toilets around the circuit. A disabled enclosure is marked on the outside just after Abbey Curve. There is even a post office located behind the pits grandstand, while ambulances are situated at Becketts, Stowe, Club and Woodcote corners.

Apart from the interest-free loans provided by members of the club (amounting to £7,500 including £2,000 from club member Harry Ferguson of tractor fame), during the year a great deal of help was also received from those sections of the motoring industry which supported racing. The Rover Car Company presented the club with a Land Rover on indefinite loan, Jaguar Cars provided an ambulance, and a second-hand two-ton Ford truck, which could be converted into a breakdown vehicle, had been provided by Mr Jack Newton.

During that first season under the BRDC, four public and 16 club meetings were staged and the short circuit was used for testing on numerous occasions. The full circuit had also been made available to Jaguar, Aston Martin and BRM. However, expenditure had greatly exceeded the original estimate and, while a reasonable profit had been made on the *Daily Express* Trophy meeting, the Grand Prix would do no better than to break even.

ABOVE *The start-finish line was moved for the 1952 season to just after Woodcote Corner. At the start of the British Grand Prix, eventual winner Alberto Ascari accelerates away in his Ferrari 500 ahead of the rest of the field. The commentator's box can be seen perched high in the distance on the outside of Woodcote. (LAT)*

ABOVE AND RIGHT

Two aerial views of Silverstone in the 1950s, with signs of its airfield heritage clearly visible in the form of dispersal points leading off from what was originally the perimeter road and is now the track. (Syd Herbert collection)

A small, but no doubt welcome, move was made in early 1953 when it was reported that Messrs Pattison Hughes had agreed to provide hot dishes in the paddock.

A problem arose from all the work done to improve the circuit, in that with the erection of pits and latrines the Northamptonshire authorities wanted to revise the rateable value of that portion of the circuit that lay within the county. The BRDC agreed to an increase of £135 per annum, rather than the £240 proposed. A considerable proportion of the increase seemed to be because of the grandstand and it was found that if it were completely dismantled after the end of each season, only part of the increase would be payable.

After the International Trophy race on 9 May 1953, John Bolster described Silverstone as: "A funny circuit, for although it looks harmless enough, it is a terror for finding out defects in roadholding." He added: "Situated as I was at the pits, I was rather concerned at the considerable difficulties that some drivers were obviously experiencing in straightening out after Woodcote corner. It may have been safer than it looked, but on more than one occasion a car first visited the grass on the left of the road and then seemed all set to shoot straight across into the pits."

His words were prescient indeed. At that July's British Grand Prix meeting, during the 500cc F3 race, Charles Headland lost control of his Martin-Headland at the end of the second lap at Woodcote, went across the grass and spun into the pit area, "collecting an unlucky reporter", as *Autosport* put it. An even more serious incident ten years later would cause a complete re-think of the pit area (see Chapter 3).

In its report of the 1953 British Grand Prix, *Autosport* said: "Silverstone on a Saturday morning presents as gay a scene as any Continental *grande épreuve*. Thousands of cars make their way into the big parks to join the vast caravan town, which has sprung up overnight. From hundreds of Calor gas cookers come the appetising odours of countless bacon and egg breakfasts. For British motor racing folk are becoming more and more like their fellow enthusiasts across the English Channel; the two big Silverstone meetings organised by the BRDC and the *Daily Express* have the proper carnival atmosphere – even to the extent of many sideshows, and the inevitable three-card trick men."

On Friday 17 July 1953, the day before the Grand Prix, Earl Howe, president of the BRDC, dedicated a memorial drinking fountain to the late Pat Fairfield. This memorial, the work of Prince Birabongse of Siam, was originally erected on the Donington Park racing circuit where Fairfield

had scored many successes, but was re-erected at Silverstone. Earl Howe paid tribute to Fairfield, who was killed racing at Le Mans in 1937, and to all other members of the club who had lost their lives in motor racing. The ceremony was attended by all the drivers taking part in the Grand Prix.

Writing 20 years later in the programme for the 1973 British Grand Prix, Jimmy Brown recalled how the Maserati driver Froilán González had caused problems that year. "He was spilling oil all over the track, but for lap after lap he ignored the black flag to bring him into the pits. By the time he did come in, all the oil had gone and he acted all innocent," he explained. "In fact González was terrific value for spectators and it was because

TOP AND ABOVE
In 1955 the oil-drum corner markers were replaced by low walls with ornamental trees behind them to help drivers' sight lines. Mike Hawthorn drives the circuit in his works D-type Jaguar. (BRDC Archive)

ABOVE *The double-decker bus which used to house the timekeepers can be seen on the far side of the track as the field gets away at the start of the Formule Libre event at the 1953 British Grand Prix meeting. (BRDC Archive)*

Club Silverstone

Throughout the 1950s, the Silverstone racing season comprised a number of sprint and race meetings organised by a variety of motor clubs.

The season commenced in April with the first of the Vintage Sports Car Club (VSCC) meetings – this being the only club that organised two events each year at the circuit. This would be followed in May by meetings organised by the Maidstone & Mid-Kent Motor Club and the Nottingham Sports Car Club. The Eight Clubs usually held their meeting in June, which was followed by the VSCC's second meeting of the year, the Motor Cycle Club's unique combined car and bike meeting and the Midland Motor Enthusiasts' Club meeting. In July the Aston Martin Owners' Club took centre stage, while in August the Bentley Drivers' Club held a meeting, followed by the 750 Motor Club's annual six-hour relay race, which became a nationally-licensed event. In September each year SUNBAC and the Peterborough Motor Club both held events, and the season rounded out at the beginning of October with the North Staffs Motor Club in attendance.

Each meeting tended to follow a similar schedule of one-hour high-speed trials followed by a number of short scratch and handicap races. *Motor Sport* commented that the club Silverstone meetings were a bit like school sports days where the same competitors kept reappearing in different events.

When it published the list of Silverstone club meetings for 1953 in its March issue, *Motor Sport* pointed out that admission to these club days was by ticket only. However, it suggested: "By lunching adequately a member of the appropriate club a few days beforehand or even addressing a begging letter to the appropriate club secretary, you will usually be able to equip yourself and friends with the required piece of pasteboard and will only be called upon to pay for parking your car."

of him that we had to erect the little walls on the inside of the runway corners. Coming up to Abbey, González used to put all four wheels on the grass, with stones showering everybody, then he'd do the same coming out of Becketts."

Towards the end of the year, Reg Parnell in an Aston Martin DB3S and Peter Whitehead in a standard Jaguar XK120 Coupé experimented with lapping the circuit anticlockwise, but neither had favoured this. Meanwhile, two trespassers who had gained access to the circuit on 14 November had tendered full apologies and agreed to make donations of £20 each to the Silverstone Parish Church Fund and to the British Motor Racing Relief Fund and to pay the club's legal expenses.

At the beginning of 1954, the club decided to spend around £1,000 on additional resurfacing, and two prefabricated concrete buildings, each 48ft x 12ft, were purchased. One was for the members' toilets and competitors' changing room, the other for Race Control. Early in the year a chicane was tried at Woodcote, but the idea was soon abandoned.

Towards the end of 1954, the RAC announced that it had awarded the following year's British Grand Prix to Aintree, near Liverpool, so that followers of the sport in the north of England should have the opportunity to see the country's premier motor race. The race would be organised by the British Automobile Racing Club (BARC). For the next seven years the event alternated between the two circuits, apart from 1961 and 1962 when it was held consecutively at Aintree because of the 50th anniversary of the BARC, albeit for the last time. From 1964 onwards, until 1986, it was to alternate between Silverstone and Brands Hatch in Kent.

The controversial announcement meant that the international *Daily Express* International Trophy meeting on 7 May would be the premier event at the circuit, and it took on a new format for 1955. Enzo Ferrari had promised to compete in the race if it was held as a straightforward event of around 300km instead of two heats and a final. He also offered to send two sports cars for an event of about 200km, so the BRDC made the decision to run the Trophy over a distance of 60 laps, to increase the distance of the sports car race to 40 laps and of the production car race to 25 laps. In the end, however, no works teams were sent by Ferrari, Maserati, Lancia or Mercedes.

Earlier in the year, a section of the track east of Club through Abbey and up to Woodcote had been resurfaced, and low breeze block walls were built on the inside of the corners to replace the old oil drum markers. Small ornamental trees were placed behind the walls to aid drivers' sight lines.

The Grand Prix returned to Silverstone on 14 July 1956 and resulted in a victory for the Lancia-Ferrari D50 of Juan Manuel Fangio, but at the start of the following year, all racing and testing was

ABOVE *Tim Parnell, in*
his Cooper-Climax T46,
chats to his father Reg
on the grid for the US
Air Force Trophy Race
at the AMOC meeting in
July 1958. Parnell went
on to win the race.
(LAT)

thrown into doubt because of the fuel shortage caused by the Suez crisis. The *Daily Express* felt that no decision could be taken regarding running the International Trophy meeting, scheduled for 4 May, until the Ministry of Fuel and Power had announced its decision regarding allocation of petrol for approved racing events.

When the Ministry eventually sanctioned petrol for a limited number of motor sport events in February, the paper believed that even with petrol for the competitors it would be impossible to organise the meeting on the normal scale to which people had become accustomed in just three months, especially as petrol-rationing still affected the general public. As a result, the event was postponed in the hope that it could be run later in the year. But despite the activities of the club being seriously impaired by the crisis, and a subsequent reduction in turnover, a greatly increased profit was made at Silverstone during the year.

More changes were put in place at the track in time for the 1958 Grand Prix on 19 July, the main one being the creation of a separate lane for cars wishing to enter the pits. This started at the beginning of Woodcote Corner and was designed to eliminate the risk posed by pit-bound cars peeling off at the apex of the corner and disturbing the drivers of faster cars at the moment of greatest strain.

In December 1958 the *Daily Express* announced that, after ten years of sponsoring the International Trophy meetings at the circuit, it was withdrawing from direct financial support. Tom Blackburn presented the BRDC with a cheque for £10,000 on behalf of the paper and said the

Express would continue to give wholehearted assistance to the club.

Because of this, the formation of a Silverstone Committee to assist in the commercial aspects of the BRDC's activities was proposed. It was felt that the implications of the club operating Silverstone without the financial backing of the *Daily Express* rendered such a committee essential for speedy decisions to be reached without the necessity of calling a general committee meeting. The potential difficulties of a members' club running a commercial operation, a situation which the BRDC would face many times in the future, were being recognised.

The International Trophy meeting in 1959 was the first to be organised by the BRDC without operational help from the *Daily Express*. The club now undertook complete control of things, such as the selling of programmes and cash control, which had previously been undertaken by *Express* staff. The event proved highly successful and a profit of £10,000 was made on the meeting.

Because of these excellent results, it was decided that the remaining 50 per cent of unsecured loans from members could be repaid, and that the club should embark on a programme of repairs and improvements, including repairs to the track surface from Copse Corner to Club Corner and modifications to Woodcote to increase safety. It was also decided to build a retaining wall of reinforced concrete on the existing yellow demarcation line in the pit area, and it was agreed to look into the possibility of a vehicle tunnel at Woodcote, but because of the short term of the lease held by the club from the Air Ministry, this idea was shelved.

LEFT *Jon Goddard-Watts gets very sideways in his Berkeley during 1959. (LAT)*

The problem of the lease had been a subject of discussion for some time. The existing lease had expired at Christmas 1958 but, under the Landlord and Tenants Act of 1954, tenancy continued until it was terminated, either by the Air Ministry or the BRDC itself. The club had been advised by its lawyers to "await events for the time being" and that a consortium with Mr Graham, the tenant farmer, might be desirable. However, while it was agreed that the club's interests would be best served by waiting, it was the general opinion of the committee that Silverstone was potentially such an excellent investment that no difficulty should be experienced in finding the necessary funds to purchase the land without becoming involved with Mr Graham.

Against this backdrop it was agreed to push ahead with further improvements. The Grand Prix circuit from Copse to Club and the Club circuit from Becketts to Woodcote would be resurfaced and the circuit would be widened at the outside of the exit from Woodcote with, if necessary, the *Motor* footbridge being moved slightly. The pit counters were to be increased in width by approximately three feet to provide greater safety for the occupants of the pits and a walkway constructed for pit personnel, including mechanics and all officials on duty in the pit area. Seats would be provided above the pits for the use of chart keepers, spotters and timekeepers. A new grandstand would also be erected at Woodcote in the position previously occupied by the *Daily Express* guests' stand.

Silverstone had firmly established itself as a world-class motor racing track, and its future looked bright.

Sir Stirling Moss

"I first went to Silverstone with a 500, and a 500 was one of the best cars to start off with because they would understeer, and if you were going too fast you would just slow yourself down with understeer, frankly. So as you get to know the circuit more, and as one's technique improved, I could lessen the disadvantage of the understeer; in other words increase my speed round because if you were going round a particular corner flat out, it does not mean you were going round there as fast as you can go, because it depends entirely on your line and the drag you get. And Silverstone was one of those because with a 500cc car at Silverstone there weren't many places you had to back off too much. We were living and learning then, and I know one time my sprocket came undone when I was in the lead.

"It was almost a modern circuit in the early days, with a spin-off area. Mike Hawthorn lost it and went right off the road opposite the pits, spun right the way down there, managed to get it back and came back on the track. It was a massive spin but he got away with it because there was a spin-off area, maybe 20 or 30 yards, which at the time was an enormous amount to have. Which, of course, with an aerodrome circuit you could do much more easily.

"It wasn't particularly bumpy because, you see, in that era we were racing road-racing cars and therefore meant to race on roads. And roads are far bumpier than aerodromes really, unless they're particularly good.

"What I used to like about Silverstone was that it was a really high-speed circuit. Originally it was quite quick around the outside. At that time we were starved of circuits, so it was very important. Silverstone filled a definite gap, a void that we had at the time."

1950

■ The Silverstone club season kicked off on 29 April with the VSCC meeting, which included four half-mile sprints and three scratch and four handicap races.

■ A record crowd turned out for Royal Silverstone on 13 May, the occasion of the Grand Prix d'Europe, which was attended by the King and Queen. The 70-lap race was won by Giuseppe Farina in a 1.5-litre Alfa Romeo 158 at an average speed of 90.95mph, followed by the other Alfas of Luigi Fagioli and Reg Parnell, whose cowling bore a dent caused by one of Silverstone's numerous hares. It would have been a one-two-three-four for Alfa had Juan Manuel Fangio not hit a straw bale at Stowe and then retired later with a broken con-rod.

BELOW *A record crowd turned out for Royal Silverstone on 13 May 1950, the occasion of the Grand Prix d'Europe. (LAT)*

■ Again, the 500cc cars opened proceedings with two five-lap heats and a ten-lap final. Stirling Moss won the first heat in his Cooper-JAP T12, while the second produced a victory for John Cooper's Cooper-JAP T11. The final was won by Wing Commander Frank Aikens in an Iota-Triumph, followed by Moss and the Cooper-Norton T11 of Peter Collins.

■ Before the Grand Prix, the much-anticipated BRM V16, which was originally entered for the race, was demonstrated by Raymond Mays.

■ The Bugatti Owners' Club meeting on 17 June comprised a 12-mile handicap for all types of Bugattis, a 1½hr relay race for teams of three sports cars, a 30-minute race for standard post-war saloons and a 72-lap F2 race.

■ At the VSCC meeting on 24 June, the 100km Seaman Trophy race for vintage and historic cars was won by G. Hartwell in an ERA Special, ahead of the Maserati Special of R. Dutt.

■ On 8 July, the 100-mile Commander Yorke Trophy race at the 500 Club's meeting was won by Ken Watkins in a Cooper MkIV ahead of Alan Rippon's Cooper and the Messenger Special of Ron Messenger.

■ The gates opened at 6am for the 150,000 people who turned out for the *Daily Express* International Trophy race on Saturday 26 August, with the main event split into two heats and a final. In the first heat, Giuseppe Farina was an easy winner, having led throughout in his Alfa Romeo 158. Peter Whitehead initially held second in his Ferrari 125 but was passed by Reg Parnell in the Maserati 4CL. Tazio Nuvolari flagged the field away in the second heat, with Juan Manuel Fangio's Alfa Romeo 158 immediately assuming the lead,

followed by the Thin Wall Special Ferrari 125 of Alberto Ascari. Rain fell heavily partway through the race, and Ascari was one of many to spin. Fangio took the flag from the ERA B-Types of Brian Shawe-Taylor and Bob Gerard. The Duke of Edinburgh watched the start of the 35-lap final in which the Alfas proved unbeatable, Farina winning ahead of Fangio, with Peter Whitehead's Ferrari 125 in third place.

■ The long-awaited BRM V16, which was due to take part, was late arriving and then its clutch broke on the starting line of the second heat.

■ The 500cc race that opened proceedings produced a victory for Stirling Moss in his Cooper-Norton T12. The supporting production car race was split into two events, for up to 2-litre and over 2-litre machinery. The two Ferrari 166MMs of Ascari and Luigi Serafini dominated the up to 2-litre event, while the over 2-litre race produced a win for Peter Walker's Jaguar XK120, with Tony Rolt's Jaguar in second. Combined results gave overall victory to Ascari from Serafini.

1951

■ Reg Parnell in his Thin Wall Special Ferrari 375 was the star of the *Daily Express* International Trophy race that took place on 5 May in atrocious weather conditions before a crowd of around 100,000, but the final had to be abandoned because of a tropical rainstorm. It was the Alfa Romeo 159 of Juan Manuel Fangio that led away in the first heat from Felice Bonetto's Alfa. Parnell was soon up to third and passed Bonetto on lap five. As he charged after Fangio, the Argentinian set a new lap record at an average of 95.4mph. He broke this again on the final lap with a speed of 96.29mph, by which time Parnell had closed the gap to just 3sec at the flag, with Bonetto back in third. The second heat was won easily by Giuseppe Farina in his Alfa, setting a new lap record of 97.19mph and finishing 31sec ahead of the similar car of Consalvo Sanesi, with Prince Birabongse's Maserati-Osca 4CLT/48 in third place.

■ A thunderstorm hit the circuit just before the start of the final but, to the crowd's delight, it was Parnell's Ferrari in the lead at the end of lap one, with Duncan Hamilton's Talbot-Lago T26C in second. When it started to hail, the lap scorers were unable to read the numbers on the cars and the track was becoming flooded. With only six laps completed the race was stopped. As the BRDC declared that the race was cancelled, there was no winner, but prizes were awarded as a gesture. Parnell was in the lead at the time, with Hamilton second, while Fangio and Graham Whitehead's ERA 'B'-Type were credited as being joint third.

■ Piero Taruffi completed a demonstration run before the main event in his record-breaking twin-boom Italcorsa.

■ In the one-hour production car race top division, Stirling Moss led home a Jaguar XK120 one-two-three-four-five. The up to 2-litre division, which had raced separately, was won by the Frazer Nash Le Mans Replica of Tony Crook, but Moss took overall honours in the combined results. Eric Brandon, in his Cooper-Norton T15, won the 500cc race ahead of Alan Brown's similar car.

■ The BBC broadcast coverage of the event on the Light Programme, the forerunner of Radio 2. A ten-minute slot from 10.50 to 11.00am covered the finish of the 500cc race, and from 11.50am to 12-noon the finish of the first heat. From 3.34 to 4.00pm, listeners could hear the finish of the

ABOVE *The start of the 500cc race at the 1951* Daily Express International Trophy *meeting. Charles Headland, in his Cooper-Norton MkV (12), gets away from the front row, with the Iota-Jap 'Tiger Kitten' of Clive Lones (35) just behind. The race was won by Eric Brandon, who started from the sixth row in a Cooper-Norton MkV, and his Ecurie Richmond team-mate, Alan Brown, was second. (BRDC Archive)*

one-hour production car race for over 2-litre cars, and from 5.15 to 5.30pm commentary on the progress of the final of the main race, and at 5.45pm the finish.

■ On 4 June, Silverstone was a meeting place for the 226 cars that had started from four different locations on the first ever RAC International Rally of Great Britain. Competitors had to complete a specified number of laps of the track in 30 minutes, maintaining an exact speed.

■ A smaller crowd than usual (50,000) turned out to see the Argentinian driver José Froilán González take the first Grand Prix victory for Ferrari in the RAC British Grand Prix on 14 July. Felice Bonetto's Alfa Romeo 159 led at the end of the first lap from González's Ferrari 375, with Giuseppe Farina's Alfa and Alberto Ascari's Ferrari in close pursuit. After five laps, González took the lead and started to pull away. Following the

ABOVE *Teammate Alberto Ascari looks on as José Froilán González makes a pit stop in his Ferrari 375 on the way to taking the marque's first-ever Grand Prix victory at the 1951 British Grand Prix. (LAT)*

ABOVE *The BRM P15 of Reg Parnell, which finished fifth in the 1951 British Grand Prix, is refuelled in the pits, overseen by Raymond Mays. (LAT)*

pit stops at 70 laps, he led the Alfa of Fangio by 1m 19.2sec, with Farina in third but a lap in arrears. After 90 laps, González took the flag with Fangio's Alfa in second and Luigi Villoresi's Ferrari third, after Farina and Ascari had both retired.

■ Farina set a new lap record of 99.99mph during the race, but race-winner González had lapped at over 100mph in practice.

■ The 20-lap race for 500cc cars was dominated by Stirling Moss in his Kieft-Norton, with Ken Wharton finishing second in his Cooper-Norton T15.

■ At the Aston Martin Owners' Club meeting on 28 July, a Mrs Howard, driving a Lea-Francis-HRG Special, was "not only easy on the eyes, but did extraordinarily well at her first essay at motor racing" according to *Motor Sport* magazine. The lady in question won her heat in the handicap race for open cars and came third in the final. In the five-lap handicap for lady drivers, she finished runner-up to Miss H. Williams in an Austin-Lotus.

■ The circuit hosted 13 club meetings during the year. Alan Brown (Cooper-Norton) and Les Leston (JBS-Norton) emerged victorious in the Half-Litre Club's two 100-mile races for 500cc cars during its 18 August meeting, while the 750 Motor Club held the first of its six-hour relay races on 25 August, with victory going to the VSCC Bentley team.

ABOVE *Farina retired from the 1951 British Grand Prix at Abbey Curve, smoke pouring from his Alfa Romeo 158, but not before he had set a new lap record of 99.99mph. (LAT)*

ABOVE *José Froilán González, known as the 'Pampas Bull', takes his Ferrari 375 to victory in the 1951 British Grand Prix, scoring the team's first-ever win. (LAT)*

1952

■ The RAC Rally speed tests, scheduled for April, had to be cancelled because of snow on the track.

■ The new shorter Club circuit was inaugurated at the VSCC meeting on 3 May, which included eight races and a one-hour high-speed trial. The new Club course ran along the top straight to Copse Corner, down to a hairpin at Becketts and back down the runway to Woodcote.

■ The *Daily Express* International Trophy race on 10 May was held for F2 cars and attracted a record crowd of 125,000 despite poor weather. There was a British victory in the final of the main event as Lance Macklin brought his HWM-Alta home ahead of team-mate Tony Rolt, with Baron de Graffenried's Maserati 4CLT/48 in third. A battle had been expected between the winners of the two heats, Mike Hawthorn in a Cooper-Bristol T20 and Robert Manzon in his Gordini 16, but Manzon broke his transmission at the start and Hawthorn suffered a broken gear lever while leading, and he dropped back. Jean Behra, in another Gordini, assumed the lead but also retired with transmission problems, leaving Macklin out in front.

■ During the day, the crowd was entertained by a 'Parade of Champions', featuring Sydney Allard in the Monte Carlo Rally-winning Allard, Stirling Moss in the second-placed Sunbeam Talbot and Donald Healey in an Invicta. Reigning 350cc motorcycle world champion Geoff Duke also demonstrated his Norton.

■ A five-lap race for identical Jaguar XK120s with star drivers from different countries was won by Stirling Moss.

■ The supporting 500cc race was run on a very wet track. Stirling Moss led the first 12 laps in his Kieft-Norton until brake problems dropped him to third behind the Cooper-Norton T18s of Stuart Lewis-Evans and Alan Brown.

■ Moss won the production touring car event in his MkVII Jaguar, with Ken Wharton's Healey Elliot in second. The highlight of the event was Dick Jacob's drive to victory in the 1100–1500 class in his MG. Moss also won the production sports car race in his Jaguar XK120C, ahead of the Aston-Martin DB3 of Reg Parnell.

■ The pits had been moved from Abbey to the straight between Woodcote and Copse, and they were now permanent brick structures with an observation roof above. The main grandstand, now covered, had also been moved to the new start-finish straight.

■ Yet another variation on the Club circuit was used at the Maidstone and Mid-Kent Motor Club's race meeting on 24 May. The track turned left after the Becketts hairpin at Tower corner, along a short straight and right again at Victory corner to rejoin the track just before Woodcote. An eight-race programme was run, with the Formule Libre event, run over 20 laps, won by Ken Downing in his F2 Connaught.

■ The HWM-Jaguar of Oscar Moore was victorious in the Formule Libre event at the Bugatti Owners' Club meeting on 14 June, setting a new Club circuit record of 74.62mph. It also won the unlimited sports car race, driven by Moore's son Terence. The all-Bugatti team, appropriately, won the one-hour relay race.

■ The VSCC ran its second meeting of the year over the short Club circuit on 12 July. In the second ten-lap handicap race, Sam Clutton's 10.6-litre Delage burst into flames as it was approaching Woodcote, and the driver attempted to steer it standing up on the seat. He stayed with the car and steered it into a ditch, where he was flung off. He was later taken to hospital with bad burns to his hands and right leg.

■ Alberto Ascari won the RAC British Grand Prix on 19 July in his Ferrari 500 on a cloudy and cool, but dry day. Ascari led away at the start and built up a strong lead from team-mate Giuseppe Farina. Both of them broke the lap record early in the race, with Piero Taruffi's Ferrari in third until Farina stopped at the pits for new plugs, then continued to fall back. Ascari thus won easily from Taruffi, with Mike Hawthorn's Cooper-Bristol T20 in third.

■ Don Parker looked as if he'd got the supporting 500cc race wrapped up until the primary chain drive broke on his Kieft with only half a lap to go, allowing Stirling Moss to take the victory in his Kieft-Norton from the Cooper-Norton T18 of Eric Brandon.

ABOVE *The 1952 British Grand Prix winner, Alberto Ascari, washes his hands under a standpipe in the paddock. (LAT)*

■ The Formule Libre event produced a victory for Piero Taruffi in the Thin Wall Special Ferrari 375, despite receiving a 30sec penalty for jumping the start. Taruffi was chased by Froilán González in the BRM V16 until he went off at Stowe Corner. The Argentinian pitted and took over Ken Wharton's sister car in fourth place. He got the BRM up into third behind Luigi Villoresi's Ferrari 375 before retiring with a broken gearbox, leaving Taruffi to take the victory, ahead of Villoresi and the Ferrari 375 of Chico Landi.

■ Immediately after the Grand Prix, spectators were entertained by the high-pitched whine of the Rover Gas Turbine car, which completed two demonstration laps.

■ John Coombs won the fourth annual 100-mile race at the Half-Litre Car Club's meeting on 23 August in his Cooper-Norton by just 2.2sec from another Cooper-Norton driven by Bob Gerard.

■ A total of 27 teams entered the 750 Motor Club's annual six-hour relay race on 30 August, and although the Ford saloons led for some time it was the Singer Owners' Club team which emerged victorious. Rather than award start money, the club instead awarded 'stopping money' to help compensate for blow-ups or other damage.

■ The SUNBAC meeting on 6 September was marred by the death of Harold Bradford, who was killed when he crashed his MG TD at Maggots during practice. It was the first fatality to occur at a club event at the circuit.

■ Les Leston won the 12-lap 500cc F3 event at the Peterborough Motor Club meeting on 20 September in his Leston Special.

■ The final club meeting of the year, organised jointly by the North Staffs Motor Club and the Nottingham Sports Car Club on 11 October, produced the best entry of any club meeting at the circuit this year, ranging from 750cc cars to an 8-litre Bentley. Les Leston again won the 500cc F3 event in his Leston Special.

BELOW *Piero Taruffi, who finished second in the 1952 British Grand Prix in his Ferrari 500, heads towards Abbey Curve. (LAT)*

1953

■ In April the circuit again played host to the RAC Rally, competitors having to complete a half-mile sprint along Club Straight.

■ The VSCC's season opener on 2 May attracted a good crowd and included the traditional hour-long high-speed trial, plus a variety of scratch and handicap races.

■ Mike Hawthorn scored a popular victory in the BRDC *Daily Express* International Trophy race on 9 May in front of a crowd reported at the time to be in excess of 100,000. Baron Emmanuel de Graffenried won an uneventful first heat in his Maserati 4CLT/48 from Stirling Moss in the Cooper-Alta, with Prince Birabongse's Maserati third. Hawthorn was an easy winner of the second heat in his Ferrari 500, from Ken Wharton's Cooper-Bristol T23 and the Connaught A-type of Roy Salvadori. At the start of the final, de Graffenried anticipated the flag, thus earning himself a one-minute penalty, but he and Hawthorn initially traded the lead before Hawthorn began to pull away. When de Graffenried was informed of his penalty on lap 17 he retired from second place in anger. Salvadori brought his Connaught home in second from the sister car of Tony Rolt.

■ The 500cc race produced a close battle between Don Parker's Kieft-Norton and Reg Bicknell's Staride-Norton, the pair swapping the lead throughout. Parker emerged the victor, with Eric Brandon's Cooper-Norton T26 in third.

■ Stirling Moss led all the way in the supporting production touring car race in his Jaguar MkVII, running out the winner ahead of Harold Grace's Riley.

■ Moss had crashed heavily in practice for the production sports car event in his Jaguar C-type at Abbey, becoming trapped underneath the car, and so was a non-starter. Mike Hawthorn led all the way in his 4.1-litre Ferrari America 340. Reg Parnell held second place initially in his Aston Martin DB3 before being passed by the Ferrari 340 of Tom Cole.

■ Sixteen races made up the Eight Clubs meeting on 6 June, which attracted an entry of 166 sports cars. Because of the large crowd, the programmes had sold out by halfway through the day.

ABOVE *Mike Hawthorn was a popular winner of the 1953* Daily Express *International Trophy race in his Ferrari 500. (LAT)*

■ A chicane made out of straw bales was installed just before Woodcote for the Motor Cycling Club (MCC) meeting on 20 June, but it was demolished by a Bentley in the *Motor Sport* handicap event.

■ Alberto Ascari led the British Grand Prix on 18 July from start to finish in his Ferrari 500. About 30min before the end, the heavens opened and flooded the track, but the rain failed to change the order at the front. Ascari finished a minute ahead of the Maserati A6GCM of Juan Manuel Fangio, with Giuseppe 'Nino' Farina's Ferrari 500 in third, two laps adrift.

■ Stirling Moss was unchallenged on his way to victory in the supporting 500cc F3 event, with Eric Brandon in second and Stuart Lewis-Evans third. All three were driving Cooper-Norton T26s.

■ Aston Martin DB3Ss finished in the top three places in the 35-lap sports car race, with Reg Parnell leading home Roy Salvadori and Peter Collins, while the first 100mph lap record was set in the supporting Formule Libre event by race-winner Giuseppe Farina driving a Thin Wall Special Ferrari 375 at 100.16mph. The BRM P15 V16s of Juan Manuel Fangio and Ken Wharton were second and third.

■ Heavy rain fell for the majority of the 750 Motor Club's six-hour relay race on 29 August. The event was won by the King's MG team but, for a short while at least, a Land Rover entered by the Surrey Sporting 'Motley' team led a race at Silverstone. The club used a specially devised 2½-mile track, utilising most of the Club circuit but with a hairpin bend at Maggot's Corner and a long downhill straight to Club Hairpin and back the other side of the runway to Woodcote and the pits via Tower Bend. The 2.6-mile variation on the Club circuit, devised by 750 Club chairman Holland Birkett, had been hired out to the Aston Martin Owners' Club for its meeting on 15 August.

■ Don Parker, in his Kieft, won the first heat of the 500cc F3 event at the SUNBAC meeting on 5 September, while Les Leston, in his Leston, took the second. The pair shared the honours as they had both averaged exactly the same time, and no final was run.

■ The North Staffs Motor Club ran the final club meeting of the year on 10 October, with large entries for the majority of the races. The Cooper of Rodney Nuckey won the 500cc F3 encounter.

ABOVE *Onofre Marimón, Giuseppe Farina and Juan Manuel Fangio in the pit lane at the 1953 British Grand Prix. (LAT)*

BELOW *Alberto Ascari scores his second consecutive British Grand Prix victory as he takes the chequered flag to win the 1953 event in his Ferrari 500. (LAT)*

1954

A crowd of around 120,000 turned up, despite poor weather, to see Froilán González win the *Daily Express* International Trophy race on 15 May in his Ferrari 625. The first 15-lap, 50-mile heat produced a win for the Argentinian from the Maserati A6GCM of Prince Bira and the Maserati 250F of Stirling Moss. Tony Rolt initially held second place in his Connaught-Lea Francis A-type but spun on the wet track on lap six. Conditions had improved by the start of the second heat, which was led initially by Reg Parnell in his Ferrari 625, closely followed by the works car of Maurice Trintignant, until lap 11 when the Frenchman took the lead. The order stayed that way to the end, with Robert Manzon's

BELOW *Eventual victor Froilán González, in his Ferrari 625, is already out of sight as the field head towards Copse Corner at the start of a very wet first heat of the 1954* Daily Express International Trophy *race. (LAT)*

Ferrari in third. Just before the start of the final, González's Ferrari refused to start, so he took over Trintignant's car. He led away at the start, pursued initially by Moss until Jean Behra's Gordini T16 got past into second. Moss managed to re-pass and he held the place until he retired with broken suspension. Behra thus took second, with the other Gordini of André Simon finishing third.

González also won the supporting 17-lap sports car race in his Ferrari 375MM ahead of the HWM-Jaguar of George Abecassis. Ian Appleyard led a Jaguar MkVII one-two-three in the touring car race, finishing ahead of Tony Rolt and Stirling Moss – all three cars breaking the lap record on the way.

Moss was victorious in the supporting 500cc F3 race in his Cooper-Norton, ahead of the similar cars of Les Leston and Jim Russell.

■ The busiest man of the Midland Motoring Enthusiasts' Club meeting on 5 June was Peter Gammon, who competed in nearly every event in his Lotus-MG Mk6, taking five wins and two second places.

■ The MCC meeting on 3 July provided the usual mix of one-hour high-speed trials for cars and motorcycles (during which passengers had to be carried), and a series of scratch and handicap races.

■ Everyone was expecting a Mercedes victory in the ninth British Grand Prix on 17 July, but it was Froilán González in the Ferrari 625 who took his second major victory of the year at the track. The all-enveloping aerodynamic bodywork of the German cars proved unsuitable for Silverstone, and it was González who led from start to finish, despite a strong challenge from the Mercedes-Benz W196 streamliner of Juan Manuel Fangio, until it dropped back with gearbox problems, the bodywork damaged from where the unsighted driver had hit the oil drums marking the circuit. Mike Hawthorn took a popular second place in his Ferrari, with the Maserati 250F of Onofre Marimón in third place. Five drivers shared fastest lap since timings were only made to a fifth of a second in those days.

■ Colin Chapman won the opening sports car race in his Lotus-MG MkVII, while the second race resulted in a one-two-three for Aston Martin, with Peter Collins in his DB3S heading Roy Salvadori and Carroll Shelby. Stirling Moss won the 500cc F3 event in his Beart Cooper-Norton MkVIIA.

■ The 750 Motor Club's annual six-hour relay race on 28 August produced a victory for the Singer Owners' Club team, with the Austin-Healey team second and the St Moritz Tobogganing Club in third place, driving XK120 Jaguars and a single 4.5-litre Bentley.

■ Ivor Bueb won the 12-lap 500cc scratch race in his MkVIII Cooper at the Peterborough Motor Club's meeting on 11 September, which was blighted by heavy rain showers for much of the day.

■ The North Staffs Motor Club meeting on 9 October closed the club race meetings for the year with a series of 13 handicap and scratch events for both sports and racing cars, the final race finishing as it was getting dark.

ABOVE *The all-enveloping bodywork of the Mercedes-Benz W196 streamliners proved unsuitable for Silverstone, the drivers being unable to judge the track limits and sustaining damage from the oil drums marking the circuit. Juan Manuel Fangio, pictured here at the 1954 British Grand Prix, eventually finished fourth after qualifying on pole position. (LAT)*

ABOVE *Froilan González takes the chequered flag in his Ferrari 625 to win the 1954 British Grand Prix, his second victory in the event. (LAT)*

1955

■ The 1955 Club Silverstone season kicked off on 16 April with the VSCC meeting. The winner of the ten-lap GP Itala Trophy race was Jim Byrom's Type 35B Bugatti, which led all the way.

■ With the British Grand Prix going to Aintree, Silverstone's biggest meeting of the year was the *Daily Express* International Trophy race on 7 May. The event was run as a single 60-lap race rather than two heats and a final. There were no works Ferraris, Lancias, Maseratis or Mercedes-Benz present, but the race produced an intense battle between the older Owen Organisation-entered Maserati 250Fs of Peter Collins and Roy Salvadori, with Collins emerging the victor, and Prince Birabongse's 250F in third. Ken Wharton suffered burns and a broken wrist when he crashed his Vanwall VW2 at Copse Corner and the car burst into flames.

■ The 40-lap International Sports Car race produced a victory for Reg Parnell's Aston Martin DB3S, ahead of Roy Salvadori's Aston. Mike Hawthorn dominated the production touring car race in his Jaguar MkVII, leading home a Jaguar one-two-three ahead of Jimmy Stewart and Desmond Titterington, while Ivor Bueb triumphed in the International 500cc F3 race in a Cooper-Norton T36.

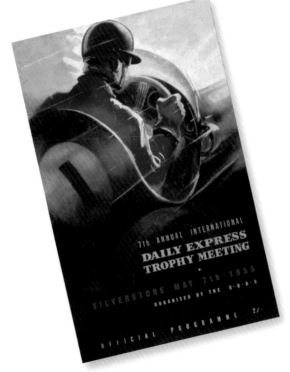

■ For the International Trophy meeting an eight-inch electric 'gong' was installed in the pit area to alert personnel of a car entering the pits.

■ A combination of icy rain, hail, thunder and lightning blighted the Maidstone and Mid-Kent Club's meeting on 14 May.

■ The annual 750 Motor Club's six-hour relay race took place on 9 July, with victory going to the 'Tinlids Team', made up of a Ford Anglia, Ford Prefect, VW and a Fiat 1100, which completed 179 laps.

■ Spectators at the Aston Martin Owners' Club sixth annual St John Horsfall meeting on 23 July basked in a heatwave while they watched a mix of half-hour regularity trials and scratch and handicap events. The highlight of the event was the participation of Roy Salvadori and Reg Parnell in the over-1500cc event in DB3S Astons, with Parnell emerging victorious.

■ The MG Car Club celebrated its silver jubilee at the circuit on 27 August. The meeting included a cavalcade of nearly 50 examples of the marque, along with eight races and a 40-minute high-speed trial.

■ The Peterborough Motor Club organised a meeting for F3, sports and production saloon cars on 10 September. The two 12-lap 500cc F3 events were won by Ken Tyrrell in a Cooper and Tom Bridger in a Kieft.

■ On 17 September, the BRSCC and the BRDC jointly organised a meeting using a new 2½-mile layout. The event included a Junior Grand Prix for children in Austin J40 pedal cars, which was won by eight-year-old Edward French, nephew of Reg Bicknell. The main event of the day, the 100-mile Commander Yorke Trophy for 500cc F3 cars, produced a victory for Jack Westcott's Cooper-Norton.

RIGHT *Reg Parnell took his Aston Martin DB3S to victory in the International Sports Car race at the 1955* Daily Express *International Trophy meeting. (LAT)*

1956

The club racing season got under way in bright sunshine with the VSCC's meeting on 21 April. The event was marred by a clash between two Lagonda Rapiers, which were fighting for the lead of a five-lap handicap race and which both ended up in the ditch at Woodcote. The driver of one, Dudley Cooke, died later.

The *Daily Express* International Trophy race on 5 May resulted in a clear win by over a lap for Stirling Moss in the revamped Vanwall VW2, watched by a crowd of 100,000. Moss won at a record speed of 100.47mph and set a new absolute lap record of 102.30mph, shared with Mike Hawthorn's BRM P25, which led before retiring. British cars filled the next three places, with Archie Scott Brown taking the runner-up spot in his Connaught B-type and Desmond Titterington's Connaught B-type in third place. Bob Gerard was fourth in a Cooper-Bristol Mk9, while the much-fancied Lancia-Ferrari D50s of Peter Collins and Juan Manuel Fangio both retired.

BELOW *The low breeze block walls on the insides of the corners can clearly be seen in this shot of Stirling Moss on his way to victory by over a lap in the 1956* Daily Express *International Trophy race, driving a Vanwall. (LAT)*

The supporting race for sports cars up to 1500cc was won by Roy Salvadori in his Cooper-Climax T39. In the over-1500cc event, Salvadori was again the winner, this time in an Aston Martin DB3S. Ivor Bueb in his 3.4-litre Jaguar MkVII won the production touring car race, while the 500cc F3 event resulted in a win for Jim Russell in his Cooper-Norton T42.

During the meeting, the Monte Carlo Rally-winning Jaguar MkVII of Ronnie Adams and the RAC Rally-winning Aston Martin DB2/4 of Lyndon Sims were both demonstrated on track.

A crowd estimated at over 85,000 attended the RAC British Grand Prix when it returned to Silverstone on 14 July. The two BRM P25s of Mike Hawthorn and Tony Brooks led away at the start, but it was the pair of Lancia-Ferrari D50s of Juan Manuel Fangio and Peter Collins, who had taken over the car of the Marquis de Portago when his own had retired, which filled the top two places at the end. Stirling Moss in his Maserati 250F

BELOW *Mike Hawthorn set a new lap record for sports cars at the 1956* Daily Express *International Trophy meeting in his long-nose D-Type Jaguar, but had to retire from the race with steering problems. (LAT)*

had assumed the lead after the BRMs retired, but he dropped back and also finally retired. Jean Behra brought his Maserati 250F home in third place, albeit two laps behind the winner. Brooks was taken to hospital after his BRM overturned and caught fire at Abbey Curve.

■ Because of the speed of the race, it ran for 13sec less than the three hours prescribed for it to officially count as an FIA-approved Grand Prix (although it still did), despite it having been increased to 101 laps this year.

■ A supporting race for the new F2 cars was won by Roy Salvadori in a Cooper-Climax T41, with Colin Chapman's Lotus-Climax XI in second place. Salvadori's car was the only actual F2 car ready, so the rest of the field comprised Lotus and Cooper sports cars.

■ Stirling Moss won the sports car race in his Maserati 300S, while Jim Russell won a wet 500cc F3 event in his Cooper-Norton T42.

■ The annual six-hour relay race organised by the 750 Motor Club took place on 18 August with a gale force wind blowing. A total of 24 teams were entered, with a variety of machinery from Aston Martin DB3Ss to Ford vans. The event had been accorded national status this year, and the need for a national racing licence precluded some club drivers from being able to compete. Victory went to the MG Magnette team, ahead of 'Shuttlecock's team of Triumphs'.

■ The BRSCC organised a meeting of six F3 and two sports car races at the circuit on 29 September. The main event of the day, the 63-lap, 100-mile Commander Yorke Trophy race, was won by David Boshier-Jones in his Cooper-Norton MkIX.

ABOVE *The Vanwall VW2 of Harry Schell passes Tony Brooks's burning BRM P25, which had crashed because of a sticking throttle and overturned at Abbey Curve before catching fire, during the 1956 British Grand Prix. Brooks, who was thrown out of the car, escaped with nothing more serious than a chipped anklebone. (LAT)*

BELOW *Juan Manuel Fangio, driving a Lancia-Ferrari D50, on his way to victory in the 1956 British Grand Prix. (LAT)*

1957

■ The club season opened on 6 April with the VSCC's first meeting of the year and, despite petrol rationing being in force, there was a good entry for the ten races. Before the first race, a new scrutineering bay was opened in the paddock in memory of the late Bentley engineer, L.C. (Mac) McKenzie. The GP Itala Trophy race was won by the 1927 4.5-litre Bentley of George Burton.

■ The first meeting to be held after the lifting of petrol rationing was the Maidstone and Mid-Kent Motor Club's event on 18 May. It proved a successful outing for Brian Naylor, who won four sports car races in his Lotus-Maserati XI. Jim Russell was victorious in both 500cc F3 encounters in his Cooper-Norton.

■ The 50-kilometre all-comers scratch race at the VSCC's meeting on 15 June was won by Nobby Spero's Maserati after a fierce battle with the ERA 'Remus' of Bill Moss – the pair swapping the lead throughout.

■ Heavy rain affected the Aston Martin Owners' Club meeting on 13 July. The St John Horsfall Trophy race was run in two parts, with victory in the pre-war event going to R. McNab Meredith in his Ulster Aston, while the post-war event provided a win for Jean Bloxham in her DB2.

■ There was more rain at the BRSCC's meeting on 27 July when Jim Russell emerged the victor in the final of the 100-mile Commander Yorke Trophy for 500cc F3 cars in his Cooper-Norton.

■ The Bentley Drivers' Club marked its 21st anniversary with its annual sprint and race meeting on 3 August. The 'All-comers' event was won by the Brooklands Riley of W.S. Bader. Among those present were two of the original 'Bentley Boys' – Sammy Davis, 1927 Le Mans winner, and John Duff, 1924 winner – together with W.O. Bentley himself. A cocktail party was held in the new McKenzie Memorial scrutineering bay after the event.

■ A revised 2½-mile course using the runways and perimeter roads was used for the 750 Motor Club's annual six-hour relay race on 17 August. This year's winners were 'The Individualists', whose team was made up of an Elva, a Jupiter, an A40 Special and a Buckler 90.

ABOVE *Ian Scott Watson in a DKW Sonderklasse during the 750 Motor Club's annual six-hour event in 1957. (LAT)*

■ Postponed from its usual April slot because of the fuel crisis, the *Daily Express* International Trophy race took place on 14 September. The choice of date meant that the event was sandwiched between races at Monza and Modena, with the entry being down as a result. The race was run for both F1 and F2 machinery, and it reverted to two heats and a final. Jean Behra in the BRM P25 was victorious in the first heat, ahead of Ron Flockhart's BRM and the Maserati 250F of Masten Gregory. The second heat produced a victory for the BRM P25 of Harry Schell, but it was Jack Brabham's F2 Cooper-Climax T43 in second place that stole the show, ahead of Jo Bonnier's Maserati 250F. The final produced a one-two-three finish for BRM, with Behra leading home Schell and Flockhart. Roy Salvadori was the first of the F2 finishers in eighth place overall in his Cooper-Climax T43.

■ The up-to-1500cc sports car race was won by Ron Flockhart in his Lotus-Climax XI, while the over-1500cc race produced a victory for Roy Salvadori in the Aston Martin DBR2. Mike Hawthorn in a Jaguar 3.4 Mk1 won the production touring car race, while Stuart Lewis-Evans was victorious in the 500cc race in his Beart Cooper-Norton T42.

RIGHT *In 1957 the* Daily Express *International Trophy race was moved from its traditional April date to September because of the Suez fuel crisis. The supporting over-1500cc sports car race was won by Roy Salvadori in his Aston Martin DBR2, seen here chasing the DBR1 of Tony Brooks, who eventually finished fourth. Noel Cunningham-Reid, in his DBR2, who finished third, follows. (LAT)*

1958

■ Advance booking for the *Daily Express* International Trophy race on 3 May opened on 17 February. An 'all-in' car ticket, including admission for all passengers, cost 25s (£1.25) booked in advance and 30s (£1.50) on the day. The pits grandstands were 30s per seat and the south stands 25s. Individual admission, not bookable in advance, was 6s (30p).

■ The VSCC's season opener on 12 April attracted a crowd of around 8,000 and an entry of 115 cars. The ten-lap 1908 GP Itala Trophy race was won by James Tozer in his 1927 Amilcar Six, while Bill Moss took his ERA 'Remus' to victory in the ten-lap all-comers scratch race. Attitudes to accidents were different in those days. *Motor Sport* reported that during one of the races, a driver rolled his car at Woodcote and lay unconscious beside the wreckage until an ambulance could be brought on to the course.

■ An eye injury to BRM P25 driver Jean Behra brought an end to a close battle between him and Ferrari's Peter Collins for the lead of the *Daily Express* International Trophy race on 3 May. A stone shattered the Frenchman's goggles, but not before both he and Collins had set a new outright lap record of 1m 40s (105.37mph). On lap 11, Behra came into the pits from the lead and, despite being in some considerable pain, rejoined the race with a new pair of goggles. This left Collins out in front, and despite a quick spin at Copse he went on to win in his Dino 246 from Roy Salvadori's Cooper-Climax T45 and the Centro-Sud Maserati 250F of Masten Gregory.

ABOVE *Drivers sprint towards their cars for the Le Mans-type start to the saloon car race at the 1958* Daily Express *International Trophy meeting. (BRDC Archive)*

BELOW *Tommy Sopwith (34) leads Mike Hawthorn (33) around Stowe Corner in their 3.4 Jaguars during the saloon car race at the 1958* Daily Express *International Trophy meeting. The pair enjoyed an epic duel, with Hawthorn emerging the victor by less than a second. (BRDC Archive/Ferret Photographic)*

■ The up-to-1500cc sports car race was won by Graham Hill, who worked his way from the back of the field in his Lotus-Climax 15 to lead a Lotus one-two-three, ahead of the MkXI models of Alan Stacey and Keith Hall. In the over-1500cc event, Masten Gregory took his Lister-Jaguar to victory ahead of the similar car of Archie Scott Brown.

■ In the Touring Car event, an epic race-long battle between the 3.4 Jaguar Mk1s of Mike Hawthorn and Tommy Sopwith resulted in a win for Hawthorn, with Ron Flockhart third in his Jaguar Mk1. Jeff Uren's Ford Zephyr Six Mk2 just fought off the Austin A105 of Jack Sears to take fourth and the 2-litre class win.

LEFT *Roy Salvadori runs towards his Lotus (6) at the Le Mans-type start for the up-to-1500cc sports car event at the 1958* Daily Express *International Trophy meeting. Next in line is eventual winner Graham Hill in his distinctive helmet in the colours of the London Rowing Club. (BRDC Archive/Geoffrey Goddard)*

■ Jim Russell won the final event of the day, the 500cc F3 race, in his Cooper-Norton T42 after early leader Stuart Lewis-Evans retired his Cooper with engine trouble.

■ Peter Collins was again the victor at the British Grand Prix held on 19 July. The Ferrari driver in his Dino 246 took the lead at the start from row two, with pole-man Stirling Moss holding second in his Vanwall until he retired on lap 25 with engine problems. This left Collins out on his own from team-mate Mike Hawthorn, while Roy Salvadori took third in his Cooper-Climax T45 after a race-long battle with the Vanwall of Stuart Lewis-Evans.

■ Stirling Moss won the supporting sports car race in his Lister-Jaguar, while the touring car race produced a one-two-three for Jaguar Mk1s, with Walter Hansgen winning ahead of Sir Gawaine Baillie and Jack Crawley.

■ Stuart Lewis-Evans was almost unchallenged on his way to victory in the 500cc F3 race in his Beart Cooper-Norton T42, ahead of the Cooper-Norton T42 of Don Parker.

BELOW *Stirling Moss takes the flag to win the sports car race at the 1958 British Grand Prix meeting in his Lister-Jaguar. (LAT)*

ABOVE *Peter Collins, in his Ferrari Dino 246, took the lead of the 1958 British Grand Prix on the first lap and held it to the finish, followed home by team-mate Mike Hawthorn. (LAT)*

■ Only a small crowd turned out for the BRSCC meeting on 9 August to see the annual 100-mile Commander Yorke Trophy race for 500cc F3 cars. Trevor Taylor emerged the winner in his Beart-tuned Cooper-Norton MkVIIA.

■ The 750 Motor Club's six-hour relay race on 16 August produced a win for the Speedwell Stable of Modified Austin A35s, with the Morgan Plus Fours only a lap behind in second place.

1959

■ Fine weather drew a large crowd to the VSCC's opening meeting of the season on 11 April, but rain soon set in and by the end of the afternoon it had become torrential, driven by a strong wind. Even so, the meeting ran to schedule and the 1908 GP Itala Trophy went to Jim Berry in his 1928 Bugatti.

■ British cars dominated the International Trophy race, now devoid of *Daily Express* sponsorship, on 2 May as Jack Brabham took his Cooper-Climax T51 to victory, with the Aston Martin DBR4/250 of Roy Salvadori in second place in its first-ever race and Ron Flockhart completing the podium in his BRM P25. Stirling Moss had led briefly in the other BRM until brake problems caused him to spin off at Copse Corner, and retire.

■ In the F2 race that ran concurrently with the main event, Jim Russell took the honours in his Cooper-Climax T51 ahead of Ivor Bueb's Cooper-Borgward T51 and Tony Marsh's Cooper-Climax T45. Innes Ireland had led much of the category in his Lotus-Climax 16 but finished fourth.

■ Stirling Moss was more successful in the supporting Grand Touring race, taking his 3.7-litre Aston Martin DB4GT to victory ahead of Roy Salvadori's Jaguar Mk1. The positions were reversed in the event for sports cars over 1100cc and under 3000cc as Salvadori took the win in his Cooper-Maserati Monaco T49, with Moss in the Aston Martin DBR1/300 second.

■ Ivor Bueb took the top step in the international production touring car race in a 3.4-litre Jaguar Mk1, followed by Salvadori in another Jaguar. Lola-Climax Mk1s took the top two places in the under-1100cc sports car event, with Peter Ashdown ahead of Michael Taylor.

■ Five-times world champion Juan Manuel Fangio flew into the circuit in a helicopter just before the start of the main race and toured the circuit in a Land Rover before dropping the Union Jack to start the race.

■ A 200-mile relay race for the David Brown Trophy was the feature event at the Aston Martin Owners' Club meeting on 23 May. Winners were the Lotus No.4 team, ahead of the Jaguar No.4 team.

■ Nearly 200 cars contested 17 races at the Eight Clubs meeting on 6 June, which was blighted by torrential rain. Gordon Lee, in a C-type Jaguar, won the *Motor Sport* Silverstone Trophy Handicap.

■ A small crowd attended the Nottingham Sports Car Club meeting on 13 June, when the 20-lap Formule Libre final was won by Tim Parnell in an F2 Cooper-Climax.

■ The usual mixed bag of events for cars and motorbikes took place at the MCC meeting on 27 June, *Motor Sport* reporting that the motorcyclists were outstanding more for their enthusiasm than ability. It also commended the club for finishing a long programme on time, despite "the interference of an overzealous official". Peter Sargent scored a hat-trick of victories in his C-type Jaguar.

■ John Freeman won the St John Horsfall Trophy at the AMOC meeting on 11 July in his Spa Special.

ABOVE *The start of the International Trophy in May 1959, with (left to right) Stirling Moss (BRM P25), Tony Brooks (Ferrari Dino 246), Roy Salvadori (Aston Martin DBR4) and winner Jack Brabham (Cooper-Climax T51). (LAT)*

■ The VSCC held its second Silverstone Club meeting on 25 July, the main race being the 12-lap All Comers scratch race for the Boulogne Trophy, which was won by Douglas Hull in a 1936 2-litre ERA. Hull also won the five-lap All Comers event later in the day.

■ The Bentley and Jaguar Drivers' Clubs combined to organise a meeting at the circuit on 1 August, consisting of 12 handicap races and one scratch event. The 15-lap All Comers handicap was won by Clive Clairmonte in his XK120.

■ Tommy Bridger was the winner of the 63-lap Commander Yorke Trophy race for 500cc F3 cars at the BRSCC meeting on 8 August in his Cooper-Norton MkIX.

■ The ninth running of the 750 Motor Club's annual six-hour relay race took place on 15 August, and for the first time it was run on the shorter Club circuit. A field of 22 teams took part, with victory going to the six-car Morgan Plus Four Team ahead of the TR Team, which was made up of two Triumph TR3s and a Peerless.

■ The final Club Silverstone meeting of the year, organised by the North Staffs Motor Club on 3 October, proved eventful for all sorts of reasons. During practice, the Austin-Healey 100 of P.D. Shanks spun at Woodcote and ended up at the paddock gate between the end of the pits and the timekeepers' box where it hit another Healey belonging to one of the officials. Both cars were badly damaged and 'Lofty' England, who was one of the stewards, was injured. Sheep invaded the track partway through the meeting, causing a delay to the proceedings. The unlimited sports car race produced a dead-heat between the Tojeiro-Jaguar of Tony Maggs and the Lister-Jaguar of Peter Mould, despite Maggs taking the flag on the grass.

1960s

"From the mid-sixties onwards, it was barley and pigs. At that time, the farm made more money than the circuit did."
Jack Sears

Silverstone entered the new decade in good financial health. At the annual general meeting of the BRDC on 16 May 1960, the treasurer's report showed that excess of income over expenditure for 1959 was higher than in 1958, which itself was double that of 1957, and that monies earned under the headings 'hire of track', 'circuit advertising', 'pit rentals' and 'catering commission at club meetings' represented an increase over all previous years.

The 1960 season proved to be Silverstone's busiest to date, with only three weekends between 19 March and 8 October when there was no on-track action from either cars or bikes. Improvements to the facilities continued to be made, and at the International Trophy meeting on 14 May, the new Benjafield hospital building (named after the late Dr Joseph Dudley Benjafield, one of the founders of the BRDC) was opened at the circuit. The building and its facilities had been given to the club by the Dunlop Rubber Company to commemorate its long association with Dr Benjafield.

The club now looked at the possibility of purchasing the property outright from the Air Ministry and also of acquiring Green Crop Conservation Ltd (the company that ran the farm on the infield of the circuit) from the farmer, Mr G.W. Graham. An independent valuation of Green Crop Conservation was obtained, and an offer of £55,000 was submitted towards the end of the

RIGHT *Eventual winner Jack Brabham, in his Brabham-Repco BT19, leads the Ferrari 312 of pre-race favourite John Surtees in the 1966* Daily Express International Trophy *race. The event was the first to be held in Britain for the new 3-litre F1 regulations. (LAT)*

year against an original asking price of £64,000. Mr Graham rejected the offer, but said that he would accept £60,000. After further negotiation, a figure of £58,750 was agreed upon.

The acquisition of the farm had been made possible by the satisfactory state of the reserves accumulated over the years, and the anticipated profits from the club's major activities. Completion of the purchase took place in mid-1961, but at the July meeting of the BRDC, Reg Parnell reported that the club appeared to have been misled by the estate agents who had carried out the valuation, regarding the state of the farm and the buildings. In particular, the grass-drying plant was inoperable on the date of the takeover, and this had caused the first crop of grass to be of a low grade. He also said that more working capital was required for Green Crop Conservation. It was agreed at the meeting that circuit manager Jimmy Brown, who at that time lived in Silverstone village, should move into the farmhouse.

Negotiations continued with the Air Ministry regarding the outright purchase of the land, but in 1962, instead of offering the entire property to the club, it was decided at ministerial level that the purely agricultural land should be offered back to the pre-war landowners on condition they leased it to Green Crop Conservation, now owned by the BRDC. The remainder of the land, that is the circuit, runways, paddock and pit areas as well as all non-agricultural land then used for car parking and spectators, would be sold freehold to the BRDC. The estimated cost of this would be £110,000. At first this figure seemed unrealistic, as it would require an additional income at the circuit of around £20,000 a year to service a loan and repay the capital.

At this point, BP stepped in and offered to loan the club £30,000, interest free, if the freehold could be purchased at a realistic figure. The club therefore had the freehold valued, based on the average net profit before rent over the previous three years, plus assessment of future income. A deduction was then made from the vacant possession value of the circuit for the rights of the BRDC under the Landlord and Tenant Act of 1954. The final figures were £41,000 representing the value with vacant possession, and £27,594 as the value without vacant possession (that is, the value to any potential outside purchaser). These figures were a long way from the £110,000 the Air Ministry was asking.

At this point the Ministry, instead of agreeing to sell the land, then proposed a new lease, embracing the land already occupied under the existing lease and also additional land already occupied under sufferance. The new lease would give the club full and unfettered use of the whole circuit without the present restrictions, so long as it continued to control Green Crop Conservation. It would also relieve the club from any liability to reinstate the site by the removal of buildings and suchlike at the end of the term. A new clause would also remove restrictions on advertising, giving the club full use of the circuit for advertising purposes, subject to appropriate planning permission, and would also include additional buildings such as certain old hangar bases not included in the present lease.

The new agreement would also allow the club much wider usage beyond strictly motor racing, such as driver training and skid pans, to which the Ministry had previously turned a blind eye. The provision for resumption of occupation for Air Force purposes would no longer apply.

The Ministry also agreed to consider permitting the landing of aircraft for competitors, mechanics and race officials at race meetings. Bizarrely, despite the fact that the land had been a former airfield, it had proved impossible to obtain permission for the landing of aircraft at Silverstone. The problem had been that the Ministry, as air traffic controller, was in difficulty over any substantial use of Silverstone for civil aviation purposes because of its proximity to an American air channel. Individual flights would have to obtain clearance by air traffic control in the usual way.

The rent proposed by the Ministry was £5,500 per annum for seven years, with a further seven at a revised rent. In August 1963, the club decided to accept a new lease on the broad basis of the Ministry's proposals, but it secured an undertaking from the Ministry to offer to the club the freehold reversion on the new proposed lease, the freehold reversion on the hangar (let out to a third party by the Ministry) and the 57 acres of agricultural land not being offered to former owners, along with first refusal on such land offered to former owners but declined.

It was also suggested that a new limited liability company be formed, Silverstone Estates Limited, to enable the borrowing of capital on a much longer term than was possible for a club limited by guarantee.

Controversy over the venue for the British Grand Prix is nothing new. In 1961 it was announced by the RAC that the 1962 event would be run at Aintree for the second year in succession to mark the 50th anniversary of the BARC. This caused a

storm of protest as the race had been alternating between the Liverpool track and Silverstone since 1955. Nevertheless, the race went ahead at Aintree that year, but was back at Silverstone for 1963, with support from the *Daily Express*, which now again wished to be officially associated with the club and Silverstone, to give full editorial backing and to assist financially.

The following extract from *Autosport* of July 1963 sums up perfectly the atmosphere of a Silverstone Grand Prix during the sixties:

"As 2.00pm approached, the vast crowd, now swollen to about 115,000, settled down to await the start. Up went the five-minute board accompanied by the raucous blast from the Lucas horns, and activity on the starting grid reached its climax. Two minutes to go, the starters whirred and engines burst into life. The track was cleared and photographers brought their cameras up to eye level. Twenty-three pairs of eyes carefully watched Kenneth Evans and his Union Jack. Up went the flag, the crescendo of noise increased, and cars began to edge forward. A clear-cut downwards sweep and the field was unleashed."

At the end of the race, Jim Clark's winning Lotus-Climax 25 was loaded on to the back of a trailer pulled by a farm tractor for a lap of honour,

while a Scots piper played 'Scotland the Brave'.

Sadly, the meeting was to be remembered for other reasons, which were to have a lasting impact on the circuit. During the GT support race, Christabel Carlisle lost control of her Austin-Healey Sprite at Woodcote and spun into the unprotected pit lane, killing scrutineer Harold Cree. Although absolved of all blame, Carlisle never raced again. The accident came only two weeks after a young driver, Mark Fielden, had been killed whilst sitting in his stationary car in the pits, when another car lost control coming out of Woodcote and crashed into it. The two accidents highlighted the danger of having unprotected pits so close to a high-speed corner. Moving the pits completely would be an expensive undertaking, but with two fatalities in the area within a fortnight, it was obvious that the BRDC had no option but to make modifications.

It moved swiftly, and on 7 August carried out tests at the circuit with the assistance of Graham Hill, Jimmy Clark, Mike Beckwith, Tony Hegbourne and John Taylor. As a result, the club took the decision to make drastic improvements during the off-season to the Woodcote Corner and pits area and to postpone the Clubmen's Championship, which was due to be run on 5

ABOVE *A colourful paddock scene at the 1962* Daily Express International Trophy *meeting.* (BRDC Archive)

ABOVE *A grid full of saloon cars stretches back around Woodcote in 1963. (BRDC Archive)*

October, until the beginning of the following season, so that work could get underway.

The improvements to be carried out were listed as follows:

1. The circuit was to be resurfaced from the main entrance through Woodcote Corner and right up to Copse Corner, and any bumps that might have contributed to potential instability were to be eradicated.
2. The pedestrian bridge was to be moved 16ft towards the outside of the circuit to remove a visual bottleneck and prevent the creation of any bottleneck in future years through rising speeds.
3. The circuit would be widened by 8ft on the outside of this area to provide a greater safety margin for drivers and cars. This would leave a grass verge of 8ft beneath the pedestrian bridge.
4. The safety ditch and bank were to be made continuous throughout the entire length of the pits grandstand area, at the same time making the bank higher, deepening the safety ditch and reinforcing the face of the safety bank to prevent natural erosion.
5. The working pits were to be moved away from Woodcote Corner, towards the pedestrian bridge, and extra pits erected at that end.
6. An Armco barrier would be erected approximately 18ft from the front of the pit counter for the entire length of the pits.
7. The radius of Woodcote would be modified to enable cars to leave the corner on a straighter, smoother and easier line.

8. The deceleration zone and pit entry road would be modified so that all competitors stopping at the pits would be inside the Armco barrier.
9. Additional warning lights would be erected from Woodcote, back towards the farm, so as to give earlier and more complete warning to drivers approaching the corner.

One aspect which was discussed further was the erection of the Armco barrier in front of the pits, as it was felt that a barrier which would provide adequate protection for cars varying from very low F1 machines to large heavy touring cars would prevent spectators in the grandstands opposite from seeing the cars in the pits.

Another solution had actually been suggested by Jimmy Brown some five or six years previously – to build a raised pit road which would keep all cars in constant view of the public and at the same time provide an impregnable barrier 20ft wide and 3ft 6in high. It would also allow existing advertising in front of the pit counters to be placed on the front of this raised road, while a ramp at each end would allow cars to enter and exit the pits. It was decided in October to push ahead with this idea. Work on the project was to start immediately and be completed in time for the International Trophy meeting the following May. In fact, all the work around the Woodcote area was completed in time to be inspected and approved by the general committee, with Jimmy Brown in attendance, at its meeting of 4 March 1964.

That year the British Grand Prix switched to Brands Hatch in Kent, instead of Aintree, but by August the RAC had still not decided on the venue for the 1965 Grand Prix. The BRDC decided that, instead of lobbying for a contract to hold it for a number of years, it was better to ask for it in 1965 and then alternate years, as this would be looked upon more favourably. The chances of getting the Grand Prix in future years was going to be subject to paying a fee of £5,000 compared to the previous year's figure of £1,325. It was suggested that the *Daily Express* be asked to assist by putting up the first £5,000.

When the offer to host the event finally arrived, the RAC wanted £8,000, but this would meet the expenses of all officials at the meeting. There were a few sticking points, including whose brokers should be used to handle legal liabilities, and the RAC also wanted the power to decide the supporting races and timing of the programme among other things. However, it was agreed that, come what may, the Grand Prix must be at Silverstone for 1965 if for no other reason than to keep the door open for 1967. The title of the event would be 'The Royal Automobile Club's British Grand Prix organised at the BRDC's Silverstone Circuit sponsored by the *Daily Express*'.

Facilities at the circuit were constantly being reviewed. Increased charges by the scaffolding company that erected the grandstands meant that planned additional stands could not now be afforded, and the provision of toilets was also an issue – the main problem being the drainage, since even during the war the air station did not have drains. Improving viewing facilities for spectators was discussed, and in 1965 ramps were built at Stowe, Club and Copse corners in time for the International Trophy meeting, and another was proposed for Becketts for the Grand Prix. During the winter of 1965–66 a number of huts were installed around the circuit for use by the St John Ambulance Brigade.

Proving that you can't please everybody, the pit facilities at Silverstone were criticised by *Motor Sport* magazine after the 1965 British Grand Prix. The elevated ramp on which the pits were built was felt to be a good safety feature, given that they were located around a blind corner, but the pit lane was deemed too narrow, and the allocation of pits also came in for criticism. Ferrari, BRM, Lotus, Cooper and Brabham occupied the first five pairs of pits at the top end of the line, while at the opposite end the private owners had plenty of space for just a single entry. The magazine felt that there was insufficient room for three works cars, the teams all being on top of one another, and that they should have been spread out more along the line of pits.

The raised ramp also meant that if a driver had to cut his engine on the approach to Woodcote, he had to ensure that he had sufficient speed to mount the ramp and coast the length of the pit road. If he was going too fast he would bottom out as he mounted the ramp, whereas too little speed would mean he could not coast to the end, and his mechanics would have to push him.

In March 1966 a new company called Silverstone Circuits Ltd was formed to run the circuit and its operations on a commercial basis. Green Crop Conservation Ltd would become a subsidiary of the new company, and BRDC Ltd would be the holding company in charge of both. This automatically meant that the members elected to the general committee of the club were still the responsible parties in control of all three companies. It also meant that the commercial affairs of Silverstone Circuits could be controlled by a small board of appointed directors, rather than by the full general committee. This would enable the commercial development of the circuit to proceed without interference with the normal operation of the BRDC as purely a members' club.

Through the sixties, the farm continued to be operated alongside the circuit and much of the south end – from Abbey down to Club, from Club to Stowe and from Stowe up to Becketts – was given over to barley.

"From the mid-sixties onwards, it was barley and pigs," explained Jack Sears, himself a farmer and, from 1966 onwards, a director of the BRDC. "At that time, the farm made more money than the circuit did. The Grand Prix brought money in, and when we had to have the Grand Prix alternating with Brands Hatch, in the Grand Prix years we made more money than the farm, but in the non-Grand Prix years, the farm made more money than the circuit because the Grand Prix was the big money-spinner. I can remember we had a combine harvester, and we used to combine the crops, and if people spun off you'd just see the head of the driver sticking out above the grain."

The proximity of the farm to the circuit caused an unusual problem in another way as well, as Norman Dewis, chief test driver for Jaguar recalled: "I was with Jaguar then as the chief development and test engineer and I used to come down to try the car out, the C-type or D-type, whichever it was we were testing and developing. I used to do the Dunlop race tyre tests and we used to spend days and days down

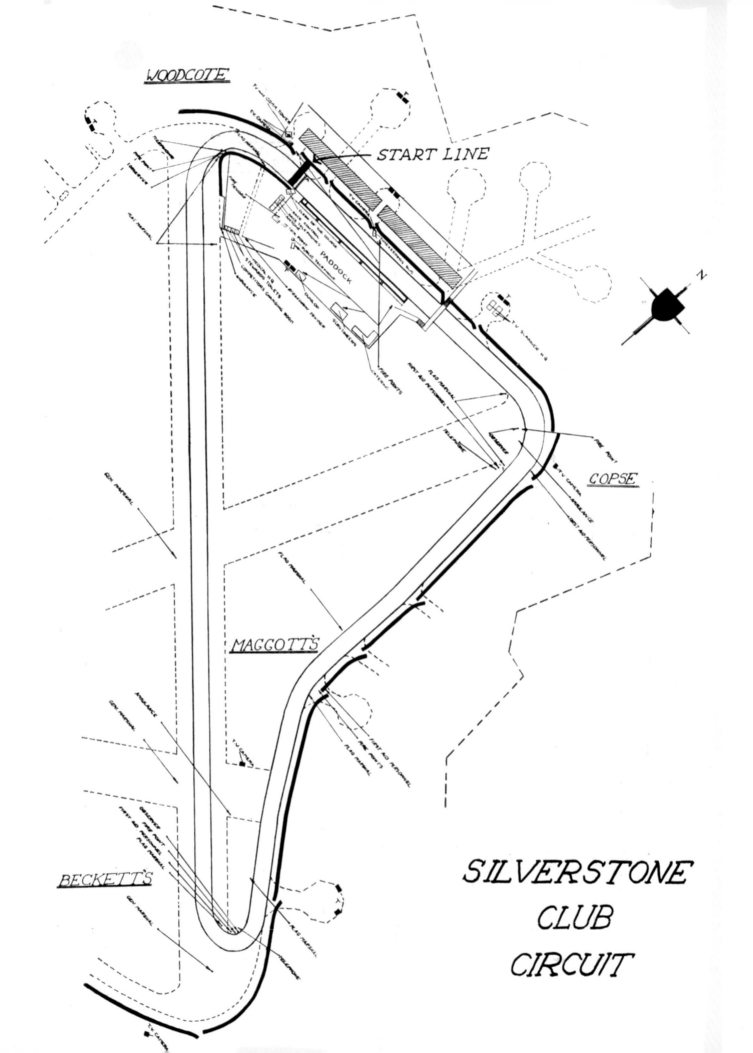

WOODCOTE

START LINE

PADDOCK

COPSE

N

MAGGOTT'S

BECKETT'S

SILVERSTONE
CLUB
CIRCUIT

at Silverstone. All we had was a track manager, Jimmy Brown, and he ran the pig farm just over at Woodcote as well. Jimmy used to run the whole show and we didn't have any marshals at all around the track. When we were doing the tests, we'd be out all day – test, test, test – and I always remember coming up over the brow to Woodcote on this one lap, and there's Jimmy Brown in the middle of the track with a pig between his legs, waving to me 'go that side!' One of his pigs had got out and it was between his knees on the centre of the track. They were great days, we used to have some fun there."

The improvements continued apace in the mid-sixties. At the International Trophy meeting on 29 April 1967, the *Daily Express* vehicle bridge over the circuit between Abbey and Woodcote corners, a feature that was to become an integral part of the Silverstone landscape for many years, was used for the first time. At the same meeting the new four-storey Dunlop Tower, situated on the outside of Woodcote and for the use of press, TV, circuit commentators and VIPs, was inaugurated. The Dunlop tyre company also had a significant presence at the circuit at this time, with a Dunlop tyre bridge located on the outside of the circuit just before Woodcote corner. Prior to the start of the 1968 season, raised spectator banks were built between Woodcote and Copse, Stowe and Club and between Club and Abbey corners.

But there was still the matter of the freehold of the land to consider. This was brought into sharp focus when, in July 1968, an article in the *Daily Telegraph* suggested that the government was considering the circuit as a possible site for a third London airport. At this stage the circuit and surrounding land was still owned by the Ministry of Defence and leased to the BRDC, and in October it was confirmed that Silverstone was on the shortlist, along with Sheppy and Foulness. It took seven months and considerable lobbying before a reprieve was announced, and it illustrated the necessity and urgency for the club to acquire the freehold.

Help was at hand, though, in the form of a trust established in 1968 to help the circuit achieve its aim. "The chairman of Ford Motor Company UK was Sir Leonard Crossland," explained Jack Sears. "He was a great supporter of ours and he spoke to a lot of leaders of the motor industry at that time – big suppliers like GKN and Dunlop, and other companies that supplied goods to the motor industry. He basically said, 'let's put some money in and then they can buy the freehold'. So they all did put substantial amounts of money in, and a trust was formed."

The four main companies that contributed to the Silverstone Trust, as it was named, were the Ford Motor Company, Dunlop, GKN and long-time supporter the *Daily Express*. A meeting took place with the Ministry of Defence in mid-1969, at which the club was told that the farmland would be offered for auction in September and that, two or three weeks prior to that date, the freehold of the racing circuit would be offered to the BRDC at a stated and non-negotiable sum. That figure would probably be in the region of £125,000, compared to a figure of £75,000–£80,000 that had been confirmed in 1963.

And so the decade ended in much the same way as it had begun, with the acquisition of the freehold of the land the major concern. It was agreed that the BRDC should acquire the freehold of the farmland at public auction, which would place it in a strong negotiating position for the racing circuit freehold, and in October 1969 it purchased 42.5 acres of adjacent land in the area behind the main grandstand and Brown car park at a cost of £240 per acre with vacant possession.

On a lighter note, *Autosport* reported in November that the firm of builders constructing a housing estate in Silverstone village had come up with the idea of naming the streets after famous racing drivers and that the idea had been agreed by the local community. Hence we had Stewart Avenue, Brabham Close, Clark Avenue, Hawthorn Drive, Moss Bank, Surtees Close and, of course, Graham Hill.

Sir Jackie Stewart

"My first visit was with my brother, Jimmy, when I was about 14 because he was driving for Ecurie Ecosse. He did the British Grand Prix in '53, and in those days I was a real enthusiast and I went to Goodwood with him, and Silverstone and Aintree. So I saw Silverstone and I thought it was big-time, because there were the transporters and there were the fancy folk.

"I always thought it to be glamorous. You can look back and say, 'well you weren't very worldly in those days', and it would be right. But it had grandstands, and when you went to Turnberry or Charterhall or Winfield up in Scotland, there weren't any grandstands to speak of, and if there were they were very modest. And here there were big grandstands and there were huge crowds.

"The crowds that went to these races in those days were damn near as big as go today. There weren't as many on the practice days as there are today, but there was still close to a hundred thousand people went to Silverstone, and the traffic congestion was colossal because the roads weren't as developed and they were country roads.

"But it looked to me very sophisticated, because if you were sitting for three hours in traffic to get into the circuit, it was a big event. Even then it had the ambience, the atmosphere of a big event. I never saw it, ever, as the primitive facility that it was later to be accused of being.

"And I was later to drive many times at Silverstone, and it is one of the race tracks that I thought was the most challenging, because there were so many fast corners. Slow corners are easy, medium-speed corners most people can do, but really fast corners take a special skill. Silverstone was loaded with those, so it was always a challenging one. For a British driver to win the British Grand Prix at Silverstone obviously was a big deal.

"My first Formula 1 win was at Silverstone, the *Daily Express* International Trophy in '65, and then I won a couple of Grand Prix there. The 1969 battle with Jochen was probably the best Grand Prix there's been there, with more than 30 lead changes.

"I think it was that many, because the ones that would be listed were at the start-finish line. In those days you draughted and passed going down Hangar and you draughted and passed going into Woodcote, coming out of Abbey. And there were 30-31 lead changes, I think. But there wouldn't be that many listed at the start-finish line.

"It was one of the best races I ever did. Outside of Monza, there was nowhere where we had lead changes of that number, because at Monza there were three places to pass on slipstreaming and there was more of a group. There couldn't be a cluster of cars at Silverstone, there were too many difficult corners to do that.

"I went off the road in practice. I was following Piers Courage and there was a kerb that was cemented into the inside of the corner. He clipped it, and for some reason it became detached and came back and took off my rear tyre, just sliced it off. In those days Woodcote was nearly flat out, not if you were following somebody, but awful fast, 150mph at least. And I did a whole lot of pirouettes and took down three rows of chain-link fencing that I had had put in. In other words I was responsible for having it done because it was railway sleepers that were in front of the grass banks, so at 150mph there was the possibility of a huge accident occurring, and that would have been a big one.

"But the chain-link fences stopped that, so it meant that I was fastest at that time, and then Jochen beat my time and I started from second on the grid.

"The whole race was just nose-to-tail passing. Jochen was a very good friend and we lived two or three hundred metres apart in Switzerland. In those days the camaraderie of drivers was different, and because we travelled together, we hoteled together, we familied together, we holidayed together, there was a much better understanding I think than there is today.

"So when, at Silverstone, we broke loose from the rest of the field, if you're racing you quite often slow each other up because you're going tight into a corner which normally you'd be going into quickly because you're on the inside, and therefore you're slowing the other car that you're passing.

"If you do it intelligently, you point where you know the guy's going to pass you anyway. Well it's better to move over, let him through, and in fact we were gaining on the opposition to a huge extent. I mean we were miles ahead of anybody and that kept increasing because our straightline speeds were faster, we weren't baulking each other in corner entries. And, therefore, I knew every lap if I were ahead going into Stowe, he would draught me going out of Abbey and, therefore, I would move over and he would go through to get the good line through Woodcote.

"It was a hell of a race because, although we were on the limit, every time you'd take the lead you'd think 'well if he makes a mistake now I'll make the break and get out of the draught', but neither of us made mistakes.

"His right rear wing endplate came undone and was touching the rear wheel. And I got alongside going down Hangar

Straight because you could draught from quite a far way before Stowe before you passed and, therefore, got in the proper racing line for Stowe – and I came alongside pointing at his rear wing endplate.

"The problem is, you know your own mirror configuration but you never know if the other person's seeing as much as you. I always had my rear-view mirrors focused on the rear wheel, because if there was a puncture you'd see it concave instead of convex. And I didn't know whether he'd be seeing it or not because he obviously hadn't felt it, because sometimes you hear these things as well as feel them, and he obviously hadn't.

"So I pointed to this and then I passed him going into Stowe. He passed me going into Woodcote and I noticed he was more often looking at the rear wing endplate, and in the end decided to come in, because it would have undoubtedly cut the tyre. In those days they were not tubeless tyres. And then, of course, he ran out of fuel after that, when he came back out. But the race was over by then.

"In 1973 it was very annoying. I got a great start and passed Ronnie going into Becketts, so I was leading at the end of the first lap by two or three seconds. But then, of course, Jody had his accident at the end of the first lap. When I came round they had the red flag out, so I stopped the car in front of the pits but not up on the pit lane, and I jumped up. It was just a hell of a lot of mess.

"After the restart I was having difficulty engaging gears. Anyway, I engaged second instead of fourth going into Stowe and it just locked up. I'd released it, but it was too late and I went into that cornfield.

"What did it take to drive a quick lap at Silverstone? Smoothness. That's why it was such a wonderful track. You had to be so gentle with the car. Because they didn't have that much horsepower, so if you scrubbed off speed you never gained it because there were long straights. If you got Copse wrong, it's quite a long drag down to Becketts. If you got Becketts wrong, it's a long drag to Stowe. Stowe was important because Club was there and Club was quite fast in those days, so again you couldn't afford to slide cars and have them hanging out. It impressed the spectators but not the bank manager. And then if you didn't get Abbey right it was another long drag uphill to go over the top towards Woodcote. So smoothness, clean driving; and I learned that all from Jim Clark really, and my brother. He was smooth."

BELOW *Jackie Stewart (Matra-Ford MS80) and Jochen Rindt (Lotus-Ford 49B) battle for the lead during the 1969 British Grand Prix. (LAT)*

1960

■ The International Trophy Meeting on 14 May was marred by the death of Harry Schell, who crashed his Yeoman Credit Cooper-Climax T51 at Abbey Curve during practice in the rain and was thrown out. Stirling Moss was another to fall victim to the conditions, spinning his Cooper-Climax T51 as he left the paddock around Woodcote and hitting one of the new Aston Martins that was parked in the pits. Both cars were badly damaged.

■ The 150-mile International Trophy race produced a victory for Innes Ireland in his Lotus-Climax 18. Moss had been the initial leader, pursued for much of the race by Ireland, with Jack Brabham's Cooper-Climax T53 third. Ireland closed relentlessly on Moss, briefly taking the lead before Moss reclaimed it. The pace told on the Cooper, though, and it eventually retired with a broken wishbone, leaving Ireland to take victory from Brabham, with Graham Hill's BRM P48 in third place.

■ The Formula Junior race was won by Jim Clark's Lotus-Ford 18, while Roy Salvadori was victorious in both the supporting production touring car race and the international unlimited sports car event, driving a Jaguar Mk2 and a Cooper-Climax Monaco T49 respectively. Meanwhile, the international 1500cc sports car race produced a victory for the Lola-Climax Mk1 of Peter Ashdown.

■ A total of 166 cars contested 16 races at the Eight Clubs meeting on 11 June, which were preceded by a series of half-hour high-speed trials.

■ Stirling Moss was flown in by helicopter from hospital, where he was recuperating from a crash during the Belgian Grand Prix, in order to act as guest starter for the British Grand Prix on 16 July, in place of regular Silverstone starter Kenneth Evans. Jack Brabham led away in his Cooper-Climax T53, but one of three drivers left on the line with stalled engines was Graham Hill in his BRM P48. Nevertheless, Hill began a storming drive through the field and on the 55th lap took the lead. Brabham hung on to his tail, though, and continued to harry him until Hill, who was suffering from fading brakes, made a mistake at Copse while passing slower cars and spun out of the race. Brabham went on to take victory, his fourth in a row, from the Lotus-Climax 18s of John Surtees and Innes Ireland.

■ Prior to the main event, spectators were treated to two parades, both of which rapidly developed into unofficial races. The first was the Grand Prix drivers circulating in Mini Minors, which ended up as a "high-speed, tight-packed traffic jam". A parade of historic racing cars had to be stopped after only two laps as officials became increasingly alarmed at the tactics of the drivers.

■ The 25-lap sports car race which opened proceedings was won by Ron Flockhart in his Cooper-Climax Monaco T49, while the Formula Junior event provided a victory for the Lotus-Ford 18 of Trevor Taylor. Colin Chapman emerged the victor from a spirited battle with Jack Sears in the production touring car race, both in Jaguar Mk2s.

■ The demise of 500cc F3 racing meant that the annual 100-mile Commander Yorke Trophy race, held at the BRSCC meeting on 6 August, was somewhat uninspiring. Gordon Jones led most of the 63 laps in his Cooper-Norton, and only one other car completed the full distance.

■ The annual 750 Motor Club's six-hour relay race took place on 13 August with 24 teams entered. However, after three of the cars from the BMC Mini team each lost wheels, the clerk of the course stopped the team from taking any further part. Victory went to the Tornado team.

■ The Peterborough Motor Club's meeting on 17 September attracted 199 entries for its 13-race programme, which had plenty of incidents, including an eight-car pile-up at Woodcote during the 1172 Formula race.

■ The North Staffs Motor Club's meeting on 24 September included the final of the *Motor Sport* Silverstone Trophy, which was won by John Anstice-Brown in his Climax-engined Halseylec. The Formula Junior event was won by Mike Spence in his Cooper-Austin T52, while the Formule Libre event went to Mike Salmon in his D-type Jaguar.

■ A soaking wet BRDC British Empire Trophy race for Formula Junior cars was held on 1 October and was won by Henry Taylor's Ken Tyrrell-entered Lotus-Ford 18 from Peter Arundell's Lotus-Ford 18.

1961

■ The opening club event of the season, the VSCC meeting on 22 April, was held in a downpour. Jim Berry's 1928 2.3-litre supercharged Bugatti T35B won the 1908 GP Itala Trophy race.

■ The *Daily Express* International Trophy race on 6 May was run to Intercontinental Formula rules over 233 miles and in heavy rain. The race provided a convincing victory for Stirling Moss in his Cooper-Climax T53P, as he finished a lap ahead of second-placed man Jack Brabham, also in a Cooper, and two laps ahead of Roy Salvadori's T53P in third place. *Autosport* described Moss's drive as: "A shattering demonstration of his unrivalled genius as a wet-weather driver."

■ Moss had already triumphed once that day in the opening sports car race, during which he broke the lap record three times in his UDT-Laystall Lotus-Climax 19. Roy Salvadori was second in his Cooper-Climax Monaco T57.

BELOW *Stirling Moss broke the sports car lap record three times on his way to victory at the 1961* Daily Express *International Trophy meeting in his UDT-Laystall Lotus-Climax 19. (LAT)*

ABOVE *Tim Parnell, Innes Ireland, Stirling Moss, Jim Clark, Jack Fairman and Lucien Bianchi walk to the start line prior to the 1961 British Empire Trophy Race for Intercontinental cars. (LAT)*

■ The Formula Junior event provided the closest racing of the day with five cars battling for the lead and the order changing almost every lap. Jim Russell in his Lotus-Ford 20 emerged the victor from the similar car of Tony Marsh.

■ Dan Gurney took pole for the production saloon car event in his Chevrolet Impala and battled hard for the lead with the Jaguar Mk2 of Graham Hill, until the Impala lost a rear wheel. Hill set a new production saloon lap record on his way to victory ahead of Mike Parkes in another Jaguar.

■ The AMOC meeting on 13 May featured the Martini 100 – a 100-mile event in which each car had to make two compulsory pit stops. Running this on the Club circuit meant that even the timekeepers had trouble keeping track of what was happening, and the results weren't declared until 30 minutes after the race finished. Mike Salmon in his D-type Jaguar was the eventual winner.

■ With the British Grand Prix being held at Aintree the following weekend, the BRDC organised the British Empire Trophy Race for Intercontinental cars on 8 July but attracted only around 50,000 spectators. The race, which was flagged away by Juan Manuel Fangio, turned into a bit of a procession, with Stirling Moss taking victory again in his Cooper-Climax T53P, ahead of the similar car of John Surtees and the BRM P48 of Graham Hill.

■ The supporting Formula Junior event attracted enough entries for it to be run as two heats. Trevor Taylor took his Lotus-Ford 20 to victory in the first heat ahead of Alan Rees in another Lotus. Peter Arundell in a Lotus-Ford 20 won heat two ahead of Tony Maggs' Cooper-Austin T59. The aggregate result produced a win for Arundell, with Taylor second and Rees third.

■ The production touring car event resulted in a win for Mike Parkes in his Jaguar Mk2, with Graham Hill's Jaguar second. The GT race went to Stirling Moss in a Ferrari 250 GT Berlinetta, ahead of Bruce McLaren's E-type Jaguar.

ABOVE *Stirling Moss leads away under the* Motor *bridge in his Ferrari 250 GT Berlinetta at the start of the GT race at the 1961 British Empire Trophy meeting. (LAT)*

■ During the meeting, Jack Brabham drove a couple of demonstration laps anticlockwise in the Indianapolis Cooper.

■ Mike Spence, driving a works Emeryson, won an entertaining 100-mile Commander Yorke Trophy race for Formula Junior cars at the BRSCC meeting on 29 July.

■ Lotus boss Colin Chapman was the guest starter of the 750 Motor Club's annual six-hour relay race on 12 August, which was won by the team of Austin-Healey Sebring Sprites, ahead of the Octagon Team of Healy 3000s.

■ The full Grand Prix circuit was used for the first time for a club event on 7 October when the first Clubmen's Championship meeting was held, organised jointly by the BRDC, AMOC, the 750 Motor Club and the Eight Clubs. Bill Moss took his Chequered Flag Gemini to victory in both the Formula Junior and Formule Libre events.

1962

■ The VSCC's Pomeroy Trophy kicked off the season on 24–25 March, and was won by Jack Williamson in his 1928 4.5-litre Bentley.

■ The Commander Yorke Trophy meeting on 31 March, organised by the BRSCC, was held in rain and snow with only nine cars out of 20 finishing in the 100-mile main event. Richard Attwood emerged victorious in his Cooper-Ford T59.

■ There was a dramatic finish to a wet *Daily Express* International Trophy race on 12 May, with Graham Hill's BRM P57 just beating the Lotus-Climax 24 of Jim Clark on the line. Clark had led throughout, but Hill had closed towards the end, despite having lost several exhaust pipes, and when Clark was held up by a back-marker at Club, it gave Hill the momentum to get on to the tail of the Lotus as they swept through Abbey and to drive around the outside of Woodcote to take the victory. John Surtees in the Lola-Climax Mk4 was third.

■ Mike Parkes, driving a Ferrari 250 GTO, won the GT race for the Scalextric Trophy, while the Formula Junior event provided an easy victory for Peter Arundell's Lotus-Ford 22.

■ Graham Hill was also victorious in the 12-lap production saloon car race, driving a Jaguar Mk2, and the meeting concluded with a 12-lap sports car race, which was won by Innes Ireland in the UDT-Laystall Lotus-Climax 19.

■ Reg Parnell completed three demonstration laps in a 1939 Mercedes Benz W163 V12 on the soaking wet track.

BELOW *Jim Clark streaks away in his Lotus-Climax 24 at the start of the 1962* Daily Express *International Trophy race, chased by Richie Ginther's BRM P57 (2), Bruce McLaren's Cooper-Climax T55 (6), Innes Ireland's UDT-Laystall Ferrari Dino 156 (9) and the BRM P57 of eventual winner Graham Hill. (LAT)*

ABOVE *The E-type Jaguar Lightweight of Graham Hill battles over second place with the Ferrari 250 GTO of Masten Gregory in the GT race at the 1962* Daily Express International Trophy *meeting. (LAT)*

■ A rather dull Formula Junior race at the Nottingham Sports Car Club's meeting on 16 June was won by Jack Pearce in a Lotus-Ford 22, with Bob Olthoff's Brabham-BMC BT2 in second place.

■ Before retiring, Frank Gardner set a new Formula Junior record of 103.31mph in his Brabham-Ford BT2 at the AMOC Martini 100 meeting on 14 July. John Fenning, in his Lotus-Ford 20, won the race. The USAF Trophy race for GT and production sports cars was won by the E-type Jaguar of Dick Protheroe by just 0.2sec from the Aston Martin DB4GT Zagato of Michael Salmon. In the 100-mile Martini 100, John Coundley's Lister-Jaguar took the honours.

■ Despite taking place on the same day as the British Grand Prix at Aintree, the VSCC meeting on 21 July drew a good crowd. The main event of the day, the 50km Boulogne Trophy, was won by the ERA of Sid Day, ahead of the similar car of Martin Morris. The meeting was marred when Morris's ERA left the track at Becketts during the all-comers scratch race, fatally injuring two marshals.

■ The 750 Motor Club's six-hour relay race on 11 August produced a thrilling battle between the Jaguar Drivers 'A' and 'B' teams and the Morgan 4/4 Club. The Jaguar 'B' team eventually secured the victory with just five minutes left to run, just beating the Morgans, with Jaguar 'A' in third place. Just two weeks before, on 28 July, the club had run its first '750 Silverstone' meeting at the track, adding another club event to the circuit's busy schedule.

■ The second Clubmen's Championship meeting, organised jointly by the AMOC, Eight Clubs and 750 MC, was held on the full circuit on 6 October. Richard Attwood, in his Cooper-Ford T59, won both the Formula Junior and Formule Libre races.

1963

■ Bill Elwell-Smith triumphed in the St John Horsfall Trophy race at the AMOC meeting on 4 May in his 1932 Le Mans Aston Martin.

■ *Motor Sport* magazine described the 15th *Daily Express* International Trophy meeting on 11 May as "a motor racing feast". Around 100,000 spectators, including HRH Princess Margaret and Lord Snowdon, saw Jim Clark drive to victory in his Lotus-Climax 25, ahead of Bruce McLaren's Cooper-Climax T66 and the other Lotus of Trevor Taylor. John Surtees, driving one of the new Ferrari 156s, was holding third until an oil leak caused his retirement.

■ In the opening GT race, Graham Hill, driving a Lightweight E-type Jaguar, led home the other E-type of Roy Salvadori after race-favourite Mike Parkes had spun out of the lead at Becketts in his John Coombs Ferrari GTO.

■ Salvadori, driving a 3.8-litre Jaguar Mk2, had to make do with second place in the production touring car race as well, as Jack Sears trounced the opposition in his 6.9-litre Ford Galaxie V8. Salvadori did claim the top spot in the unlimited sports car event, though. Driving a Cooper-Climax Monaco T61 he beat the Lotus-Climax 19 of Innes Ireland into second place.

■ The Formula Junior event produced a victory for Denny Hulme, driving a Brabham-Ford BT6, after a close battle with David Hobbs, who finished second in a Lola-Ford Mk5A.

■ *Autosport* reported that, despite pleas by commentator Peter Scott-Russell, the crowds in front of the pits wouldn't move to give paying customers in the grandstands a chance to see Jim Clark receive his trophy after the main event. It suggested that it might be an idea to have a portable rostrum in time for the Grand Prix.

■ The Martini Trophy meeting, organised by the Aston Martin Owners' Club on 6 July, was marred by an accident during practice when the Hon. James Dawnay spun his Aston Martin DBR1 at Woodcote, hitting the Lotus 17 of Mark Fielden, which was stationary in the pits, killing its driver. The accident highlighted the danger of having unprotected pits so close to a high-speed corner. On race day, John Dunn was fatally injured during the Formula Junior event when he crashed his Brabham-Ford BT6 on a soaking wet track.

ABOVE *Photographers could stand right at the edge of the track in those days, as this shot of Graham Hill in his BRM P57 leading the Ferrari 156 of John Surtees around Woodcote during the 1963 British Grand Prix clearly shows. (Michael Hewett)*

■ The main event of the meeting, the Martini International Trophy for sports, sports-racing and GT cars, was reduced from 52 to 30 laps, owing to the torrential rain, and was easily won by Mike Parkes in the Maranello Concessionaires Ferrari 250 GTO, who finished a lap ahead of the rest of the field.

■ Only two months after the International Trophy race, the F1 cars were back at the track for the British Grand Prix on 20 July, which produced the fourth Grand Prix victory in a row for Jim Clark in the Lotus-Climax 25. It was the Brabham-Climax BT7s of Jack Brabham and Dan Gurney that led initially, but Clark moved to the front on the fourth lap and was thereafter never headed. The Ferrari 156 of John Surtees was second, passing Graham Hill's BRM P57, which was running out of fuel, on the last lap.

■ Peter Arundell won the supporting Formula Junior race in his Lotus-Ford 27, while Jack Sears again won the production touring car race in his Willment-entered Ford Galaxie V8. The event for sports and GT cars produced a victory for Roy Salvadori's Cooper-Climax Monaco T61.

RIGHT *John Surtees, in his Ferrari 156, claimed second place from Graham Hill's BRM P57, which was low on fuel, on the last lap of the 1963 British Grand Prix. (LAT)*

■ During the GT support race, Christabel Carlisle lost control of her Austin-Healey Sprite at Woodcote and spun into the unprotected pit lane, killing scrutineer Harold Cree. Although absolved of all blame, Carlisle never raced again.

■ During the lunch interval, the crowd was treated to a demonstration run by Graham Hill in the Rover-Turbine in which he had competed at Le Mans the previous month. Following this, French stunt driver José Canga completed a lap of the track on two wheels in his Simca.

■ In its report of the VSCC meeting on 27 July, *Motor Sport* magazine observed that, with the recent fatalities in the Silverstone pits, it was surprising to see people still standing on the counters during the racing. This time it noted, though, that the only casualty was someone who fell off the pit-counter and broke his arm.

■ The Tornado Talismans ran out the winners of the 750 Motor Club's six-hour relay race on 10 August. The dangerous nature of the position of the pits was again highlighted when a Triumph TR3 driver spun off at Woodcote and hit the unused area of the pits backwards, the driver being half flung out. Fortunately he was uninjured. Prior to the race, a minute's silence was observed for club chairman Holland 'Holly' Birkett, who had organised and run the event since its inception and who had perished along with his wife Margaret in an aircraft accident the previous month.

■ In order for safety work to commence as soon as possible, the Clubmen's Championship meeting, due to take place on 5 October, was postponed until the beginning of the following season, meaning that the club season finished on 28 September with the North Staffs Motor Club meeting.

ABOVE *Innes Ireland spins his BRP-BRM Mk1 in front of the unprotected pits during the 1963 British Grand Prix. (LAT)*

BELOW *Lotus boss Colin Chapman joined his victorious driver Jim Clark on the podium at the 1963 British Grand Prix. (LAT)*

1964

The 16th *Daily Express* International Trophy race on 2 May was run over 52 laps and produced a thrilling 'Silverstone-type finish' as Jack Brabham in a Brabham-Climax BT7 and Graham Hill's BRM P261 crossed the line side-by-side. Brabham, who also set a new lap record at 1m 33.6s, an average speed of 112.58mph, was given the victory, although the pair were awarded identical times by the timekeepers. Jim Clark had initially led in his Lotus-Climax 25B but fell back with engine problems after a few laps, allowing Dan Gurney in his Brabham-Climax BT7 to head the pack until he retired. This left Brabham in front for three laps before he was passed by Hill, who then led until the final lap when Brabham just beat him to the line. Peter Arundell brought his Lotus-Climax 25B in third.

ABOVE *Max Aitkin, chairman of Beaverbrook Newspapers, congratulates Jack Brabham on his victory in the 1964* Daily Express *International Trophy race. (LAT)*

Mike Salmon should have won the opening GT race in his Aston Martin DB4GT, but he spun on the opening lap, dropping 22 places. He managed to work his way back through the field and into second place, but was unable to catch the leading Ferrari 250 GTO of Graham Hill.

Bruce McLaren won the sports car event in his Zerex Cooper-Climax T53, while Jack Sears took his Willment-entered Ford Galaxie to victory in the saloon car event. Jackie Stewart won the F3 race in his Ken Tyrrell-entered Cooper-BMC T72.

The Eight Clubs meeting on 13 June was marred by the death of Peter Rose, whose Austin-Healey 100 suffered brake failure coming into Woodcote Corner and hit the bank during Friday practice.

Roger Nathan, in his Brabham-Climax BT8, won the 150-mile Martini Trophy held on the full Grand Prix circuit at the AMOC meeting on 4 July.

The 750 Motor Club's annual six-hour race on 8 August was renamed the Birkett 6 Hour Relay in honour of the club's former chairman Holly Birkett, who had died the year before. The Hagley Minis emerged the winners, beating the Cherwell Imps.

Another fatality occurred during the North Staffs Motor Club's meeting on 26 September when the Lotus Seven of Nick Robinson crashed at Copse and overturned during the sports racing car event.

Roger Mac won both the F3 and the over-1600cc GT races in a Brabham-Ford BT2 and E-type Jaguar, respectively, at the Club Championship meeting on 3 October.

1965

The Senior Service 200 meeting on 20 March, organised by the BARC, was eventually abandoned mid-afternoon because of the appalling weather conditions before the main event for F2 cars could be held. Prior to that, the F3 race had been won by Warwick Banks in the Tyrrell team Cooper-BMC T76. The following sports car race was reduced from 25 to 18 laps and resulted in a victory for Jim Clark's Lotus-Ford 30, after battling hard through the heavy rain with the Lola-Chevrolet T70 of John Surtees. No other races were run.

No fewer than six drivers qualified inside the existing lap record for the BRDC *Daily Express* International Trophy meeting on 15 May. Jackie Stewart scored his first-ever F1 victory in a BRM P261, ahead of reigning world champion John Surtees in his Ferrari 158 and the Lotus-Climax 33 of Mike Spence. Stewart's team-mate Graham Hill was the early leader, challenged by the Brabham-Climax BT11 of Jack Brabham, who eventually took the lead. Hill retired soon after with a dead engine, while Stewart and Surtees battled over second place. This became a fight for the lead when Brabham also retired after losing all his oil. Stewart took the flag, but Surtees set a new lap record of 1m 33s (a speed of 113.30mph).

Piers Courage, driving a Brabham-Ford BT10, was the winner of the supporting F3 event, while Bruce McLaren set a new outright circuit record of 1m 31.6s (115.03mph) in his McLaren-Elva-Oldsmobile M1A on his way to victory in the sports car race, the first time that the lap record had fallen to a sports-racing car.

Roy Pierpoint's Ford Mustang led all the way in the 'Senior Service' touring car race, beating Sir Gawaine Baillie's Mustang into second place.

BELOW *Mechanics and spectators look on as the 1965 British Grand Prix gets underway. (BRDC Archive)*

ABOVE *The pit board shows that Jim Clark is 21sec in the lead of the 1965 British Grand Prix in his Lotus-Climax 33. (LAT)*

■ A new lap record for the Club circuit was set at the Nottingham Sports Car Club's meeting on Whit Monday, 7 June, by Chris Summers in his Lotus-Chevrolet 24, with a time of 1m 04s (an average speed of 95.84mph).

■ The BARC organised its first club meeting at the circuit on 19 June. The F3 event was won by David Cole in his Brabham-Ford BT15.

■ Jim Clark won his fourth British Grand Prix in a row on 10 July, taking victory ahead of Graham Hill in the BRM P261, but it was a close-run thing towards the finish. Clark's Lotus-Climax 33 had been losing oil and developed a misfire, allowing Hill to slowly close in. By coasting through the corners and only accelerating down the straights, Clark was able to nurse his car home, despite the best efforts of the chasing Hill who, along with team-mate Jackie Stewart, had fitted rain tyres on the rear wheels. Along the way, Hill set a new (but not outright) F1 lap record of 1m 32.2s (a speed of 114.29mph). John Surtees brought his Ferrari 158 home in third place.

■ The supporting sports car race produced a runaway victory for John Coundley in his McLaren-Elva-Oldsmobile M1A. Ford Mustangs led the way in the Britax touring car race, Sir Gawaine Baillie finishing ahead of Mike Salmon, with the Lotus Ford Cortinas of Sir John Whitmore and Jack Sears dead-heating for third. Roy Pike won the F3 event in a Brabham-Ford BT15.

■ Chris Amon, deputising for the injured Bruce McLaren, took his McLaren-Elva-Oldsmobile M1A to victory in the Martini International Trophy race at the Aston Martin Owners' Club meeting on 24 July. McLaren had suffered burns to his neck and shoulders after the front carburettor on the car had worked loose and caught fire during Friday's practice. Pole-man John Surtees, in a Lola-Chevrolet T70, had led until lap seven when it stopped on Hangar Straight, but not before Surtees had lowered McLaren's outright circuit record by 0.4sec, leaving it at 1m 31.2s (a speed of 115.54mph). Amon thus assumed a lead he was never to lose.

RIGHT *The Ford Anglia Supers of Mike Young (2) and Chris Craft (3) lead the BMW 1800 of Keith Greene (38) around Club Corner during the production touring car race at the 1965 British Grand Prix. (BRDC Archive)*

ABOVE *Despite losing oil and developing a misfire, Jim Clark nursed his Lotus-Climax 33 home to victory in the 1965 British Grand Prix. (LAT)*

1966

The 35-lap *Daily Express* International Trophy race, which took place on 14 May, was the first F1 race in Britain held to the new 3-litre regulations, and it produced a victory for Jack Brabham in his Brabham-Repco BT19. Pre-race favourite had been the Ferrari 312 of John Surtees, but he had to settle for second, with Jo Bonnier's Cooper-Maserati T81 finishing third.

The supporting sports car race was won by Denny Hulme in a Lola-Chevrolet T70, while the saloon car event produced a win for the Ford Falcon of Sir John Whitmore. Radio London, the pirate radio station, sponsored the F3 encounter, which provided the closest race of the day. Roy Pike, in the Lucas Team Lotus-Ford 41, was the winner by just 0.8sec from Chris Irwin's Chequered Flag team Brabham-Ford BT18.

The AMOC's annual Martini International on 9 July was held in atrocious conditions and provided a convincing victory in the 150-mile race for Denny Hulme in Sid Taylor's Lola-Chevrolet T70. The supporting F3 event produced a one-two for the Chequered Flag Brabham-Ford BT18s of Mike Beckwith and Chris Irwin, the pair crossing the line just 0.2sec apart. Roy Pierpoint won the saloon car race in his Ford Falcon, while Mike de Udy won the sports and GT event in his Porsche Carrera 6.

The first-ever Sunday meeting was held at the circuit on 24 July and was organised by the BARC, but it had to be halted after the second event because of torrential rain and an inch of standing water at Woodcote. When conditions improved, racing resumed, and the final of the feature event, the W.D. & H.O. Wills Trophy for F3 cars, was won by Robin Widdows in his Brabham-Ford BT18.

Chris Lambert took his Brabham-Ford BT15 to victory in the wet F3 event at the Eight Clubs meeting on 1 October, held on the full Grand Prix, circuit after a thrilling dice with Jackie Oliver and Derek Bell, who followed him home in their Lotus-Ford 41s.

BELOW *Jack Brabham in his Brabham-Repco BT19 leads the 1966* Daily Express *International Trophy race, winning from pre-race favourite John Surtess in his Ferrari 312. The event was the first to be held in Britain for the new three-litre Formula One regulations. (LAT)*

ABOVE *The front row of the grid had already gone as a very wet F3 race at the Martini International Trophy meeting in July 1966 gets underway. The Lotus-Ford 41s of Jackie Oliver and Charles Lucas (29) and the Brabham-Ford BT18 of Peter Gethin (7) are followed by the Brabhams of Charles Crichton-Stuart (5) and Chris Lambert (18). The race was dominated by the Brabham BT18s of Mike Beckwith and Chris Irwin. Other famous names in the race included Jacky Ickx, Derek Bell, Mo Nunn and Dave Walker. (Ian Wagstaff)*

LEFT *A varied grid for a 10-lap scratch race for GT cars at the Peterborough Motor Club meeting in September 1966 includes a De Sauto-Stevens (70) alongside a Marcos GT and a Diva GT, while behind them another Diva (75) shares row two with a Lotus 11 (67) and a Mini Marcos. (Ian Wagstaff)*

1967

■ Having competed at Snetterton on Good Friday, the new 1600cc F2 championship decamped to Silverstone for the W.D. & H.O. Wills Trophy meeting on Easter Monday, 27 March. The event was run in two parts, each of 20 laps, with the result being decided on aggregate. The first heat was won convincingly by Jochen Rindt in his Winklemann-run Brabham-Cosworth BT23, with team-mate Alan Rees second. John Surtees, driving a Lola-Cosworth T100, completed the podium. The start of the second heat was delayed by five minutes to allow live coverage by ITV, enabling Graham Hill's mechanics to complete repairs to his Lotus-Cosworth 48, which had suffered rear suspension failure in the first heat. Hill started from the back of the grid but worked his way up to second at the flag, behind Rindt but ahead of third-placed Surtees. Rindt was the overall winner, with Rees second and Surtees third.

■ The supporting Wills Trophy F3 race, which opened proceedings, produced a terrific scrap between Kurt Ahrens, Peter Gethin, Chris Williams and Alan Rollinson, all driving Brabham-Cosworth BT21s, but after both Williams and Rollinson retired it was Morris Nunn in a Lotus-Cosworth 41 who took the honours, ahead of Gethin.

■ The *Autosport* Group 4 sports car race was won by Denny Hulme in a Ford GT40. In the Group 5 saloon car event, Jackie Oliver overcame a snowstorm to emerge the winner in his Ford Mustang, ahead of early leader Frank Gardner who had spun his Alan Mann Ford Falcon.

■ Morris Nunn won the F3 encounter at the BARC meeting on 15 April in his Lotus-Ford 41 after a classic slipstreaming battle with the Brabham-Ford BT21 of Tony Lanfranchi, who finished second, and the Brabham-Ford BT18 of Peter Gaydon, who was just beaten to third place by David Cole in his BT18.

■ The proximity of the Monaco Grand Prix affected the entry for the *Daily Express* International Trophy race on 29 April, with neither Cooper-Maserati nor Eagle present and BRM, Lotus and Ferrari sending single entries. The race resulted in a victory for Mike Parkes' Ferrari 312 after a close tussle with

BELOW *Eventual winner Jochen Rindt (right – Brabham-Ford BT23) side-by-side with John Surtess (left – Lola-Ford T100) during the second 20-lap part of the W.D. & H.O. Wills Trophy F2 championship race on Easter Monday. (LAT)*

the BRM H16 of Jackie Stewart until he retired. Jack Brabham came second in his Brabham-Repco BT20, with Jo Siffert's Cooper-Maserati T81 third.

■ The supporting Caravans International F3 race was won by Peter Westbury in a Brabham-Ford BT21. David Piper won the W.D. & H.O. Wills Trophy for sports cars in his Ferrari 275LM, while the Ovaltine Trophy for saloon cars went to Frank Gardner in the Ford Falcon.

■ The meeting marked the opening of the new *Daily Express* vehicle bridge over the circuit between Abbey and Woodcote corners. The impressive new Dunlop press and TV tower on the outside of Woodcote was also inaugurated, while the Red Arrows display team entertained the crowd in their Hawker Siddeley Gnat Trainers.

■ Paul Hawkins seized the lead at the first corner of the Martini International Trophy race for Group 4 sports cars on 20 May, and simply drove away to victory in his Ford GT40. Derek Bell won the F3 race in his Brabham-Ford BT21, and Frank Gardner was victorious in the saloon car event in his 4.7-litre Ford Falcon Sprint.

ABOVE *Yet another British Grand Prix victory for Jim Clark – his fifth in total, and the third consecutive win at Silverstone – this time in a Lotus-Cosworth 49 at the 1967 event. (LAT)*

LEFT *With spinning rear wheels wreathed in tyre smoke, the Lotus-Ford 49s of Jim Clark and Graham Hill, together with the Brabham-Repco BT24 of Jack Brabham, lead away at the start of the 1967 British Grand Prix. (Michael Hewett)*

RIGHT *Denny Hulme took his Brabham-Repco BT24 to second place at the 1967 British Grand Prix, behind Jim Clark's Lotus 49. Hulme went on to win that year's World Championship.* (LAT)

BELOW *Timing equipment at the 1967 British Grand Prix.* (LAT)

ABOVE *Jim Clark and the Lotus team set off on their lap of honour, towed behind a tractor, after winning the 1967 British Grand Prix.* (Ian Wagstaff)

■ The BARC-organised meeting on Sunday 18 June included the first-ever Formula Vee race to be run in the country, and a display by the Red Devils free-fall parachute team.

■ The British Grand Prix was back at Silverstone on 15 July, and a crowd of around 120,000 turned out. Prior to the main event, spectators were treated to a five-lap demonstration run by members of the Club Internationale des Anciens Pilotes de Grands Prix, including Louis Chiron in a Bugatti T35, Duncan Hamilton in a D-type Jaguar, Tony Brooks in a Vanwall, Baron Emmanuel de Graffenried in a Maserati 250F, Juan Manuel Fangio in a Mercedes-Benz W196 and Stirling Moss and Denis Jenkinson in a Mercedes-Benz 300SLR.

■ In the Grand Prix itself, Jim Clark gave the new Lotus-Ford 49 another win, with Denny Hulme's Brabham-Repco BT24 second and the Ferrari 312 V12 of Chris Amon third. At one point it had looked as if it would be a Lotus one-two as Clark and his team-mate Graham Hill lapped at the front of the field until Hill's Lotus suffered rear suspension failure on lap 54 while he was leading.

■ Charles Lucas won the supporting F3 event in his Lotus-Ford 41, despite spinning, while Richard Attwood's Ferrari 275LM was victorious in the W.D. & H.O. Wills Trophy for sports cars, and Frank Gardner's Ford Falcon Sprint won the Ovaltine Trophy for touring cars.

■ The Birkett 6 Hour Relay race on 5 August was won by the Austin-Healey Club's team of Sprites.

■ The Clubmen's Championship meeting, organised by the 750 Motor Club on 14 October, had to be abandoned after six of the eight races had been run, because of heavy rain and standing water around the track.

1968

■ Motor Racing Stables began running courses at the circuit in February on the first and third Sundays of each month. Chief instructors were Peter Arundell and Trevor Taylor.

■ Club racer Robin Smith suffered a heart attack in his Ford Mustang and died during practice for the BARC's meeting on 6 April.

■ A smaller field than usual gathered for the 20th *Daily Express* International Trophy race on 27 April. Prior to the main event, a minute's silence was held in memory of Jim Clark, who had been killed at Hockenheim earlier in the month, with each driver standing beside his car on the grid while a lone piper played a lament. The race ended in a one-two for McLaren, with Denny Hulme leading home Bruce McLaren in their Ford-powered M7As, followed by the Ferrari 312 of Chris Amon in third place. Mike Spence's BRM P126 had been an early leader while his team-mate Pedro Rodriguez in a P139 and the Gold Leaf Team Lotus-Ford 49 of Graham Hill had both offered a challenge to the McLarens before all three retired. Hulme's victory was particularly impressive since a stone had smashed the right-hand lens of his goggles early in the race, causing him to drop to seventh place, before fighting his way back to the front. Amon set a new lap record of 1m 25.1s (a speed of 123.82mph).

■ Hulme also won the Players Group 4 sports car race in a Lola-Chevrolet T70, while the Duckhams saloon car trophy was won by Brian Muir in a Ford Falcon Sprint. The Caravans International Trophy F3 event provided a narrow victory for John Miles in the experimental Lotus-Ford 41X.

■ Denny Hulme's winning ways at Silverstone continued at the Martini International meeting on 27 July when he took his Sid Taylor Lola T70 to victory in the feature Martini 300 event for Group 4 and Group 6 sports cars. A massive entry of 88 cars had been received for the 36 places on the grid, including a single Alan Mann Racing Ford F3L for Frank Gardner. The Australian held the lead with Hulme right on his tail for the first 42 laps, until he retired with engine failure, leaving the New Zealander to take victory by two laps over the Ford GT40 of Paul Hawkins.

ABOVE *The Group 5 saloon car race at the 1968 Martini International Trophy meeting produced a win for David Hobbs in his Ford Falcon Sprint, ahead of the similar car of Brian Muir. (LAT)*

■ Tetsu Ikuzawa won the F3 encounter in his Brabham-Ford BT21B, and David Hobbs won the Group 5 saloon car race in his Ford Falcon Sprint. An invitation saloon car race, which opened proceedings, was won by Rauno Aaltonen in a Mini Cooper S.

■ Spectators at the Bentley Drivers' Club meeting on 31 August were treated to an air display by the RAF Vipers Jet Provost aerobatics team, and demonstrations of the Hoverhawk hovercraft and Tik Tickner's Geronimo dragster.

■ The Formule Libre event at the SUNBAC meeting on 7 August was won by a certain Max Mosley, driving a Brabham-Cosworth BT23C.

■ The following day, 8 August, the circuit played host to the finale of the Players No.6 Autocross Championship with an 1,100-yard course laid out in the Red car park. BTD went to Eric Clegg in his Minivan-based 1.3 Leda-BMC 1 Special, but Rod Chapman secured the 1968 Autocross title in his 1.6 Lotus Cortina.

1969

■ For the first time, the *Daily Express* International Trophy was held on a Sunday, 30 March, in order to give more people a chance to attend. A heavy shower just before the start left the track wet, but Jack Brabham led from the off and had the race under control until, towards the end, his Brabham-Ford BT26 began cutting out as it was low on fuel. Nevertheless, the Australian managed to nurse it to the line, finishing just 2.2sec ahead of the Gold Leaf Team Lotus-Ford 49 of Jochen Rindt, who had been delayed by a misfiring engine in the early laps but had stormed through the field. Jackie Stewart brought his Matra-Ford MS10 into third place.

ABOVE *An example of how close drivers used to get to the breeze block walls on the inside of the corners. This is Jack Brabham just kissing the wall with the front tyre of his Brabham-Ford BT26 on his way to victory during the 1969 International Trophy race. (Michael Hewett)*

■ The supporting Group 4 sports car race was won by Denny Hulme in a Lola-Chevrolet T70 Mk3B GT, while the Group 5 saloon car event provided a win for the Ford Escort Twin Cam of Frank Gardner.

■ Heavy rain blighted the Martini International Trophy, organised by the Aston Martin Owners' Club, on 17 May. Chris Craft emerged the winner of the 65-lap feature race in a Lola T70 Mk3. The F3 event was won by Charles Lucas in a Titan-Ford Mk 3A.

■ The first Guards F5000 Championship race at the circuit took place on 15 June at the BRSCC-organised meeting. Mike Walker took the honours in his Lola-Chevrolet T142 after early leaders Peter Gethin, in a McLaren-Chevrolet M10A, and Trevor Taylor, in a Surtees-Chevrolet TS5, both retired.

■ Advertisements for the British Grand Prix to be held on 19 July showed that special trackside enclosures cost 17s 6d (87.5p) in advance, or 20s (£1) on the day. Children under 14 were 5s (25p) each. Reserved grandstands opposite the pits and at Woodcote cost 50s (£2.50), while those at the south end of the circuit around Stowe were 40s (£2.00). Paddock transfers cost 10s (50p).

■ The Grand Prix itself produced an epic battle between the Gold Leaf Team Lotus-Ford 49 of Jochen Rindt and the Matra-Ford MS80 of Jackie Stewart. The pair had started from the front of the grid and were immediately in a class of their own, pulling away from the rest of the field and swapping the lead. The battle was resolved when Rindt had to pit towards the end in order to have his rear wing endplate, which was coming loose, removed. He rejoined in a distant second place but then had to pit again to take on fuel, dropping him to fourth. Second place, albeit a lap behind the triumphant Stewart, was Jacky Ickx in a Brabham-Ford BT26 while Bruce McLaren took third in his McLaren-Ford M7C.

ABOVE *As usual, the pit lane, together with the spectators' balcony behind it, is packed during the 1969 British Grand Prix. (BRDC Archive)*

ABOVE *An epic battle at the 1969 British Grand Prix between the Gold Leaf Team Lotus-Ford 49 of Jochen Rindt and the Matra-Ford MS80 of Jackie Stewart came to an end when the Austrian driver had to pit to remove a broken rear wing endplate, which can be seen rubbing on his tyre in this photograph. Stewart went on to win the race by over a lap, while Rindt finished fourth. (LAT)*

■ The Grand Prix was notable for having four four-wheel-drive F1 cars make the start, these being the Lotus-Ford 63s of John Miles and Jo Bonnier, the Matra MS84 of Jean-Pierre Beltoise and the McLaren-Ford M9A of Derek Bell. Both Beltoise and Miles made it to the finish, albeit in ninth and tenth places out of the ten finishers, and six and nine laps behind the winner respectively.

■ The supporting F3 event provided another epic Silverstone slip streamer, with eight cars battling for the lead. Alan Rollinson emerged the victor in his Chevron-Ford B15 just 0.4sec ahead of the Lotus-Ford 59 of Tetsu Ikuzawa. Roy Pierpoint won the Group 5 saloon car race in his Chevrolet Camaro Z28.

■ Ford Anglia driver Graham Bean was presented with the Clubman of the Year award at the BRDC-organised Gold Leaf Clubmen's Championship meeting on 18 October, for his consistent domination of his class at the circuit during the year.

BELOW *Allan Rollinson, in a Chevron-Holbay B15, seen here leading the Tecno-Novamotor 69 of Ronnie Peterson and the rest of the F3 pack, emerged victorious from an eight-car scrap at the 1969 British Grand Prix meeting. (LAT)*

1970s

"*To get a quick lap at Silverstone you need smooth driving, and ask the mechanics to tighten up the belts to really squeeze your balls.*"
Emerson Fittipaldi

The pits balcony at Silverstone in the early seventies afforded good views. Spectators could not only look down at cars in the raised pit lane below them, but also see them exiting the crushingly fast Woodcote Corner, often teetering on the edge of adhesion as the drivers fought to keep the cars under control, sliding in spectacular fashion.

The greatest exponent of this skill at the sport's top end was the Swedish racing driver Ronnie Peterson, and one of the iconic sights of Silverstone's past is of him in 1973, his glorious black and gold JPS Lotus-Ford 72E on full opposite lock as he hurtled through Woodcote at around 150mph. At the John Player British Grand Prix that year, Peterson claimed pole position and went on to finish second behind the Yardley McLaren-Ford M23 of Peter Revson in the restarted race.

Motor Sport captured the drama of the start of the 1973 British Grand Prix perfectly: "The real activity began to occur about 1.30pm when the cars and drivers began to gather for the entrance into the pits, with the lucky chief mechanics having the honour of driving the cars from the paddock round to the pits. The drivers then drove round the circuit to the starting grid, where everyone was marshalled into their grid position, and then a fine parade was carried out in front of the main grandstand. Row by row the cars were wheeled along the track by the mechanics,

RIGHT *Seen here coming down Hangar Straight approaching Stowe, Jackie Stewart dominated the 1971 Woolmark British Grand Prix in his Tyrrell-Ford 003, setting a new outright lap record along the way. (LAT)*

while the drivers and the team managers or team owners walked alongside and the commentator 'presented' the contestants to the 'Tribune d'Honneur'. It was as good as a bullfight and gave you the feeling of participation in the great manifestation that was about to begin.

"The drivers then donned their helmets and gloves, were strapped in their cars by their mechanics and set off on a serious warm-up lap in grid formation. It was a splendid sight as the 28 cars in rows of three-two-three appeared under the bridge before Woodcote in an orderly array, just like an Indianapolis rolling start. They paused on the dummy-grid and then moved forward to the starting-grid, the Union Flag went up, was lowered and amidst smoke and rubber dust the British Grand Prix was under way."

Under way it might have been, but it didn't last very long and as the pack completed the opening lap, with Jackie Stewart's Tyrrell-Ford 003 leading Peterson's Lotus-Ford 72E across the line, Jody Scheckter, who had started eighth in his Yardley McLaren-Ford M23 but was now up to fourth, ran wide on the exit of Woodcote and slid on the grass. To the horror of the crowd and everyone in the pits, his car slid broadside across the track and buried its nose in the three-foot high pit wall, causing those standing just above him at the point of impact to recoil.

Scheckter's car rolled back into the middle of the track, the South African waving his hands furiously in the air to try to warn others but it was too late. Some cars went either side of him in avoidance, but then he was clipped and all hell broke loose.

The event marked the first-ever race at Silverstone for John Watson, who was driving a Brabham-Ford BT37 run by Hexagon of Highgate. "When I came round on the opening lap, the marshals were extremely vigorous in their flag waving," he recalled. "Normally when a driver sees the yellow flag he always imagines to himself he knows better, but this time I suddenly thought 'this is serious'. So you back out of it as much as you feel is appropriate, and when I came around the corner and got on to the pit straight it was like an aircraft accident. I'd never, ever seen an accident in my life like it. There were cars everywhere, bits of cars everywhere, bits of cars still up in the sky, and fortunately, because I was sufficiently far back at the end of the first lap, I managed to thread my way through it without hitting anything or being hit by anything. Then, of course, the race was red-flagged and they had to restart it two hours or something later."

Lord Alexander Hesketh, who at that time had just started running James Hunt in a March-Ford 731, also remembers the incident well: "One of the most outrageous pieces of driving," he said. "The crash went on and on, and James Hunt was nearly decapitated. We would have won the race if it hadn't been for that crash, because it took off the first piece of aerodynamics we did, which was the narrow Harvey Postlethwaite airbox. All the Marches had those ugly airboxes and we had this very tall, narrow one, which was worth about 400–500rpm on the fast straights. Someone's wing came off and took the whole airbox off – sliced it

like a knife through butter. You could see the mark on the top of James' helmet – it was scratched where it had gone through. We had to put a March standard airbox on after the accident, and in the race there was just this group of four cars nose-to-tail with Revson in front. James always said afterwards that he should have won the race, but he felt he'd just got so few miles in an F1 car, or even an F2 car, that he just didn't dare do it. Because he knew that even with the crap airbox he was quicker but didn't want to go and screw it up."

Remarkably, the only casualty from the accident was the Italian driver Andrea de Adamich, who was trapped in his Brabham-Ford BT42 for nearly an hour with a broken ankle before he could be cut free and taken to hospital. But the accident sent out signals to the world – Silverstone, or rather Woodcote Corner in particular, was getting too fast, and by the next time the Grand Prix was held there, the first major track modification since 1950 would have been made and a new pit and paddock complex built.

A year previously, during the Formula Ford final at the 1972 *Daily Express* International Trophy meeting, Scheckter's older brother Ian had lost control of his Merlyn coming through Woodcote

Stuart Graham

LEFT *Stuart Graham, who competed at Silverstone on both two wheels and on four, won the prestigious Tourist Trophy in his Brut-sponsored Chevrolet Camaro Z28 for the second consecutive year in 1975. (LAT)*

"There are one or two circuits that are considered or accepted to be the 'classic' circuits around the world, and Silverstone certainly is the one for England.

"With bike racing, because of the nature of the circuit – and this is a good thing about fast-flowing circuits – there were huge slip streaming bunches, and the races were close with six people trying to get round the corner all at the same time. It's a wide circuit and when you've got width and you've got fast corners then you're going to get close racing, so it was always a good fast circuit and always good racing. I loved it.

"You speak to most bike racers and they'll usually remember some incident or moment at the old Woodcote, which was a hugely quick corner and was nearly flat out, depending on how brave you were and how quick your bike was. There was a slight dip in the middle if I remember rightly, not far from the apex as you were going in, which always unsettled something just at the wrong moment. So we've all probably had a fairly scary moment there, thinking we'd got through flat, to find that we didn't quite and we very nearly didn't get through at all.

"Bikes and cars obviously take different lines to a degree but it's still the same challenges – a fast corner is a fast corner – and when I started racing cars it was basically still the same circuit with the old Woodcote, so it was just as big a challenge. We were running the big Camaros then, and a 7-litre Camaro through those sort of corners was extremely entertaining. It was very quick.

"I think we did 103mph in practice for one of the TTs, which wasn't bad going for a saloon car, and it just indicated just how quick the course was. And, of course, I'm talking pre-chicanes,

and then the chicanes came, but it always retained this high-speed nature, which any racer, of course, loves.

"The first Tourist Trophy win was interesting because we'd never done a longish race with the Camaros up until that point, and they had a reputation for being quick but slightly fragile, and they didn't normally survive long distances. We were confident that we could do it, but we had to drive it sensibly. The brakes were always the weak link with the Camaro and, of course, tyre wear. And so I drove it single-handedly rather than with a second driver, mainly because I knew I had to conserve things and drive it sensibly, which you do with a long-distance race anyway. So it was a very satisfying race to win because people didn't think it could be done with that sort of car.

"The second year, in '75, we had a more modified Camaro for the European championship regulations, and that was easier because the car was so much quicker. We were three seconds a lap quicker than anything else, for pole and practice, which is slightly embarrassing. And BMW had got some works-supported coupés, all the usual European hotshots came over, so of course everyone was saying that we blew everybody away but that it wouldn't last. Well it did.

"I drove on my own that year as well. I was probably too mean to share any money or something, but I always felt it was easier to do it myself than to try and get somebody else in, who probably would have done a decent job but there was always that added risk. We were running bigger wheels and tyres in '75, and what that did was increase the grip, so that you put more strain on the driveshafts. Again, it was another reason you had to be pretty sensible how you drove it."

and had spun in front of the pack, kissing the pit wall. The Jamun of Mike Sirett hit the Armco barrier opposite the pits, flew right across the track under the *Motor* bridge, ending up beyond the pits and taking two other cars with it. Sirett escaped with a fractured ankle. So it could be argued that the younger Scheckter was only following the example set a year earlier by his older brother.

But this is jumping ahead. Throughout 1970, the BRDC continued with its attempts to purchase the freehold of the site from the Ministry of Defence, and at the BRDC annual dinner-dance at the Dorchester Hotel on 4 December that year, the club's president, Gerald Lascelles, announced that the club had acquired the freehold of the circuit and other lands at Silverstone, amounting to around 398 acres, for the sum of £125,000 from the Ministry of Defence.

The purchase had been funded jointly, with the Silverstone Trust making its funds (amounting to £65,000) available on an interest-free basis to the BRDC, while the Midland Bank had agreed to the club having overdraft facilities of up to £50,000 for 12 months, plus an additional £30,000 for three months. An additional £10,000 came from the operating companies.

Jack Sears recalled the negotiations that had taken place with the Ministry over the purchase of the land: "We let it be known to the Ministry of Defence that we were interested in buying the freehold, and at that time they were quite keen to sell it, really.

"They put in a price that seemed to me, as a farmer, to be very high. There were about 700 acres and a lot of it was farmland, a lot of it was asphalt. I was a director of the BRDC and also a director of Silverstone Circuits, who were really doing the negotiations, and I had a chartered surveyor friend called Philip Hall, and I asked the fellow directors if they'd let me get him over to do a valuation and negotiate on our behalf to get a fair and reasonable price. He went all round the place and saw everything with Jimmy Brown and came back with a valuation that was far less than was being asked for by the Ministry of Defence.

"So the time then came to meet the Ministry of Defence people, and there was Jimmy Brown, myself and Philip Hall, and Gerald Lascelles was there as president of the club. We sat across the table with the government people and negotiated, and we finally put our price down on the table, which in the end they accepted. So that was very satisfactory.

"We had the money from the Trust and we bought the freehold, paid for it, and my recollection of events is that the companies who donated all this money never did ask for it back. To start with, it was a contribution towards us buying, and a trust was formed so we couldn't spend the money on something else, but in the end it became a donation."

Silverstone was finally secure and work pressed ahead on improvement, the circuit announcing its long-term plans in early 1971. *Autosport* had described Silverstone as having "fallen into a rut over recent years, with the same meetings year in, year out". A new team, consisting of Peter Clark as chairman, George Smith as circuit manager and Pierre Aumonier as the press and publicity officer, was embarking on an ambitious plan to change that. The following season there would be a distinct difference between true clubmen's meetings and promoted championship meetings. For clubmen's meetings the circuit would be offered free of charge as long as there was no commercial backing, and no prize donor would be allowed to publicise the meeting for commercial purposes. These meetings would continue to be held on a Saturday and, while spectators were welcome to attend, the meetings were designed purely for the club competitor. There would also be a number of larger meetings, mainly held on Sundays, organised by the bigger clubs and including sponsored championship races.

Having finally acquired the freehold of the land, the club was seeking to acquire even more with the intention of establishing a leisure centre, and a meeting was held in March 1971 to decide whether or not to purchase a further 258 acres of land.

A report to the meeting stated: "When the club started trying to purchase the freehold, its motives were simply to obtain physical security of tenure. At that time we had no idea that the money-earning potential of the land, as a means of deriving income from sources other than motor racing, could eventually become a vital factor in assuring the survival of the circuit and the club financially.

"Thus when we acquired Green Crop Conservation, we thought in terms of getting rid of a troublesome neighbour and strengthening the bargaining position with the Ministry with regard to the ultimate purchase of the land. We did not foresee the extent to which the farm income would be a factor in the club's overall solvency.

"Today the club administration, consisting of one man, two girls and three small rooms, costs around £10,000 per annum to operate, towards which subscriptions contribute in round figures about £2,000. In other words the club could not exist without the farm and circuit earnings.

"Circuit earnings, based upon motor racing and allied activities, have in recent years been eroded by ever-increasing demands of competitors, to the point that we make a loss in a non-Grand Prix year and a modest profit in a GP year. Thus our motives for purchasing freehold land have shifted from merely seeking physical security of tenure, towards broadening the basis of our earnings by the intelligent use of that land for other compatible purposes.

"398.5 acres were purchased last November, but because of the bits missing in the middle and elsewhere, we may not have the best possible situation for other profit-earning developments until we obtain the remaining 258 acres now on offer to us."

The asking price for the remaining land was £65,000, including a farmhouse and cottages, but £58,000 was regarded as acceptable. If a serious offer was not made to the Ministry by 1 April they could sell to a third party.

During June, discussions were held about a proposal for the formation of a new company – Silverstone Leisure Ltd – to admit outside participation and be charged with profitable development of the remainder of the estate for non-motoring purposes. Silverstone Circuits would remain a wholly-owned subsidiary of the BRDC and would operate the racing circuit and the 'Northants infield' for motor sporting purposes. Silverstone Leisure would develop the rest of the estate for 'non-motoring' leisure by sale of leases and franchises to what was described as 'best-reputed operators'.

In July, a letter was sent to all members informing them that the club had been offered the freehold of lands at Silverstone at present being farmed. When the purchase was completed, the BRDC would own a 700-acre estate costing nearly £200,000. Members were offered the opportunity to purchase shares in the new company. By November, completion of the purchase of the remaining land had taken place.

In its 1971 British Grand Prix report, *Motor Sport* noted the changing face of Silverstone. Whereas the shape of the circuit had not altered, the edge of the track had constantly evolved. In the early days there had been complaints about the inside of the corners being featureless, particularly where they crossed the ends of the runways, so they were marked out using five-gallon oil drums. These were replaced by low brick walls on the inside of the corners, which made sighting easier and more clearly defined the line of the track. However, as a result of consultations with the Grand Prix Drivers' Association and the RAC, the low walls on the inside of Copse, Becketts and Club corners had been replaced over the winter of 1969–70 with plastic markers, as already in place at Woodcote. These moves didn't meet with everyone's approval, though. At the Nottingham Sports Car Club meeting on Easter Monday 1970, a Mini spun at Copse towards the infield, scattering officials and St John Ambulance personnel, and the British Motor Racing Marshals' Club had expressed its concern over safety.

As *Motor Sport* pointed out, the removal of the walls had made Silverstone more like a perimeter track again and less like a road circuit. Another change was that ditches, which had been dug to keep errant cars out of the spectator areas, had been filled in and the earth banks on the outside of the track reinforced with some 7,500 railway sleepers buried into the ground on end and faced with Armco barriers to act as a rubbing strip. It was noted that, while the spectators were now safer, anyone having a high-speed accident stood a good chance of being badly hurt.

Even so, the Grand Prix Drivers' Association had initially just requested that additional Armco barriers be installed, but circuit manager George Smith felt it better to give competitors as much run-off area as possible, rather than have the barrier right up against the side of the track, so the earth banking at Copse was moved back and Armco barrier erected between Maggots and Becketts. All remaining concrete protection for flag marshals had been removed, as requested by the governing body, the CSI (Commission Sportive Internationale de la FIA), and new signalling posts were established on the outside of corners.

Other circuit alterations included new toilets and the surfacing of the paddock and the spectator access roads to the main grandstands. The erection of new permanent grandstands and other amenities would be spread over a number of years because of the cost, and would commence in 1972.

Meanwhile, an all-weather ring road was to be constructed to improve traffic flow around the Grand Prix circuit. Looking ahead, it was felt that an underpass was needed to the centre of the circuit, along with new pits and a technical centre. Ideas for a 'leisure centre' were also mooted, but details were scarce.

Emerson Fittipaldi

"My first memory from Silverstone was a Formula Ford race in 1969 that was just slipstreaming all the race and there were no chicanes – it was the old Silverstone, very fast – and during the race I was working out what position should I be before Woodcote, the last corner, and Woodcote was nearly flat in Formula Ford. And I thought if I come into Woodcote in third place I'll be able to overtake second and be on the inside of the first and win the race.

"I had everything worked out. And I come into Woodcote, third place, everything is perfect. I slipstream second place, I overtake three cars side-by-side. I was on the inside line, with nearly two wheels on the grass, into Woodcote. It's perfect, I'm going to win the race. But to my surprise, there was a car with four wheels on the grass overtaking on the inside. And he spun halfway through Woodcote – I remember his eyes looking at me in the visor, going backwards through Woodcote and he finished second and I was only fourth!

"Silverstone was also my first experience in Formula 1 in 1970. Just before the British Grand Prix I tested a Lotus 49 with Jochen Rindt as my teacher. Silverstone was also my last Grand Prix win, in 1975. It was my first Grand Prix experience and my last Grand Prix win. When it rained I was the first one to put wet tyres on and I survived.

"In 1973, the big crash at Woodcote; Jody Scheckter spun completing the first lap. It was the first time my mother watched a race. Whenever myself and my brother raced, she always stayed in the car park, inside the car. She never wanted to watch a race, she just listened. When the racing finished, 'how is Emerson and Wilson, are they OK?' was her first question. And I keep telling her, 'Mummy, you have to watch the race, it's much safer than you think'. And for the first time she decided to watch the British Grand Prix at Silverstone, right on garage number one at Woodcote, and then there was that strike from Jody.

"Silverstone was very challenging. The best corner was Woodcote. Woodcote I remember with the JPS 72 when I was team-mate with Ronnie. We challenged each other to see if we could take it nearly flat. We were very close, and I remember we put the car sideways there. It was a fantastic corner. But the safety changes meant you had to make the chicane before Woodcote, but Woodcote was a challenge, very difficult.

"To get a quick lap at Silverstone? Smooth driving, and ask the mechanics to tighten up the belts to really squeeze your balls. And then hold tight coming to Woodcote and you make a quick lap.

"I would say it's a classic track. One of the most classic tracks in Grand Prix racing. Very fast in my time when I raced there. I would say at that time it was one of the fastest tracks, and average speed must be very high – I don't remember – but always very fast. I think it was Monza, the fastest, and then Silverstone."

Jochen Mass

"I think the first time I raced at Silverstone was in Formula 3 in '71. I liked the old Silverstone a lot. It had a sort of classic feel of a fast circuit: to slipstream and a few corners to focus on. It was less technical, but it was more sort of man-to-man with the tow and the slipstream, so I think for the public it was more interesting to watch.

"And I enjoyed it tremendously. Of course, you grow up with fast circuits – Spa, of course, and the old Nürburgring, as curvy as it was, but it was very quick nevertheless. So I loved these sort of circuits. And then you grow up with circuits like this in your mind and sort of ingrained in your system; it's difficult to start liking these watered-down, modified versions.

"It's very difficult for me now to see Silverstone as a particularly attractive circuit. I think it's very technical, sure, but on the other hand it doesn't really do much does it?

"In 1973 there were 12 cars eliminated. With the big wings you couldn't see very far, and I was still in this bulk of cars, and they backed off and I backed off and then they accelerated and I accelerated – next moment was mayhem. Nothing really happened except that Andrea de Adamich broke his ankle, but we were really lucky that nothing more happened.

"But this was part of the fast circuit. Woodcote was, of course, a very severe corner in a way. It was damn quick and the outside was immediately grass, no kerbs, so if you put your foot wrong then this sort of thing happened. But it didn't happen often.

"After the start, the right-hander [Copse] was important and, of course, Becketts was always quite challenging because of this long straight following. Then you had Hangar, the right-hander at the bottom of Hangar, which was Stowe; that was a good corner, leading up to Club. Club was important because you had this long sort of straight, because Abbey was not really a corner for us, it was all flat out.

"Woodcote was fantastic. Oh yeah, that was wonderful. It was seriously a good gut feeling corner – you really knew it was right, and it felt good and you could slipstream and you could slide a little bit and all that. It was wonderful, and I regret that we did away with all these circuits now, we have all similar tracks, and Silverstone now is one of them.

"In '72 in a Formula 3 race, Roger Williamson was ahead and he pulled away and I was in a bunch of guys behind. There were six, seven, eight of us. I started overtaking before Woodcote on the very last lap before the finish, just coming out under the bridge I towed myself and, of course, they tried to close the door and I went over the grass on the right, and I managed to keep my foot down and got to the inside so I won that second place.

ABOVE *Damage to the rear bodywork caused Jochen Mass to crash the Essex Porsche 936 he was sharing with Brian Redman while leading the 1979 Silverstone 6-Hours. (LAT)*

"I had a big shunt in '78 [Mass broke his knee and thigh in a testing accident driving an ATS] and I spent some time, but not that long, in Northampton hospital. My first race after that was the six-hours in '79 and I drove the 936 with Brian Redman. Brian had a little get-together with somebody, and damaged the rear wing and then I took over, and going down to Club and then Abbey the rear bonnet opened and I started to fly, because with no lift, we were doing 300kph. So I started to fly and I flew under the bridge. I thought I would hit it but I didn't, and then sort of landed in the embankment on the left and the car disintegrated, but only the bodywork. It was not a hard impact. It looked spectacular but it was quite harmless for the driver. But it looked good because I took off, a good height, and I flew around, and my only thought was 'not Northampton hospital again', but nothing happened.

"In my last McLaren year, '75, when Emerson won it, I would have won if I had just finished that lap. I didn't spin off but I couldn't stop at Stowe. I was trying to, but skidded, skidded, skidded, aquaplaning, and I couldn't slow enough to make it half way round the corner. So I went on to the grass and got stuck in the green there, and I couldn't reverse out of it. And right over my head was a big banner saying that some small village in Germany greeted me, Jochen Mass. So I said 'Hi guys!'

"The old Silverstone was one of the very good circuits. Silverstone was a very fast, very satisfying circuit. It gave you so much. I loved it, honestly, and I think it was one of the good circuits in the world, and now it's just one of many."

In March 1972, plans were announced for a new four-storey pits and paddock complex to be completed in time for the following year's Grand Prix. The ground floor of the building would consist of lock-up garages and the first and third floors would provide spectator decks. The second floor would house private hospitality suites for teams and sponsors, and work on the cars would be carried out from a 'work island' separated from the main building by a three-lane service road.

The same year, a four-layered 'catch fence' was installed as an experiment at Woodcote Corner with the intention of avoiding repetitions of an accident that had befallen Patrick Lindsay on the Club circuit, but without impeding the Grand Prix circuit in any way. It was first used on 22 July at the VSCC meeting, when drivers were reported to have "glared rather balefully at it and then turned right", suggesting that it had perhaps acted as a deterrent.

The fencing, which was 1.2 metres high, was made from 8.5 gauge plastic-coated wire, woven into two-inch mesh and wired on to three-inch wooden posts spaced ten feet apart and set two feet into the ground. Four rows of this fencing were erected at the end of Club Straight, and at the BRSCC's 30 July meeting, Formula Ford driver Derek Lawrence became the first to test the new system when he went straight on at Woodcote. Instead of hitting the sleepers at high speed, his Titan Mk6 tore through the first layer of fencing but was stopped by the second layer. Lawrence was able to drive back to the pits afterwards, and repairs to the fence, consisting of the replacement of broken posts, were quickly carried out.

Another safety initiative was the erection of debris fencing for the protection of spectators in the pits grandstands. This was installed towards the end of the year from Woodcote to the end of the grandstand by the *Motor* bridge. By having its own contractors design and fabricate a special mesh from a special wire, the circuit had tried to minimise interference with visibility for spectators, even when looking at an oblique angle. It was noted, though, that psychologically the fence gave a 'caged-in' sensation that was unpopular, and that it also interfered with photography.

And so to 1973. This was silver jubilee year for Silverstone and the circuit was busier than ever. Along with the John Player British Grand Prix in July, the track played host as usual to the GKN-*Daily Express* International Trophy in April, F5000 in August and a number of championship race meetings, seven organised by the BRDC, four by

the BARC, two by the VSCC and one by AMOC. In addition, a total of ten Saturday amateur club meetings were held.

The circuit also staged more off-track entertainment and provided improved camping and caravanning facilities. Banking was elevated almost all the way around the circuit, and the four-layer catch fencing, having proved successful, was retained.

Obtaining planning permission for a proposed motel and leisure centre was proving slow because the circuit straddled the county boundary between Northamptonshire and Buckinghamshire. Plans for the new pits complex had been put on hold at the end of 1972, but a lot of work had been completed in time for the start of the new season and a considerable amount of improvements had been made at the circuit. All the entrances had been modified in order to improve traffic flow, and several decrepit old buildings by the main entrance had been demolished, and a lay-by created for incoming traffic held for admission-ticket queries. Almost all the old buildings throughout the estate had now been demolished, apart from those that it was intended to restore – the premises housing the Jim Russell Racing Driver's School being an example of an old building renovated. The state of all the car parks was being progressively improved by levelling, grading and filling-in of hollows, while three further toilet blocks had been converted to a 'super-flush' system.

"The toilets were always a sore point because they were a bit primitive," recalled Jack Sears. "We were always wanting to improve the toilets so people came and felt that they were being looked after in that respect, because there was a time when lavatories got blocked and we had to lay on sewage wagons to pump out all the cesspits on a regular basis through a Grand Prix weekend."

Other improvements included new spectator embankments between Club and Abbey and at the entrance to Woodcote, and a new arrangement for traffic behind the grandstands allowed better and safer access by pedestrians. The medical HQ was also increased in size by 50 per cent and its facilities upgraded, while the pits and paddock area was significantly extended and the paddock cafeteria doubled in size, providing a waitress-service restaurant section as well as an improved self-service area. A similar facility behind the pits grandstand was planned to cater for the public.

The most visible improvement, though, was the erection of the new *Motor* pedestrian bridge over the circuit on the main straight, which was completed in time for the Grand Prix. It was much

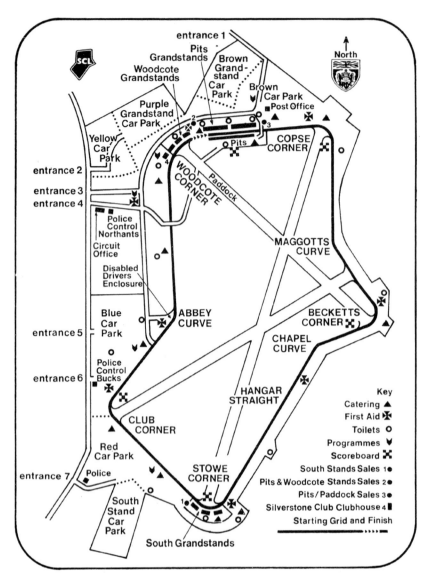

Labels on map:

entrance 1
Pits Grandstands
Woodcote Grandstands
Brown Grandstand Car Park
Brown Car Park
Post Office
SCL
North
Purple Grandstand Car Park
Yellow Car Park
entrance 2
entrance 3
entrance 4
Pits
Paddock
COPSE CORNER
WOODCOTE CORNER
Police Control Northants
Circuit Office
Disabled Drivers Enclosure
MAGGOTTS CURVE
Blue Car Park
entrance 5
ABBEY CURVE
BECKETTS CORNER
CHAPEL CURVE
Police Control Bucks
entrance 6
HANGAR STRAIGHT
CLUB CORNER
Red Car Park
entrance 7
Police
STOWE CORNER
South Stand Car Park
South Grandstands

Key
Catering ▲
First Aid ✠
Toilets ○
Programmes ⌄
Scoreboard ✕
South Stands Sales 1●
Pits & Woodcote Stands Sales 2●
Pits / Paddock Sales 3●
Silverstone Club Clubhouse 4■
Starting Grid and Finish ▪▪▪▶

ABOVE *In the seventies, the car parking at Silverstone continued to be divided into five sections: Brown, Purple, Yellow, Blue and Red. The Brown car park was for the Pits Grandstand and Copse areas; the Purple for Woodcote and Pits Grandstand areas; the Yellow for the Abbey to Woodcote spectators; Blue for the Club to Abbey spectators; and Red for the Stowe to Club spectators. Designated routes brought spectators into the relevant part of the circuit.*

wider than the old one, and the supports were set further back so that the sleepers on the Pit Straight could run all the way down to Copse Corner. Its added height also allowed better vision towards Copse and a clear view from the grandstands and the Dunlop Tower. The new bridge proved to be a godsend at the Grand Prix as it was felt that, had the old bridge been in place at the time of the multiple accident at the end of the first lap, the situation could have been much worse.

On a lighter note, during the Grand Prix several criticisms were made of the amount of air-time used by the French commentator, Jean-Charles Laurens, and it was recommended at a subsequent meeting of the BRDC that "some control be exercised over the gentleman in the future".

Attendance at the Grand Prix had been 65,000, and the popularity of the event was demonstrated by the fact that British Rail had run a Grand Prix special to Silverstone, with a train leaving

London's Euston station at 8.06am, stopping at Watford at 8.25am and arriving at Northampton at 9.25am, with a special bus to transfer passengers to the circuit. The cost was £1 for adults and 70p for children.

The fuel crisis over the winter of 1973–74 meant that all scheduled races and practice sessions for the new season would be reduced by 20 per cent, and work on a new pits complex was postponed until the autumn. Also, the two traditional sponsors of the International Trophy meeting, GKN and the *Daily Express*, withdrew their support this year as they felt unable to continue in the present national emergency. Instead, Silverstone Circuits and the BRDC would promote the meeting themselves.

In October 1974, the circuit announced plans for a new pits complex to be completed by February of the following year. The £120,000 complex, which would bring the circuit's facilities into line with current requirements, was to include 44 new pit garages, each 20ft x 20ft, stretching along the whole of the main straight from the exit of Woodcote to the entrance of Copse – twice the length of the existing buildings. The pit lane was to be brought back down to ground level and widened to 50ft to incorporate four lanes: a fast and slowing-down lane, a working lane and an officials and team members walkway in front of the pits. In addition, a 6ft safety wall and signalling area would separate the pit lane from the track itself. The pit exit was also to be moved so that cars would rejoin the circuit after Copse Corner, and the start-finish line moved 100yds towards Copse, with a new timekeepers' box alongside it. The paddock area behind the pits was also to be extended. The bulldozers started work on 23 October, and the existing pit buildings were completely demolished by the following day.

The new complex was officially opened by HRH the Duke of Edinburgh at the following year's International Trophy meeting on 13 April, but it wasn't the new pits buildings that would be the major change at the circuit during 1975.

"The biggest changes came when Bernie Ecclestone got control of Formula 1 in the seventies," explained Jack Sears. "Up until that point the start money for the Grands Prix was negotiated by the circuit with the Formula 1 teams. Suddenly it all changed when Bernie said they should form themselves into an association and speak as one voice.

"He agreed to do it, and that was the start of FOCA, the Formula 1 Constructors' Association.

Win Percy

"Even as a kid before I ever thought of being involved in motor sport, let alone a racing driver, Silverstone to me was British motor sport.

"I first went there in the sixties when the Alan Mann Escorts were there, and I went with Tony Birchenhough, who had a little Fiat Abarth he used to race. I went up just to be with him and the team and I remember seeing these Escorts go round, and I was absolutely amazed that chaps could go round this track consistently within point something of a second close together, because in those days I was an Autocross driver and then I went to Rallycross and I was rallying, and consistency wasn't the art. The art was doing a very fast lap or two and that's it. To see them do it lap after lap after lap was amazing.

"The first time that I actually went to Silverstone as a competitive person myself was '69 to the Player's No.6 Autocross championship finals in the Red car park, which was by Club Corner. So we were using a grass car park and I was representing the south-west in my 1650 Ford Anglia, and between runs I walked up and stood on the bank and looked down at the tarmac surface, and I thought, 'my god, how on earth do they do that?'

"And years and years later, in 1986, I was in the Silk Cut Jaguar approaching Club Corner. The Formula 1 lap record then was 1m 9.9s. Raul Boesel had just gone out in the sprint Silk Cut Jaguar and done a 1m 9.8s, and I was approaching Club and that lap I remember I did 1m 10.2s, and it brought back memories of me, a skinny kid on the bank thinking 'God, how do they do that', and I suddenly thought, 'I'm doing it now'.

"My first time on the tarmac would have been in 1974. I was given the drive in Big Sam, the Datsun 240Z, and it lunched its engine in practice, so Spike Anderson of Samuri gave me his road-going Datsun to compete in, and that was in the Blue Circle Modified Sports Car Championship against Nick Faure,

especially, in a works Porsche. And I won the class that day in basically a road car.

"The old circuit was all about high speed, and getting a car that could handle those speeds through Stowe, through Club and through Abbey was amazing – the most squeeze of the bum experience you can imagine, especially after a couple of laps when the tyres start to ease off a bit.

"You needed to be smooth to be fast at Silverstone. Flowing speed, not over-braking, it was brushing the pedal, settling the car, don't be aggressive, but your exit speed was important all the time.

"My favourite race would have to be the Grand Prix support in '87 in Andy Rouse's Sierra. Andy was off doing the World Touring Car series. He said, 'I need someone reliable who's not going to make a fool of himself to drive my Sierra because Ford really wants some good publicity at the Grand Prix support race', and he asked if I would do it. I said, 'yeah'.

"So we did a day's testing, talked to Dunlop, and they said, 'Win you're very good on tyres, these will do the race, 18 laps, but they will only just do it. So be smooth, be sensible, and you will do it.' I put the car on pole position and didn't want to wreck the rear tyres off the start line, so tried to pull away gingerly. Stalled it. Completely stalled it.

"Every single car went by me. I'm trying to restart it. I hit the wipers, I hit this, I hit that, eventually it started. The Minis had gone; everything had gone. Of course, then I had to fight through some 30 odd cars, so I put more wear into my tyres than I thought. Anyway, luckily, I won the race – made quite an exciting race of it. On the slowing down lap both rear tyres deflated. In parc fermé, when Andy Rouse's guys came to get the car, all four tyres were flat. They were completely worn through. That has to be one of the most memorable races I think."

ABOVE *The drivers'
briefing before each
Grand Prix used to
take place down by
the start-finish line.
In 1975 Jochen Mass,
Carlos Pace, Mario
Andretti (obscured by
Emerson Fittipaldi),
Clay Regazzoni, Jody
Scheckter, John Watson,
Lella Lombardi and
Niki Lauda all pay
close attention. In
the background are
Wilson Fittipaldi,
Jim Crawford, John
Nicholson and Brian
Henton. (Michael
Hewett)*

And then, of course, he started making demands.
So things had to get better, and changes were
made to the infrastructure and so on over a
period of many years."

Concerns had been raised that F1 cars were
now going around Woodcote at nearly 160mph.
It was felt that there was a risk to the public in
the grandstands if parts of a car became airborne
during a collision, and that heavy items could
burst through the debris fence. The circuit felt
that, since the matter had been raised officially,
there was no alternative but to take action, and
an 'S-bend' chicane was installed at the corner in
time for the British Grand Prix on 19 July.

"We, as directors, were getting very worried
about increasing speeds as well," explained Sears.
"So we said 'let's put a chicane in at Woodcote,
which is probably the most dangerous corner of
all'. There was quite a big run-off out of Abbey, and
at Stowe, even at Club. But there wasn't much of a
run-off at Woodcote, and it was such a fast corner.
So that's why the first chicane was created there."

The alteration to the track was the first since
1950, when Club Corner had been changed, and
that evocative sight of racing cars teetering on
the edge of adhesion through Woodcote was
lost forever.

The BRDC celebrated its golden jubilee in
1977, and in an interview with *Motor Sport*
chief executive and managing director Jimmy
Brown explained about the 'schizophrenic
outlook' he had to adopt in order to keep the
business commercial enough to make profits to
be ploughed back into the circuit, while at the
same time satisfying the feelings of the dedicated
enthusiasts which made up the BRDC.

"The shareholders we are responsible for
are other BRDC members who are interested in
motor sport," he explained. "Provided we make
a profit to keep on developing the situation they
are happy. At the same time we are looking after
the promotion and the needs of motor sport. I'm
not sure that it isn't harder to make a profit *and*
look after the needs of motor sport!

"We promote race meetings that some of the
other organisers wouldn't – and say we're mad
to do so. But we do it because we think that it's
the right thing for the sport at that particular
time. Certainly, Formula 2 is a marginal case at
the moment – everybody knows we lost money
on the last F2 race. Now there is only one non-
championship F1 race per year, to be held
here alternate years, what else can we run the
International Trophy for but F2? Since 1949 it

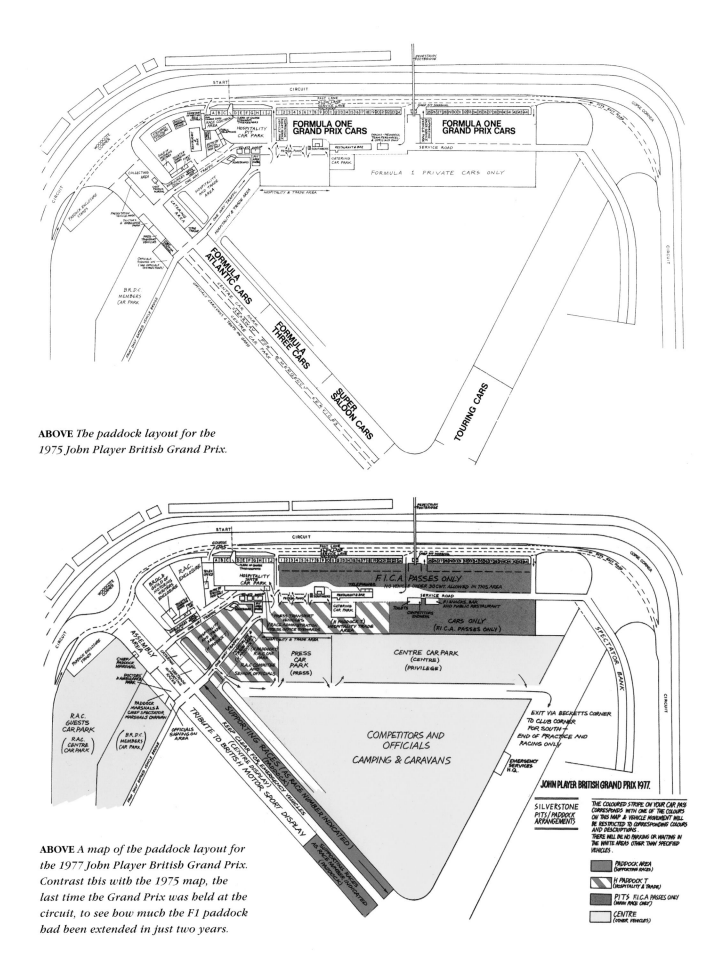

ABOVE *The paddock layout for the 1975 John Player British Grand Prix.*

ABOVE *A map of the paddock layout for the 1977 John Player British Grand Prix. Contrast this with the 1975 map, the last time the Grand Prix was held at the circuit, to see how much the F1 paddock had been extended in just two years.*

has always been run for the foremost European formula, and where do you go after F1 and F2?

"Some people think the World Championship of Makes is a marginal case, too, but we consider that Britain should be represented in every international formula. It is fair to say that in 1977 the BRDC will have a representative race of just about all these formulae: F1 with the Grand Prix; the International Trophy for F2; a European F3 round at Donington in August; Group 2 at the TT; and Group 5 in the World Championship of Makes round in May. In between, we'll fill in with everything from Formula Ford to Historics.

"We are able to do this by spreading the financial load over the year – over successful and unsuccessful meetings. We are happy if at the end of the season we have produced enough profit to develop the circuit."

On the subject of safety matters he said that on many occasions the club had been ahead of the legislation. "We did catch fencing our own way, putting up seven rows in echelon on our fast corners instead of three or four normal rows as recommended, because if a car goes off on a fast corner it describes an arc. We've got more catch fencing here than anywhere else in Britain."

It was pointed out in the article that, with catch fencing costing £30 a row and with little of it salvageable when a car went into it, it was an expensive business to provide this extra protection.

As a culmination of its celebrations, the BRDC couldn't have hoped for a better outcome to the British Grand Prix, with a home victory for James Hunt in his Marlboro McLaren-Ford M26, after a race-long duel with the Martini Brabham-Alfa Romeo BT45B of John Watson. The event was a huge success, with 85,000 race day spectators and around 113,500 fans in attendance over the weekend, and there were stories of cars being abandoned miles from the circuit as people tried to get in. The same year, the first British Motorcycle Grand Prix was held at the circuit, bypassing the chicane at Woodcote, with victory going to the American rider Pat Hennen, on a Suzuki.

The following year, conditions at the 1978 International Trophy race in March demonstrated just how difficult it is to run a major event when the weather doesn't cooperate. The circuit had been covered in four inches of snow only two days before, resulting in problems in the car parks, with spectators complaining later of being charged £5 to be towed out. But the major issues had occurred on track, which was flooded by a deluge of rain, particularly at Abbey where a large lake formed.

Two of the front runners – Ronnie Peterson and Niki Lauda – spun out on the warm-up lap in the atrocious conditions, while others such as James Hunt and Mario Andretti fared little better. The race was eventually won by Keke Rosberg in the Theodore-Ford TR1. Part of the problem was that water wasn't draining off the track, which had been completely resurfaced over the previous winter with Dunlop Delugrip at a cost of £150,000.

Ironically, Gerald Lascelles, BRDC president, had referred to the new track surface in the programme notes for the meeting, saying that: "There is no doubt that it will enable all types of car here to go slightly faster – possibly two seconds per lap quicker on the Grand Prix circuit. The texture provided by Delugrip should reduce spray and hopefully will make Formula 1 cars seem less prone to off-course excursions when suddenly confronted by a sharp shower of rain in the middle of the race."

BELOW *A map of the Club circuit layout from 1978.*

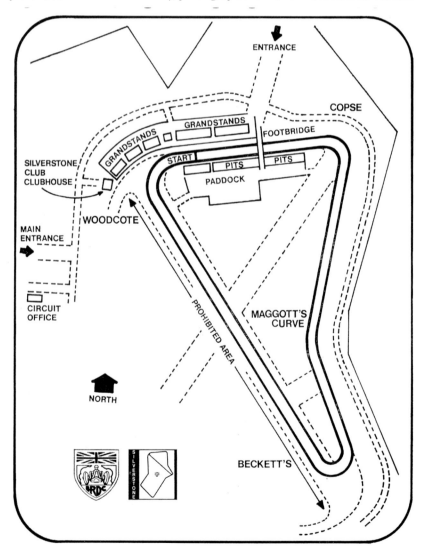

Jimmy Brown felt that the surface was probably more slippery than it would normally have been since it hadn't had enough time to wear off the bitumen, and that cambering of the surface had not been considered as it would have doubled the cost. In the wake of all the problems, it was announced in April that parts of the track would be resurfaced again under the 'rectification clause' of all Tarmac contracts.

By the end of 1978, plans were in hand for a new medical centre, together with a new scrutineering bay that would allow four lanes of cars to be scrutineered. In addition, a total of 11 new hospitality units were being constructed, extending into the old Stewards' Enclosure at Woodcote Corner. And after 30 years in the old Nissen hut offices, the administrative staff were to have a new 4,000sq ft building to be positioned in the area between the competitors' and spectators' entrances to the circuit.

The new medical centre was opened at the 1979 British Grand Prix meeting by Jackie Stewart, and a cheque for £2,500 was presented to equip the resuscitation room. This money had been raised by the memorial fund for Nigel Tan and David Allen, two marshals who had died at the circuit the previous year. The race itself provided a hugely-popular first win for the Williams team, with Clay Regazzoni taking his Ford-powered FW07 to victory.

The future of the International Trophy, for 31 years one of the circuit's flagship events, was uncertain, however, as a second year of poor weather had resulted in a loss of around £12,000. When Bernie Ecclestone decided that the F1 Constructors' Association wouldn't support the event in 1980, it was agreed that it should run as a round of the Aurora National F1 championship instead.

Times were indeed changing as the decade drew to a close.

ABOVE *Keke Rosberg steers his Theodore-Ford TR1 through the spray in atrocious conditions to win the International Trophy race on 19th March 1978, his first F1 victory. (sutton-images.com)*

1970

■ The opening club event of the season, due to be run by the Nottingham Sports Car Club on 14 March, was cancelled because of snow flurries.

■ Dave Walker, driving a Gold Leaf Team Lotus-Ford 59, won the opening round of the Forward Trust Formula 3 Championship on 5 April on a slippery track.

■ Anticipating a small entry of F1 cars for the GKN *Daily Express* International Trophy race on 26 April, the BRDC opened up the event to F5000 cars as well. The event was run in two 26-lap parts as the F5000 cars did not have large enough fuel tanks to run for a full 52-lap race. The first

BELOW *The STP March-Ford 701 of eventual race winner Chris Amon (15) gets away from pole position at the start of heat one of the 1970 GKN* Daily Express *International Trophy. Sharing the front row of the 4-3-4 grid is the Tyrrell-entered March-Ford 701 of Jackie Stewart (1), who finished second, the McLaren-Ford M14A of Denny Hulme and Peter Gethin's F5000 McLaren-Chevrolet M10B. (BRDC Archive)*

heat produced a victory for Chris Amon in the new STP March-Ford 701. Jackie Stewart in the Tyrrell-run March finished second after Jack Brabham's engine blew in his Brabham-Ford BT33 when it looked as if he would take the runner-up spot. Piers Courage in the Frank Williams-entered De Tomaso-Ford 505 was third. In the second heat it was Stewart who took the flag ahead of Amon, with Courage again third. The aggregate result gave Amon the overall win, from Stewart and Courage.

■ Mike Hailwood, driving a Lola-Chevrolet T190, won the overall F5000 category after Peter Gethin in a McLaren-Chevrolet M10B won the first part and Frank Gardner in another Lola the second, with Hailwood the runner-up in each part.

■ Gardner won the supporting RAC British Saloon Car Championship round in a Ford Boss Mustang from Brian Muir's Chevrolet Camaro Z28. The sports car event was won by Jo Bonnier's Lola T210 after a race-long tussle with the Chevron B16 of John Burton.

■ The two works Gold Leaf Team Lotus-Ford 59s of Dave Walker and Bev Bond broke away from the rest of the field in the GKN F3 event, but Ian Ashley in his Chevron-Ford B15 managed to keep with them and snatch second place from Bond at Woodcote on the last lap. In a last ditch effort to regain the place, Bond crashed but was still credited with third place.

■ The Nottingham Sports Car Club's meeting on Bank Holiday Monday, 25 May, was marred by the death of hill-climber Martin Brain, who crashed his ex-works Cooper-BRM T86 F1 car in the single-seater event.

■ Mike Beuttler in his Brabham-Ford BT28 was the victor in the *Motor Sport*/Shell F3 Championship race at the Martini Trophy meeting on 6 June. He led the Lotus-Ford 59s of Dave Walker and Carlos Pace across the line in a typical 'Silverstone finish', with 12 cars covered by barely 3sec after 25 laps. Brian Muir won the RAC British Saloon Car Championship round in his Chevrolet Camaro Z28.

■ The RAC *Daily Express*-Fordsport Tourist Trophy was held on 27 June for Group 2 international touring cars and counted towards both the RAC and European Touring Car Championships. The event was run in two two-hour heats, with the first race being won by Brian Muir in his Chevrolet Camaro Z28, ahead of the Ford Capri 2300GT of Rolf Stommelen and the Alfa Romeo GTAm of Toine Hezemans. In the second heat, Muir again took the honours with Frank Gardner putting in a storming drive through the field in his Ford Boss Mustang, beating Hezemans to the runner-up spot. Aggregate results gave Muir the overall win from Hezemans and Gardner.

■ The 20th running of the Holland Birkett 6 Hour Relay race, organised by the 750 Motor Club on 8 August, provided a victory for the Aston Martin Jubilee Team which just beat the mod-sport Spridget team by a few yards.

ABOVE *The annual* Daily Express *International Trophy race was opened up to F5000 cars for the first time in 1970. Peter Gethin, who won the F5000 class in heat one of the event in his McLaren-Chevrolet M10B, is seen here ahead of the De Tomaso-Ford 505 of Piers Courage, who finished third overall. (LAT)*

■ Frank Gardner was the decisive winner of the round of the Guards F5000 Championship held on 15 August. He took his Lola-Chevrolet T190 to victory in both of the two ten-lap heats, with Reine Wisell's McLaren-Chevrolet M10B taking second in heat one and Graham McRae in another M10B the runner-up in heat two. The aggregate result gave victory to Gardner ahead of Wisell and McRae.

■ David Prophet smashed the Club circuit lap record by 3.2sec at the SUNBAC meeting on 5 September, taking his F5000 McLaren-Chevrolet M10B round in 54.0s (a speed of 107.20mph) during the Formule Libre event.

BELOW *Chaos at Copse Corner during the* Motor Sport/*Shell F3 Championship round at the 1970 Martini International Trophy meeting. Carlos Pace, at left of picture in his Gold Leaf Lotus-Ford 59, finished third. (Mike Hayward)*

1971

■ Dave Walker, driving the Gold Leaf Team Lotus-Ford 69, won the opening round of the Forward Trust Formula 3 Championship at the BARC meeting on 4 April, ahead of Roger Williamson's March-Ford 713M.

■ Graham Hill in his 'lobster-claw' Brabham-Ford BT34 was the surprise, but popular, winner of the GKN *Daily Express* International Trophy race on 8 May. The event was run in two 26-lap heats for both F1 and F5000 cars, and Jackie Stewart, driving the sole Elf Tyrrell-Ford 003, romped away to an easy victory in the first part, ahead of the Yardley BRM P160 of Pedro Rodriguez and Hill's Brabham. In the second part, however, the throttle on the Tyrrell jammed open as Stewart lifted for Copse on the first lap and he slid with all four wheels locked up into the bank on the outside of the circuit, right beneath the TV camera, giving television viewers a close-up view of his misfortune. After battling with Rodriguez, Hill took the lead and held it to the finish, with Chris Amon bringing his Matra MS120B home second and Emerson Fittipaldi, driving the Gold Leaf turbine-powered Lotus-Pratt & Whitney 56B, finishing third. The aggregate result gave Hill the overall victory ahead of the McLaren-Ford M14A of Peter Gethin, with the Brabham-Ford BT33 of Tim Schenken in third place. The first F5000 car home was the Surtees-Chevrolet TS8 of Mike Hailwood in fifth place overall.

ABOVE *Graham Hill, driving the 'lobster-claw' Brabham-Ford BT34, was a popular winner of the 1971 GKN* Daily Express International Trophy. *(Mike Hayward)*

■ Bev Bond, in a works Ensign-Ford LN1, won the GKN Forgings Trophy for F3 cars, while Brian Muir scored a convincing win in the touring car event in his Chevrolet Camaro Z28. The most exciting race of the day was the 2-litre Group 5 and 6 sports car event, with Chevron-Ford B19s dominating. John Miles just beat John Hine, with Chris Craft, who had spun at Copse on the opening lap, in third place.

RIGHT *Jackie Stewart hits the banking at Copse Corner as the throttle on his Tyrrell-Ford 003 jams open at the start of the second heat of the 1971 GKN* Daily Express International Trophy *race. Pedro Rodriguez in the BRM P160 goes past. (Mike Hayward)*

■ Britain's round of the European 2-litre sports car championship for Group 5 and 6 cars was held at the circuit on 5 June when the Aston Martin Owners' Club held its Martini Trophy meeting. The Chevron-Ford B19 of John Burton was an early leader of the first heat until he hit one of Silverstone's notorious hares. This left Chris Craft's Chevron-Ford B19 in front, but he spun at Stowe, leaving Toine Hezemans in another B19 to take victory. Ronnie Peterson's Lola-Ford T212 won the second heat, but Hezemans' third place was enough for the aggregate victory.

■ The supporting F3 race was won by Dave Walker in the Gold Leaf Lotus-Ford 69, taking his fourth successive F3 victory. Frank Gardner dominated the touring car event in his Chevrolet Camaro Z28.

■ Jackie Stewart made up for his disappointment in the International Trophy by taking an emphatic win in glorious weather at the Woolmark British Grand Prix on 17 July. It

BELOW *The start of the 1971 Woolmark British Grand Prix. Pole-sitter Clay Regazzoni (5), in his Ferrari 312B2, leads away from the Tyrrell-Ford 003 of eventual winner Jackie Stewart (12), the Yardley BRM P160 of Jo Siffert (16), the Gold Leaf Team Lotus-Ford 72D of Emerson Fittipaldi (1), the March-Ford 711 of Ronnie Peterson (18), who finished second, the Brabham-Ford BT33 of Tim Schenken (8), the Ferrari 312B2 of Jacky Ickx (4), the McLaren-Ford M19A of Denny Hulme (9), the Tyrrell-Ford 002 of François Cevert (14) and the Matra Simca MS120B of Chris Amon (21). (BRDC Archive)*

was the Ferrari 312B2s of Clay Regazzoni and Jacky Ickx that led away at the start, though, with Stewart's Elf Tyrrell-Ford 003 following, but within three laps the Scot was ahead and proceeded to disappear into the distance. Ronnie Peterson brought his March-Ford 711 into second, ahead of the Gold Leaf Lotus-Ford 72D of Emerson Fittipaldi, the two Ferraris having both retired with engine problems. Stewart set a new lap record of 1m 19.9s (an average speed of 131.88mph).

ABOVE, TOP RIGHT AND RIGHT

Three classic views of F1 cars on the limit through the old Woodcote Corner during the 1971 Woolmark British Grand Prix: the race-winning Tyrrell-Ford 003 of Jackie Stewart, the Ferrari 312B2 of Clay Regazzoni, who qualified on pole but retired with oil pressure problems, and the Yardley BRM P160 of Jo Siffert, who finished ninth. (Michael Hewett)

■ The 100,000 spectators were treated to a full day's entertainment, including the Red Arrows display team, a parade of historic racing cars and Chris Barber's jazz band to round off the day. A new initiative was a three-hour broadcast over the PA system by two members of the British Forces Broadcasting Service, which included interviews with drivers, information on practice times and music.

■ Dave Walker scored an impressive victory in the Shell Super Oil F3 support race in his Gold Leaf Lotus-Ford 69 after another thrilling slipstreaming race, with cars sometimes five abreast going into Woodcote. Pierre-François Rousselot brought his Brabham-Ford BT35 into second place.

■ Brian Muir was an easy winner of the RAC Touring Car Championship round in his Chevrolet Camaro Z28 after Frank Gardner retired his Camaro on the first lap. Martin Thomas took second in another Camaro ahead of the Ford Capri RS2600 of Gerry Birrell. However, following an RAC tribunal the following month, the Camaros were excluded on a technicality, elevating Birrell to winner.

■ Mike Hailwood won the Esso Uniflo Trophy for F5000 cars on 14 August in his Surtees-Chevrolet TS8, beating the Lola-Chevrolet T300 of Frank Gardner.

1972

■ HRH Princess Anne was the guest of Jackie Stewart at the circuit on Monday 20 March to watch him and team-mate François Cevert testing their Tyrrell F1 cars. Princess Anne herself drove a Ford Escort Mexico around.

■ For the first time the GKN *Daily Express* International Trophy meeting spanned three days, with practice on the Friday and racing on both Saturday 22 and Sunday 23 April. The meeting comprised a total of eight races for F1, F5000, F3, Formula Ford, saloons and historic cars, but the main race attracted the smallest number of F1 cars ever entered for the event, partly because of the Spanish Grand Prix being held the following weekend. Only ten F1 cars were entered, the rest of the field made up of F5000 machines. The Marlboro-BRM P160s of Jean-Pierre Beltoise and Peter Gethin led away, smoking their tyres off the grid, but Emerson Fittipaldi in the JPS Lotus-Ford 72D soon passed the pair of them. Mike Hailwood in the Surtees-Ford TS9B was also on the move and caught and passed the Lotus for the lead, only to retire shortly afterwards. Fittipaldi therefore ran on to victory, with Beltoise second and the other TS9B of John Surtees third. Despite retiring from the race, Mike Hailwood set a new outright lap record of 1m 18.8s (a speed of 133.72mph).

■ The F5000 cars had their own race on the Saturday, with Graham McRae in a Leda-Chevrolet LT27/GM1 emerging the winner. The F3 race provided Roger Williamson with a win in his GRD-Ford 372.

■ The saloon car event, a round of the Wiggins Teape Paper Chase Saloon Car Championship, the forerunner of today's BTCC, was won easily by Frank Gardner in his SCA-backed Chevrolet Camaro Z28, ahead of the Wiggins Teape Ford Capri RS2600 of Brian Muir.

■ A new event for 1972 was the Super Sports 200, a round of the European Interserie championship for Group 7 Can-Am type cars, held on 21 May. Willie Green won the first heat in his JCB-entered Ferrari 512M, but could only manage fourth in the second heat leaving Leo Kinnunen in the Porsche 917/10 the overall winner from Green.

■ There was confusion over the aggregate result of the Martini International on 17 June, Britain's round of the

ABOVE *Mike Hailwood, in the Surtees-Ford TS9B (seen here chasing the JPS Lotus-Ford 72D of eventual winner Emerson Fittipaldi) took the lead of the 1972 GKN* Daily Express *International Trophy race only to retire shortly afterwards, but not before setting a new outright lap record. (LAT)*

European 2-litre sports car championship, when the organising AMOC decided to work out the results on a points basis from the two heats, rather than the usual method of aggregate times. The first heat provided a win for Dieter Quester's Chevron-BMW B21, but in the second part he was caught out by torrential rain, along with many others, and spun off. Arturo Merzario, who had finished fourth in the first heat in his Abarth-Osella 2000, put on a magnificent wet-weather display, lapping the entire field on his way to victory and thus earning overall honours.

■ Dutch driver Gijs van Lennep won a shortened Rothmans European Formula 5000 Championship race on 6 August driving his Speed International Surtees-Chevrolet TS11 to victory in torrential rain. John Cannon's March-Oldsmobile 725 was less than a second behind at the finish.

■ Masami Kuwashima won the final of the Lombard North Central F3 Championship round on Bank Holiday Monday, 28 August, in his GRD-Holbay 372. It was the Japanese driver's first F3 win.

■ The Tourist Trophy returned to Silverstone on 24 September as Britain's round of the European Group 2 Touring Car Championship and provided a dominant victory for the works German Ford Capri RS2600 of Jochen Mass and Dieter Glemser. Mass had won the first two-hour part ahead of the Capris of Brian Muir and Toine Hezemans, while Glemeser's own car had blown its engine. He therefore took over Mass's car for the second part and finished second behind Hezemans. Overall victory therefore went to Mass/Glemser, with Hezemans in the runner-up spot.

■ It was announced at the end of the year that the Jim Russell Racing Drivers' School would be extending its operations to Silverstone during 1973 using a fleet of Merlyn Mk20A Formula Ford cars.

1973

■ Alan Jones won the second round of the Lombard North Central F3 Championship on 18 March in his DART GRD-Ford 372 ahead of Russell Wood's March-Ford 733.

■ It was bitterly cold for the 25th running of the GKN *Daily Express* International Trophy race on 8 April. Ronnie Peterson in his JPS Lotus-Ford 72E made a perfect start from the middle of the front row, with Jackie Stewart's Tyrrell-Ford 006 in hot pursuit. Peterson's team-mate and reigning world champion, Emerson Fittipaldi, crept off the line with a burnt-out clutch. Stewart managed to pass Peterson, who then spun at Becketts, dropping to sixth. The Swede then proceeded to put in an inspired drive, moving back up to second before a brief snow flurry caused him to spin at Becketts, handing the lead and the race win to Stewart. Peterson recovered to take second place, ahead of the Marlboro-BRM P160E of Clay Regazzoni. The first F5000 car home was the Lola-Chevrolet T330 of Gijs van Lennep.

■ The F5000 runners had had their own race the previous day, with victory going to David Hobbs in the Lola-Chevrolet T330. Brian Muir took victory on race day in the touring car event in his Alpina BMW 3.3 CSL, while Russell Wood won the F3 race in his Chequered Flag March-Ford 733. Further snow after the main event caused the final two races of the day, for Formula Ford and historics, to be cut to just five laps each.

BELOW *During a snow flurry, Ronnie Peterson spins away the lead of the 1973 GKN* Daily Express *International Trophy race in his JPS Lotus-Ford 72E. The Swede finished second behind the Tyrrell-Ford 006 of Jackie Stewart. (LAT)*

ABOVE *The Surtees-Ford TS14A of Jochen Mass and the Marlboro BRM P160E of Jean-Pierre Beltoise lie wrecked on the track, as Carlos Pace, whose Surtees had also been involved in the nine-car accident, can be seen climbing over the wall to safety. (Author)*

■ Leo Kinnunen scored his first Interserie win of the year on 20 May in the Martini International Super Sports event in his Porsche 917/10, beating the similar car of Willi Kauhsen on aggregate after the two 35-lap parts. Kinnunen had won the first heat ahead of Kauhsen, with the positions reversed in the second encounter.

■ Tony Brise scored a convincing win in the Forward Trust F3 race on 10 June in his March-Ford 733.

■ The circuit held its first major air show – Silverstone Sky Day – on Saturday 23 June, featuring displays by the Red Arrows and the Barnstormers Flying Circus, along with flypasts of various aircraft, including a Lancaster, Vulcan, Spitfire, Hurricane and Nimrod. The following day the National Drag Racing Club held the first international drag meeting at the circuit, with some 180 vehicles present.

■ Ronnie Peterson enthralled the crowd during practice for the British Grand Prix on 14 July, sliding his JPS Lotus-Ford 72E through Woodcote Corner at around 150mph, lap after lap, earning himself pole position. The race was stopped after a nine-car pile-up at the end of the first lap, caused by Jody Scheckter losing control of his Yardley McLaren-Ford M23. When the race was restarted, it was his team-mate Peter Revson who emerged the narrow victor ahead of Peterson and the other McLaren of Denny Hulme, with James Hunt, who also set the fastest lap in his Hesketh March-Ford 731, in fourth place – this group covered by just 3.4sec at the flag. Jackie Stewart, who had started as one of the favourites in his Elf Tyrrell-Ford 006 spun into the cornfield at Stowe after the restart and eventually finished tenth.

ABOVE *At the restart of the 1973 British Grand Prix, the JPS Lotus-Ford 72E of Ronnie Peterson and the Yardley McLaren-Ford M23 of Denny Hulme smoke their tyres, while the race-winning McLaren of Peter Revson is already out of shot. Jackie Stewart's Tyrrell-Ford 006 and the other JPS Lotus of Emerson Fittipaldi get away from the second row of the grid, while Carlos Reutemann's Brabham-Ford BT42, obscured by Fittipaldi, makes a good start from row three. Niki Lauda's Marlboro BRM P160E, François Cevert's Tyrrell, Clay Regazzoni's BRM and Howden Ganley's Iso Marlboro-Ford IR follow. (Michael Hewett)*

RIGHT *The condition of the track was very different from the standards required today. Here, Ronnie Peterson's JPS Lotus-Ford 72E is chased by the Yardley McLaren-Ford M23 of Denny Hulme past a drain cover on the inside of Woodcote Corner during the 1973 British Grand Prix. (Michael Hewett)*

ABOVE *Peter Revson took his maiden Grand Prix victory at the restarted 1973 British GP in his Yardley McLaren-Ford M23. (LAT)*

ABOVE *Peter Revson celebrating victory in the paddock after the 1973 British Grand Prix. (Author)*

■ The F3 final resulted in a victory for Tony Rouff in a GRD-Ford 373, while Frank Gardner won the British Touring Car Championship round in his SCA Chevrolet Camaro Z28. The race was marred by a horrific accident involving the Ford Capri RS2600 of David Matthews, the Ford Escort RS1600 of David Brodie and the BLMC Mini of Gavin Booth, which was being lapped. All three cars were written off and the drivers hospitalised.

■ The F5000 race on 5 August had to be called off after torrential rain left standing water and rivers across Club Straight. The rest of the meeting could be run, but it was deemed too dangerous for the 5-litre cars with their wide tyres to compete.

BELOW *Derek Bell and Harald Ertl won the 1973 RAC Tourist Trophy in their Alpina BMW 3.0 CSL. (LAT)*

■ The Lombard North Central F3 event on a wet Bank Holiday Monday, 27 August, provided a win for Alan Jones in his GRD-Ford 373. The weather was very different two weeks later on 9 September when Brian Henton took his Ensign-Ford LNF3 to victory in the Forward Trust F3 encounter.

■ The RAC Tourist Trophy on 23 September resulted in victory for the Alpina BMW 3.0 CSL of Harald Ertl and Derek Bell. The event, which was both the final round of the European Touring Car Championship and the penultimate round of the British Touring Car Championship, was run in two two-hour heats, with the result being decided on aggregate. Ertl took victory in the first heat, ahead of the Ford Capri RS2600 of Jochen Mass, while team-mate Bell took victory in the second from the other CSL of Brian Muir. Overall, Bell and Ertl took the honours with Mass's Capri RS2600 second.

1974

■ Brian Henton took the F3 honours at the BRDC meeting on 17 March in his works March-Ford 743, challenged strongly by Tony Rouff's GRD-Ford 373.

■ Local hero James Hunt qualified his Hesketh-Ford 308 on pole for the *Daily Express* International Trophy race on 7 April, and 32,000 spectators came to see him score a hugely popular first F1 victory. Hunt had initially suffered problems getting off the line and dropped to the back of the field, but stormed his way back to the front, taking the lead from Ronnie Peterson's JPS Lotus-Ford 76 at Woodcote Corner to cheers from the crowd on lap 28. Peterson retired soon after and Hunt took the flag ahead of Jochen Mass in the Surtees-Ford TS16 and the Shadow-Ford DN3 of Jean-Pierre Jarier. The first F5000 car home was the Chevron-Chevrolet B28 of Peter Gethin, which finished seventh overall, a lap behind the winner.

■ The previous day, Gethin had finished second in the F5000 race, behind the Lola-Chevrolet T332 of Brian Redman. Stuart Graham in a Chevrolet Camaro Z28 won the supporting touring car event ahead of Richard Lloyd in another Camaro.

■ British Leyland managing director John Barber presented the keys of a brand new Jaguar XJ12 fire tender to BRDC president Gerald Lascelles at the International Trophy meeting. The fully equipped vehicle was the world's fastest fire engine and carried 180 gallons of light water, which could be discharged in 70sec. The car followed the field round on the first lap of each race.

■ Brian Henton triumphed again in the F3 race on 5 May in his March-Ford 743, despite heavy rain half way through, and was again chased home by the GRD-Ford 373 of Tony Rouff.

■ The Martini Trophy meeting on 12 May provided a victory for Willi Kauhsen in his Porsche 917/10, beating the Martini-sponsored 917/10 of Herbert Müller, which had won the preceding sprint event. Vince Woodman won the round of the Castrol Anniversary Touring Car Championship in his Chevrolet Camaro Z28.

■ The F3 tables were turned on 9 June when Tony Rouff brought his GRD-Ford 373 home ahead of Brian Henton's March-Ford 743 in another rain-affected race. Three months later, on 8 September, it was the Antiguan driver Mike Tyrrell who emerged victorious in a March-Ford 733.

■ During the five-lap Repco Caravan race at the BARC meeting on 9 June, John Heppenstall's Opel Commodore-towed Bessacar Milano overturned at Woodcote depositing broken glass all over the track. The event was won by Andrew Higton, driving a Vauxhall VX4/90 with a Bailey Prototype in tow.

■ Stuart Graham became the first man to win the Tourist Trophy on both two wheels and four when he triumphed in the 107-lap Access RAC TT on 22 September, driving the whole distance himself in his Brut-sponsored Chevrolet Camaro Z28. Graham had previously won the Isle of Man TT on a 50cc Suzuki in 1967. Vince Woodman and Jonathan Buncombe came in second in their Camaro.

RIGHT *The Martini Porsche 917/10 turbo of Herbert Müller and the McLaren-Chevrolet M20 of Helmut Kelleners lead away at the start of the sprint heat of the 1974 Martini International Trophy race. (Author)*

1975

■ With such a good entry for the *Daily Express* International Trophy on 13 April, there was no need to bolster the field with F5000 cars. The race produced a mesmerising battle between the Ferrari 312T of Niki Lauda and the Marlboro McLaren-Ford M23 of reigning world champion Emerson Fittipaldi. The previous year's winner, James Hunt, had started from pole position and had led for over half the race until the engine in his Hesketh-Ford 308 blew as he crossed the line at the start of lap 26, leaving Lauda and Fittipaldi, who had been keeping close watch, to battle to the finish. The Brazilian made one last attempt around the outside at Woodcote on the final lap, but Lauda just hung on to take victory by a tenth of a second, with the Parnelli-Ford VPJ4 of Mario Andretti in third place.

■ Before the start of the main event, HRH the Duke of Edinburgh was driven around the circuit in a Triumph Stag by Jackie Stewart after having officially opened the new pits complex.

■ Richard Lloyd won the round of the RAC Southern Organs Touring Car Championship in his Chevrolet Camaro Z28, while Tony Brise triumphed in the Formula Atlantic encounter driving a Modus-Ford M1.

■ On the previous day, the 25-lap F5000 race had been won by the Durex-sponsored Lola-Chevrolet T400 of Richard Scott. Scott's car had to run with its sponsor's name removed as the BBC threatened not to televise the event if it was displayed, stating that "there are certain advertisements which we feel may give offence or seem unacceptable to certain members of the public".

BELOW *The 1975* Daily Express *International Trophy developed into a thrilling dice between the Ferrari 312T of Niki Lauda and the Marlboro McLaren-Ford M23 of Emerson Fittipaldi after early leader James Hunt had retired his Hesketh-Ford 308. Lauda just held on to take victory by a tenth of a second.* (sutton-images.com)

■ Danny Sullivan took his Modus-Ford M1 to victory in the round of the BP Super Visco F3 Championship on 27 April after early leader Larry Perkins suffered a puncture on his Ralt-Ford RT1.

■ The round of the Southern Organs Touring Car Championship on Bank Holiday Monday, 26 May, was run in two parts with the grid split so that the up-to-1600cc and 1601-2500cc had their own race, while the 2501-4000cc and over 4000cc classes ran together in a separate event. Andy Rouse won the first part in his Triumph Dolomite Sprint, while Stuart Graham took his Chevrolet Camaro Z28 to victory in the second race.

■ Tom Pryce was quickest in pre-Grand Prix tyre testing on 4–5 June in his UOP Shadow-Ford DN5. Experiments were conducted using a chicane at Woodcote during the Goodyear-run tests because of concerns about debris flying into the grandstands in the event of a crash at the high-speed corner. At the end of June it was announced that a chicane would be installed at the corner in time for the Grand Prix in July.

■ The John Player British Grand Prix on 19 July ended chaotically with 11 competitors buried in the catch fencing after rain hit the circuit partway through. The red flag was shown and Emerson Fittipaldi, who was in the pits at the time changing tyres on his Marlboro McLaren-Ford M23, was declared the victor on count-back. Carlos Pace had been the initial leader in his Martini Brabham-Ford BT44B from pole-sitter Tom Pryce's Shadow-Ford DN5/2A. At the end of lap 13, Clay Regazzoni in his Ferrari 312T2 took the lead at Woodcote, but a few laps later he damaged his rear

ABOVE *A chicane was introduced at Woodcote prior to the 1975 British Grand Prix in order to reduce speeds through the corner. (BRDC Archive)*

BELOW *Graham Hill announced his retirement from F1 driving at the 1975 British Grand Prix, and completed a lap of honour prior to the race in his Embassy Hill-Ford GH1. (LAT)*

ABOVE *Marshals and fire crews attend to Wilson Fittipaldi's Fittipaldi-Ford FD03 and the Hesketh-Ford 308 of James Hunt, which have both crashed during a heavy rain shower at the 1975 John Player British Grand Prix. (LAT)*

BELOW *Emerson Fittipaldi emerged the surprised winner of the 1975 John Player British Grand Prix in his Marlboro McLaren-Ford M23 when the red flag fell as he was in the pits changing tyres. A heavy rain shower had caused 11 cars to crash late in the race, and the results were declared at the end of the previous lap. (LAT)*

wing on being caught out by a shower of rain, as was Pryce who crashed at Becketts. Many cars now headed for the pits to change tyres, while others stayed out on slicks carefully negotiating the damp track, though the rain had now stopped. Jody Scheckter in the Elf Tyrrell-Ford 007 assumed the lead, but as the track dried he had to change back on to slicks. When the rain returned with a vengeance a few laps later, three cars slid off at Stowe and another eight at Club, injuring one marshal, and a spectator was also hit by flying debris. Fittipaldi had stopped for wet tyres at the end of lap 56 but the results were declared at the end of lap 55, giving him the win from Pace and Scheckter.

■ Gunnar Nilsson won the BP F3 Championship round in his March-Toyota 753, while Stuart Graham won the touring car event in his Chevrolet Camaro Z28.

■ A 'pit stop challenge' between the McLaren and Tyrrell teams on the Friday resulted in a win for the Tyrrell mechanics, who changed all four wheels in just 12.8sec, a far cry from the times achieved today.

■ Prior to the main event, demonstration laps were run by Graham Hill, who had announced his retirement from Grand Prix racing that weekend, in his Embassy Hill-Ford GH1, and by Derek Bell in the Le Mans-winning Gulf-Ford GR7.

■ Eddie Cheever scored his first F3 victory in only his fourth F3 outing on Bank Holiday Monday, 25 August, in his Modus-Ford M1. Cheever had taken the lead by driving around the

outside of Alex Ribeiro's works March-Toyota 753 at Woodcote on the Club circuit, a move that earned him the Man of the Meeting award as well.

■ The first of what was billed as Silverstone's 'Autumn Internationals' took place on 31 August when the first F2 race since 1967 was held at the circuit. A poor crowd of just 7,000 saw Michel Leclere take victory in his March-BMW 752, ahead of Gerard Larrousse in the Elf-BMW 2J. A popular third was Brian Henton, driving Tom Wheatcroft's Donington Collection-backed Wheatcroft-Ford 002.

■ Concern was raised about the safety of catch fencing when Hervé Regout was hospitalised after crashing at Copse in the supporting F3 event. As the car was caught by the fencing, one of the posts struck Regout's helmet and split it open. Eddie Cheever won the race in his Modus-Toyota M1.

■ *Autosport* magazine celebrated its 25th anniversary with a special meeting at the circuit on 7 September. Geoff Friswell won the *Autosport* Trophy in his Mallock U2 Mk11B/14.

ABOVE *Gerry Marshall, in his Vauxhall Magnum, goes kerb-hopping at the Woodcote chicane during the production saloon car race at the European F2 meeting in August 1975. (Author)*

■ Alan Jones was the winner of the Shellsport European F5000 event run on the Grand Prix circuit on 28 September in his RAM March-Ford 751, with David Purley bringing his Chevron-Ford B30 home in second place. The F3 event was won by Gunnar Nilsson in his works March-Toyota 753.

■ Stuart Graham won the Access RAC Tourist Trophy on 5 October for the second year running in his Brut Chevrolet Camaro Z28, leading all bar the first of the 107 laps. The BMW 3.0 CSi of Jean Xhenceval and Hughes de Fierlandt came in second a lap in arrears.

BELOW *Jean-Pierre Jabouille enters the pit lane in his Elf-BMW 2J during the first F2 event to be held at the circuit since 1967. Jabouille retired from the race with engine problems. (Author)*

1976

■ The International Trophy race on 11 April was named the Graham Hill International Trophy, in memory of the driver who had won the event in 1962 and 1971 and who had been killed, along with five members of his team, including Tony Brise, in a plane crash the previous November. The event was sponsored by the *Daily Express* plus both John Player and Embassy, which had both sponsored Hill during his career. James Hunt was a popular winner of the 40-lap event in his Marlboro McLaren-Ford M23 and received the winner's trophy from Hill's widow, Bette. The Italian Vittorio Brambilla brought his March-Ford 761 home in second, ahead of Jody Scheckter's Tyrrell-Ford 007.

■ The supporting Shellsport F3 event was won by Bruno Giacomelli's March-Toyota 763, while Gordon Spice won the Keith Prowse RAC Touring Car round in his Ford Capri II after on-the-track winner Chris Craft in another Capri was disqualified following scrutineering.

■ There was an exciting conclusion to the inaugural Silverstone 6-Hours on 9 May, when the Hermetite BMW 3.5 CSL of Tom Walkinshaw and John Fitzpatrick just managed to hold off the Kremer Porsche Turbo of Bob Wollek and Hans Heyer to take victory. The race favourite, the works Martini Porsche Turbo of Jacky Ickx and Jochen Mass, had destroyed its clutch at the start, leaving Ickx to coast around to Becketts Corner. He and Mass then pushed the car back down Club Straight to the pits where, 1¾hr after the race had started, it rejoined, setting fastest lap and finishing tenth. With less than ¼hr left, the Kremer car, which had just taken the lead from the BMW, had to make a 'splash-and-dash' pit stop. It emerged 24sec adrift of Fitzpatrick in the BMW and with nine minutes left on the clock. Heyer was at the wheel and he closed

BELOW *The Kremer Porsche 935 Turbo of Bob Wollek and Hans Heyer sits in the pit lane prior to the 1976 Silverstone 6-Hours. (Author)*

relentlessly on Fitzpatrick, but the 'home' car just held on to win by a margin of 1.18sec after six hours of racing. A true 'Silverstone-type finish'.

■ Walkinshaw was not present to witness the exciting end or take part in the victory celebrations. He had already left to fly by helicopter to Thruxton where he was driving a Ford Capri in the British Touring Car Championship round, which he also won.

■ Bruno Giacomelli set a new F3 Club circuit lap record of 55.6s (104.12mph) on his way to victory in the BP Super Visco round on 6 June, driving his works March-Toyota 763. The Italian triumphed again two weeks later on 20 June.

■ John Lepp set a new outright lap record for the Club circuit of 51.6s (112.19mph) at the BRSCC meeting on 4 July, driving his Ensign-Cosworth N174 in the Formule Libre event.

■ The Access Tourist Trophy on 19 September marked the debut of the Jaguar XJ12 5.3C, and hopes were high for a home victory when Derek Bell, who was sharing with David Hobbs, put it on pole position. Alas, its challenge was short-lived as it began to fade with tyre problems during the race, resulting in a puncture. It retired later with driveshaft failure. The race was won by the Luigi BMW 3.0 CSL of Jean Xhenceval, Pierre Dieudonne and Hughes de Fierlandt. Geoff Lees scored his maiden F3 victory in the supporting Shellsport Championship round driving a Chevron-Toyota B34.

BELOW *Tom Walkinshaw and John Fitzpatrick won a thrilling Silverstone 6-Hours in 1976 in their Hermetite BMW 3.5 CSL, just holding off the Kremer Porsche 935 Turbo of Bob Wollek and Hans Heyer at the flag to take victory by a mere 1.18sec. (Author)*

1977

■ With the F1 Constructors Association having decreed that there could only be one non-championship F1 race per year this was allocated to the Brands Hatch Race of Champions, as Silverstone had the Grand Prix for 1977. This meant that the *Daily Express* International Trophy race on 6 March was run for F2 cars and was the first round of the European Championship. René Arnoux in his Martini-Renault Mk22 won the main event, having taken the lead with only seven laps left to run. Ray Mallock was second in his Chevron-Hart B40 and Patrick Neve, who had led until just eight laps from the end when he had to pit with a loose wheel nut, was third in the March-BMW 772P.

■ The supporting Vandervell International F3 race was won by Stephen South in his unsponsored year-old March-Toyota 763, while Gordon Spice won a spirited Tricentrol British Saloon Car Championship opening round in his Ford Capri II after battling with Chris Craft's Capri II until it became stuck in top gear.

■ Geoff Brabham won the BP F3 Championship round on the road on 3 April, only to be disqualified when the airbox on his Esso Ralt-Toyota RT1 failed the vacuum test in scrutineering. This handed the win to Ian Taylor's Unipart March-Triumph 773.

■ Porsche made up for its disappointment of the previous year at the Kosset Silverstone 6 Hours on 15 May when Jacky Ickx and Jochen Mass scored a runaway victory in the Martini-liveried 935-77 model. Bob Wollek and John Fitzpatrick were second in a Kremer-entered 935 ahead of Rolf Stommelen and Toine Hezemans in the Gelo 935. The crowd's favourite, though, was the fourth-placed BMW 320i, driven spectacularly by Ronnie Peterson, alongside Helmut Kelleners.

■ Geoff Brabham also made up for his earlier disappointment by winning the Vandervell F3 Championship race on 7 June in his Esso Ralt-Toyota RT1. Stuart Graham won the round of the Tricentrol British Saloon Car Championship in his Brut-sponsored Ford Capri II.

■ Around 85,000 spectators turned up for the British Grand Prix on 16 July (the event was still run on a Saturday in those days) and were rewarded with a popular home win for reigning world champion James Hunt in his Marlboro McLaren-Ford M26. The event had also been given the prestigious title of 'Grand Prix of Europe'. As was usual in those days, the grid stretched back as far as the Woodcote chicane, and the cars

ABOVE *The 1977 John Player British Grand Prix marked the debut of the first turbocharged car to be run in F1– the Renault RS01, driven by Jean-Pierre Jabouille. The Renault qualified 21st and retired after 16 laps with turbo problems. (Author)*

completed a final warm-up lap, missing out the chicane, the fencing for which was hastily put in place as soon as they had started. John Watson's Martini Brabham-Alfa Romeo BT45B took an early lead ahead of Niki Lauda's Ferrari 312T2 and the Wolf-Ford WR1 of Jody Scheckter, with pole-sitter Hunt down in fourth. He soon passed the Wolf and closed on the leaders and out-braked Lauda at the chicane at the end of lap 23. Despite his best efforts, he was unable to pass Watson, though, until the Brabham's fuel pressure dropped on lap 50 causing Watson's eventual retirement. Hunt thus won his home Grand Prix, ahead of Lauda and the JPS Lotus-Ford 78 of Gunnar Nilsson.

■ Prior to the official practice and qualifying sessions, an additional day was set aside to allow those smaller teams not part of the F1 Constructors' Association to be allowed to qualify for qualifying, the idea being that the fastest five would be allowed to take part in the rest of the weekend's proceedings. As it was, the fastest seven were allowed through. This pre-qualifying session was marred by an accident that befell David Purley, driving the Lec-Ford CRP1, when the throttle stuck open going into Becketts Corner. Purley was trapped in the car for some time and sustained serious leg injuries, which ultimately ended his racing career. Among those who went through to qualifying were Patrick Tambay in an Ensign-Ford N177 and Gilles Villeneuve in a McLaren-Ford M23. Both would make their Grand Prix debuts in the race, which also marked the first appearance of the 1.5-litre turbocharged Renault RS01, driven by Jean-Pierre Jabouille.

■ The supporting Tricentrol British Saloon Car Championship round was dominated by Tony Dron's Triumph Dolomite Sprint, leading all bar three of the 20 laps. Anders Olofsson took victory in the final of the Vandervell F3 round in his Ralt-Toyota RT1 after Derek Daly's Chevron-Toyota B38 and the March-Toyota 763 of Stephen South clashed at Chapel Curve on lap 15 while battling for the lead, hospitalising South.

■ Drivers from the European F3 Championship who had taken part in a BRDC-organised round at Donington Park on 27 August, headed for Silverstone to join the regular Vandervell British F3

ABOVE *James Hunt completes his lap of honour after winning the 1977 John Player British Grand Prix. (Author)*

runners two days later on Bank Holiday Monday, 29 August, for a non-European championship race. The race resulted in a win for Beppe Gabbiani in his Trivellato Chevron-Toyota B38.

■ The Access Tourist Trophy on 18 September, which was Britain's round of the European Touring Car Championship, was open to both British Group 1 cars and European Group 2 machinery, resulting in a 60-plus entry for the 44 places on the grid. The two Leyland Jaguar XJ12Cs of Andy Rouse/Derek Bell and Tim Schenken/John Fitzpatrick headed the front row, but it was to be a BMW victory after Rouse lost control on a damp track while closing on the leader just nine laps from the end, leaving the Alpina BMW 3.0 CSL of Dieter Quester and Tom Walkinshaw to take the win.

■ Brett Riley won the final round of the Vandervell F3 Championship on 2 October driving a March-Toyota 773 after Derek Warwick, who was leading in his Ralt-Toyota RT1, slid wide at Stowe on the last lap. Meanwhile, a young Nigel Mansell clinched the Brush Fusegear Formula Ford title with victory in his Crosslé 32F.

■ In December the F1 Constructors' Association awarded the RAC the prize for the John Player Grand Prix at Silverstone as the best-organised event of 1977.

BELOW *Gordon Spice spins his Ford Capri II as the similar car of Chris Craft goes past during the Tricentrol British Saloon Car race at the 1977 British Grand Prix meeting. (Author)*

1978

■ There were only 12 starters for the opening round of the Vandervell F3 Championship on 5 March, which was led from start to finish by Derek Warwick in his Ralt-Toyota RT1, setting a new lap record of 54.28s (106.65mph) along the way.

■ The 13th running of the *Daily Express* International Trophy race on 19 March produced a surprise victory for the Theodore-Cosworth TR1 of Keke Rosberg after a downpour flooded the track, particularly at Abbey where a large lake formed. The big names – James Hunt, Mario Andretti, Patrick Depailler, Clay Regazzoni, Ronnie Peterson and Niki Lauda – all crashed out, the last two on the warm-up lap. At one point it looked as if Derek Daly in the Hesketh-Ford 308E would win, until he lost his visor and went off at Woodcote leaving Rosberg to demonstrate superb car control as he kept the Copersucar Fittipaldi-Ford F5A of Emerson Fittipaldi at bay over the final few laps. Tony Trimmer was third in a McLaren-Ford M23, and only five of the original 14 starters were still running at the end.

■ The supporting Vandervell F3 Championship round was stopped part way through and restarted because of the dire conditions. Derek Warwick had been leading in his Ralt-Toyota RT1 when the red flag came out, but he spun out at the restart, leaving Nelson Piquet to take the victory in his similar car. Tony Dron dominated the Tricentrol Saloon Car Championship race in his Triumph Dolomite Sprint.

■ Chico Serra won the Bank Holiday Monday F3 encounter on 1 May, taking his Project 4 March-Toyota 783 to victory.

■ Porsche scored a comprehensive victory in front of a crowd of 12,000 in the Silverstone 6 Hours on 14 May, with the winning Martini-sponsored 935-78 of Jacky Ickx and Jochen Mass leading from start to finish. The car, nicknamed 'Moby Dick' because of its long, swooping tail, finished seven laps ahead of the second-placed Kremer Porsche 935-77A of Bob Wollek and Henri Pescarolo.

■ The Ford Capri IIs of Gordon Spice and Chris Craft dominated the late May Bank Holiday round of the Tricentrol British Touring Car Championship on 29 May. The up-to-1600cc class had its own race and was won by Richard Lloyd's VW Golf ahead of the Toyota Celica of Win Percy.

■ The international press awarded Silverstone its 'Prix d'Orange' for the best press facilities and circuit co-operation of any Grand Prix during 1977.

■ Nelson Piquet led the BP F3 Championship race from flag to flag on 9 July in his Ralt-Toyota RT1, chased home by fellow Brazilian Chico Serra in his March-Toyota 783.

■ Two marshals, Nigel Tan and David Allen, were killed and another two seriously injured on 19 August at the British Motor Racing Marshals' Club 21st anniversary meeting when an E-type Jaguar, braking because the race had been red flagged, went out of control and struck them.

■ Nelson Piquet was again victorious in his Ralt-Toyota RT1, this time in the round of the Vandervell F3 Championship on Bank Holiday Monday, 28 August, beating Derek Warwick's Ralt.

■ BMW scored a fourth successive victory in the Diners Club International Tourist Trophy on 17 September, courtesy of the Luigi 3.2 CSL of Eddy Joosens and Raymond van Hove.

LEFT *The race-winning Martini Porsche 935-78 'Moby Dick' of Jacky Ickx and Jochen Mass sits in the pit lane prior to the 1978 Silverstone 6-Hours. (Author)*

■ It was Nelson Piquet who triumphed yet again at the Vandervell F3 round on 23 September. The Brazilian was also victorious a week later on 30 September.

■ Only a small crowd turned out to see the USAC Indycars at the circuit on their first visit to the UK. The race was scheduled to be run on Saturday 30 September but was postponed to the following day because of rain. During practice, the Hawaiian driver Danny Ongais lapped 2.5sec under the lap record held by James Hunt and took pole position in his Parnelli-Cosworth VPJ6B. Ongais led the early laps until a driveshaft snapped, but not before he set a new outright lap record of 1m 18.45s (134.55mph). This left the Lola-Cosworth T500 of Al Unser in front until he ran out of fuel and lost time crawling back to the pits. A.J. Foyt, meanwhile, had been on the move in his Coyote-

ABOVE *A.J. Foyt in his Gilmore Racing Coyote-Foyt 78 took victory in a rain-interrupted race when the USAC Indycars visited the circuit during the autumn of 1978. (Author)*

Foyt 78 and was up to second behind the Penske-Cosworth PC6 of Rick Mears when it started to rain and, after a lap behind the pace car, the cars came into the pits. After about 30 minutes the rain had stopped and the race was back on, Foyt soon taking the lead until the rain returned and the race was declared over. Foyt, therefore, took the victory from Mears.

BELOW *Pole-sitter Danny Ongais in his Parnelli-Cosworth VPJ6 and the Lola-Cosworth T500 of Al Unser go round Woodcote side-by-side at the start of the 1978 USAC Indycar event. (Author)*

1979

■ The opening round of the Vandervell British F3 Championship on 4 March provided plenty of excitement and a win for Chico Serra in his Project 4 March-Toyota 793. Michael Roe, driving a Chevron-Toyota B47, took a well-deserved second place on his F3 debut.

■ On 25 March, Eddie Cheever won a very wet Marlboro *Daily Express* International Trophy race, the first round of the European F2 Championship, in his Beta Osella-BMW FA2/79 after a close-fought battle with Derek Daly's ICI March-BMW 792. After five laps the race had to be stopped and restarted when one car ended up beached on the Woodcote chicane, its suspension broken.

■ The supporting F3 race was won by Nigel Mansell in his Unipart March-Dolomite 783/793, with team-mate Brett Riley in second place. Andrea de Cesaris had taken the flag in his March-Toyota 793 but a ten-second penalty for missing

BELOW *The Essex Porsche 936 of Jochen Mass and Brian Redman (seen here) dominated the 1979 Rivet Supply Silverstone 6-Hours until damage to the rear bodywork caused Mass to crash heavily at Woodcote, destroying the car. (Author)*

the chicane dropped him to third. The Tricentrol British Touring Car event provided a one-two for the Gordon Spice-run Ford Capris, Spice leading home Chris Craft.

■ Porsche sent a single 936 to the Rivet Supply Silverstone 6 Hours on 6 May, and the car (driven by Brian Redman and Jochen Mass) dominated most of the race until, with 3¾hr gone, Redman suffered brake failure at Stowe and slid off, damaging the rear bodywork. About 15 minutes were lost on repairs, but the car rejoined still in the lead. With just an hour left to run and with Mass at the wheel, it then crashed heavily at Woodcote, totally writing-off what had been the very chassis which had won at Le Mans in 1977 and 1978. This left Bob Wollek, John Fitzpatrick and Hans Heyer to take victory in their Gelo Porsche 935 ahead of the de Cadenet Cosworth of Alain de Cadenet and François Migault.

■ Bernard Devaney led home a Chevron one-two in the Vandervell F3 race on Bank Holiday Monday, 28 May, in his Toyota-engined B47B, with the B47 of Michael Roe second. Winner on the road, though, had been Andrea de Cesaris in a March-Toyota 793, but he was penalised a minute for starting beyond his front row grid slot.

■ Jeff Allam won the Tricentrol RAC Touring Car round in his Capri MkIII, with Tom Walkinshaw bringing his rotary-engined Mazda RX7 into second place.

■ After 'winning' on the road twice at Silverstone earlier in the year, only to lose the place, Andrea de Cesaris finally triumphed in the Vandervell F3 Championship race on 1 July in his Marlboro March-Toyota 793 with a perfectly judged drive.

■ Clay Regazzoni scored the first win for Frank Williams at the Marlboro British Grand Prix on 14 July in his Saudia Williams-Ford FW07. His team-mate, Alan Jones, had been the initial leader ahead of the Renault RS10 of Jean-Pierre Jabouille, who eventually pitted for new tyres. This left a Williams one-two at the head of the field until the end of lap 40 when the engine in Jones's car blew up. Regazzoni held on to take a popular victory ahead of the Renault RS10 of René Arnoux, with Jean-Pierre Jarier's Candy Tyrrell-Ford 009 third.

■ Mike Thackwell won the supporting F3 event in a March-Toyota 793 ahead of the similar car of Chico Serra. The British Touring Car Championship round was a Ford Capri benefit, with the cars filling the top six places. Four drivers took their turn at the head of the field, but it was Gordon Spice who emerged victorious, ahead of Chris Craft.

ABOVE *Clay Regazzoni scored the first victory for Frank Williams' Grand Prix team at the 1979 Marlboro British Grand Prix in his Williams-Ford FW07. (sutton-images.com)*

■ A good crowd turned out on Bank Holiday Monday, 27 August, for the Vandervell F3 Championship round, with Chico Serra emerging the winner after a spirited battle with Stefan Johansson, both driving March-Toyota 793s.

■ The Pentax RAC Tourist Trophy on 17 September produced yet another victory for BMW in the shape of the 3.2 CSL driven by Martino Finotto and Carlo Facetti. The event marked the car racing debut of Barry Sheene who, before retiring, impressed in a VW Golf GTi he shared with Richard Lloyd.

■ The Vandervell British F3 round on 7 October ended in carnage, with nine cars in the catch fencing at Woodcote after rain deluged the circuit partway through the race. Stefan Johansson won in his Marlboro March-Toyota 793, despite spinning at Woodcote himself and continuing. When the red flag came out, the Swede was declared the winner, with Mike Thackwell's March-Toyota 793 second.

1980s

"When the car was right there was nothing so satisfying as doing a really hot lap round Silverstone."

Derek Bell

Silverstone, with its long straights and sweeping bends, was always known for being a fast circuit, second only to Monza in Italy on the Grand Prix calendar for outright speed. In 1973 Ronnie Peterson's pole position speed for the Grand Prix in his JPS Lotus-Ford 72E had been 138.102mph, prompting the introduction of a chicane at Woodcote two years later, dropping the pole lap for that year's race, set by Tom Pryce in a Shadow-Ford DN5, to 133.004mph. Slowly it began to creep back up. In 1977 (remember Silverstone only hosted the Grand Prix on alternate years in those days) it was 134.478mph, set by James Hunt in his McLaren-Ford M26. Another two years and speeds had rocketed with the development of ground-effect aerodynamics and turbocharged engines. Alan Jones, albeit in a normally-aspirated Williams-Cosworth FW07, averaged 146.845mph in 1979, with René Arnoux's turbocharged Renault RE30 achieving 148.665mph in 1981.

The trend continued. It was Arnoux on pole again in 1983, this time in a turbo Ferrari 126C3, breaking the 150mph barrier with an average speed of 151.956mph. And then came 1985 and Keke Rosberg in a Williams-Honda FW10.

RIGHT *René Arnoux in his Renault RE30 leads from teammate Alain Prost at the start of the 1981 British Grand Prix. (sutton-images.com)*

Silverstone–Le Mans challenge

One of the established events on the calendar during the eighties was the Silverstone 1000km long-distance sports car race, held each May. The event immediately preceded the prestigious Le Mans 24 Hours and so was often used by teams as a chance for a final shakedown of their cars. In 1982, the BRDC and Le Mans organisers, the Automobile Club de L'Ouest (ACO), instigated the Silverstone–Le Mans challenge for the best-placed driver in the two races, to celebrate the 50th anniversary of the French race. The first winner was Jacky Ickx, with subsequent winners being Derek Bell ('83), Klaus Ludwig ('84) and Hans Stuck ('85, '86, '87).

There had already been talk in May that year of the possibility of major changes to the circuit because of rising lap speeds. It was felt that the Woodcote chicane, introduced ten years previously, was now itself too fast and one plan was to route the circuit right after the *Daily Express* bridge and then sharp left to join the existing Club Straight and on to Woodcote. At Stowe, a right-left at the end of the Hangar Straight would slow the cars for that corner. But these were plans for the future.

During tyre testing in June, Ayrton Senna lapped 1.7sec faster than Arnoux's pole time from 1983, at an average speed of 155.77mph in his JPS Lotus-Renault 97T, and it was realised that a 160mph lap was on the cards for qualifying.

Twenty minutes into the session a short shower left the track damp, but as the wind dried the surface Rosberg went out on his first set of qualifying tyres. He was visibly quicker than anyone else as he went through the chicane at the end of the lap, stopping the clock at 1m 05.967s, an average speed of 160.007mph – the first-ever 160mph lap recorded at the circuit. What was even more remarkable was the fact that he had achieved the time with a left-front tyre that was starting to deflate and with spots of rain again beginning to fall on the track.

But the rain stopped, and at first Nelson Piquet in his Brabham-BMW BT54 and then Ayrton Senna's Lotus began to get closer. Five minutes from the end, Rosberg went out again, and on a still damp track set a stunning lap of 1m 05.591s, averaging 160.925mph. When asked how fast he had been going down the straights, Rosberg replied: "Straights? What straights?"

But spectacular as the lap was, it reinforced the argument that changes would have to be made.

Not that the circuit had stood still during the first five years of the decade. In June 1980 a new BRDC suite was opened at Woodcote Corner at a cost of £70,000, and at the end of the year a new assembly area for competing cars was built in the paddock, with spoil from that area being used to build a spectator bank on the inside of Woodcote.

In order to encourage more spectators, grandstand charges were waived for all of the circuit's own 16 race meetings throughout 1982, and accompanied children under 15 were admitted free. This meant that a family of four with two children under 15 buying admission, grandstand and paddock tickets for the International Trophy race, would pay just £17 as opposed to the £31 it would have cost for the same tickets in 1981.

Silverstone's wide-open spaces have always meant that it and its spectators are susceptible to the weather. After the 1983 *Grand Prix International* 1000km race in May, Jimmy Brown wrote to *Autosport* apologising to the 11,000 fans who attended for problems caused by the weather in gaining access to and exit from the car parks. It wasn't the last time that such a problem would affect the circuit.

But the Silverstone spectators were used to minor inconveniences like the weather. What they weren't expecting when they turned up for the 1983 British Grand Prix in July was to find the paddock cordoned off behind high security fencing. The correspondence pages of the motor sport press the following week were full of letters of complaint from spectators who had paid £3 to cross the Shell Oils Bridge, only to be confronted by security guards and find the paddock inaccessible. It was likened to a prisoner of war camp, and people commented that there had always been a relaxed atmosphere at the Grand Prix prior to this. The move, of course, was not instigated by Silverstone, but was one of the ever-increasing requirements being placed on circuits by Bernie Ecclestone.

"It was a requirement of Bernie," explained Jack Sears. "Jimmy Brown was the managing director at that time and he got on very well with Bernie. Gerald Lascelles (BRDC president) and myself got on very well with Bernie, so really we did whatever he wanted us to do without making a fuss about it. He decided that he wanted to have the paddock area clearer, and therefore he cordoned it all off and issued special passes for those people who could go the other side of the wire, so to speak.

"I think probably the public were a bit disappointed they couldn't get right into the pits. We still had the pit road walkabout, though, that was organised for BRDC members and for members of the public. That was at specific times; they couldn't just do it anytime they wanted."

On the plus side, a new vehicle entrance from the A413 Whittlebury Road on the east side of the circuit was opened in May 1985, along with a new perimeter road to ease the flow of traffic. Other improvements that year included the installation of closed circuit television cameras all the way around the track, while the run-off area at Becketts was extended for safety reasons. An innovation at the Grand Prix was Radio Silverstone, where the commentary, together with driver interviews and music, was broadcast on 1602kHz medium wave.

On 24 May 1986 it was announced that Silverstone had secured an exclusive five-year contract to host the British Grand Prix, ending a 22-year run of alternating with Brands Hatch. The announcement caused considerable furore as the deal had been done in secret without the knowledge of the RAC, Brands Hatch or Donington Park, which had been trying to secure a Grand Prix itself for some time. A statement from Silverstone simply said: "Brands Hatch have advertised the fact that they have had five Grands Prix in five years, and we have taken steps to ensure that we have a Grand Prix for each of the next five years."

Bernie Ecclestone said: "Silverstone has undertaken to build a totally new pit complex, expand the paddock and complete long-term improvements that will really make it the centre of British motor racing."

Stuart Graham was a board member in those days and recalls that the deal was done between Jimmy Brown and Bernie Ecclestone. "I remember the meeting when Jimmy informed us as a board that he'd come to an arrangement with Bernie that the Grand Prix would be exclusively at Silverstone for a period of five years, which Jimmy thought was a good deal," he said.

"There's always been politics going on, which is inevitable – it's a business and there was always a certain amount of rivalry between Brands and Silverstone," he continued. "There was always a threat that Brands would either snatch our Grand Prix or vice versa, so there was a competition, so we could never be complacent, and one of the things we were always worried about was losing our Grand Prix.

"I think at the time, possibly Bernie with his foresight could already see that it was going to grow and grow and grow, and I think most people would accept the fact that Silverstone was one of the few places in England with the actual room to do what needs to be done at a Grand Prix."

It is also quite likely that Jimmy Brown, with his own foresight, was heading off the possibility of the Grand Prix being shared between Silverstone, Brands and Donington, an idea favoured by the RAC but one which the circuits felt to be unsustainable. Earlier in the year FISA's F1 Commission had proposed that there should be a ban on rotating Grands Prix venues in individual countries, and it had been felt that Brands would be the favoured circuit if this came to pass, but Brown had got in first.

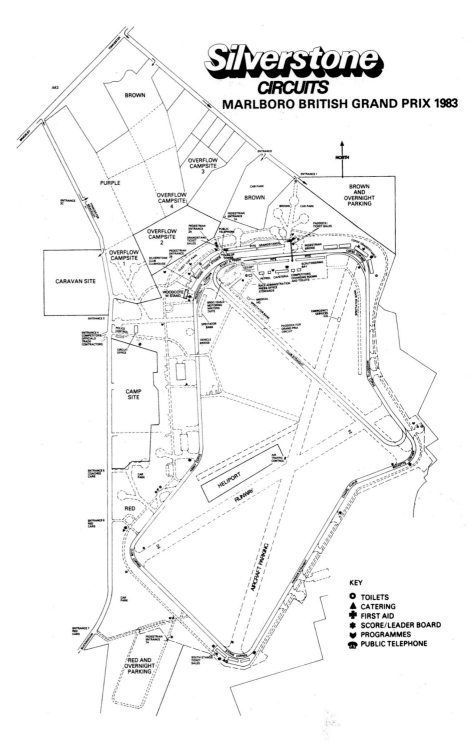

ABOVE *The circuit in 1983, as shown in the programme for the Marlboro British Grand Prix.*

Desiré Wilson

"At the 1980 6-Hours race I was driving the de Cadenet with Alain de Cadenet and we'd just come off a win at Monza so we were pretty high. The only thing was, we had an old engine in the car, so we weren't quite sure if it would actually make the whole race.

"During practice I remember coming up across a Porsche 935. It was terribly fast on the straights and terribly slow in the corners. And although I was two seconds a lap faster than him, I couldn't get by him. So I thought, 'Oh no, this is tough', but that played a big role in my win later on, which I didn't even know at the time, of course.

"Alain started the race, did the first three hours then handed over to me in the lead, and the car was still running really well. Then, a little way into the race it started getting a bit of a misfire, so I was a little perturbed but not too much. I was in the lead and I think it was before the last pit stop, because I had to come in and do one pit stop.

"But what happened was, I came up into the chicane behind somebody and braked too hard and missed the chicane and landed up in the middle of it. So I thought, well I know there's a penalty, but if I stop dead to show them I'm taking a penalty and then drive out, maybe it'll be a ten-second penalty, something like that.

ABOVE *Alain de Cadenet and Desiré Wilson took their de Cadenet-Cosworth LM to victory at the 1980 Silverstone 6-Hours. (LAT)*

"Well, they gave me a full lap penalty so I actually dropped down the field again, so I basically just drove really, really hard. And right towards the end of the race I was chasing Sigi Brunn's Porsche 908, which was now in the lead and I knew I had to actually pass him twice to take the lead because I was a lap down.

"He was also having a few issues and I was having a few issues, and we were catching this 935 that was somewhere in the race. And I got past the 908, not for the lead of the race but on the lead lap, and then we caught this 935 and I said to myself: 'The second I catch this car I am driving right by it, I don't care how I do, because I know from practice if I don't I'm doomed.'

"Because by now I had a misfire, and Sigi was having troubles, and I remember just dive-bombing past the 935 into the chicane and then sort of giving him a little brake job to slow him down, and then off I went. I dropped a gear and I drove away, because I knew I had to get rid of him. And Sigi got stuck behind him and couldn't do a thing.

"And I made up a complete lap and then passed the 908 again. I made up the full lap and I'm positive it was mainly because of him being stuck behind the 935."

In return for the long-term deal, Silverstone had undertaken to build a completely new pit and paddock complex, and work began in November to demolish the existing concrete pit garages, which had been in place since 1975 and cost £120,000 to build at the time. Work continued through the winter of 1986–87, and in addition to the 40 new pit garages, a twin access tunnel was excavated at Copse, and the *Daily Express* vehicle access bridge at Abbey was widened to take two lanes of traffic with pedestrian walkways either side. A new bridge, with link roads, was also installed over Club Straight. Prior to this, vehicles had had to wait to leave the paddock until racing was over.

But that 160mph lap by Keke Rosberg in 1985 had also had an effect, and the £1 million the BRDC was investing in new developments, as it celebrated its diamond jubilee in 1987, included a modification to the track between Abbey and Woodcote. A new dog-leg, left-right corner was introduced in order to slow cars down. The left-hander after the *Daily Express* bridge was followed by a sharp right-hander that led into Woodcote, where the chicane would no longer be used.

It meant that Silverstone had something it hadn't had since the chicane at Club was removed in 1950 – a slow corner. Cars were decelerating from around 190mph as they came under the *Daily Express* bridge to about 60mph for the new section.

The revised circuit was used for the first time at the International Trophy meeting over the weekend of 11–12 April, but when the F1 drivers tried out the new layout on 2–4 June at a mid-week tyre test, there were mixed views. All were unhappy with the new pit lane entrance, which was on the racing line into the new section, and it was agreed that it would be moved to after the new corner in time for July's Grand Prix.

In 1987 a familiar landmark changed, with the Dunlop Tower rebranded the Shell Oils Tower – the old *Motor* bridge having already become the Shell Oils bridge in 1981. The year marked the first of the five-year contract to run the British Grand Prix, and the programme notes for the event contained a few interesting facts about the circuit. At this time, Silverstone had 14,000 permanent grandstand seats, with a further 9,000 erected for the Grand Prix. The circuit's own licensed helipad became the busiest airport in the country at Grand Prix time, with some 2,800 helicopter and 250 fixed wing movements. The increasing popularity of corporate hospitality meant that to deal with the demand around 200,000sq ft of canvas would be erected, and some 10,000 lunches served to guests.

However, the circuit came under fire from Bernie Ecclestone in an interview with BBC Radio 2. "We made a contract with Silverstone under specific conditions," he said. "They were going to change a lot of the facilities, which they haven't done. They were going to build a new pits complex, and they've given us things like lean-to garages. They were going to provide a new press centre, and they've given us a tent. They were going to build new commentary booths, and if you go and look at them you'll see that they're a complete joke. They have done very little of what they were supposed to do.

"This circuit was OK until a couple of years ago, but Formula 1 is now a top-level sport on a worldwide basis, and it is essential that all the circuits press ahead with us. If we find that these people can't do what they said they were going to do, then we'll have to look at somewhere else.

"Now, Brands Hatch are saying that they are willing to make the necessary changes. At the time we signed our contract with Silverstone, it wasn't obvious that Brands Hatch was in a position to do these things: we were moving towards entering into long-term contracts with Formula 1 circuits, and we felt it was necessary to sign a contract for five years with people who could do the job we needed. We gave Silverstone the opportunity to bring their circuit into the nineties with us and they haven't taken it.

"The trouble with the people in England is that they think they have a divine right to have a Grand Prix. Just because most of the teams happen to be based in England, it doesn't necessarily mean that we have to race here."

In its response, the circuit pointed out that it had made all the safety requirements requested by FISA and that the new pits were built to FISA/FOCA dimensions. As to the press centre, that had always been part of the second phase of development and would be completed in time for the following year's Grand Prix.

It wouldn't be the last time that Silverstone was criticised by the boss of F1, though. Not by a long way.

Ecclestone wasn't the only one with gripes, either. After the Grand Prix, *Motoring News* initiated a reader survey, which contained many unfavourable comments, while a disgruntled spectator wrote to *Motor Sport* magazine complaining of the time that it had taken him to get out of the Red car park at the south of the circuit at the end of the meeting. "…the only notice of exit was a painted board at one end of the field," he wrote, adding: "This led single-file traffic through an empty field into another car park (each with approximately 20,000 cars)…Traffic was stationary for hours and not an official to be seen."

At the end of 1987, work began on phase two of the circuit's development programme, which included the new media centre located at the Woodcote end of the pit lane straddling the existing pit garages, debris fencing and improved spectator facilities. But one person who wouldn't be around to see the completion of the work was the man who had been instrumental in guiding Silverstone through the past 40 years – Jimmy Brown.

On 19 April 1988, the man who had been track manager at that very first Grand Prix in 1948 and who went on to become chairman of Silverstone Circuits, passed away in hospital at the age of 67. When the new media centre was opened by Bernie Ecclestone on the eve of the British Grand Prix, Friday 8 July, it was named the Jimmy Brown Centre, and Ecclestone was joined by Brown's widow, Kay.

In his place, Tom Walkinshaw was appointed chairman, while Pierre Aumonier remained as deputy chairman, responsible for the day-to-day running of the group. Jimmy's son Hamish became managing director of the Silverstone group of companies.

The circuit celebrated its 40th anniversary in 1988, and in May it was awarded the AMRA (Accessory Manufacturers' Racing Association) trophy in recognition of its cooperation with the trade during the 1987 Grand Prix, while in December it won the FOCA Trophy for the best-organised Grand Prix of the year.

In January 1989, the Silverstone Racing School was renamed the John Watson Performance Driving Centre and was based at a new centre near Abbey Corner. The new fleet included 16 Formula Fords, 12 MG Montegos, a pair of Volvo skid cars and a few rally cars, the intention being to provide a broader opportunity of experience as well as standard race instruction.

Also in January, plans for changes to the Club circuit were announced. A new left-hand corner named Brooklands, just before the end of Club Straight, took the cars away from the approach to Woodcote, rejoining the existing track just after the *Daily Express* bridge at a right-hander named Bridge, and the layout was renamed the National circuit. A mini-oval for use by the skid training school was also planned, while the shorter Club circuit would still be used for smaller meetings.

At the same time, a new southern circuit was also announced for general testing and the racing school – allowing Silverstone to run two layouts at the same time. The track left the existing circuit at Abbey, where it turned right and ran up a straight past the helicopter pad. It then turned right to run a short distance parallel to Club Straight before turning right again to rejoin the track at Chapel Curve. The new facility was opened on 14 April 1989 when the Jaguar sports car team tested there, along with the Onyx, Brabham and Leyton House F1 teams.

Other work included the construction of a new vehicle bridge, with pedestrian underpass, over Hangar Straight, and new spectator terraces were built at Copse, Maggots and Becketts. The terrace at Copse and the walkways behind were concreted, and viewing areas to accommodate wheelchairs were added for the disabled. New toilet facilities were also

Derek Bell

"I won two races at Silverstone on Whit Monday 1964 in my Lotus 7, at the Nottingham Sports Car Club meeting, and it immediately became something special in my life because there I was, on this phenomenal Silverstone Grand Prix circuit, winning two races in one day.

"After that I had this great passion for Silverstone and, of course, loved the old track. I raced there in Formula 3, I did the British Grand Prix once and the *Daily Express* Trophy, and then, of course, all my sports car races.

"John Wyer had me there testing the Porsche 917 during 1971, before we went off to the races. The Gulf racing team truck would open up and out would come the 917, and it didn't really need much testing. So I would spend about an hour and a half in it doing different things and John would say, 'OK, that'll do Bell', and out would come this bloody Mirage which had been designed and built by Len Bailey, and which at one stage ended up with a V12 engine as a hill climb car and a Can-Am car.

"So this car was being developed to do Can-Am, and every time it was rolled out I would think, 'Oh, blast, I've got to drive that thing again,' and I remember I used to get in it, drive off and on my first lap I always went off into a field of wheat. I would come to Club, turn into the corner and just keep on turning and go round, and have to come into the pits and pull all the green wheat out. I said, 'It always wants to eat something,' and John Wyer didn't find that very funny. 'Oh, carry on Bell, don't keep on about it.'

"Anyway, this thing had a mind of its own and if you touched a seam in the road, of which there were many at Silverstone – those awful little two inch high kerbs around the ends of the runways which were the apexes of corners. If you touched them the car would just go out of control.

"The last time I ever drove it, John said, 'OK, we're going to spend a day with the Mirage and if we can get down to a certain time by the end of the day we're going to go and race in America with it in Can-Am.' And even at that point I didn't think I could race this thing anywhere else because I'd got to know where every bump was at Silverstone and where I was likely to spin off. You couldn't go to a new track, it would take you another three weeks to build up confidence to go fast.

"I went round, changing stuff all the day, and at a-quarter-to-five we're still not doing terribly well. So I said, 'Tighten everything up – shock absorbers all hard, roll bars right up tight, everything we can do – make it like a go-kart.' So we tightened it up and I went out.

"On my timed lap I came down to Stowe and turned in and I was absolutely flying. I kept it neat and tidy, slightly understeered through the corner and then down to Club, leaping down to Club, turned in and touched the little kerb. I went round and round, hit the bank backwards, the car exploded in the air, all the bits flew everywhere and I remember sitting on top of the bank with oil pouring down my face – this was in the days of goggles and helmet – thinking, 'Oh sugar, what have we done here?'

"I got out of the car and nobody appeared – there were no marshals, I could have been dead – and eventually one of the marshals turns up, and meanwhile I've been picking up the pieces, bits of bodywork, putting it all together to make the car look neater, as if it wasn't such a big crash. I couldn't do much about the car being on the bank though.

"JW had a Mustang, or whatever, and he cruised around and came up beside me, and I was still standing there picking bits of plastic up, and he said, 'Don't worry Bell, I saw it all,' and he drove off and left me there with the car. But afterwards he said, 'Do you know, up until that point, that was the quickest lap you'd done?'

ABOVE *The Porsche 956, a car which would go on to dominate Group C sports car racing, made its debut at the 1982 Pace Silverstone 6-Hours in the hands of Jacky Ickx and Derek Bell. Fuel regulations prevented it from running at its true pace, however, and the works car finished second to the Group Six Lancia Martini of Michele Alboreto and Riccardo Patrese. (LAT)*

"As a track to drive it was very, very demanding. Those fast corners. It was a glorious track and was always brilliant in the Porsche 962 because it was so fast. When the car was right there was nothing so satisfying as doing a really hot lap round Silverstone. The drifting out of Becketts was fantastic, obviously wanting to get it on to the straight neatly so you got maximum speed down Hangar Straight, and then back up the other side to Abbey. Going through Abbey flat. Whatever you drove, Abbey always seemed to be just flat, but probably not every lap. It was just a very demanding track and one of the fastest in the world. The races were always very hard and the satisfaction when you won the 1000km at Silverstone, you knew you'd done it. But, of course, it was one of the quickest races we did because it was so fast, averaging whatever it was, 130mph. It was all over fairly quickly, so we liked Silverstone from the point of view that we got home earlier."

installed around Stowe, Club and Abbey. On the downside, the popular spectator area on the inside of Woodcote was removed.

Two giant Avesco Starvision TV screens had been used at the Grand Prix for the first time in 1988 and had proved so popular with spectators that five were to be provided for 1989 – the largest number ever at one location. They were 20ft high, and two were to be located between Stowe and Club, with others at Woodcote, Copse and Becketts, providing not only the BBC coverage but also Silverstone's own specially filmed footage as well, including the support races. At the same time Radio Silverstone was increasing its daily commentaries.

But all this work had to be paid for somehow, and when the ticket prices for the Shell Oils 1989 British Grand Prix were announced, spectators were dismayed to find that they had risen by 67 per cent to £30 for basic admission. "The prices have been brought into line because they had become totally out of step with the costs of putting on a Grand Prix," explained Silverstone Circuits chairman Tom Walkinshaw at the time in an interview with *Autosport*. "They didn't take account of the increases inflicted on us by outside parties, and even with this increase we are only now in line with the other European Grands Prix.

"We had to take a good look and see how we could use the facility in order to make it pay. That's why we will soon have two circuits that can operate at the same time. It's not just testing but corporate days and the school."

When Silverstone was granted the five-year deal to host the British Grand Prix from 1987 onwards, it had to agree to a raft of demands from FISA. In the first phase, it had to concentrate on fulfilling the very basic demands, such as a new press centre, safety fencing and closed-circuit television all around the track for safety reasons. The debris fencing, in particular, was unpopular with spectators, restricting both their view and the opportunity for photography. But, as Walkinshaw explained in the interview, they didn't just wake up one morning and decide to spend several thousand pounds on fencing. "The governing body says that the standards for a Grand Prix include debris fencing, so we did it, there was no option.

"The press centre was not a priority of our choosing, but FISA said that they wanted it, along with the television link around the circuit," he added.

To improve the spectator's experience, the terracing from the start line, around Copse and towards Becketts was raised and concreted, and other sections were also raised, but the concreting of these had to wait until the following year to allow the ground to settle.

In a separate interview with *Motor Sport* Walkinshaw said: "FISA has made it clear that only circuits which develop will grow with the sport, and we know what that means. We made all the changes to date to comply with our agreement with FISA. The latest changes, however, have nothing to do with that. They are being made because we want to bring motor racing in Britain into the nineties, and to bring our facilities up to the standard of those in other areas of the sport or entertainment business."

John Watson

"I think the first time I visited Silverstone was in the late sixties, it might have been '67 or '68 for the International Trophy, and my best friend and I went over because his sister worked for John Surtees or Lola or something. So we got taken up to the circuit and then tucked into the back of a van, covered by tyres and blankets, and got taken into the pits. So we were on the inside of the circuit, and that was the first time I'd been there.

"There was a Formula 1 race, but there was also a big sports car race and I was watching through a little gap between the pit wall and the timing and scoring at Woodcote, and it was such a visual experience. Woodcote was still a fast corner and I'd never seen racing cars travelling at that level of speed, and the sound of the V8s was very powerful.

"The first time I raced there was '73 in the Grand Prix, and that was in a Brabham, which Hexagon of Highgate had leased from Bernie and painted in the international racing colours of Highgate, North London, which was brown.

"I managed to avoid being caught up in the notorious Jody Scheckter drop in Woodcote, where he was just too quick, too wide and too inexperienced.

"In 1977 the Brabham BT45B was a very effective Grand Prix car, with the flat 12 Alfa Romeo engine, and the nature of that circuit played to the strengths of the car. I was on the front row with James Hunt, and I led off the line, and for 30 odd laps James and I had a battle for the lead.

"But we had a fuel pick-up problem so I went into the pits and they put more fuel in. I went back out again and within another ten or so laps, I had to retire – a huge disappointment. I think it was very generous of James to say later that he was doing all he could to find a way past, but he couldn't achieve that. Had he found a way past then I don't know what would have happened.

"That home win in 1981 was a very special win, a very special day. The lead-up to that Grand Prix was that at the Spanish Grand Prix at Jarama, which was two races prior to Silverstone, I finished third and scored the first podium finish for the McLaren MP4/1. At the French Grand Prix at Dijon I finished second, and then I thought, well we're coming to Silverstone, a circuit that primarily is a power circuit, so the turbo-charged cars are going to be at an advantage. Nevertheless, the media were asking, will you win at Silverstone?

"And I don't know what I expected. Obviously I had hopes, but the pace of the Renaults in particular, and to a lesser degree the Ferraris, meant I was somewhere on the fourth or fifth row

of the grid. When the race started I was running behind Alan Jones, who was running directly behind Gilles Villeneuve, and I described Villeneuve's driving that day as being like that of a hyperactive child.

"His Ferrari was a dog, and that's a compliment – it's an insult to a dog – and in the chicane he had the car bouncing over kerbs. To watch, it was amazing to see the car control, but he was holding up Alan, certainly holding me up and inevitably he lost control of the car at Woodcote. Alan was so close behind he couldn't see where Villeneuve was through the tyre smoke. I was far enough behind and I was looking through the corner to the exit as well as watching what was happening here.

"Anyway, I managed to slow down enough to avoid everything, but in the process of doing so the engine stalled, so I had to quickly think – fuel pump on, select a lower gear and bump start it. It just caught and off I went again. And my team-mate, Andrea de Cesaris, who was directly behind me, had been looking at the gearbox of my car. He hadn't been looking through the corner, which is what he should have done. Andrea could have won his first Grand Prix but he realised there was an accident, hit the brakes and turned sharp left, and had his own accident.

"So I then started all over again, having to re-pass people I'd already overtaken. Eventually, Piquet had an accident, something on his car failed going up into Becketts, Prost had a problem with the Renault and then Arnoux, who was leading, had a problem as well. I was catching him at a point when his problem was evolving, overtook him, and I think he then retired before the end of the race.

"At the point when I got into the lead of the race I could see all around the circuit, suddenly there was a mass rising. I was acutely aware of it, but what I was also aware of was that some four years earlier at Dijon I'd been at the point of having my second Grand Prix win and on the last lap ran out of fuel. So what I did was to shut down the expectations or the premature acknowledgement, as I didn't want to let what was going on, which I was aware of, interfere or intrude into my focus.

"By then I had a comfortable lead and Ron Dennis was hanging over the pit wall slowing me down, and the only way I felt to do that without losing rhythm was to reduce the rpm, because if you lose rhythm you make mistakes. So for the last three or so laps I was only revving the engine to 9,000rpm, as opposed to 10,600rpm. And it made hardly any difference whatsoever to the lap times, but the key was to maintain the momentum and the rhythm and not start to try to brake earlier or do other things. And then, once finally I took the chequered flag, I was able to acknowledge what had been happening around the circuit for the previous eight or ten laps.

"I'd never been on a lap of honour during a track invasion. I'd seen it because you were used to the crowd coming on to the track at Monza after the race, but I'd never been on the flat-bed truck that took you round on the lap of honour as the winner and suddenly receiving this level of adulation. And I thought, Jesus Christ, I've never seen this in my life – is this for me? I was a relatively self-effacing person and I turned to Jacques Laffite and said, 'What is this all about?' And he said, 'Look, this is their way of saying we've had a good day and thank you very much.'

He added: "The cost of staging the Grand Prix has risen considerably on a number of fronts. We have no control over any of them, we simply pay the increased rates. Overall, it's gone up some 85 per cent. Nowadays the public expects better facilities, but bringing them into line costs money. The two factors have led to the need to put our prices up."

After the International Trophy meeting in April 1989, the circuit ran advertisements apologising for the fact that rain, hail and snow in the lead-up to the meeting had meant that car parks had been flooded in places, and that resurfacing of the car parks and approach roads had been delayed. A planned courtesy shuttle service to take spectators around the perimeter road had also been unable to complete a full circuit because of incomplete surfacing of the road. The intention at future meetings was to have five shuttles operating for people to jump on and off.

Ticket prices might have risen, but the timetable for the 1989 British Grand Prix on 14–16 July demonstrated how full a programme spectators were treated to, compared to today.

On race day, Radio Silverstone was on air from 6am, and a pit lane walkabout for holders of centre transfers took place from 7.30 to 9.30am. At 10am there was the half-hour F1 warm-up, a feature long gone from Grands Prix these days. This was followed by the first race of the day, for GM Lotus Euroseries and Vauxhall Lotus, and then a round of the Coupe de France 309 Peugeot Esso Championship. A parade of winners from Saturday's races (British F3 and Esso Metro Challenge) was followed by track parades and demonstrations, including the John Watson Performance Driving Centre, Russ Swift's Montego Display Team and various historic F1 cars, while in the air entertainment was provided by a Sea Harrier and the Red Arrows, a regular feature at the Grand Prix each year.

The race itself began at 2.30pm and was followed by a round of the Esso British Touring Car Championship. Afterwards, bands located at Woodcote, Copse, Stowe and the mall between the main car parks provided entertainment as spectators left the circuit.

BELOW *View of Woodcote with surrounding grandstands and Shell Oils Tower at the 1989 Shell Oils British Grand Prix. (Author)*

Alain Prost

"I first raced on the club track in Formula 3 in 1978. When you are racing in Europe and then you come to England for the first time, you realise what racing in England means. You have a completely different atmosphere, and it was the first time that I raced on a track where you have a large straight, and in Formula 3 we were five or six cars all together, and I was not used to doing this kind of racing. It was hard racing, harder than we used to have in France, for example. It was a good experience, but I didn't win.

"The thing I liked about the old Silverstone was that it was a really challenging track, because it was fast and dangerous, with fast corners – but also technically it was really something different.

"What I liked in the old days was that you had different cars, for example the turbo cars were better at Silverstone than at Monaco. What I also liked was the fact that we had really low-speed tracks, then you had average speed, and then you had high-speed tracks. And every time you had to change the set-up of the car and the set-up of the engine. Silverstone was really demanding, very different, because you had no low speed corners. At the time you had to take care of the tyres because when you had a very low downforce you had to be a bit careful. It was really challenging, and that is what I like. Maybe because I was really motivated by the set-up of the car and trying to get something perfect, I was maybe more competitive on a track like Silverstone.

"I remember '85 very well because it was a very big domination [Prost lapped the entire field]. In '89 I was behind Ayrton and my car was as usual a little bit less quick in qualifying, but in the

ABOVE *Alain Prost on his way to winning the 1985 Marlboro British Grand Prix in his McLaren-TAG MP4/2B. (LAT)*

race condition I was very good and was behind him and pushing, pushing and then he spun. You know there's a few races that you are fighting with the car or you know that it is going to be difficult, and some races that you know that it's going to be OK. I was second behind him and I knew that one way or another I would have won because I was quicker in the race.

"It was the same in '83 with the Renault, fighting with the Ferrari. I remember very well because I made a good choice of the tyres, was maybe a little less quick at the beginning of the race, but slowly I came back and overtook the Ferrari.

"I can only talk about the old track, but on that it was obvious you needed a very precise driving style, an accommodation between the set-up of the car and your style. We had many problems with the tyres at the time on this track because of the long corners, especially after Hangar. Club was really the most difficult corner. When I say difficult, that's the place where you could gain or lose time a lot. When you started to have problems with the tyres, especially with a low downforce car, that is where you had to work a lot in private testing to try to understand how the car would be after 20 or 30 laps, and that is what you need the most at Silverstone.

"When I was racing I always said that of the great tracks in the world, if you had to choose three you would say Silverstone, Spa and the old Interlagos. Also, there is an atmosphere that as a driver you can like or dislike. Silverstone was one of my favourite tracks."

1980

■ Stefan Johansson dominated the first round of the Vandervell British F3 Championship on 2 March in his Marlboro Project Four March-Toyota 803.

■ This year's International Trophy, held on a bitterly cold 20 April, was a round of the national Aurora AFX F1 Championship and was won by the Chilean driver Eliseo Salazar in a RAM Williams-Ford FW07. Another Williams FW07 was second in the hands of Emilio de Villota, with Ray Mallock's Surtees-Ford TS20 third. The race was a dull affair and a sad reflection of the former glory days of the International Trophy.

■ In contrast, the supporting Tricentrol British Saloon Car Championship round provided plenty of entertainment, even though it was cut short because of an accident involving the Vauxhall Magnum of Tony Lanfranchi. Andy Rouse emerged the victor in his Ford Capri ahead of Rex Greenslade's Rover Vitesse. Kenny Acheson took the honours in the F3 encounter in a March-Toyota 803.

■ Alain de Cadenet and Desiré Wilson, in their de Cadenet-Cosworth LM, scored a well-deserved win at the Silverstone 6-Hours race, the fifth round of the World Championship of Makes, on 11 May. The initial leader had been the pole-sitting Kremer Porsche 935 K3/80, driven by John Fitzpatrick, Guy Edwards and Axel Plankenhorn, until it began to smoke around the halfway point and the de Cadenet moved into the lead, though this too developed a misfire. When Wilson was docked a lap for missing the chicane, the Porsche 908/3 of Jürgen Barth and Siegfried Brunn assumed the lead, but Wilson then put in a storming drive, closed the gap to the Porsche and retook the lead with just 23 minutes left to run.

■ Stefan Johansson took pole position and then went on to score his second Silverstone win of the season in the Vandervell F3 round on 26 May in his March-Toyota 803b, narrowly beating the older March-Toyota 793 of Kenny Acheson.

■ Derek Warwick scored his first F2 win in the 47-lap Marlboro F2 Trophy race, the sixth round of the European F2 Championship, on 8 June. Warwick led from start to finish in his BP Toleman-Hart TG280, with Andrea de Cesaris in a March-BMW 802 second. The supporting British F3 event was won by Kenny Acheson in a March-Toyota 793, while Andy Rouse was victorious in a very wet Tricentrol British Saloon Car Championship race in his Ford Capri.

■ There was heartbreak for Mike White at the Tricentrol F3 meeting on 6 July when he was disqualified from first place for a leaking airbox on his March-Toyota 803b. White's misfortune handed the victory to Thierry Tassin's Argo-Toyota JM6.

■ The Vandervell F3 contenders were back at Silverstone on 25 August, and this time Thierry Tassin won on merit in his Argo-Toyota JM6, narrowly beating Kenny Acheson's March-Toyota 803b.

■ Just two weeks later, on 7 September, F3 was back yet again with a combined round of the British Vandervell and European championships, run as two 15-lap heats with the overall result declared on aggregate. Mike White emerged the overall victor in his March-Toyota 803b, having also won the first heat, while heat two winner Rob Wilson in a Ralt-Toyota RT3 was runner-up.

■ BMW scored a fifth successive win at the Halfords Tourist Trophy, Britain's round of the European Touring Car Championship, on 14 September in front of a crowd of around 8,000. The Italia-entered 635 CSi of Umberto Grano, Heribert Werginz and Harry Neger took the flag ahead of the Zakspeed Ford Escort of Jürgen Hamelmann and Klaus Ludwig, which was later excluded for a suspension irregularity. This handed runner-up spot to the BMW 320i of Helmut Kelleners and Siegfried Müller Jr.

■ The Aurora AFX F1 Championship visited the circuit again on 5 October for the Pentax Trophy meeting, which provided a victory for Emilio de Villota's RAM Williams-Ford FW07B, after his team-mate Eliseo Salazar crashed out heavily while the pair were dicing for the lead.

1981

■ Jonathan Palmer won a very wet opening round of the Marlboro British F3 Championship on 1 March in his Ralt-Toyota RT3, beating the March-Toyota 813 of Mike White into second. The meeting had to be abandoned early as darkness descended.

■ Mike Thackwell, driving a Ralt-Honda RH6, won the Marlboro *Daily Express* International Trophy race, the opening round of the European F2 Championship, on 29 March, despite having to stop for slick tyres on a drying track, and later clashing with his team-mate Geoff Lees, who was a lap down. The early leader had been the Swiss privateer Jurg Leinhard in his March-BMW 802, whose Goodyear wet tyres proved ideal for the conditions, but he was eventually sidelined by battery failure.

■ Ford Capris finished one-two-three in the Tricentrol RAC British Saloon Car Championship round, in the hands of Andy Rouse, Gordon Spice and Vince Woodman, after pole-sitter and early leader Win Percy suffered gearbox failure on his Mazda RX7. Jonathan Palmer was again victorious in the F3 round in his Ralt-Toyota RT3.

■ The pole position car at the Silverstone 6 Hours on 10 May didn't even make it to the end of the first lap, Jochen Mass crashing the Joest Porsche 908-80 that he was sharing with Reinhold Joest and Volkhert Merl on a streaming wet track at Woodcote. Victory went to the Porsche 935 of Dieter Schornstein, Harald Grohs and Walter Rohl, with the EMKA BMW M1 of Derek Bell, Steve O'Rourke and David Hobbs in second place.

■ Thierry Tassin won the round of the Marlboro British F3 Championship on Bank Holiday Monday, 25 May, in slippery conditions, starting from seventh on the grid and taking the lead after just seven laps in his Ralt-Toyota RT3/81.

■ A month later, on 25 June, Roberto Moreno took his debut F3 win at the Marlboro European F3 Trophy meeting, which included a round of the British championship. The Brazilian scored a lights-to-flag victory in his Ralt-Toyota RT3/81. In the supporting Tricentrol British Saloon Car Championship round, Peter Lovett gave TWR Rover its first win as he took his 3.5 Rover V8 to victory.

ABOVE *The EMKA BMW M1 of Derek Bell, Steve O'Rourke and David Hobbs finished second in the Silverstone 6-Hours on 10 May 1981. (LAT)*

■ It was Raul Boesel's turn to win an F3 encounter, this time on the Club circuit at the Marlboro British F3 round on 5 July in his Ralt-Toyota RT3.

■ John Watson scored a hugely popular win at the Marlboro British Grand Prix on Saturday 18 July, in his Marlboro McLaren-Ford MP4/1, after the leading Renault RE30s of Alain Prost and René Arnoux both retired with engine problems. Watson had been delayed by a multi-car accident at the end of lap four, triggered when Gilles Villeneuve spun his Ferrari 126CK at Woodcote and was hit by the Williams-Ford FW07C of reigning world champion Alan Jones. Watson managed to brake to a virtual standstill without hitting anything, but he dropped to tenth place, whereas his team-mate, Andrea de Cesaris, went off in avoidance. Watson started to make up places and, aided by retirements in front of him, was soon up to third. When Prost retired he was second and chasing the other Renault of Arnoux, which had a healthy lead until it too began to slow, allowing Watson to catch it and take the lead on lap 61. Arnoux retired soon after, leaving Watson to win ahead of the Williams-Ford FW07 of Carlos Reutemann and Jacques Laffite's Talbot Ligier-Matra JS17.

■ Roberto Moreno won the supporting F3 event in his Ralt-Toyota RT3/81, only to be excluded later for a fuel irregularity. Thierry Tassin's similar machine therefore inherited the victory. Peter Lovett led a TWR Rover V8 one-two ahead of Jeff Allam in the Tricentrol British Saloon Car race.

RIGHT *At the end of the first lap of the 1981 Marlboro British Grand Prix, Gilles Villeneuve lost control of his Ferrari 126CK, triggering a multi-car accident. The Marlboro McLaren-Ford MP4/1 of Andrea de Cesaris has locked up trying to avoid the mêlée, as has the Williams-Ford FW07 of Alan Jones. De Cesaris' team-mate John Watson, who was also delayed by the accident, went on to take victory. (BRDC Archive)*

BELOW *Watson celebrates on the podium. (LAT)*

■ Dave Scott took a maiden F3 victory on Bank Holiday Monday, 31 August, at the Marlboro British F3 round, leading every lap in his Ralt-Toyota RT3/81. Jeff Allam won the round of the Tricentrol British Saloon Car Championship in his Rover V8 ahead of Win Percy's Mazda RX7.

■ For the first time since 1975, BMW was beaten in the RAC Tourist Trophy on 13 September, the laurels going to the rotary-powered Mazda RX7 of Tom Walkinshaw and Chuck Nicholson. With only a few laps to run, Walkinshaw took the lead from the BMW 635 CSi of Helmut Kelleners and Umberto Grano, which had led from the start, and the pair finished just 5sec apart. The winning car was initially disqualified after the race, but was later reinstated on appeal.

■ Raul Boesel took an easy win in the British F3 encounter on 4 October in his Ralt-Toyota RT3/81. The supporting final round of the British Saloon Car Championship was marred by a series of protests after the race concerning the eligibility of the TWR-run Rovers of Peter Lovett and Jeff Allam, which had finished one-two on the road, but the results were eventually confirmed.

ABOVE *The start of the Tricentrol British Saloon Car round at the 1981 Marlboro British Grand Prix meeting. Peter Lovett, in his TWR Rover V8, won the race ahead of team-mate Jeff Allam. (Author)*

1982

■ The Marlboro British F3 Championship kicked off at Silverstone on 7 March with a healthy grid of 20 cars for a 20-lap race on the Club circuit, with victory going to Tommy Byrne in his Ralt-Toyota RT3C/81.

■ Stefan Bellof won his first-ever F2 race, the Marlboro *Daily Express* International Trophy on 21 March, driving a Maurer-BMW MM82, taking the lead from Thierry Tassin's Toleman-Hart DS1 with just two laps to run. A rain shower just before the start meant the field began on rain tyres, and pole-sitter Stefan Johansson in the Spirit-Honda 201 built an early lead until his Bridgestone tyres began to overheat. Tassin, running on Avons, was on course to take victory until he was caught and passed by the flying Bellof, who had started ninth. Tassin's Toleman was later excluded, handing second place to Satoru Nakajima's March-Honda 812, ahead of Beppe Gabbiani's Maurer-BMW MM82.

■ Jeff Allam dominated the opening round of the Tricentrol British Saloon Car Championship in his Rover V8, while Dave Scott took victory in the Marlboro British F3 encounter in a Ralt-Toyota RT3C/81 after early leader Tommy Byrne had spun his similar car at the Woodcote chicane.

■ The Pace Silverstone 6-Hours on 16 May was run for the new Group C category of endurance sports car racing and marked the world debut of Porsche's latest challenger, the mighty 956. Fuel regulations, however, meant that the pole-sitting Rothmans-backed works car of Jacky Ickx and Derek Bell was unable to run at its true pace during the race. This handed victory to the Group 6 Lancia Martini of Michele Alboreto and Riccardo Patrese, with Bell and Ickx having to settle for second ahead of the Belga Porsche 936C of the Martin brothers, Jean-Michel and Philippe, together with Bob Wollek.

ABOVE *A pit stop for the winning TWR Jaguar XJS of Tom Walkinshaw and Chuck Nicholson, which led home teammates Peter Lovett and Pierre Dieudonne at the 1982 Canon Tourist Trophy. (LAT)*

LEFT *The victorious Lancia Martini of Michele Alboreto and Riccardo Patrese enters parc fermé at the end of the 1982 Pace Silverstone 6-Hours. (Author)*

■ Roberto Moreno won the Bank Holiday Monday, 31 May, round of the Marlboro British F3 Championship in his Ralt-Toyota RT3D/82 ahead of pole-sitter James Weaver's older RT3C/81.

■ A fortnight later, on 13 June, the European F3 contenders combined with the British championship, producing a victory for Emanuele Pirro in his Euroracing-Alfa Romeo 101. The supporting British Saloon Car encounter produced a thrilling race, with Jeff Allam's Rover V8 just beating the Ford Capri of Vince Woodman.

■ Roberto Moreno won again at the 27 June round of the Marlboro British F3 Championship in a Ralt-Alfa Romeo RT3D/82, beating the Toyota-powered RT3D/82 of Enrique Mansilla, but it was the Argentinian who won in atrocious conditions at the Bank Holiday Monday meeting on 30 August. Because of the conditions the race had to be stopped after 11 laps, and was restarted. Martin Brundle had been leading in his Ralt-VW RT3D/82 but retired with a flat battery, leaving Mansilla to take his Toyota-powered RT3D/82 to victory.

■ Jaguar scored a one-two at the Canon Tourist Trophy on 12 September, with the XJS of Tom Walkinshaw and Chuck Nicholson leading home team-mates Peter Lovett and Pierre Dieudonne.

■ There was a thrilling three-way battle for honours in the Marlboro British F3 race on 3 October between Enrique Mansilla, Dave Scott and eventual winner Tommy Byrne, all driving Ralt RT3D/82s, with Scott just taking the runner-up spot. The final round of the Tricentrol British Saloon Car Championship produced a one-two for Rover as Peter Lovett just held off Brian Muir.

1983

■ David Leslie put his new Magnum-Toyota 833 on pole for the opening round of the Marlboro British F3 Championship on 6 March, but it was the Brazilian driver Ayrton Senna da Silva who won convincingly in his West Surry Racing Ralt-Toyota RT3E/83. A close battle for second resulted in Martin Brundle's Eddie Jordan Racing, Toyota-powered RT3E/81 just beating the VW-powered example of Davy Jones to the place.

■ Only nine cars finished in the International Trophy, the opening round of the European F2 Championship, on 20 March, with victory going to Beppe Gabbiani driving a March-BMW 832. He was chased hard towards the end by the Maurer-BMW MM83 of Stefan Bellof, but the German was thwarted when his throttle cable broke at the end of the penultimate lap. Second place thus went to Mike Thackwell in a Ralt-Honda RH6/83H, ahead of the March-BMW 832 of Christian Danner.

■ A very wet supporting F3 race produced another victory for Ayrton Senna da Silva, with Martin Brundle again being his closest challenger. Steve Soper took the honours in the opening round of the Trimoco British Saloon Car Championship in his TWR-run Rover Vitesse, ahead of team-mate Jeff Allam.

■ Senna took his sixth win out of six starts at the 24 April round of the F3 Championship, leading from pole and never headed. Davy Jones claimed the runner-up spot in his Murray Taylor Racing Ralt-VW RT3E/83.

■ The annual six-hours endurance race morphed into a 1000km event for the second round of the FIA World Endurance Championship on 8 May and was backed by *Grand Prix International* magazine. The two works Martini Lancia LC2s of Michele Alboreto/Riccardo Patrese and Piercarlo Ghinzani/Teo Fabi were the early runaway leaders of the rain-affected race, but eventually they retired with overheating problems. This left the works Rothmans Porsche 956 of Derek Bell and Stefan Bellof to take victory, albeit just 53sec ahead of the Marlboro Porsche 956 of Bob Wollek and Stefan Johansson. Third went to the Canon Porsche 956 of Jan Lammers and Thierry Boutsen.

BELOW *The field streams down into Woodcote for the start of the wet 1983 Grand Prix International 1000km. The two cars at the front – the Rothmans Porsche 956 of Derek Bell and Stefan Bellof and the Marlboro-backed 956 of Bob Wollek and Stefan Johansson – eventually finished first and second. (Author)*

ABOVE *The Martini Lancia LC2 of Piercarlo Ghinzani and Teo Fabi comes down the pit lane during the 1983* Grand Prix International *1000km. The car, together with that of team-mates Michele Alboreto and Riccardo Patrese, led the race early on before retiring with overheating problems. (Author)*

ABOVE *Flame out from the Lancia LC1 of Massimo Sigala and Oscar Larrauri during the 1983* Grand Prix International *1000km. (Steve Rendle)*

■ F3 was becoming a Senna benefit, as the Brazilian won yet again on Bank Holiday Monday, 30 May, in a tedious race with Brundle again second. The spell was finally broken on 12 June at the Marlboro European F3 Trophy race when Brundle took a magnificent victory for the Eddie Jordan team, ahead of team-mate Tommy Byrne. Senna had already spun while fighting for second place and then crashed out at Woodcote a couple of laps later.

■ The supporting Trimoco British Saloon Car Championship round produced a great scrap between the Rover Vitesse duo of Steve Soper and Peter Lovett and the BMW 635 CSi of Frank Sytner, who finished second on the road behind Soper but dropped to third after a ten-second penalty for missing the Woodcote chicane.

■ The 25th anniversary of Mike Hawthorn's World Championship victory was celebrated at the VSCC's Hawthorn Memorial Trophy meeting on Saturday 2 July. Neil Corner won the feature race in a Ferrari Dino.

■ Silverstone basked in a heatwave for the Marlboro British Grand Prix on Saturday 16 July, and René Arnoux took pole position in his Ferrari 126C3 with a scorching lap time of 1m 09.462s (an average speed of 151.956mph). It was his team-mate Patrick Tambay who led initially, though, ahead of Arnoux, but the two Ferraris soon dropped back with tyre wear problems, allowing Alain Prost in his Renault RE40 to cruise round to victory ahead of Nelson Piquet's Brabham-BMW BT52B. Tambay managed to salvage third.

■ Steve Soper easily won a dull Trimoco British Saloon Car Championship round, leading home a Rover Vitesse one-two-three, ahead of Peter Lovett and Jeff Allam. Ayrton Senna da Silva was back on top for the F3 encounter in his Ralt-Toyota RT3E/83, narrowly beating Martin Brundle's Ralt-Toyota. He repeated the victory on Bank Holiday Monday, 29 August, with Brundle again runner-up.

ABOVE *Alain Prost cruised to victory at the 1983 Marlboro British Grand Prix in his Renault RE40, after the Ferrari 126C3s of Patrick Tambay and René Arnoux dropped back with tyre wear problems. (LAT)*

■ There was victory for Rover in a rain-affected Canon Tourist Trophy on 11 September as the TWR-run Vitesse of René Metge and Steve Soper took the honours. They were chased home by the BMW 635 CSi of Jonathan Palmer and James Weaver. A close battle between Weaver and the other Rover of Peter Lovett and Jeff Allam ended when the pair touched coming out of the Woodcote chicane, sending Lovett into the pit wall.

■ The presence of the BBC television cameras meant a slightly larger entry than normal, but it was the same names at the front in the penultimate round of the Marlboro British F3 Championship on 2 October. This time Martin Brundle just beat his rival Ayrton Senna to victory and, by taking fastest lap, moved himself to the top of the points table for the first time. The final round of the Trimoco British Saloon Car Championship provided a win for Jeff Allam's Rover Vitesse.

1984

The season kicked off on 4 March with the opening round of the Marlboro British F3 Championship at which Johnny Dumfries scored his maiden F3 victory in a Ralt-VW RT3/83 in very wet conditions.

In March, at a secret test, HRH Princess Anne drove a Williams FW08 at the circuit. A Williams spokesman said: "It was simply a private opportunity for HRH Princess Anne to enjoy the experience of driving a Formula 1 car, and we wanted to make sure it could be done in absolute privacy."

The two Ralt-Hondas of Mike Thackwell and Roberto Moreno totally dominated the Marlboro *Daily Express* International Trophy race on 1 April, the opening round of the European F2 Championship. The pair still put on a show for the crowd, swapping the lead several times until they clashed at the chicane on the final lap. Despite it having been agreed beforehand that Moreno should take the victory, he spun and stalled, but was able to restart and still take second ahead of the Martini-BMW 002 of Michel Ferté.

Andrew Gilbert-Scott finished first on the road in his Ralt-VW RT3/84 in the F3 encounter, which took place amid snow sweeping across the circuit, but was penalised for overstepping his pole position grid slot. Therefore victory went to Johnny Dumfries once more in his Ralt-VW RT3/83. Tony Pond took outright victory in the Trimoco British Saloon Car race in his Rover Vitesse.

There was a record 46-car entry, including 24 Group C cars, for the *Grand Prix International* 1000km race on 13 May, which caused problems for the front runners because of the speed differential between them and some of the slower Group B cars. The pole-sitting Martini Lancia LC2-84 of Bob Wollek and Riccardo Patrese was the early leader until it developed a misfire and eventually retired. By this time the Canon Porsche 956 of Jonathan Palmer and Jan Lammers was at the front of the field and built up a healthy lead over the Rothmans Porsche 956-83 of Jacky Ickx and Jochen Mass until contact while lapping the third-placed Skoal Bandit Porsche 956 of Thierry Boutsen and David Hobbs caused an oil line to come adrift. This left the Rothmans car to take the flag ahead of Klaus Ludwig and Henri Pescarolo's Joest-entered Porsche 956, with the other Skoal Bandit 956, driven by Rupert Keegan and Guy Edwards, in third place.

BELOW *Lancia leads Porsche 956s through the Woodcote chicane during the 1984* Grand Prix International *1000km event. (Steve Rendle)*

ABOVE *The Canon Porsche 956 of Jonathan Palmer and Jan Lammers built up a healthy lead during the 1984* Grand Prix International *1000km until contact while lapping the third-placed Skoal Bandit Porsche 956 of Thierry Boutsen and David Hobbs caused an oil line to come adrift. (Steve Rendle)*

■ Mario Hytten and Tony Trevor both gambled on fitting dry tyres for the Marlboro British F3 round on Bank Holiday Monday, 28 May, despite a damp track and rain threatening. The pair finished the first lap in 10th and 12th places respectively but moved up to first and second as the track dried. Hytten, therefore, took his Ralt-VW RT3/84 to victory, despite the drizzle returning, ahead of Trevor's VW-powered RT3/83.

■ A fortnight later, at the Acorn Computer Trophy European F3 round on 10 June, Johnny Dumfries was back on the winner's step in his Team BP Ralt-VW RT3, while Russell Spence set a new lap record on his way to second in his similar car. The supporting Trimoco Saloon Car race produced a victory for Andy Rouse in his Rover Vitesse.

■ Jaguar looked on course to win the Istel RAC Tourist Trophy on 9 September, with the three TWR XJSs of Tom Walkinshaw/Hans Heyer, Win Percy/Chuck Nicholson and Enzo Calderari/David Sears occupying the first three places

on the grid, but that wasn't reckoning with the torrential rain which fell on lap 60. With the track awash and a number of cars, including Nicholson's Jaguar, in the Woodcote catch fencing, the pace car was deployed. The leader at this point, thanks to a timely pit stop for wet tyres, was the BMW 635 CSi of Dieter Quester and Hans Stuck, with Walkinshaw's Jaguar, which began to lose power running slowly behind the pace car, down in third. When racing resumed, the man on the move was second-placed Gianfranco Brancatelli in the BMW 635 CSi he was sharing with Helmut Kelleners and he took the lead on lap 90. Walkinshaw began to eat into the BMW's lead and looked on target to take the win until his engine finally gave up seven laps from the end. Kelleners and Brancatelli thus took the win ahead of the Calderari/Sears Jaguar.

■ The Marlboro Championship meeting on 7 October included the final rounds of both the British F3 and Trimoco Saloon Car championships. Johnny Dumfries wrapped up the F3 title by taking a decisive win in his BP/Dave Price Racing Ralt-VW RT3/84. The race was red-flagged and then restarted after Ross Cheever crashed heavily at Club Corner. Dave Brodie emerged the on-road winner of a close-fought saloon car encounter in his Colt Starion Turbo just ahead of championship-winner Andy Rouse's Rover Vitesse. But, some two months later, Brodie was excluded from the results, handing the victory to Rouse.

LEFT *Torrential rain affected the 1984 Istel Tourist Trophy, which resulted in victory for the BMW 635 CSi of Gianfranco Brancatelli and Helmut Kelleners. (Author)*

1985

■ As usual the season began with the opening round of the Marlboro British F3 Championship, which was on 3 March. Pole-man Andy Wallace, driving a Reynard-VW 853, led from start to finish on a wet track, totally dominating the race.

■ The Marlboro *Daily Express* International Trophy race on 24 March was the opening round of the new FIA European F3000 Championship and resulted in a third International Trophy win for Mike Thackwell, ahead of team-mate John Nielsen in their Ralt-Cosworth RT20s. A heavy rain shower soaked the track just before the start, and it was Thackwell on wet tyres who got away first, quickly building up a lead over Michel Ferté's March-Cosworth 85B. As the track dried, Ferté assumed the lead until the rain returned, when Thackwell moved ahead again. Ferté spun into the catch fencing at Woodcote, allowing Nielsen into second place, but was able to resume and finish third.

■ Russell Spence conclusively won the supporting F3 encounter in his Warmastyle Reynard-VW 853, ahead of Andy Wallace's similar car. A close battle between Frank Sytner's BMW 635 CSi and the Rover Vitesse of Neil McGrath in the Trimoco British Saloon Car opener resulted in a win for Sytner. Motorcycle ace Barry Sheene, who was making his debut in the championship, finished fifth, driving a Toyota Celica Supra.

■ John Brindley broke the Club circuit lap record on 21 April in his March 821 in the Formule Libre encounter, setting a time of 49.4s (an average speed of 117.18mph).

■ Jacky Ickx and Jochen Mass took their Rothmans Porsche 962C to victory in the Silverstone 1000km event on 12 May, but only after the early leaders had all struck problems. Jonathan Palmer and Richard Lloyd lost a front wheel from their Canon Porsche 956B while leading – a problem that afflicted a number of the privately-run 956s in the race. This left the two Martini Lancia LC2 85s of Riccardo Patrese/Alessandro Nannini and Bob Wollek/Mauro Baldi first and second until they ran into problems. Ickx and Mass thus finished ahead of team-mates Derek Bell and Hans Stuck, with Patrese and Nannini in third. During qualifying, Patrese had taken pole position with a time of 1m 10.84s (an average speed of exactly 149mph).

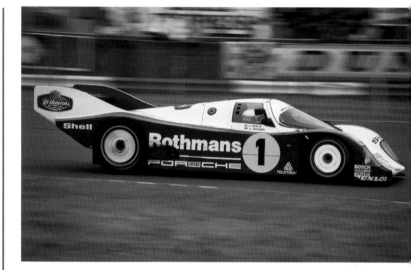

ABOVE *The Rothmans Porsches were victorious yet again at the Silverstone 1000km event in 1985, this time Jacky Ickx and Jochen Mass leading home team-mates Derek Bell and Hans Stuck in their brace of 962Cs. (Author)*

BELOW *The winning Rothmans Porsche 962C of Jacky Ickx and Jochen Mass enters parc fermé at the end of the 1985 Silverstone 1000km. (Author)*

RIGHT *Keke Rosberg set the first-ever 160mph lap at Silverstone to take pole position for the 1985 Marlboro British Grand Prix in his Canon Williams-Honda FW10. (Steve Rendle)*

■ A century of world motoring was celebrated at the Motor 100 over the Bank Holiday weekend of 25–27 May. HRH Prince Michael of Kent conducted the official opening of the three-day event, which included displays of cars, motorcycles, commercial vehicles, racing and rally cars, dragsters and land speed record breakers.

■ Mauricio Gugelmin scored a maiden F3 win at the 9 June round of the Marlboro British F3 Championship in his WSR Ralt-VW RT30. Andy Rouse took his Ford Sierra Turbo to victory in the Trimoco British Saloon Car Championship round.

■ The Marlboro British Grand Prix took place on 21 July. Trackside enclosure prices were just £14 for an adult and £3 for a child up to 15 years old. Centre transfers cost an extra £6, while grandstands ranged from between £30 to £40 each for adults and £21 to £31 for children. Keke Rosberg took pole position in his Canon Williams-Honda FW10 with a stunning lap of 1m 05.591s (an average speed of 160.925mph). The race itself initially developed into a battle between the JPS Lotus-Renault 97T of Ayrton Senna, who snatched the lead at the start, and Rosberg, until the Finn retired with engine problems. Alain Prost in his Marlboro McLaren-Tag MP4/2B then took up the challenge, taking the lead five laps from the end as the Lotus ran out of fuel. Prost thus secured his second British Grand Prix victory ahead of the Ferrari 156/85 of Michele Alboreto and the Ligier-Renault JS25 of Jacques Laffite. The race came to a premature end when the chequered flag was waved after only 65 laps of the 66-lap race.

■ Gerrit van Kouwen won the supporting Marlboro F3 round in his Ralt-VW RT30, while Andy Rouse again won the Trimoco Saloon Car encounter after a close scrap with the Colt Starion Turbo of Dave Brodie.

■ Over the three days, attendance at the Grand Prix was a record 135,000, and the crowds on race day could enjoy free coach trips around the circuit from 6.30 until 10.30am. A two-hour pit lane walkabout took place from 8.30 to 10.30am for holders of centre transfer tickets, while other attractions included the Red Arrows, the Marlboro Pitts Specials aerobatic team and the Royal Marines free fall parachute display team. An innovation at the Grand Prix was the introduction of Radio Silverstone, broadcasting commentary together with interviews, news and traffic reports, throughout the event on 1602kHz medium wave.

■ Dave Scott won the Bank Holiday Monday, 26 August, F3 race in his Ralt-VW RT30, chased all the way by pole-sitter Andy Wallace in his Reynard-VW 853.

■ Tom Walkinshaw and Win Percy won the Istel RAC Tourist Trophy on 8 September in their Rover Vitesse, ahead of team-mates Jean-Louis Schlesser and Steve Soper. The Volvo of Gianfranco Brancatelli and Thomas Lindstrom had started seventh but soon moved its way up into the lead, which it opened out until the pace car was deployed to move a crashed BMW from a dangerous position at Woodcote. This bunched the field up, and slick work at the pit stops by the TWR crew allowed the two Rovers to slip ahead, leaving the Volvo drivers to finish third.

■ Mauricio Gugelmin clinched the Marlboro British F3 title by winning the final round on 13 October in his Ralt-VW RT30, ahead of Andy Wallace's Reynard-VW 853. Champion-elect Andy Rouse won the final round of the Trimoco Saloon Car Championship in his Ford Sierra Turbo, but was made to fight all the way by the Colt Starion Turbo of Dave Brodie.

BELOW *Gerrit van Kouwen won the round of the Marlboro British F3 Championship at the 1985 British Grand Prix meeting in his Ralt-VW RT30. (Author)*

1986

■ The season-opening British F3 round on 2 March had to be cancelled because of snow, and was rescheduled for 23 March. When it did take place it resulted in a win for Andy Wallace in his Madgwick-run Reynard-VW 863.

■ The opening round of the FIA European F3000 championship took place on 13 April at the International Trophy meeting, but the rain-affected race was cut short after 24 of the 44 scheduled laps following an accident involving the March-Cosworth 86B of Thierry Tassin and the March-Cosworth 85B of Dominique Delestre, both of whom suffered broken arms. The race, which had already been red-flagged once after just three laps, resulted in a narrow win for Pascal Fabre in his Lola-Cosworth T86/50. Fabre actually finished 1.7sec behind the March-Cosworth 86B of Emanuele Pirro but had been 2.9sec ahead at the end of the first part, and so won on aggregate. John Nielsen took third in his Ralt-Honda RT20.

■ The supporting Lucas British F3 Championship round was won by Maurizio Sandro Sala in his Eddie Jordan-run Ralt RT30/86. Andy Rouse and Dennis Leech swapped the lead throughout the opening round of the RAC British Saloon Car Championship, with Rouse's Ford Sierra Turbo taking the flag ahead of Leach's Rover Vitesse.

■ The 26,000 spectators who braved a showery Bank Holiday Monday on 5 May to attend the Kouros 1000km endurance race witnessed the first victory for Jaguar since 1957, as the TWR Silk Cut XJR-6 of Derek Warwick and Eddie Cheever took the flag after nearly five hours of racing. The Jaguar pairing had battled with the pole-sitting Martini Lancia LC2-86 of Andrea de Cesaris and Alessandro Nannini for much of the race until it suffered fuel pressure problems, leaving the works Rothmans Porsche 962C of Derek Bell and Hans Stuck to take second ahead of the Kremer Porsche 962C of Jo Gartner and Tiff Needell.

■ Brazilian driver Mauricio Sandro Sala took victory in the Lucas British F3 encounter on 26 May in his Ralt-VW RT30/86, beating the Reynard-VW 863 of Andy Wallace by just 0.17sec. Two weeks later, on 8 June, Wallace was the winner, with Mark Galvin second in his Ralt-VW RT30/86.

■ Martin Donnelly emerged the deserved winner of a saturated Bank Holiday Monday Lucas British F3 round on 25 August in his Ralt-VW RT30/86, beating the Reynard-VW 863 of Andy Wallace. The conditions were so bad that the meeting was abandoned shortly afterwards.

■ Denny Hulme and Jeff Allam won the 50th running of the Tourist Trophy, the world's oldest motor race, on 7 September, in their TWR Rover Vitesse, beating the BMW 635 CSi of Dieter Quester and Roberto Ravaglia. It was Hulme's fourth victory in the event, the first having been 21 years before.

■ Andy Wallace took his eighth victory of the season in the Lucas British F3 final on 5 October in his Warmastlye Racing for Britain Reynard-VW 863, thereby clinching the championship. In the British Saloon Car Championship event, pole-man Andy Rouse retired his Ford Sierra Turbo while battling hard with the Colt Starion Turbo of Dave Brodie, who went on to win.

RIGHT *Derek Warwick's TWR Silk Cut Jaguar XJR-6 out-brakes the Martini Lancia LC2-86 of Alessandro Nannini to take the lead of the 1986 Kouros 1000km event. Warwick, together with his co-driver Eddie Cheever, went on to score Jaguar's first victory since 1957. (Author)*

1987

■ For the second year in succession, the VSCC and F3 meetings scheduled for 7 and 8 March were both cancelled because of a heavy snowfall.

■ A new left-right dog-leg section of track between the bridge just after Abbey and Woodcote Corner was used for the first time on Thursday 2 April at a test day for F3000 cars, in advance of the International Trophy meeting.

■ Mauricio Gugelmin, in his works Ralt-Honda RT21/87, won the Marlboro International Trophy F3000 race on 12 April, with team-mate Roberto Moreno finishing third behind the Lola-Cosworth T87/50 of Michel Trolle. Moreno had led until five laps from the end when he suffered gearbox problems. Ralts were also successful in the supporting Lucas British F3 event, where Gary Brabham and Bertrand Gachot finished one-two in their RT31s. In the British Touring Car race, Andy Rouse took his Ford Sierra Cosworth to victory ahead of Dennis Leech's Rover Vitesse.

■ It was another home win for Jaguar in the Autoglass 1000km on 10 May, as the TWR-run Silk Cut XJR8s finished one-two in the hands of Eddie Cheever/Raul Boesel and Jan Lammers/John Watson. The Kouros Sauber-Mercedes C9 of Mike Thackwell and Henri Pescarolo was the early leader, but it dropped back with a misfire and eventually retired with rear suspension failure.

■ Nigel Mansell was fastest in pre-Grand Prix testing on 2–4 June in his Canon Williams-Honda FW11B. It was the first time that the F1 teams had had a chance to try out the new circuit configuration, and spectators were admitted to the three-day midweek test for the first time as well.

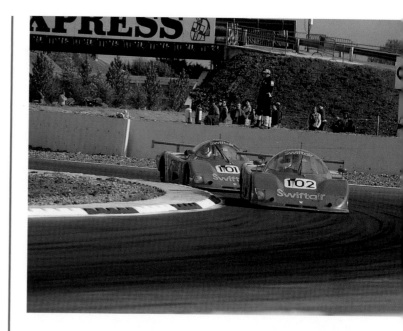

ABOVE *David Leslie in his Swiftair Ecosse-Cosworth C286 leads team-mate Johnny Dumfries through the new dog-leg corner just after the* Daily Express *bridge between Abbey and Woodcote during the 1987 Autoglass 1000km. (Author)*

■ Johnny Herbert won the feature F3 race on the Grand Prix circuit at the BRDC's Diamond Jubilee meeting on 7 June in his Reynard-VW 873. The Diamond Jubilee Trophy race itself, for Can-Am and Sports Cars, was won by Mike Wilds and Ian Flux in their Lola T530 while Tim Harvey took the honours in the Dunlop British Touring Car race in his Rover Vitesse.

LEFT *Eddie Cheever leads team-mate Jan Lammers to a Silk Cut Jaguar one-two in their XJR8s in the closing stages of the 1987 Autoglass 1000km. (Author)*

ABOVE *Nelson Piquet leads Nigel Mansell in their pair of Canon Williams-Honda FW11Bs during a thrilling 1987 Shell Oils British Grand Prix. Despite making a pit stop to change tyres, Mansell caught Piquet and took the lead two laps from the end. (Author)*

RIGHT *Sparks fly from Andrea de Cesaris's Brabham-BMW BT56 during the weekend of the 1987 Shell Oils British Grand Prix. The Italian retired from the race early on after a split fuel line caused a fire. (Steve Rendle)*

■ A record 180,000 people attended the Shell Oils British Grand Prix over the weekend of 10–12 July. The two Canon Williams-Honda FW11Bs of Nelson Piquet and crowd favourite Nigel Mansell were on the front row, and once the lights went out no one else got a look in. Halfway through, Mansell had to stop to change tyres because of a bad vibration. He still rejoined in second place but was now some way behind his team-mate. Ignoring his fuel consumption read-out Mansell began to haul in Piquet by about a second a lap, and on lap 63 out of 65 approaching Stowe he dummied to the outside and then dived inside as Piquet tried to cover the move. The crowd went wild, Mansell took the flag, and promptly ran out of fuel on the slowing down lap. Ayrton Senna finished third in his Camel Lotus-Honda 99T.

■ Win Percy won a thrilling Dunlop RAC British Touring Car Championship round in his Ford Sierra RS Cosworth. Pole-man Percy stalled on the line and got away dead last, but then drove through the field to take the lead on the fourth lap and win, despite a puncture on the very last lap. Bertrand Gachot won the Lucas British F3 Championship round in his West Surrey Ralt-Alfa Romeo RT31.

■ Thomas Danielsson won the round of the Lucas British F3 Championship on 31 August in his Madgwick Reynard-Alfa Romeo 873.

■ Enzo Calderari and Fabio Mancini were the surprise winners of a very wet RAC Istel Tourist Trophy on 6 September in their CiBiEmme BMW M3, after Luis Sala, sharing another M3 with Olivier Grouillard, spun away a 45sec lead and stalled at Stowe on the penultimate lap of the race.

■ John Foulston, the chairman of Brands Hatch Leisure, was killed on 29 September when he crashed his McLaren-Offenhauser M15 Indycar at Club Corner during testing.

■ Steve Kempton won the prestigious FIA European F3 Cup on 4 October in his Reynard-Alfa Romeo 873, becoming the first Briton to do so. Peter Hall won the supporting Dunlop RAC British Touring Car Championship round in his Ford Sierra RS500.

ABOVE *The Canon Williams-Honda FW11B of Nigel Mansell kicks up a shower of sparks on the way to victory in the 1987 Shell Oils British Grand Prix. (LAT)*

BELOW *Second place finisher Damon Hill (Intersport Racing Ralt-Toyota RT31) battles for the lead with winner Thomas Danielsson (Madgwick Reynard-Alfa Romeo 873) during the Lucas British F3 Championship round on 31 August. (sutton-images.com)*

1988

■ JJ Lehto, in his Pacific Marlboro Reynard-Toyota 883, won the Lucas British F3 encounter on 27 March. Ford Sierra RS500 driver Jerry Mahony was the winner of the supporting Dunlop RAC British Touring Car Championship round.

■ Jimmy Brown, chairman of Silverstone Circuits Ltd, passed away on 19 April at the age of 67, having been at the circuit for 40 years.

■ JJ Lehto continued on his winning way in his Reynard-Toyota 883 in the British F3 round on 2 May, beating the Ralt-Toyota RT31 of Martin Donnelly.

■ Eddie Cheever and Jaguar made it a hat-trick of victories at the *Autosport* 1000km on 8 May, in front of a crowd of around 35,000. The TWR Silk Cut XJR9 of Cheever and team-mate Martin Brundle ran out the winners ahead of the pair of AEG Olympia Sauber-Mercedes C9-88s of Jean-Louis Schlesser/Jochen Mass and Mauro Baldi/James Weaver.

■ After the drivers' briefing at the *Autosport* 1000km, 'Silverstone Syd' Herbert was presented with the 1987 Jaguar Driver of the Year award by former Jaguar team manager 'Lofty' England.

■ Roberto Moreno won the 40th BRDC International Trophy race, the fourth round of the International F3000 Championship, in his Reynard-Cosworth 88D on 5 June. The supporting British F3 Championship round once again went to JJ Lehto, who scored his fifth win of the season. British Touring Car Championship honours went to Andy Rouse in his Ford Sierra RS500.

■ Official tyre testing for the British Grand Prix on 27–28 June was opened up to the public at a cost of £4 per day. Gerhard Berger topped the times in his Ferrari F187/88C.

RIGHT *The TWR Silk Cut Jaguar team was victorious for the third year running at the 1988 Autosport 1000km. Here, the winning XJR9 of Eddie Cheever and Martin Brundle and the Sauber-Mercedes C9/88 of Jean-Louis Schlesser and Jochen Mass lead at the start. (LAT)*

ABOVE *Gerhard Berger qualified on pole for the 1988 Shell Oils British Grand Prix in his Ferrari F187/88C, but he had dropped to ninth by the end of the rain-affected race. (Author)*

ABOVE *A feature of the 1988 Shell Oils British Grand Prix was the two Avesco Starvision television screens located at Woodcote and between Stowe and Club corners. (Author)*

■ Tickets for the Shell Oils British Grand Prix on 10 July cost just £18 in advance or £20 on the day. Spectators were treated to a pit lane walkabout from 7.30 to 9.30am, followed at 10am by the F1 untimed warm-up session. Races for Renault Elf Turbos, Alfa Romeo 164s and the Vauxhall Lotus Challenge preceded the main event that took place at 2.30pm, with the day's events being rounded off by a round of the British Touring Car Championship. Two giant television screens located at Woodcote and between Stowe and Club corners allowed spectators to follow the action more closely.

■ Race day itself was wet and miserable, but the crowds were treated to a magnificent display of wet weather driving by Ayrton Senna in his Marlboro McLaren-Honda MP4/4 and pole-sitter Gerhard Berger in his Ferrari F187/88C, until the latter had to slow to conserve fuel. Local hero Nigel Mansell battled from 11th on the grid in his Williams-Judd FW12 to take second place in the treacherous conditions, much to the crowd's delight.

BELOW *Ayrton Senna put on a magnificent display of wet-weather driving during the 1988 Shell Oils British Grand Prix to take victory in his Marlboro McLaren-Honda MP4/4. (LAT)*

ABOVE *F3 cars in parc fermé after the round of the Lucas British F3 Championship at the 1988 Shell Oils British Grand Prix meeting. (Author)*

■ The supporting Dunlop British Touring Car Championship round provided another victory for Andy Rouse in his Ford Sierra RS500, while Damon Hill took his Ralt-Toyota RT32 to victory in the Lucas British F3 round held on the Saturday (9 July) of Grand Prix weekend.

■ On Friday 8 July, the new media centre, named after Jimmy Brown, was opened by his widow Kay and Bernie Ecclestone.

■ Once again it was the Reynard-Toyota 883 of JJ Lehto that emerged victorious at the British F3 round on Bank Holiday Monday, 29 August, ahead of Ross Huckenhull's Ralt-VW RT32.

■ The 52nd running of the Fina RAC Tourist Trophy on 4 September, the penultimate round of the European Touring Car Championship, provided a victory for the Kaliber-backed Ford Sierra RS500 of Andy Rouse and Alain Ferté. RS500s filled the first six places.

ABOVE *Damon Hill, driving a Ralt-Toyota RT32, took victory in the round of the British F3 Championship at the 1988 Shell Oils British Grand Prix meeting. (Author)*

■ The final round of the British Touring Car Championship on 2 October produced a win for Gianfranco Brancatelli's Texaco Ford Sierra RS500 after Andy Rouse suffered a tyre blow-out in his RS500. Gary Brabham won the season finale of the Lucas British F3 Championship driving a Ralt-VW RT32.

1989

■ Thomas Danielsson won the *Motoring News* International Trophy race, the first round of the FIA International F3000 Championship, on 9 April in his Reynard-Cosworth 89D. Philippe Favre took second in a Lola-Cosworth T89/50, while JJ Lehto was disqualified from third in his Reynard-Mugen 89D, promoting the Reynard-Cosworth 89D of Mark Blundell into the position. The supporting British Touring Car Championship round provided a victory for Andy Rouse in his Ford Sierra RS500. David Brabham won the F3 encounter in his Ralt-VW RT33.

■ Derek Higgins won the round of the Lucas British F3 Championship on 1 May in his Ralt-Mugen Honda RT33, beating Rickard Rydell's Reynard-VW 893.

■ With no round of the World Sports-Prototype Championship this year, Silverstone instead played host to the German SAT1 Supercup on 14 May. Only 16 cars took part in the 45-lap BRDC Supersprint, with the Joest Porsche 962C of Bob Wollek emerging the winner.

■ Allan McNish took the honours at the F3 encounter on 4 June in his Ralt-Mugen Honda RT33, while Robb Gravett won the supporting British Touring Car round in his Sierra RS500.

■ Alain Prost won the Shell British Grand Prix on 16 July for the third time in his Marlboro McLaren-Honda MP4/5 after team-mate and pole-sitter Ayrton Senna had spun out of the lead on lap 12 at Becketts with gearbox problems. Nigel Mansell, in his Ferrari 640, piled on the pressure until delayed by a puncture, but still managed to finish second ahead of the Benetton-Ford B189 of Alessandro Nannini.

■ The supporting British F3 round was won by Derek Higgins in a Ralt-Mugen Honda RT33 after on-track winner Allan McNish was excluded, along with second-placed David Brabham. Meanwhile, Andy Rouse took the honours in the British Touring Car Championship encounter once again in his Sierra RS500.

RIGHT Ayrton Senna gives a brief talk to guests of Courtaulds, sponsors of the McLaren team, in the F1 Paddock Club area, prior to the 1989 Shell Oils British Grand Prix. (Author)

■ Gary Brabham won the British F3000 round on 30 July in his Reynard-Cosworth 88D, beating the similar car of Andrew Gilbert-Scott by just 0.26sec on the National circuit.

■ With the demise of the European Touring Car Championship, it was decided in August not to hold the RAC Tourist Trophy, Britain's oldest motor race, which was scheduled to be run on 10 September. The BRDC blamed lack of competitor support for the planned non-championship event.

■ David Brabham took his Ralt-VW RT33 to victory in the 28 August round of the Lucas British F3 Championship, leading from start to finish.

■ John Cleland clinched the British Touring Car Championship on 8 October after taking class victory in his Vauxhall Astra GTE. Overall winner of the race, as usual, was Andy Rouse in his Sierra RS500. David Brabham won his sixth F3 race of the season in his Ralt-VW RT33 in the penultimate round of the British championship.

ABOVE *Alain Prost won his third British Grand Prix in 1989 in his Marlboro McLaren-Honda MP4/5 after his team-mate and early leader Ayrton Senna spun out with gearbox problems after only 11 laps. (LAT)*

RIGHT *McLaren mechanics prepare the cars prior to the 1989 Shell Oils British Grand Prix, while guests on the pit lane walkabout watch from outside. (Author)*

1990s

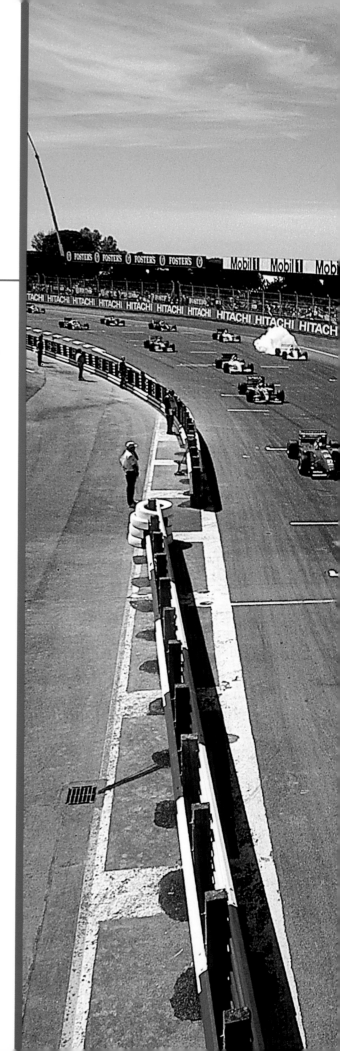

"Silverstone is a famous old place with great tradition, like Monza. But it, like Britain, has no divine right to a Grand Prix."
Bernie Ecclestone

The nineties was a period of both great change and controversy for the circuit. In January 1990, the FIA confirmed that Silverstone had taken up its option to host the British Grand Prix for a further five years after the existing contract expired in 1991, taking it through to 1996, but it was conditional upon major changes being made to the track.

The alterations would be the biggest to the circuit since 1949 and involved the construction of a new infield section between Abbey and Woodcote, together with major revisions at Becketts and Stowe, increasing the length of the Grand Prix circuit from 2.975 miles to 3.2 miles. It was intended that the work would be completed in time for the first international meeting of 1991.

The reasoning behind the changes was two-fold: first to slow the cars down for safety reasons, and second to provide a better experience for the spectator, with three distinct viewing areas – one at Becketts, one around Stowe and Club and the third at a new 'stadium' area between Abbey and Woodcote.

The circuit remained the same up to Maggots, where a series of fast right-left-right curves would replace the old Becketts Corner, before rejoining the existing track at Chapel Curve. By moving the new section of track inwards it provided increased space and a better flow of spectator traffic around that area.

Stowe was to be tightened up, the track turning further right and dropping down into

RIGHT *Damon Hill's Rothmans Williams-Renault FW16 and the Benetton-Ford B194 of Michael Schumacher lead away at the start of the 1994 British Grand Prix. In the background, the Peugeot engine in the Marlboro McLaren MP4/9 of Martin Brundle blows up in spectacular fashion. (LAT)*

a section called Vale, where a gentle left led on to a short straight running parallel to the old course. Club Corner now became a sharp left, followed by a right, where the track rejoined the old circuit.

"At Stowe and Club the cars were going so fast they were taking Club flat in qualifying," explained BRDC chairman Tom Walkinshaw at the time. "The safety aspect is very important with Grand Prix cars getting faster and faster, and we obviously had to do something. We've tightened up the exit to Stowe, and the track will now drop down 12ft into the infield. That'll still be a very demanding corner."

After Abbey and Farm Straight, which were unchanged, the cars dropped down under a new vehicle bridge, sweeping right through the slightly banked Bridge Bend into the new stadium section. Here the sharp left-hander of Priory led on to a short straight into another left-hander, Brooklands. This, in turn, led to the double right-handers of Luffield One and Luffield Two, which brought the cars back on to the old circuit at Woodcote, where the chicane had been removed.

On 1 August 1990, BRDC president Gerald Lascelles flagged off a bulldozer driven by Walkinshaw to begin work on the new infield section. Meetings on the National circuit were unaffected by the work, and track-laying of the new section was completed by October. The work progressed throughout the winter and the new-look Silverstone was shown off to the press on 9 January 1991, just five months after work had begun. It represented an investment of £1.8 million by the BRDC, and Bernie Ecclestone formally opened the new circuit the following day before being driven around by Derek Warwick in a Jaguar XJR15.

In addition to the above changes, the run-off area at Copse had also been increased substantially by tightening the entry to the corner and rerouting the track. The first major event that took place on the new layout was the round of the World Sportscar Championship on 18 May.

The run-up to a Grand Prix is always a busy time for the circuit, but 1991 proved to be particularly trying for the management. During the week of the F1 tyre tests in June, contractors severed power cables to the infield and smashed a water main, but the biggest headache was the crane that toppled over on to the roof of a newly-constructed toilet block on the outside of Copse. The operator had been positioning his 50-ton, 12-wheel vehicle in order to lift roof sections on to a temporary grandstand when the cesspit cover that the crane was standing on collapsed.

In 1992 there began an unhappy period in Silverstone's history, as the BRDC was acrimoniously split in two, with the break-up of long-standing friendships, over a proposed business venture.

On 21 April, Silverstone and Tom Walkinshaw Racing (TWR) jointly launched the Silverstone Motor Group (SMG). Walkinshaw already owned a chain of high-street car dealerships around the country, and Silverstone Circuits paid £5.3 million to purchase a 50 per cent shareholding in the TWR Group's motor retailing franchises.

This news was not well-received by BRDC members, many of whom viewed a move into the motor trade at a time when the industry was depressed as a bad idea. Others, while admiring Walkinshaw's business and organisational abilities, concluded that he was both buyer and seller in the deal. Some members were also disgruntled at the way the deal seemed to have been done in secrecy, without them being privy to the sums of money involved.

Matters came to a head a few days later at the annual general meeting of the club on 24 April. The deal had not been on the agenda, but Ken Tyrrell had obtained the signatures of 50 members forcing it to be discussed. After much heated debate, Walkinshaw was ousted as a board member but remained chairman of Silverstone Circuits.

In his defence, Walkinshaw argued that, as chairman of Silverstone Circuits, he, together with the other directors, was tasked with maximising the commercial potential of that group of companies. "We take decisions on financial matters on a regular basis," he said. "We have board meetings every month and management meetings in between, and that is what we have done in this instance.

"To doubly ratify it we put it to the board of the BRDC and they also concurred. That is 14 different people, there are seven on the board of Silverstone and 14 on the board of the BRDC, and they unanimously voted in favour of this transaction. We went to great lengths, I should say extreme lengths, to ensure that everything was handled correctly and that nothing was done or influenced that was improper."

Walkinshaw believed that, in order for the circuit to fulfil its contractual obligations to run the British Grand Prix for the next five years, and to ensure that it remained at a standard whereby the contract would be renewed in 1997, heavy investment had to be made. "Without that, we won't get the Grand Prix again, it's as simple as that. We need to make massive investment," he said.

Johnny Herbert

"When I won the British Grand Prix in 1995 it was a bit difficult. Qualifying went OK, I think I was fifth, and then the morning was a bit damp. I came out of Copse – it was very weird – I had a bit of a slide and then shot left on the exit of Copse and I hit the wall on the left, so they had to repair the car before the race.

"I got a nice start, moved up to third and sat there for quite a while. Then, of course, Michael got launched by Damon and it obviously took them off and I passed them, saw it, and only realised about half a lap later, 'Oh, hang on, then I'm in the lead.' So that was a nice realisation.

"And David Coulthard got a penalty for speeding in the pit lane, and so I remember Ross Brawn came on the radio and said 'don't fight David because he's got a drive-through penalty', so I didn't have to worry about him. Jean Alesi, I think, was a lot further back and so it made my race a lot easier because I didn't have to fight David in any way. I did a little bit when he passed me, I'm not just going to let him go, but I didn't have to fight tooth and nail and block him or anything else, so it made it easier. It was a shame because I'm sure it would have been a nice little ding-dong we would have probably had with about only ten laps to go when he got pulled in.

"Seeing everybody in the last five or so laps, seeing the Union Jacks flying, seeing the emotion with the hands and gestures that were going on, so all that side of it was absolutely awesome, to have that type of thing. We still had damn good crowds in those days as well, and for me, first Grand Prix victory and it being Silverstone – just incredible.

"I think from the whole incarnation of Silverstone to the present day, to me the biggest thing they've ever done is the ability to adapt to everything that is needed nowadays to become an ongoing Formula 1 venue. OK, they're lucky it's an old World War Two airfield, so they've got room and space, compared to Brands Hatch where you have to dig the banks out and flatten all the trees and everything else to do something to it. I think Silverstone is still that special high-speed track that it's always been famous for."

RIGHT *Johnny Herbert celebrates on the podium after winning the 1995 British Grand Prix. (LAT)*

Martin Brundle

"My first memories are as a kid, queuing with my uncle, standing on the bank at Copse Corner. We always used to take these sort of boxes and things you take down to the beach, anything you could get a little bit of height from, so you could see above everybody else's little creations, and watching Jim Clark, Jackie Stewart, Graham Hill, in the sixties.

"My first race there would have been 1977, probably supporting the British Grand Prix in the Toyota Celica GT. I did the British Touring Car Championship round there in the 1600 class. We used to be parked all down the Club Straight and it was great. We were part of the Grand Prix weekend then, which was magnificent.

"Two memories stand out immediately. One would be when I drove Ross Brawn's Jaguar there in 1990, when we had a throttle cable break. I think I lost ten minutes, and I had to drive it solo for the rest of the race because they couldn't put Derek Warwick back in it, otherwise he couldn't score points if he drove two different cars, so I had to drive it myself. I unlapped myself, I think twice against my sister Jag, three times against the works Peugeot, five times against Schuey in his Mercedes, and had an amazing race and finished on the podium. They had to lift me out of the car at the end.

"And then not very long later, in 1992 when Nigel won the race, Patrese was second for Williams and I was third. I had an epic fight with Senna, but I've got a lot of memories with Senna at Silverstone. And I finished third. That's when the crowd invaded the track. Absolutely bizarre experience where a guy wanted to stop me for my autograph! I'm coming out of Club Corner towards Abbey, and he had his kiddie in his arms. He almost stuck his kiddie out to give me a reason to stop, so it was really bizarre.

"It's always been a very high-speed track and it's always been particularly affected by the wind conditions, the weather in general and track temperature. But it's always been massively fast, which is why the drivers love it, and whichever configuration you look at, as they've tried to slow it down and give it run-off areas over the years, it's still remained incredibly fast.

"It takes a balanced car to get a quick lap there. Some of the fast corners you can't carry a single-seater through there. If you haven't got a balance you just can't make the difference in a long, very high-speed corner, because soon the car's going to get out of shape. So there's that aspect, then in the medium speed corners and in the chicanes you've really got to attack hard. You need a good car. You can't outperform your car very well round there but you can maximise it, that's for sure.

"Silverstone very rarely gets mentioned in the top three greatest tracks in the world. People always say Monaco, Spa. I personally say Macau and Le Mans. I think Silverstone, like Le Mans, doesn't get good billing – doesn't get good press in that respect, but I would certainly say that it's easily in the top five in the world."

His fears were well founded, since Bernie Ecclestone had stated at the Monaco Grand Prix at the end of May that: "Silverstone is a famous old place with great tradition, like Monza. But it, like Britain, has no divine right to a Grand Prix. It is up to Tom Walkinshaw and Silverstone to do something about it themselves. They've got to keep their promise to continue developing the circuit."

At the same event, Walkinshaw, BRDC secretary Peter Warr, and board member John Watson addressed the media, saying that the circuit needed £15–£20 million to fund improvements over the coming five years and that it could lose the British Grand Prix if the track was not upgraded. If that happened, the circuit would close within three years, they claimed. The three believed that the Silverstone Motor Group was the best way to raise that money.

An extraordinary general meeting (EGM) of the club was organised for 30 June to consider two resolutions. One, proposed by the directors, asked the membership to ratify the deal. The other, proposed by opponents of the deal, was for the directors to take 'all lawful steps available' to terminate it. If the board got 50 per cent support at the EGM, the SMG agreement would be ratified.

Leading up to the meeting, the BRDC held four regional seminars so that members could ask questions about the proposal. In addition, a 28-page document entitled 'The Investment by Silverstone Circuits Limited in Silverstone Motor Group Limited' was issued to the members on 22 June. This projected a profit of £5.3 million by 1996, for an investment of a similar amount (£3.3 million for 500,000 'A' shares and £2 million for two million preference shares). If the SMG was floated by 1996/97, its potential value was estimated to be in excess of £63 million.

No dividend would be paid by SMG for several years, and Walkinshaw's TWR Group continued to own the freeholds of the dealerships, with the BRDC paying rent of £1 million a year for 20 years.

The need for investment and upgrades was also emphasised, including resurfacing the track, upgrading the pits and paddock area, providing new media commentary positions, a new race control and administration centre, timekeepers' and stewards' offices, grandstands and other spectator facilities such as improvements to the car parks. The Silverstone by-pass was also scheduled for 1995 and the cost of these required upgrades was estimated to be in the region of £15–£20 million.

But many members, including Ken Tyrrell and Innes Ireland, still felt that diversifying into the motor trade was against the interests of the members. A committee, chaired by Tyrrell, was set up and a letter circulated to members stating: "The distributorship subsidiaries acquired by SMG from TWR Group had losses in 1990 of £2.2 million and in 1991 of £1.4 million, and in the first two months of this year [1992] of £103,000.

"BRDC has purchased for £5.3 million a 50 per cent share in a business having total net assets of £4.3 million, which is making a loss and has made a substantial loss for its last two accounting periods.

"BRDC has to fund the interest on the £3 million which it has borrowed. There is, however, a statement that no dividends will be paid by SMG in the initial years; the Joint Venture Agreement indicates until 1996. During this period BRDC will have to fund the interest on the loan with no matching income from its investment.

"BRDC accepted the rental value (which in the first year comes to £979,489) placed on the leases by experts instructed by TWR. If, as seems likely, the TWR Group chooses to sell the portfolio of leases granted to SMG there is a provision that on the first rent review there will be a minimum increase in rents of 27 per cent regardless of market rates at that time."

Walkinshaw disputed the accuracy of the document.

Prior to the EGM, Bernie Ecclestone arranged a meeting between Walkinshaw and Tyrrell at which Walkinshaw repeated an offer he had made before the AGM, which the BRDC board had rejected, to underwrite the deal.

At the meeting, attended by more than 250 of the 510 voting members, 75 per cent voted against the board's recommendation to ratify the SMG deal, and over 80 per cent voted in favour of attempting to unravel the deal. There was great hostility towards Walkinshaw, with a reported 'lynch mob' attitude, at the meeting. Some apparently saw the deal as a plot by both Walkinshaw and Ecclestone to eventually acquire the circuit from the BRDC.

Afterwards, Walkinshaw stated: "There has been a total lack of understanding how this deal came about, who decided what. I don't believe that some people basically wanted to understand it.

"I was originally going to do the deal with another party, but the Silverstone board, which had been seeking investment opportunities for a couple of years, asked to examine the proposition. From the outset, I stood down from the Silverstone Circuits board at all times when it was evaluating the offer it eventually made. I saw none of the working papers and did not speak to a single director in connection with it.

"The BRDC set up Silverstone Circuits to manage the commercial side of the business, but you can't create a subsidiary, hire a board of directors and task them with maximising revenue for the group and then bitch when they go ahead and do it."

At the meeting, Walkinshaw had repeated his offer to underwrite the deal and to make other concessions to members in the light of their objections, but this was rejected. Ecclestone, who was also in attendance, then stood up and offered to underwrite any losses incurred, provided any profits were signed over to him. He was shouted down.

This point should not be glossed over. Ecclestone did not take kindly to the manner in which his offer was rejected, and it sowed the seeds for the difficulties which the circuit was to encounter over negotiations with him for the next 20 years.

John Watson remembers the occasion well. "Bernie stood up and said, 'Look, I don't think you should be in the motor business. I've been in it, some of you have been in it, but I'll give you the £5.2m after five years. I'll give you your money back, but I own the business. If the business makes a profit, I'll keep the profit, if it makes a loss I'll still give you your £5.2m.'

"But the members had a go at Bernie, and told him to stick his money. And that is in part why Silverstone has had to deal with Bernie being so outspoken, because he realised this place has more chance of being struck by lightning than it ever has of getting its act together. He runs Formula 1 and the buck stops with Bernie. He is answerable to all his other shareholders, but they mandate him to run Formula 1 on their behalf.

"He walked in and saw small-mindedness, pettiness, malice – whatever. Who can he do a deal with at Silverstone to run a Grand Prix? How can you run a company that's trying to run a Grand Prix on a five-year contract where you've got members who can, at any whim or fancy, form a quorum and call an EGM? You can't do that."

It transpired that the BRDC board had been misadvised by its own lawyers about whether or not it had to consult the membership over the SMG deal.

"The crux of the matter," said Watson, "was that Tom was seen to be the beneficiary of club assets at a difficult economic time. And there were many members who were struggling in their businesses, and here was the chairman of the board of the British Racing Drivers' Club structuring a deal to the benefit of his businesses. And it was this part

of the advice the club's legal advisors got wrong, as they had interpreted the articles of the club to mean that the board was free to make that business judgement without reference to the membership.

"So, Tom was getting a direct benefit and the board were mistaken, based on the advice provided by their solicitors, and it set off a very unpleasant period in the club's history. On top of which Tom was a very competitive racing driver and very competitive team manager. He used the rule book very much to his advantage, and wasn't universally popular amongst the membership because some of them feel that he stuffed them, and there was an element of vindictiveness so that, when we had the night of the long knives, old scores were settled.

"But from the members' perspective, and I'm a member of the club as well, the advice that was given by the solicitors was incorrect, and ultimately this then went to court because the club sued the solicitors who then fell back on their insurers."

Jack Sears, BRDC chairman, and the entire board were also voted out at the EGM. Stuart Graham was one of the board members who was ousted at the time. "I spent a long time on the board back in the eighties and it was very interesting," he said. "But as the circuit became more and more commercial, as they have to do, there was always an element of conflict between BRDC the club and the members and what their priorities were, and the commercial realities of actually running an international racing circuit.

"Of course, once you've got a Grand Prix contract, as we all know, the ante's upped every year on that, and so it became more and more demanding. It was not easy, there were all sorts of things and there was always the threat that Brands Hatch would take the Grand Prix, and there were the usual sort of rumours and Machiavellian sort of things.

"So we were always very conscious that we'd got to protect our interests, and part of the problem was realising that if we weren't careful, we only had a one-trick pony here. We only had the Grand Prix, which was the thing that made the money, and very little else did, and so we had to then start looking at ways and means to either diversify or come up with more commercial activities to try and generate money.

"There were various schemes, some which were good, some which weren't, but all of which of course had an element of risk to them.

"I was very involved in the Silverstone Motor Group, and at the time it looked like a good

Mika Häkkinen

"I spent so much time at Silverstone with the testing programmes that they did with the McLaren, and one thing comes back to me when I was testing there. The people who were working there were very professional, very strict with the rules, and I was a young guy, of course, and a bit of a hooligan when I was driving there, and quite a few people gave me a bollocking quite often, for what I was doing.

"But it was a beautiful racetrack, and at that time – we're talking about ten years ago, maybe more – Silverstone was definitely one of the greatest racetracks and still is a great, great racetrack. It was always great to come to race there because I was driving for the British team, we always had a beautiful welcome from the people and it was always great to come to Silverstone.

"One of the key issues was to make the tyres work. You have a long lap before you're starting your timed lap, you really had to understand the timing when you could start pushing with your car. If you do it too early, you destroy your tyres; too late, then the pressure goes too low and you are not quick because of that."

RIGHT *Mika Häkkinen celebrates on the podium after winning the 2001 Foster's British Grand Prix. (LAT)*

idea on the basis that we needed to diversify the Silverstone business and brand away from just running a Grand Prix into areas where we thought that the brand could actually be exploited commercially in other areas. And at that time a motor group looked a reasonable way of going forward and to generate some serious money and some serious capital, which could then be ploughed back into the circuit operations. But, unfortunately, it probably was a bit too clever too soon, and I think the difficulty is, as latter boards have found, it's very difficult to try and have a mandate for circuit companies to go away and do commercial operations.

"That mandate can be a little bit cloudy at times and people don't always understand and, of course, a lot of commercial things involve an element of confidentiality that you then can't tell people. When you are able to tell people and it has to go before the members, you'll find that it's almost presented as a fait accompli and then, of course, people get a bit upset, which is understandable. So it's a catch-22 and it's interesting that subsequent boards have had exactly the same problem. You can't have 750 people on a committee, you'll never get a result. But we've had probably 20 years of problems, a bit of conflict, and all of it involves the wretched

Grand Prix unfortunately because that's where all the stakes are."

A tripartite meeting between the lawyers representing the members, Silverstone Circuits and TWR was set up to try to sell BRDC's stake in the SMG. It was believed that the directors could be liable for any shortfall if no buyer could be found. The BRDC was also suing the original lawyers who had advised them on the deal.

At another EGM, held on 1 October 1992, Innes Ireland was voted in as president of the BRDC, together with a new set of directors.

Discussions about how the club could extract itself from the SMG deal laboured on throughout 1993, and in November Denys Rohan was appointed managing director and chief executive of Silverstone Circuits. He met with Walkinshaw on 2 December and started negotiations, which finally resulted in a settlement. Walkinshaw agreed to buy back Silverstone Circuit's shares in SMG for £3.2 million, with both parties paying their own costs and making a contribution towards the directors' costs as well. At the club's AGM on 22 April 1994 the members gave their approval to the settlement and the sorry saga was finally over.

The postscript to this was that on 23 May 1996 Silverstone Circuits won a £3.5 million settlement from the High Court after its solicitors were proved to have been negligent in their advice regarding the purchase of the Silverstone Motor Group.

Perhaps the saddest part of all of this is that it had been the late Jimmy Brown, the man who had lived and breathed Silverstone for so long, who had asked Walkinshaw specifically to take over as chairman of Silverstone Circuits from him. Apparently, when Walkinshaw first visited Silverstone in 1968, he did so after having collected a tractor at Lincoln and then driven his truck to the circuit to look around. He was apparently asked to move on by Jimmy Brown, but the two engaged in a conversation from which a long-standing mutual respect developed.

Meanwhile, with all this going on in the background, developments at the circuit continued. Towards the end of 1992, plans were announced for the A43 to be rerouted around Silverstone village in order to reduce traffic congestion at major meetings. Construction on the Silverstone by-pass was due to commence in autumn 1994 or spring 1995.

In March 1993 plans were announced for a proposed 1.8-mile high-speed oval circuit to be built at the south end of the track, but in January the following year these were postponed as it was felt that the prospects for Indycar racing in Europe were a little way down the road and that there were other improvements to be made which were more important.

These improvements centred around a deal that was struck between the circuit and Bernie Ecclestone in April 1993 that would allow the British Grand Prix to remain at Silverstone until 2001. The long-term agreement would allow the BRDC to press ahead with a multi-million pound expansion scheme that would include an extension to the back of the pits complex, with a hospitality suite and conference centre built above the pits. Spectator banking was to be built around the southern end of the circuit, using earth from the construction of the proposed A43 dual carriageway.

In 1994, further modifications were made to the track in the light of the fatal accident which befell Ayrton Senna at Imola on 1 May that year. A huge programme of improvements was undertaken and completed in just 18 days. Copse Corner was re-profiled, making it tighter and increasing the run-off area and gravel trap while, instead of being a sweeping corner, Stowe now became a slower, sharp right-hander, also with an increased gravel trap. In order to slow the cars at the fast Bridge Bend, a left-right corner was added at Abbey, and Priory was also altered to create more run-off area. The track at Vale was extended down its left-hand side to allow more overtaking into Club, while gravel traps were also extended in other areas, and the entrance to the pit lane was moved.

Floodlights were installed to allow the contractors to work round the clock in order to complete the revisions in time for the F1 test session on 21 June. Prior to all this, a three-storey block of ten hospitality suites and a 180-seat restaurant overlooking Brooklands Corner was opened in time for the International Trophy meeting in May.

The next phase of the redevelopment of the circuit was completed with the opening on 5 April 1995 by HRH Prince Michael of Kent (who had recently taken over as president-in-chief of the BRDC from the Duke of Edinburgh) of a new pits and paddock complex, comprising larger, fully-equipped pits, a new paddock diner and shop, new scrutineering bay and medical centre. The £650,000 (7,000sq ft) centre contained its own treatment room, x-ray room, operating theatre and burns unit, together with two four-bed wards, a drug-testing room and, hopefully never to be used, a mortuary.

At the southern end of the circuit, the 0.795-mile self-contained Stowe circuit was opened on the infield, intended for use by the Silverstone Driving Centre, but also for smaller race meetings while the National circuit was also in use. This brought the total number of available circuit layouts at Silverstone up to four. The Stowe circuit hosted its first event on Saturday 10 June, and then over the weekend of 5–6 August it was used for a 24-hour kart race, a round of the RacePro British Zip Endurance Championship, with 75 karts entered.

Also in 1995, new offices and workshops for the Silverstone Driving Centre were constructed alongside the Hangar Straight to allow all activities, including the rally stage, corporate karting and the four-wheel drive and skid courses to be run together from the same site. At the British Grand Prix, the Shell Oils Tower was rebranded the *Autosport* Tower. Tickets for that year's event had been limited to 90,000 on race day. Advance bookings for the race had been up 300 per cent and all but 2,000 of the grandstand seats had been sold by March, four months ahead of the race.

In 1996 the new 2.2-mile 'International' track layout, formed by linking the Grand Prix circuit between Becketts and Abbey, was opened, while a revised 3.106-mile 'Historic' circuit was used for the Coys International Historic Festival on 2–4 August. This eased the approach to Club Corner through Vale and restored the old Abbey Corner. Both changes were aimed at reducing stress on brakes and transmissions of the older cars. The early Festivals had been run on the original section of track from Stowe to Club.

Changes were also made that year to Stowe Corner, which had become a tight right-hander in 1994. It was now eased, making a more flowing line. Similar changes to Copse would be made in 1997, while Stowe was re-profiled again in time for the 1996 British Grand Prix.

In January 1997, further changes were made to the circuit. Priory was eased and the straight between it and Brooklands increased slightly in length. Luffield now became one sweeping, constant radius corner instead of two sharp right-handers linked by a short straight, while Copse now had an earlier entry to restore the high-speed flow of the corner. For spectators, a new bank of

ABOVE *During the 1994 Grand Prix weekend, the circuit's Club Straight was used as a paddock for the support races. Here, the contenders in the Porsche Supercup line up prior to their race. (Author)*

open seating for 5,000 was built between Abbey and Bridge corners. In April the circuit was granted another five-year extension to its contract to host the British Grand Prix, taking it up to 2006.

Also in 1997, a new twin-track Superspecial rally stage, located on the outside of the circuit near Becketts Corner, was opened and it hosted its first event, the Mintex/Elf Rallysprint, on 30 August. The 1.93km track, which the following year was named after BRDC director and rally driver Roger Clark, would be used by the circuit's rally school, and the twin tracks meant that cars could run side-by-side for about 60 per cent of the stage, with a crossover to ensure each side was of equal length. The stage also featured a jump and a water-splash.

Silverstone Television was launched at the start of the 1997 season, with its own dedicated studio and team of reporters and presenters. At the British Grand Prix in July it was on air for 39 hours from Friday through to Sunday. Ten cameras around the circuit sent pictures to giant screens located around the track and at the hospitality units and the BRDC suite.

It was the circuit's 50th anniversary in 1998, and to celebrate, the grid for the 1948 RAC Grand Prix was recreated at the Coys Historic Festival on 24–26 July, with 19 of the original 26 cars present. Towards the end of the year plans were revealed for a new BRDC clubhouse, to be located overlooking Brooklands and Woodcote corners, with extensive viewing facilities, while on track the Ireland esses on the International circuit were straightened to give cars a smoother run out of Becketts and on to the straight towards Abbey.

But the circuit's 50th anniversary also heralded the start of another period of uncertainty.

In November 1998 it was rumoured that a takeover bid had been made for the circuit. BRDC secretary John Fitzpatrick was confident that the £41-million bid, backed by HSBC Private Equity, would be turned down by the membership, rejecting claims by some members that the circuit needed a cash injection. A similar

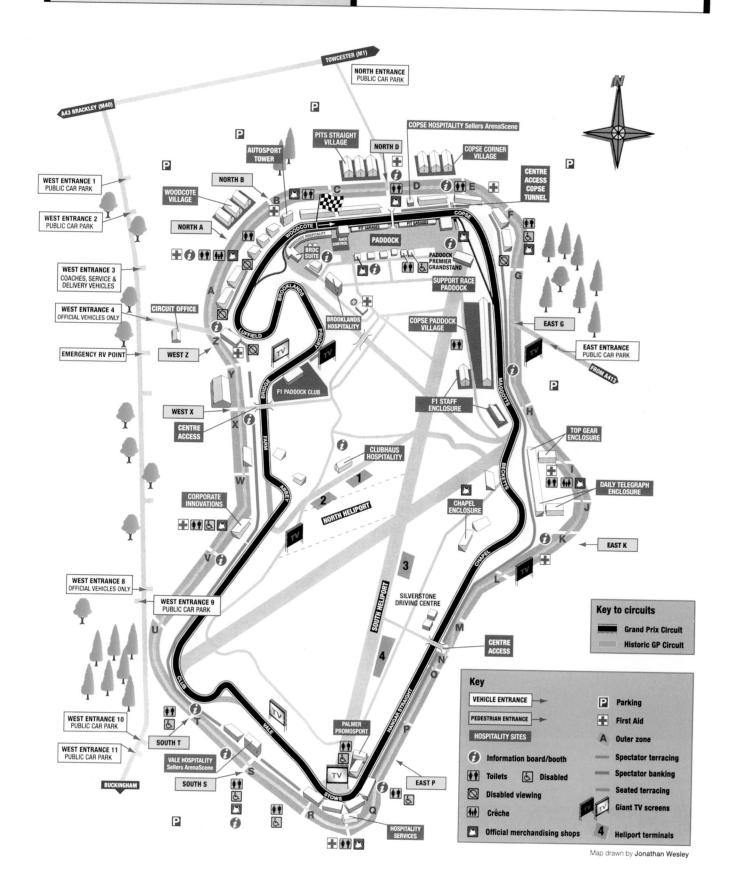

Map drawn by **Jonathan Wesley**

ABOVE *FIA president
Max Mosley was driven
around the circuit in
the two-seater McLaren-
Mercedes MP4-98T at
the 1998 RAC British
Grand Prix meeting.*
(Author)

bid by property developer Colin Sullivan had
been unanimously rejected in April 1997 and was
described at the time by BRDC president Lord
Hesketh as "not much better than an IOU from
the bank of Toytown".

The new bidder was property developer John
Lewis, himself a BRDC member and chairman of
Silverstone Estates, who dismissed rumours that
the site would be developed and lost to racing.
He claimed that the bid contained guarantees
to ensure motor racing would continue and that
the BRDC always had a place at the circuit. The
bid threw up deep divisions within the club over
whether or not to sell, with some members feeling
that the time was right for the club to realise its
assets, plough the money into supporting aspiring
drivers and championships and let someone else
run the circuit. Others felt that selling would be a
dreadful mistake.

Shortly afterwards, Sullivan's company, SMC
Investments, joined in with another offer, and

the circuit engaged merchant bank Dresdner
Kleinwort Benson to evaluate all potential
proposals, with interested parties having to place
their bids by 22 January.

In January 1999, Silverstone chief executive
Denys Rohan denied that bids were being
invited for the sale of the circuit. "It's grossly
exaggerated," he said. "There's a review process
going on and a number of people have expressed
an interest in acquiring all parts of Silverstone.
We're just providing information. In due course,
the board can go back to its members and say
'this is the situation'." He added that it was all part
of a review process to look at all the options open
to the circuit and that one of those was to see if
people were prepared to bid.

But, as Lord Hesketh commented later: "The
fact that someone had made an offer meant that
Silverstone was, as they say in the corporate
world, in play."

It certainly was. Also in January news broke that
Nicola Foulston, chief executive of Brands Hatch
Leisure (BHL), had made a bid to buy Silverstone
and had entered into negotiations with Bernie
Ecclestone to try to get the British Grand Prix
returned to Brands Hatch if she was unsuccessful
in her attempts to acquire the circuit.

Rob Bain, at that time finance director of BHL,
takes up the story: "When we made our approach
to the BRDC, one of its members also made an
approach," he said. "He was a property developer,
and then all of a sudden we were hearing about
various media groups being interested. The only
way we could take those other options away from
the table was by securing a Grand Prix contract.
That contract effectively closed the door on any
other bidder."

What Foulston knew, but others apparently
didn't, was that Silverstone's contract with
Ecclestone to hold the British Grand Prix
contained a change of ownership clause. In other
words, if Silverstone changed hands, Ecclestone
could take the Grand Prix away. Anyone thinking
of bidding for the track needed his approval.

She therefore set up a meeting with him and
negotiated a deal whereby not only would he
approve her bid for the circuit, but that he would
only accept her bid. In an interview with *Autosport*,
Ecclestone said that the circuit hadn't done enough
to keep up to the required standards for a modern
Grand Prix venue. "When you have a good look at
Silverstone," he said, "you come to the conclusion
that it's one of the worst circuits we've got. It's not
what you'd call a premier prestige circuit. It would
be nice if they were prepared to do what they
promise to do; it would be all right."

He also added that Britain did not have a "God-given right" to host a Grand Prix at all, and also confirmed that if Silverstone was sold to anyone other than Foulston, the contract to run the Grand Prix would expire immediately.

In March, the BRDC circulated its members with a plan to restructure, which would involve splitting the commercial side from the club itself, with members receiving shares in a new company. The board had been considering such a plan for over a year and recommended this as an alternative to accepting a takeover bid from Brands Hatch.

Under the scheme, Silverstone Circuits Group would split from the club with members receiving the entire share capital of the business. A 'golden share' right of veto would prevent anyone controlling more than a 10 per cent shareholding. The circuit freehold and trademark would be ring-fenced as protected assets and the lease and licensing of those assets to the Silverstone Circuits Group would provide an income.

The plans were opposed by a number of people, and at their AGM in April, BRDC members rejected the idea of selling the circuit but voted in favour of a restructuring, though not for giving members shares in the new company.

In April, Foulston lodged a formal bid for the circuit. She had secured a deal with Ecclestone to hold the British Grand Prix, either at Brands or at Silverstone if she could take it over. If Silverstone was sold it had to be sold to her, because that was the only way it could retain the Grand Prix. If the BRDC wouldn't sell the circuit to her, she would run the race at Brands Hatch.

Sceptics pointed out that Brands had less than half the land that Silverstone had available to it on a race weekend and that, since the circuit had last hosted a Grand Prix 13 years previously, all the hospitality that now accompanied such an event could not be accommodated at the Kent circuit.

"The trouble was the members got very scared by Nicola Foulston's bid," explained Lord Hesketh, "and I said 'you must be mad. Brands Hatch has got no more chance of being compliant as an F1 track in the modern world as I have of being selected for the astronauts' programme'. And this was ably demonstrated by one of our directors, Martin Colvill, who came in one day and he put down a map that covered the entire acreage of Silverstone, and then he put down another map, to the same scale, of the entire acreage of Brands Hatch, which just about filled the helicopter landing strip. And I said, 'There you are – that's the proof. That's what I've been saying all along.'"

In May, Foulston withdrew her offer to purchase Silverstone, instead pushing ahead with plans to hold the British Grand Prix at Brands Hatch from 2002 onwards, but in July she reopened her bid of £43 million. The deal would provide each BRDC member with a £60,000 windfall and give the club responsibility for administration of all BHL's motorsport activities. In return, BHL would acquire a 50-year lease on Silverstone, together with the BRDC's commercial activities. BRDC insiders regarded the move as an indication that the BHL boss was beginning to get desperate, as she had a deadline to meet to get planning permission for work at Brands Hatch.

Two months later, in September, Foulston did another about-turn and announced that she had abandoned plans to take over Silverstone, claiming that "we have bigger fish to fry". Revised plans for changes to Brands were revealed and submitted to the local district council for planning permission.

"It was another step to turn up the heat on Silverstone," explained Rob Bain. "We'd knocked all the other bidders away from the table but they still wouldn't come to the negotiating table with us, so we decided to raise the pressure. We had two Grand Prix contracts, one to run at Silverstone, one to run at Brands Hatch, and then we pursued planning permission. Obviously we were confident, we were spending a vast amount of money trying to secure planning permission, and we were successful."

In October, Lord Hesketh resigned as BRDC president after failing to come to an agreement with the board concerning the restructuring of the club, and Ken Tyrrell succeeded him as BRDC president.

To complicate matters further, in November, Nicola Foulston sold Brands Hatch Leisure to the Interpublic Group (IPG), one of the world's largest advertising and marketing communications groups. Its specialist motorsports division, Octagon Motorsports, already owned and managed several international motorsports series, including the World Superbike Championship.

But even more unsettling news had come in October when the FIA announced that the 2000 British Grand Prix would take place on Easter Sunday, 23 April, instead of the traditional July date. The revised scheduling would mean fewer hours of daylight for the circuit to fit its programme into, although the number of support races had already been reduced, the traditional F3 encounter having been dropped.

Silverstone was facing a very uncertain start to the new millennium, but if the nineties had been turbulent for the circuit, it was nothing compared to what the decade ahead was to hold.

Nigel Mansell

"I probably first went to Silverstone back in the sixties, but racing-wise it was in 1976 in Formula Ford. It was just awesome. The old circuit where Stowe and Club were open and flat out – Woodcote was obviously pretty flat out as well; just an awesome circuit.

"In 1977, I won the Brush Fusegear Formula Ford Championship, stepped up to Formula 3 and won my first Formula 3 race there.

"It's home advantage. It's racing in your home country and basically I love very fast circuits – I call them ballsy circuits where you have to hang it out there, and if something goes wrong obviously you pay the highest price because it would be a very high-speed accident. But I just love Silverstone.

"In the 1987 British Grand Prix we had a big vibration problem and we were going to do the whole race on a set of tyres but I pitted halfway through – I couldn't drive the car anymore, I couldn't see where I was going. And I put a new set of tyres on and was immediately a lot quicker, some two seconds a lap quicker. I did the quick maths and there were 20-something laps to go and I could catch about a second and a bit a lap, and maybe with two laps to go I might catch Nelson (Piquet) who was 24 seconds ahead, and that's exactly what we did. We broke the track record 11 times in the last 15 laps and I passed him with a lap to go before the finish and won the race. It was one of the most brilliant overtaking manoeuvres and a very satisfying win.

"The fuel read-out was showing minus and the team were telling me to slow down as well, but you can't slow down when you're potentially going to win the home Grand Prix. I just kept going.

"I ran out of fuel on the slowing-down lap, and so I went round on a motorbike with a policeman for a lap of honour, and that's when I got off and kissed the track where we overtook, it was wonderful.

"The opening lap in 1992 was a banzai, and I just got an advantage and held it. It's what I call people power, and if you use people power to your advantage you get half a second in your pocket. You have to not get uptight, to embrace the fans and enjoy it, and then they give you an extra adrenalin rush, and it worked for me over every single year I raced there in front of my home crowd. They enjoyed it, I enjoyed it and, of course, getting the results was even better.

"The slowing-down lap was just sensational. It was one of the best moments in my life because it's money-can't-buy moments. You can't prompt 120,000 people to invade the circuit; you can't prompt their enjoyment and satisfaction. It's something that happens spontaneously; it's just wonderful, wonderful occasions.

"I think the great thing is that Silverstone for me is one of the best, if not the best Grand Prix circuit in the world. It has the most demanding corners, attacking corners, it has great overtaking opportunities, and so it's a spectacle, and that's what Grand Prix racing should be all about.

"There were corners where you needed to be super smooth, and there were others you needed to gorilla the car round, because then we didn't have power steering, so the driver and his strength was mega important.

"The endearing memory I'll have of every single race, even when I'm not racing there, is the crowd at Silverstone. They are the most educated, most supportive and just brilliant, brilliant supporters of all British drivers, and all other drivers too. And it's like one big family when they come to the British Grand Prix at Silverstone, and everybody's just great."

RIGHT *Nigel Mansell scored a famous victory at the 1987 Shell Oils British Grand Prix in his Canon Williams-Honda FW11B. (LAT)*

1990

■ Plans for major revisions to the track were announced as it was revealed that Silverstone would continue to host the British Grand Prix for a further five years after its existing contract expired in 1991.

■ The two rounds of the British F3 Championship on 8 April and 7 May both produced wins for Mika Salo in his Ralt-Mugen Honda RT34.

■ The International Trophy meeting on the weekend of 19–20 May included rounds of both the FIA F3000 championship, for the International Trophy itself on the Saturday, and of the Sports-Prototype World Sports Car Championship, for the British Empire Trophy, on the Sunday. Allan McNish took victory in the former, driving a DAMS Marlboro Lola-Mugen T90/50 to a narrow victory over team-mate Erik Comas.

■ Meanwhile, Jaguar maintained its perfect record when it took its fourth victory from four starts at the 480km Sports-Prototype British Empire Trophy race. Martin Brundle and Alain Ferté brought their Silk Cut XJR-11 home a lap ahead of team-mates Jan Lammers and Andy Wallace as the team scored a perfect one-two finish. The much-fancied Mercedes C11 of Jean-Louis Schlesser and Mauro Baldi retired from the lead with engine failure after 40 laps.

■ Steve Robertson was the victor at the 10 June round of the British F3 Championship in his Ralt-VW RT33, while Robb Gravett took the honours in his Ford Sierra RS500 in the supporting Esso British Touring Car round.

■ An estimated crowd of 100,000 turned out in beautiful weather for the Foster's British Grand Prix over the weekend of 13–15 July in the hope of seeing Nigel Mansell take victory at the last Grand Prix to be held on the old track layout. The Englishman had been in a class of his own in qualifying, taking pole position in his Ferrari 641/2, but was out-dragged at the start by the McLaren MP4/5B of Ayrton Senna and the two gradually pulled clear of the rest of the field. On lap 12 Mansell took the lead and shortly afterwards Senna spun at Copse, dropping three places. Mansell's hopes of a home victory were dashed, however, when his semi-automatic gearbox began to play up, allowing his team-mate Alain Prost into the lead, and the Englishman eventually retired on lap 56 as his car lost all drive as he went into Copse Corner.

ABOVE *Nigel Mansell led the 1990 Foster's British Grand Prix, in his Ferrari 641/2, until he retired with gearbox failure. Here he leads Gerhard Berger and Alain Prost in the early stages of the race. (LAT)*

ABOVE *A crowd of around 100,000 turned out for the 1990 Foster's British Grand Prix, many of them hoping for a home win for Nigel Mansell in his Ferrari. (LAT)*

Mansell climbed from his car, threw his gloves into the crowd, and walked away. Prost took the flag, ahead of the Williams-Renault FW13B of Thierry Boutsen and Senna's McLaren. Immediately after the race, a disconsolate Mansell announced that he was retiring from racing.

■ The supporting British F3 championship round was won by Mika Salo in his Ralt-Mugen Honda RT34. Robb Gravett again triumphed in the British Touring Car Championship round in his Sierra RS500.

■ The first Christie's International Historic Festival was held on 28–29 July with 12 races as the old Grand Prix circuit was used for the very last time. Events included vintage aircraft displays, historic Grand Prix and touring car events and the International Supersports Cup.

■ Work started on construction of the new infield complex at Woodcote on 1 August. Tom Walkinshaw, chairman of Silverstone Circuits, drove a Marshall 'heavy angle' bulldozer to begin the excavation work.

ABOVE *Ayrton Senna's Marlboro McLaren-Honda MP4/5B outdragged Nigel Mansell's Ferrari 641/2 at the start of the 1990 Foster's British Grand Prix to take the lead going into Copse Corner, with Gerhard Berger's McLaren, the Williams-Renault FW13B of Thierry Boutsen, Alain Prost's Ferrari and the rest of the field, giving chase. (LAT)*

■ It was the two Mikas at the front of the British F3 round again on 27 August, this time Häkkinen beating Salo to the flag, both driving Ralt-Mugen Honda RT34s.

■ Pedro Chaves was crowned British F3000 champion when he won the very wet penultimate round on 30 September in his Reynard-Langford & Peck 90D.

■ It was Mika Häkkinen who won the final round of the British F3 Championship on 7 October, his Ralt-Mugen Honda RT34 leading home the similar car of Christian Fittipaldi. Robb Gravett gave the Ford Sierra RS500 a final victory in the British Touring Car Championship round, as regulation changes would render it ineligible the following year.

RIGHT *Alain Prost crosses the line in his Ferrari 641/2 to win the 1990 Foster's British Grand Prix. (LAT)*

1991

■ The new-look Silverstone was shown off to the press on 9 January, just five months after work had begun. The modifications to the track had increased the length from 2.97 to 3.02 miles. FIA vice president (promotional affairs) Bernie Ecclestone formally opened the new circuit on 10 January and was driven around by Derek Warwick in a Jaguar XJR15.

■ Rickard Rydell, driving a TOM'S-TOM'S Toyota 031F was the surprise winner of the opening round of the British F3 Championship on 17 March, beating the Ralt-Mugen Honda RT35 of Hideki Noda.

■ Will Hoy dominated the opening round of the Esso British Touring Car Championship on Easter Monday, 1 April, in his BMW M3, beating the Vauxhall Cavalier GSi of Jeff Allam.

■ The first major event to be held on the new layout was the round of the World Sportscar Championship on 18 May, which resulted in victory for the Silk Cut Jaguar XJR-14 of Derek Warwick and Teo Fabi. The Mercedes C291 of Michael Schumacher and Karl Wendlinger took second, ahead of the Jaguar of Martin Brundle.

■ The round of the Esso British Touring Car Championship on 9 June ended in chaos as the race was red-flagged after just ten laps because of torrential rain. John Cleland was declared the winner, despite his Vauxhall Cavalier GSi being buried in the tyre wall at Brooklands. The equally wet British F3 Championship round was won by the Ralt-Mugen Honda RT35 of David Coulthard.

■ Brazilian driver Oswaldo Negri was lucky to escape uninjured after his Bowman-VW BC1 was launched over the top of another car and barrel-rolled on the first lap of the British F3 Championship round on 29 June. The race was won by Gil de Ferran in a Reynard-Mugen Honda 913.

■ Nigel Mansell led all but the first half-lap of the Foster's British Grand Prix on 14 July to take a decisive victory in his Canon Williams-Renault FW14. He had taken pole position but was beaten off the line by Ayrton Senna's Marlboro McLaren-Honda MP4/6. Mansell got by him at Stowe and that was the last anyone saw of him. He took the flag 59 laps later and stopped to give Senna – whose car had run out of fuel at Club Corner on the last lap – a lift back to the pits. Gerhard

ABOVE *The Seven-Up Jordan team was based at Silverstone and was in its first year of Grand Prix motor racing in 1991. Its Ford-powered 191 sits in the pit lane prior to the British Grand Prix. (Steve Rendle)*

Berger's McLaren thus inherited second place, ahead of the Ferrari 643 of Alain Prost.

■ The supporting British F3 round was won by Gil de Ferran in his Reynard-Mugen Honda 913, and Steve Soper took the honours in the Esso British Touring Car Championship encounter driving a BMW M3.

■ The second Christie's International Historic Festival was held on 27–28 July in glorious sunshine, the event having already established itself as an important part of the historic racing calendar.

■ Hideki Noda became the first Japanese driver to win an F3 race outside of his home country when he triumphed in the British championship round on Bank Holiday Monday, 26 August, in his Ralt-Mugen Honda RT35.

■ The round of the British F3000 Championship on 22 September was won by Fredrik Ekblom in a Lola-Cosworth T90/50.

■ Rubens Barrichello took pole position and set fastest lap on his way to winning the British F3 Championship round on 6 October in his Ralt-Mugen Honda RT35. Tim Harvey won the final round of the Esso British Touring Car Championship in his BMW M3 as Will Hoy clinched the title.

ABOVE *Nigel Mansell takes the lead in his Canon Williams-Renault FW14 from the Marlboro McLaren-Honda MP4/6 of Ayrton Senna going into Stowe on the first lap of the 1991 Foster's British Grand Prix, as the rest of the field, led by Roberto Moreno's Benetton B191, streams down Hanger Straight. (LAT)*

LEFT *Nigel Mansell stopped on his slowing-down lap, after winning the 1991 Foster's British Grand Prix, to give Ayrton Senna, whose Marlboro McLaren-Honda MP4/6 had run out of fuel at Club Corner on the last lap, a lift back to the pits. (LAT)*

1992

■ John Cleland won the opening round of the Esso British Touring Car Championship on 5 April in his Vauxhall Cavalier GSi, fighting off the challenge of the Toyota Carinas of Andy Rouse and Will Hoy, who eventually spun and dropped to fourth behind Jeff Allam's Cavalier. Gil de Ferran won the British F3 encounter in his PSR Reynard-Mugen Honda 923.

■ The British Empire Trophy meeting on 10 May featured rounds of both the Sportscar World Championship and the FIA F3000 Championship. Silverstone had proposed that the SWC round be reduced from 500km to 200km in a bid to attract more entries and make the event more entertaining for spectators. The idea was blocked by Toyota, however, and only 11 cars started the event, which was won by Derek Warwick and Yannick Dalmas in their Peugeot 905B. Only five cars finished. Jordi Gene dominated the F3000 race in his Marlboro Reynard-Mugen Honda 92D.

■ Gil de Ferran took his Reynard-Mugen Honda 923 to victory on Bank Holiday Monday, 25 May, at the British F3 round after on-the-road winner and pole-sitter Oswaldo Negri was adjudged to have jumped the start in his similar car. Two weeks later, on 7 June, it was Philippe Adams who took victory in his Ralt-Mugen Honda RT36, with de Ferran second.

BELOW *Nigel Mansell utterly dominated the 1992 Foster's British Grand Prix in his Canon Williams-Renault FW14B, causing excited fans to invade the track at the end of the race while some cars were still at racing speed. (Steve Rendle)*

■ Nigel Mansell set a pole position lap of 1m 18.965s (a speed of 148.043mph) for the Foster's British Grand Prix on 12 July, the fastest ever on the new configuration of track. Driving his Canon Williams-Renault FW14B, Mansell went on to utterly dominate the race, pulling out a lead of over 3sec by the end of the first lap. He steadily increased the gap to the rest of the field until after just ten laps he was already 20sec clear. Behind him, the battle for second was won by his team-mate Riccardo Patrese, with the Benetton-Ford B192 of Martin Brundle in third. At the end, one fan ran across the track on the start-finish straight as soon as Mansell had crossed the line, and others followed suit, streaming on to the circuit while other cars were still completing their final lap. Future world champion and BRDC president Damon Hill made his Grand Prix debut at the event, driving a Brabham-Judd BT60B. He finished 16th.

■ The supporting British F3 event was won by Warren Hughes in a Ralt-Mugen Honda RT36 from ninth on the grid. Jeff Allam won the Esso British Touring Car Championship round in his Vauxhall Cavalier GSi.

■ A crowd of 27,000 people attended the third Christie's International Historic Festival on 25–26 July, firmly establishing its position as the world's foremost historic meeting. Former world champions Phil Hill, John Surtees and Jody Scheckter were among those in attendance, as was Stirling Moss.

■ Philippe Adams won the British F3 encounter on 31 August in his Ralt-Mugen Honda RT36, but runner-up Gil de Ferran, driving a Reynard-Mugen Honda 923, was crowned champion.

■ Yvan Muller clinched the Halfords British F2 title on 13 September by taking second place in his Reynard-Cosworth 91D. The race was won by the similar car of Enrico Bertaggia.

■ Tim Harvey clinched the Esso British Touring Car Championship title in controversial circumstances on 4 October. The BMW 318i driver finished fourth, but title rival John Cleland, who was in fifth place in his Vauxhall Cavalier GSi and set to take the championship himself, was knocked off track by Harvey's team-mate Steve Soper. The race was won by Andy Rouse in a Toyota Carina. Meanwhile, Gil de Ferran won the final round of the British F3 championship in his Reynard-Mugen Honda 923.

1993

■ Kelvin Burt won the first round of the British F3 Championship on 21 March in his Paul Stewart Racing Reynard-Mugen Honda 933. Burt was initially disqualified for contact with the Reynard of pole-man Andre Ribeiro, but was later reinstated.

■ The Schnitzer-run BMW 318is of Steve Soper and Jo Winklehock finished one-two at the opening round of the *Auto Trader* British Touring Car Championship on 28 March.

■ Philippe Adams won an incident-packed British F2 race on 25 April in his Reynard-Cosworth 92D.

■ The BRDC International Trophy race on 9 May, the second round of the FIA International F3000 Championship, was led from start to finish by Gil de Ferran in his Paul Stewart Racing Reynard-Cosworth 93D, with the Pacific Racing Reynards of David Coulthard and Michael Bartels finishing second and third.

■ The round of the British F3 Championship on Bank Holiday Monday, 31 May, resulted in a commanding win for Oliver Gavin in a Dallara-Vauxhall 393.

■ There was disappointment for the smaller-than-usual home crowd, and heartbreak for Damon Hill, at the Foster's British Grand Prix on 11 July, when the engine in his Williams-Renault FW15C blew up while he was leading the race. Hill's team-mate, Alain Prost, went on to score his 50th Grand Prix victory, with Michael Schumacher second in his Benetton-Ford B193B. Riccardo Patrese, in the other Benetton, inherited third place after Ayrton Senna, in his Marlboro McLaren-Ford MP4/8, ran out of fuel on the final lap.

■ Toyota team-mates Julian Bailey and Will Hoy clashed while leading the supporting *Auto Trader* British Touring Car Championship round, with Hoy rolling out of the race. Keith O'dor and Win Percy went on to take a one-two for Nissan in their Primera eGTs. Oliver Gavin won the British F3 round on 10 July in his Dallara-Vauxhall 393.

■ Coys took over sponsorship of the fourth annual Historic Festival, which was held on 24–25 July and included a demonstration of the 1953 Le Mans-winning Jaguar C-type, with drivers Duncan Hamilton and Tony Rolt in attendance.

■ Kelvin Burt clinched the British F3 title by winning the round on 5 September on the National circuit in his Paul Stewart Racing Dallara-Mugen Honda 393. Meanwhile, two F1 teams – Footwork and Lotus – conducted testing on the South circuit at the same time, demonstrating Silverstone's adaptability. Burt repeated his victory at the 3 October round.

■ The final round of the *Auto Trader* British Touring Car Championship on 19 September produced a one-two for the Ford Mondeo Sis of Paul Radisich and Andy Rouse, but eighth place was enough for Jo Winklehock, in his BMW 318i, to clinch the title.

1994

■ Benetton F1 driver JJ Lehto suffered a fractured vertebra after a high-speed accident while testing his Ford-powered B194 at the track on 21 January. The Finn crashed heavily at Stowe corner in damp conditions.

■ Dario Franchitti scored a dominant lights-to-flag victory in the opening round of the British F3 Championship on 27 March in his PSR Dallara-Mugen Honda F394.

■ *Autosport* sponsored the International Trophy race, the opening round of the FIA F3000 Championship on Bank Holiday Monday, 2 May. The race was won by Frank Lagorce in his Reynard-Cosworth 94D, ahead of David Coulthard's similar car. The two supporting rounds of the British F3 Championship were both won by Jan Magnussen's Dallara-Mugen Honda F394.

■ The double-header of *Auto Trader* British Touring Car Championship races on 15 May produced victories for Gabriele Tarquini's Alfa Romeo 155 TS and the Ford Mondeo Ghia of Paul Radisich.

■ The Lotus-Mugen Honda 107C of Pedro Lamy crashed during testing at the circuit on 24 May, vaulting the fences and ending up in the pedestrian tunnel on Farm Straight after it spun at the exit of Abbey. Lamy broke both knees in the accident, which was blamed on a rear wing failure.

■ Damon Hill scored a popular victory in front of his home crowd at the British Grand Prix on 10 July, which was attended by HRH Diana, Princess of Wales. Hill led away from pole in his Rothmans Williams-Renault FW16, chased by the Benetton-Ford B194 of Michael Schumacher, who was subsequently given a 10sec stop-go penalty for overtaking Hill during the parade lap. By this time, the German had leapfrogged Hill at the first pit stops to take the lead, but dropped 20sec behind after serving his penalty. Jean Alesi finished third in his Ferrari 412 T1, but this became second when Schumacher was later excluded from the results for initially ignoring the black flag. This elevated the Marlboro McLaren-Peugeot MP4/9 of Mika Häkkinen to third.

■ The British F3 Championship race the previous day was won by Vincent Radermecker in a Dallara-Mugen Honda F394. The supporting *Auto Trader* British Touring Car Championship round was won by Jo Winklehock in his BMW 318i, after the race had to be restarted following a first corner pile-up.

ABOVE *Damon Hill's 1994 British Grand Prix didn't get off to a very good start on the first morning of practice when he suffered front suspension failure on his Rothmans Williams-Renault FW16 on his first lap out of the pits. The weekend got better, however, with Hill going on to take victory in the race. (Author)*

RIGHT *Carnage at the first corner of the* Auto Trader *British Touring Car Championship round at the 1994 British Grand Prix, as both Julian Bailey (Toyota Carina E) and Giampiero Simoni (Alfa Romeo 155 TS) both spin in front of the pack at Copse. (Author)*

ABOVE *Damon Hill picked up a Union Flag to carry on his parade lap, after taking victory in his Rothmans Williams FW16 at the 1994 British Grand Prix. (LAT)*

■ Radio Silverstone switched from 1602kHz medium wave to be broadcast for the first time on 87.7MHz FM, and Eddie Jordan hosted a concert in the paddock after the race and was joined on stage by Damon Hill and Johnny Herbert.

■ Wet weather on the Sunday failed to spoil the fifth running of the Coys Historic Festival on 30–31 July with 13 races over the two days.

■ Jan Magnussen was crowned British F3 champion on Bank Holiday Monday, 29 August, after winning both rounds of the double-header meeting in his Dallara-Mugen Honda F394, equalling the late Ayrton Senna's record of 12 wins in a single season. Five weeks later, at the final meeting on 2 October, he took his 14th victory in torrential rain.

■ Gabriele Tarquini clinched the *Auto Trader* British Touring Car Championship title in his Alfa Romeo 155 TS by winning the second of the two rounds on 11 September. Tim Harvey took victory in the first race in his Renault Laguna.

1995

■ Ralph Firmin Jr., driving a Dallara-Mugen Honda F395, won both of the opening rounds of the British F3 Championship at the Spring Trophy meeting on 26 March.

■ HRH the Duke of Kent opened the new pit and paddock complex at the circuit on 5 April. The refurbishment included new pit garages, medical centre and scrutineering bay.

■ A healthy crowd of 21,000 turned out in fine weather for the *Autosport* International Trophy on 7 May, the first round of the FIA F3000 Championship. The race produced a one-two for the Super Nova team, pole-sitter Ricardo Rosset leading home team-mate Vincenzo Sospiri in their Reynard-Cosworth 95Ds. Allan McNish finished third in his PSR-run Reynard.

■ A week later, on 14 May, Volvo's Rickard Rydell won the first of two *Auto Trader* British Touring Car Championship rounds in his 850, while Paul Radisich took victory in the second in his Ford Mondeo Ghia.

■ Jeremie Dufour took his maiden F3 victory at the Bank Holiday Monday, 29 May, round of the British Championship in his Dallara-Mugen Honda F395, beating the similar car of Ralph Firmin Jr.

■ The new 0.796-mile Stowe circuit was used for the first time on 10 June. The BRDC ran an eight-race programme, while the National circuit was hosting a VSCC meeting at the same time.

■ Benetton driver Johnny Herbert was a surprise winner of the British Grand Prix on 16 July in his Renault-powered B195. Damon Hill had taken the lead at the start in his Rothmans Williams-Renault FW17, with Jean Alesi's Ferrari 412T2 in second place ahead of Herbert's team-mate Michael Schumacher. Hill had opted for a two-stop strategy to Schumacher's one and lost the lead when he pitted for the second time, emerging right on the German's tail. A few laps later he attempted to pass at Priory but hit the Benetton, pitching them both into the gravel. Hill's team-mate, David Coulthard, looked set to take a maiden Grand Prix victory until he was given a stop-go penalty for exceeding the pit lane speed limit. This left Herbert to win his home Grand Prix ahead of Alesi, with Coulthard third. The event was a sell-out, the circuit having limited admission to 90,000.

ABOVE *The grid lines up around Woodcote for the start of the 1995 British Grand Prix. (LAT)*

■ John Cleland won a wet *Auto Trader* BTCC encounter in his Vauxhall Cavalier, while the previous day's British F3 round went to Gualter Salles in a Dallara-Mugen Honda F395 after on-track winner Gonzalo Rodriguez was excluded from the results because of a damaged airbox on his Mitsubishi-powered F395.

■ Beautiful weather greeted spectators and competitors at the Coys Historic Festival on 28–30 July and, as *Motor Sport* magazine pointed out, the paddock alone would have made a visit worthwhile, let alone two days of top-class historic racing.

■ Andy Wallace and Olivier Grouillard won a wet British Empire Trophy race, a round of the Global Endurance GT Series, on 17 September in their Harrods-backed McLaren F1 GTR, despite having to serve two stop-go penalties during the four-hour event for speeding in the pit lane. The Ferrari F40s of Michel Ferté/Olivier Thevenin and Anders Olofsson/Luciano Della Noce were second and third.

■ Alain Menu and team-mate Will Hoy took a win and a second place apiece in their Williams-run Renault Lagunas in the final two rounds of the *Auto Trader* British Touring Car Championship on 24 September, to give Renault the manufacturers' title. New champion John Cleland was third each time in his Vauxhall Cavalier.

■ Warren Hughes in an Alan Docking-run Dallara-Mitsubishi F395 and Oliver Gavin in an Edenbridge Dallara-Vauxhall F395 were the winners of the two rounds of the British F3 Championship at the Autumn Gold Cup meeting on 8 October.

BELOW *Johnny Herbert acknowledges the crowd after taking victory in the 1995 British Grand Prix. (LAT)*

1996

■ The new 2.215-mile International circuit, designed to host championship meetings, was used for the first time on 31 March at the BRDC's Spring Trophy meeting. Guy Smith won the opening round of the British F3 Championship in his Fortec Dallara-Mitsubishi F396, while Jamie Davies won round two in his TWR Dallara-GM F396.

■ Andy Wallace and Olivier Grouillard took their Harrods McLaren F1 GTR to victory in the British Empire Trophy race, a round of the Global Endurance GT Championship, on 12 May. The pair started tenth on the grid but, with a perfect race set-up, worked their way to the front of the four-hour event to take the flag ahead of the Lotus Esprit of Jan Lammers and Perry McCarthy.

■ Kelvin Burt drove his Volvo 850 to victory in race one of the *Auto Trader* British Touring Car Championship meeting on 19 May, while Frank Biela took the honours in his Audi A4 in race two.

■ Damon Hill spun out of the British Grand Prix in his Rothmans Williams-Renault FW18 on 14 July when a wheel nut worked loose, leaving his team-mate Jacques Villeneuve to take the victory. Hill had made a poor start from pole, dropping to fifth, but was up to third at the time of the accident. Gerhard Berger finished second in his Benetton-Renault B196, while Mika Häkkinen completed the podium in his Marlboro McLaren-Mercedes MP4/11.

ABOVE *The BTCC contenders stream up from Club towards Abbey during the support race for the 1996 British Grand Prix. (Author)*

LEFT *McLaren mechanics at work in the pit garage at the 1996 British Grand Prix. (Author)*

■ Roberto Ravaglia scored his first *Auto Trader* British Touring Car Championship victory in Saturday's supporting race in his BMW 320i, while David Leslie gave Honda its first-ever BTCC win driving his Accord on Sunday. Darren Manning, in a Dallara-Mugen Honda F395/96, just held off the similar car of Ralph Firmin Jr. to take victory in Saturday's British F3 Championship encounter.

■ Eddie Jordan hosted a post-race party in the paddock after the Grand Prix, and Tony and Cherie Blair were guests at the race itself.

■ A revised 'Historic' circuit was used for the Coys International Historic Festival on 2–4 August, which eased the approach to Club Corner through Vale and restored the old Abbey Corner. Both changes were aimed at reducing stress on the brakes and transmissions of the older cars. The early festivals had been run on the original section of track from Stowe to Club.

■ Kenny Brack won the *Autosport* International Trophy, a round of the FIA International F3000 Championship, on 17 August in convincing style in his Super Nova Lola-Zytek Judd T96/50.

■ The International Touring Car Championship paid its first visit to the circuit on 17–18 August, with the Zakspeed Opel Calibra of Klaus Ludwig leading home the JAS Alfa Romeo 155 V6 TI of Gabriele Tarquini in the first encounter. Tarquini went one better in the second race, as Ludwig was delayed on the grid, taking a deserved win ahead of the Rosberg-run Opel Calibra V6 of JJ Lehto.

■ Nicolas Minassian dominated the final round of the British F3 Championship on 13 October in his Dallara-Renault F396, taking the chequered flag over 7sec ahead of second-placed Jonny Kane's Dallara-Mugen Honda F395/96.

1997

The tyre barriers on the exit of Copse Corner had to be extended after the Dallara-Spiess F397 of Paula Cook crashed heavily into the concrete wall during qualifying for the *Autosport* British F3 Championship race on 6 April. Nicolas Minassian, driving a Dallara-Renault F397, took a dominant lights-to-flag victory in a race that was red-flagged twice – first when Mario Haberfeld barrel-rolled his Dallara-Opel F397 at Becketts, and then after a two-car collision on the main straight caused the result to be declared early.

Swiss driver Alain Menu dominated both rounds of the *Auto Trader* British Touring Car Championship on 20 April in his Williams Renault Laguna, with Rickard Rydell bringing his TWR Volvo S40 home in second place each time.

At the British Empire Trophy meeting on 9–11 May, the circuit hosted rounds of the FIA International F3000 Championship, the *Autosport* British F3 Championship and the new FIA GT Championship. Conditions were so bad for the British Empire Trophy race itself, the second round of the new FIA GT Championship, that the race was red-flagged 40 minutes early. There had already been nine different leaders and a long period behind the safety car before the race was brought to a premature end, handing victory to the Schnitzer team's McLaren-BMW F1 GTR driven by Peter Kox and Roberto Ravaglia by just over half a second from the pole-sitting AMG Mercedes-Benz of Bernd Schneider and Alex Wurz. The Mercedes had just taken the lead but results were declared on count-back to the previous lap, denying them the victory.

The first ten laps of the *Autosport* International Trophy race, the first round of the FIA F3000 Championship, was also run on a soaking wet track. The race was led by the RSM Marco Lola-Zytek T96/50 of Juan Pablo Montoya until the safety car was deployed after 12 laps when Gareth Rees crashed his Durango Lola. Montoya led away at the restart but skated off the track at Club Corner, leaving Ricardo Zonta to take victory in his Super Nova-run T96/50 from the Auto Sport Racing entry of Tom Kristensen. A month later Zonta was stripped of his victory as his car did not have a functioning first gear, handing the win to Kristensen.

The supporting *Autosport* British F3 round, held on a wet but drying track, produced a crushing victory for Jonny Kane in his PSR Dallara-Mugen Honda F397. National class runner

Martin O'Connell, driving a Dallara-TOM'S Toyota F395/6, took an excellent second place.

Jacques Villeneuve won his second British Grand Prix in succession on 13 July in his Rothmans Williams-Renault FW19, and in doing so scored the 100th victory for the Williams team at the same circuit where it had scored its very first, back in 1979. Villeneuve had led initially, chased by the Ferrari F310B of Michael Schumacher, but a problem during a pit stop had dropped him to seventh place. Schumacher retired with wheel-bearing failure and West McLaren-Mercedes MP4/12 driver Mika Häkkinen looked set to take the victory until his engine expired with less than seven laps to go. This left Villeneuve to take the win ahead of the two Benetton-Renault B197s of Jean Alesi and Alexander Wurz. The event was another sell-out, and Eddie Jordan once again hosted a post-race party in the paddock, with Damon Hill one of the many guests performing on stage.

The round of the *Autosport* British F3 Championship, held on 12 July, produced a win for Mario Haberfeld in his Dallara-Opel F397, with Mark Webber's Dallara-Mugen Honda F397 second. For the first time in years, the BTCC wasn't among the many support races for the British Grand Prix, which instead featured British GTs, Renault Spiders, Formula

BELOW *The giant television screen at Stowe shows the field for the supporting GT race at the 1997 British Grand Prix. (Author)*

Opel, Porsche Supercup and 1950s and 1960s Grand Prix cars, alongside the traditional F3 encounter.

■ The Coys Historic Festival on 25–27 July featured the largest gathering of Ferraris ever seen in Britain. Froilán González demonstrated a Ferrari 375, similar to the one in which he won the 1951 British Grand Prix at the circuit.

■ Silverstone's new twin-track Superspecial rally stage, located on the outside of Hangar Straight, hosted its first public event, the Mintex/Elf Rallysprint, on 30 August and was praised by the majority of competitors. The event was won by Marcus Dodd in a Ford Escort RS.

■ The circuit cancelled the rest of its Summer Festival over the weekend of 30–31 August as soon as news broke of the death of Diana, Princess of Wales. The following weekend's HSCC meeting was also cancelled out of respect for the Princess, whose family home was in Northamptonshire.

■ The Williams Renault Laguna pairing of Alain Menu and Jason Plato battled furiously throughout the two final rounds of the *Auto Trader* British Touring Car Championship on 21 September. Menu took victory in the first encounter as his team-mate dropped to third, but Plato got his revenge in race two, winning ahead of Menu.

■ Nicolas Minassian, driving a Promatecme Dallara-Renault F397, took another F3 victory at the circuit in the 5 October round of the *Autosport* British Championship, setting fastest lap on the way and beating his team-mate Enrique Bernoldi into second.

■ Silverstone played host to the Network Q RAC Rally on 25 November, with stages Three and Four of the event being held on a special layout which incorporated both the Grand Prix circuit and a large extent of the infield, providing a mix of tarmac and gravel for the competitors. Stage Eight was also held at the track, this time on the twin-track Rallysprint Superspecial stage located on the outside of the Hangar Straight. Juha Kankkunen (Ford Escort WRC) and Richard Burns (Mitsubishi Carisma GT) shared the honours on SS3, while Didier Auriol (Toyota Corolla WRC) was quickest on SS4. Honours in the Superspecial stage were shared by Kankkunen and Colin McRae (Subaru Impreza 555 WRC97), who went on to win the rally overall with co-driver Nicky Grist.

ABOVE *Jacques Villeneuve's Rothmans Williams-Renault FW19 leads Mika Häkkinen's West McLaren-Mercedes MP4/12 away at the start of the 1997 British Grand Prix. The Canadian went on to win his second RAC British Grand Prix in succession after Häkkinen's engine expired just seven laps from the end. (LAT)*

1998

■ Will Hoy won the Celebrity TV Challenge, held on the Superspecial rally stage on 7 February, just beating fellow BTCC runner Tim Harvey by 0.19sec in identical F2 Ford Escort rally cars. Other competitors included Tiff Needell, British Superbike rider Jim Moody and 1979 F1 world champion Jody Scheckter.

■ Mario Haberfeld won the round of the *Autosport* British F3 championship on 5 April in his PSR Dallara-Mugen Honda F397/98.

■ David Leslie and Will Hoy were the winners in the pair of *Auto Trader* British Touring Car rounds on 26 April. Leslie took his Nissan Primera to victory in race one, beating the Honda Accord of James Thompson, while Hoy, driving a Ford Mondeo, beat the Renault Laguna of Jason Plato in race two.

■ Once again the British Empire Trophy meeting, on 15–17 May, hosted three major championships. The *Autosport* International Trophy race on 16 May, a round of the FIA International F3000 Championship, provided a relatively easy

victory for Juan Pablo Montoya in his Super Nova Lola-Zytek T96/50. The Colombian eased out a lead over the West Lola of Nick Heidfeld until a safety car period bunched the field up again. At the restart, Montoya had no problem opening out the gap again to cruise home to the flag.

■ It was a Porsche versus Mercedes battle in the British Empire Trophy on 17 May, a round of the FIA GT Championship. Allan McNish and Bob Wollek took pole in their Porsche 911 GT1 98 and led the first 12 laps before a turbo problem caused their retirement. This left the DAMS Panoz GTR-1 of David Brabham and Eric Bernard in first place until it clashed with the other Porsche of Uwe Alzen and Jörg Müller, leaving the Mercedes CLK-GTR of Bernd Schneider and Mark Webber to take victory. The *Autosport* British F3 round resulted in a dominant win for Enrique Bernoldi, driving a Promatecme Dallara-Renault F397/8.

BELOW *The Mercedes CLK-GTR of Bernd Schneider and Mark Webber won the 1998 British Empire Trophy, Britain's round of the FIA GT Championship. (sutton-images.com)*

■ There was controversy at the end of the RAC British Grand Prix on 12 July as Michael Schumacher took victory while serving a stop-go penalty at the end of the final lap, crossing the finish line before reaching his pit. The German had been given a 10sec penalty for overtaking under a yellow flag in his Ferrari F300, but the stewards had failed to notify the team within the prescribed time limit, hence the stop-go. Mika Häkkinen had led much of the race in his West McLaren-Mercedes MP4/13 but eventually spun on a streaming wet track, handing the lead, and victory, to Schumacher. The German's team-mate, Eddie Irvine, finished third.

■ Darren Manning was the winner of the supporting *Autosport* British F3 round on 11 July, taking his Dallara-Mugen Honda F397/8 to victory over the Renault-powered example of Warren Hughes. The race was red-flagged after a crash and restarted over just two laps with the results decided on aggregate.

■ Fifty years after the event, the grid of the 1948 RAC Grand Prix was recreated at the Coys Historic Festival on 24–26 July with 19 of the original 26 cars present. Drivers present who had taken part in the original event were Baron Emmanuel 'Toulo' de Graffenried, who won the following year's race, Roy Salvadori, Geoff Richardson, Tony Rolt and Bob Ansell.

■ The runner-up spot in the first of the two final *Auto Trader* British Touring Car Championship rounds on 20 September was enough to clinch the title for Rickard Rydell in his Volvo S40. Honda Accord driver James Thompson won the first race, while the Nissan Primera duo of Anthony Reid and David Leslie scored a one-two in the second, with new champion Rydell in third.

■ The circuit celebrated its 50th anniversary at the Hill House Hammond Golden Jubilee meeting on 3–4 October. Newly-crowned *Autosport* British F3 champion Mario Haberfeld took victory in the final round in his PSR Dallara-Mugen Honda F397/8 – his sixth win of the season.

■ Silverstone again played host to the Network Q RAC Rally on 21–22 November on both the main circuit and the Rallysprint stage. Colin McRae, in a Subaru Impreza WRC98, won the first two Silverstone stages (SS3 and SS4), while Carlos Sainz in a Toyota Corolla WRC was fastest on the Superspecial (SS7). McRae then took the next Silverstone stage (SS8), with Didier Auriol in his Toyota fastest on SS9.

1999

■ Marc Hynes won the second round of the *Autosport* British F3 Championship on 28 March in his Dallara-Mugen Honda F399.

■ Laurent Aiello and Jason Plato were the two victors in the *Auto Trader* British Touring Car Championship meeting on 18 April. The Frenchman took his Vodafone Nissan Primera to victory in the sprint race, while Jason Plato won the feature event in his Nescafé Williams Renault Laguna.

■ The Silverstone 500 on 9 May, the second round of the FIA GT Championship, provided a dominant one-two for the Oreca team. Karl Wendlinger and Olivier Beretta shared the winning Chrysler Viper GTS-R with David Donohue, Jean-Philippe Belloc and Justin Bell taking the runners-up spot after five hours and 500 miles of racing. The first hour of the race was led by the Lister Storm of Julian Bailey, Tiff Needell and Bobby Verdon-Roe, but this eventually retired from second place with driveshaft failure.

■ The RAC British Grand Prix was held over four days, from 8–11 July, with qualifying for F3, F3000 and GTs on the Thursday, along with a pit road walkabout. The F1 action kicked off as usual on the Friday with two practice sessions and qualifying on the Saturday, along with the F3000 race. Grand Prix day itself consisted of the F1 warm-up at 8.30am, followed by a Porsche Supercup race and the drivers' parade. The Red Arrows provided their usual breathtaking display at midday, and the Grand Prix kicked off at 1pm. After that there were races for GT and saloon cars to round off the day.

■ The race itself had to be red-flagged on the opening lap after Michael Schumacher suffered brake failure and crashed his Ferrari F399 heavily at Stowe, breaking his right leg. The

BELOW *Silverstone is often used for the launch and media days of various championships. Here the contenders for the 1999 Auto Trader British Touring Car Championship perform tracking shots for the cameras. (Author)*

RIGHT *The Red Arrows enthralled the crowd, as usual, prior to the 1999 RAC British Grand Prix. (Author)*

LEFT *David Coulthard won the 1999 RAC British Grand Prix in his West McLaren-Mercedes MP4/14 after his team-mate and early leader Mika Häkkinen was delayed at a pit stop and eventually lost a wheel. (Author)*

BELOW *The crowd cheers as David Coulthard scores a home victory at the 1999 RAC British Grand Prix in his West McLaren-Mercedes MP4/14. (Author)*

race was restarted three-quarters of an hour later, and pole-sitter Mika Häkkinen looked on course for victory in his West McLaren-Mercedes MP4/14 until problems changing his left rear wheel during his pit stop delayed him. A second stop failed to solve the problem and the wheel eventually parted company with the car as he approached Woodcote on lap 29. By this time his team-mate David Coulthard had assumed the lead and went on to take a popular home victory ahead of Eddie Irvine's Ferrari, with Ralf Schumacher's Winfield Williams-Supertec FW21 in third.

■ Nicolas Minassian gave Kid Jensen Racing its first victory of the year in his Lola-Zytek B99/50 in the supporting F3000 round on the Saturday, beating Bruno Junqueira in the Petrobras Junior team entry, while Marc Hynes took another victory in the *Autosport* British F3 encounter in his Dallara-Mugen Honda F399, beating the Dallara-Sodemo Renault of Jenson Button by just 0.383sec after a race-long battle.

■ A total of 66,000 spectators attended over the three days of the Coys International Historic Festival on 30 July–1 August, the central theme of which was 'Fifty years of BRM'.

■ The 40th anniversary of the Mini was celebrated at the Computacenter SummerFest on 21–22 August. The two-day event included rounds of the BRDC Junior Single Seater and the Privilege Insurance British GT Championships, together with a night-time parachute display from the Red Devils and a firework finale on the Saturday night.

■ Volvo S40 driver Rickard Rydell won both the sprint and feature races at a very wet *Auto Trader* British Touring Car Championship meeting on 19 September, but it wasn't enough to stop Laurent Aiello from clinching the crown in his Vodafone Nissan Primera.

■ The Bank One Silverstone Autumn Gold Cup meeting on 10 October provided a win for Jenson Button in the *Autosport* British F3 Championship encounter. Button took his Promatecme-run Dallara-Sodemo Renault F399 to victory ahead of the Fortec Dallara-Mugen Honda F399 of Matt Davies.

RIGHT *The 1999 RAC British Grand Prix was red-flagged on the first lap after Michael Schumacher crashed his Ferrari F399 heavily at Stowe Corner, breaking his right leg. (LAT)*

2000s

The first year of the new millennium was dominated by controversy surrounding the British Grand Prix. The race had been moved from its traditional July slot in the calendar to 23 April, Easter Sunday, a move suspected by some to be Bernie Ecclestone's way of reminding the BRDC just who was in charge.

Two weeks before the event, the BAR-Honda 002 of Ricardo Zonta crashed at Stowe Corner after suffering suspension failure at 190mph during testing. It vaulted the barriers, coming to rest upside-down just in front of the grandstands, albeit in a prohibited area where spectators would not be allowed. Zonta was uninjured, but the incident raised concerns for the safety of spectators and marshals alike.

But it was the heavy rain that fell in the weeks prior to the event that caused the biggest problems. Car parks became a quagmire, and the circuit was forced to close them on the Saturday in the hope of giving the ground time to recover for Sunday. This unprecedented step of effectively keeping spectators away on qualifying day, and having to promise refunds on all Saturday tickets, meant that the circuit would take a huge financial hit. Only 20,000 spectators were in attendance on the Saturday, a massive drop on the usual numbers.

The plan didn't work, however, and the car parks had not dried out by the following day. By

RIGHT *The cars assembled on the grid in front of the huge crowd for the 2009 Santander British Grand Prix. (LAT)*

9.20am on race day, the Northamptonshire police were advising people not to set out for the circuit. Many abandoned their cars at the roadside and tried to walk in, but thousands of fans still missed the Grand Prix because they were stuck in five-hour traffic jams that stretched for 18 miles.

To compound the problems, the F1 warm-up on race day morning had to be delayed because fog was preventing the medical helicopter from being able to fly. It also meant that corporate guests, used to being flown in, had to join the ordinary spectators in the long queues to the circuit.

Bernie Ecclestone claimed it was not his fault that the race had been given an April date, despite the fact that he was solely responsible for the F1 calendar. He cited congestion on the fixture list as the reason, though most people were sceptical about this. He also blamed the BRDC for not being prepared for bad weather. "Silverstone has done what it normally does and has not taken the weather into consideration," he said at the time. "I get the blame for most things, but I don't deserve it for this."

Denys Rohan, Silverstone's managing director said: "This weekend has underlined the problems of racing at this time of year, and I hope people will understand that we have done everything we possibly can. You simply cannot tarmac 200 acres of land." He had a point regarding the time of year. The last time a Grand Prix was held in the UK over the Easter weekend – the 1993 European GP at Donington – it was horrendously wet as well.

The circuit was called before the FIA's World Council on 21 June, but escaped without punishment. Despite fears that the following year's race would be removed from the calendar, it was given a provisional date of 13 May 2001, and the circuit was required to provide proof by October that changes had been made to the way the event was organised and that solutions had been found to traffic and parking problems. A month later, the circuit announced that it was to restrict the number of cars allowed into the circuit at the Grand Prix to just 18,000 instead of the 30,000 which had been reached in the past.

In October, with the necessary assurances in place, the World Motor Sport Council announced that the British Grand Prix would revert to its traditional July date after all, rather than the provisional one in May. Rohan explained: "We had the wettest winter for 260 years and the wettest April since the year dot. The chances of us having these problems again in July are much less, but we are planning on the worst-case basis. We will be issuing a number of car passes and everything

will be done in advance. There will be no tickets sold on the gate, because that would not allow us to plan."

It was unfortunate that the 2000 British Grand Prix had also marked the opening of the BRDC's new clubhouse, overlooking Brooklands and Woodcote corners. The building had been funded from the damages received over incorrect advice from the club's solicitors about the Silverstone Motor Group a few years previously, but it added fuel for the circuit's detractors, such as Ecclestone, who claimed that the money could have been better spent.

The club was trying, though. By June it had restructured its operation, and the commercial arm of Silverstone was to be split, with a new company to work independently of the BRDC, thereby separating commercial risks from the club itself.

In October, the circuit announced ambitious plans for a new £8.5 million pits and paddock complex on the infield adjacent to the Hangar Straight, with Stowe becoming the first corner, provided the British Grand Prix remained at the track. The facility was to include state-of-the-art garages, offices, large hospitality areas and a new media centre. The existing pits complex would be retained and used for support races, while a new centre, exclusively for F1 teams (with garages allocated for their use whenever they wanted), would be created. In addition, a new access road from the entrance on the A413 on the east side of the circuit would be built, exclusively for the use of F1 personnel.

The current pits complex had been opened in 1995 and the circuit had spent £24 million since then, but the plans would remain in limbo unless a deal was struck with Octagon, the IPG's motor sports division, for the Grand Prix to be run at Silverstone, a scenario which was beginning to look more likely.

In January, Nicola Foulston had resigned as chief executive of Brands Hatch Leisure and Rob Bain had taken over the position. He soon entered into discussions with the Donington circuit in Leicestershire about the possibility of hosting the British Grand Prix there, a move that was designed to put more pressure on the BRDC, since Donington was a far more viable option as a venue than Brands Hatch, but nothing came of the talks.

The BRDC was in a strong position now, since Octagon had had its planning application for Brands Hatch called in for review, meaning that time was running out to develop the circuit in time for the 2002 Grand Prix. The company, remember, had signed a deal with Ecclestone to run the event and was now obliged to find somewhere to hold it. Rob Bain, managing director at BHL, explained: "The only way the Grand Prix could be saved would be for the Brands Hatch Group to lease the Silverstone circuit under what I would describe as favourable terms. That happened."

At an EGM on 18 December 2000, the membership approved a deal for the British Grand Prix to be run at Silverstone and for Octagon to take over the operation of the circuit under a 15-year lease. The deal was said to be worth £8 million a year, with the BRDC retaining the clubhouse and the members all of their rights.

It meant that the day-to-day running of the circuit would now be handled by BHL, and one of the consequences was redundancies at Silverstone. *Autosport* reported in February 2001 that up to 50 staff could lose their jobs at the circuit because of duplication of roles within the group. Silverstone at that time employed 160 people.

In March 2001, the circuit announced that it intended to replace its gravel traps with high-grip concrete run-offs as part of a revamp to take place after that year's British GP, and then three months later, on 20 June, Octagon Motorsports and the BRDC announced phase one of a master plan for Silverstone, intended to be completed in time for the 2003 British Grand Prix. Instead of a new pit and paddock complex being built on the Hangar Straight, it was now to be situated between Club and Abbey corners, with a new track configuration that turned sharp right and then left at Abbey Corner, taking cars along a straight to join the existing Club Straight close to the Becketts esses. The track then rejoined the existing Grand Prix circuit at Brooklands. The intended layout was very close to the one finally adopted and built ten years later in 2011.

Other proposed changes included a banked final turn at Club Corner and it was still intended that the new pits should be dedicated to F1 teams, allowing them a permanent base for testing. The £40 million development was to be jointly funded by Octagon, Bernie Ecclestone's Formula One Management (FOM) company and the BRDC.

In addition, the long-awaited link road between the M1 and M40, which had been approved by the local council in March 2000 and would cut through the circuit's northern car park, was to be built in 2002, with a four-lane entrance road connecting this to the circuit.

The new configuration was part of a five-year plan, which included a visitor centre, leisure park, hotel, retail outlets and drivers' academy and

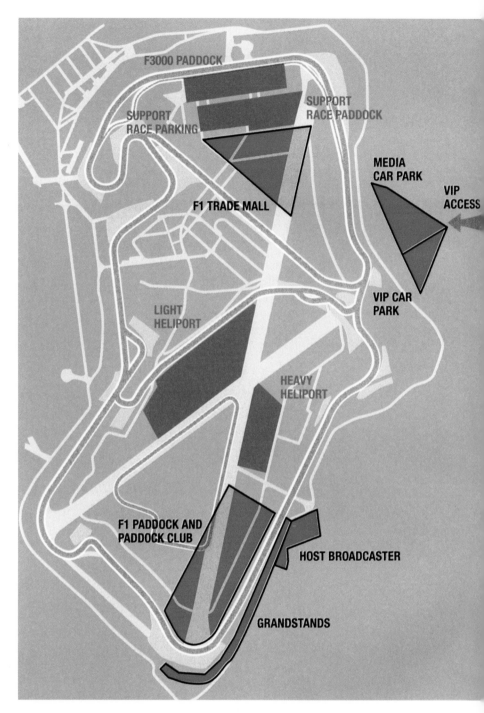

technology centre. Former world champion Jackie (by now Sir Jackie) Stewart was lobbying hard for the government to match the money that was already being put into the scheme. He had met with Prime Minister Tony Blair twice in eight days during December 2000 in an attempt to get £40 million of government money to invest in British motorsport to match the same amount already committed to Silverstone by Octagon, FOM and the BRDC.

The proposed new layout would not affect national and club racing, which would be able to continue. "The BRDC has been an immense

ABOVE *The initial plans for a new pit and paddock complex, as published in* Autosport *in October 2000, had the start line moved to Hangar Straight.*

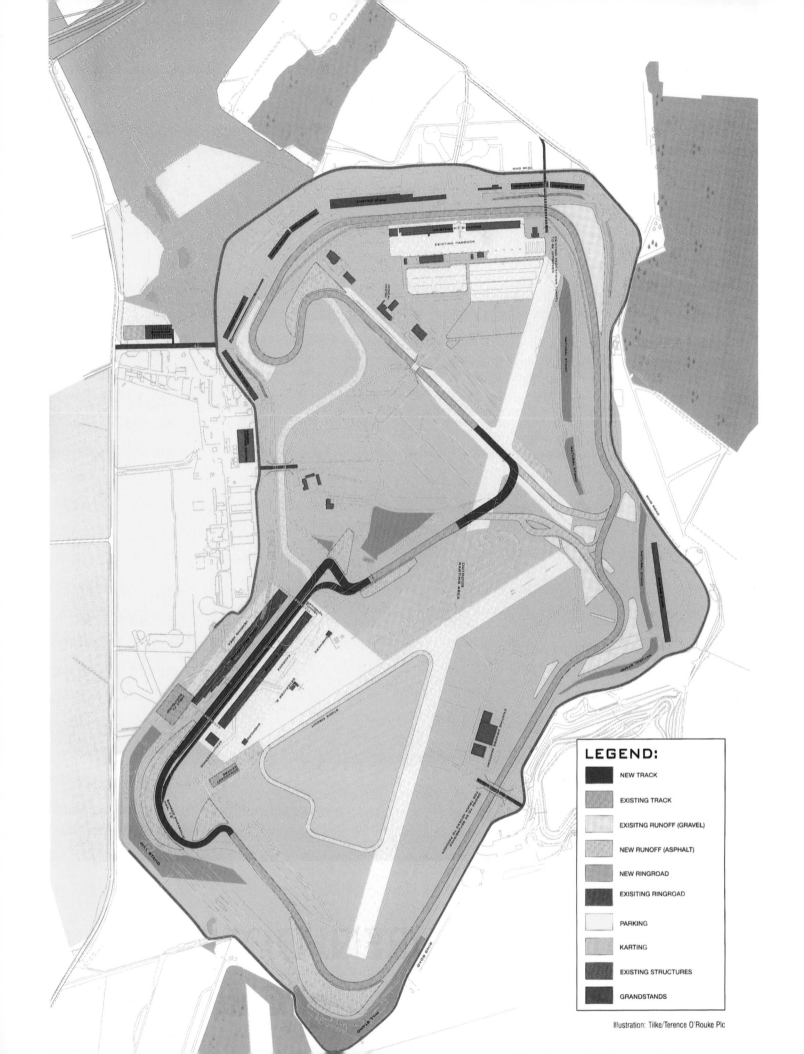

LEGEND:

- NEW TRACK
- EXISTING TRACK
- EXISITNG RUNOFF (GRAVEL)
- NEW RUNOFF (ASPHALT)
- NEW RINGROAD
- EXISITING RINGROAD
- PARKING
- KARTING
- EXISTING STRUCTURES
- GRANDSTANDS

Illustration: Tilke/Terence O'Rouke Plc

supporter of grassroots motorsport and we'll continue to be so," said Stewart. "It is an important part of the growth of motorsport, and the design of the new facility has been created specifically for that benefit. We are hoping to cause as little disruption as possible to the rest of the activities at the circuit, and that includes the driving school."

For the 2001 British Grand Prix, in order to ensure there would be no repeat of the previous year's problems, attention was focused on short-term parking and improvements in the traffic flow. Gateways were to be widened, six kilometres of new access roads into the car parks built and 660,000sq ft of reinforced meshing laid in the car parks themselves.

Tickets for the event were available only in advance, with none on the gate. The circuit also operated a park-and-ride scheme, with a dedicated fast-track lane for coaches, but charged £29 per person for it. Despite this, access to and from the circuit still proved difficult, and the FIA demanded to know why. Rob Bain admitted that mistakes had been made regarding the traffic arrangements, but claimed that they had been inherited from the previous management and promised to make changes.

And changes were made – when the FIA published the 2002 calendar in October, the British Grand Prix was only given a provisional date of 7 July, but at the end of the month Silverstone announced that the maximum crowd for the 2002 Grand Prix would be cut from 90,000 to just 60,000, in a bid to overcome the traffic congestion problems. Park-and-ride facilities would be provided free, but a car park ticket could be purchased for £45, albeit with the same limit of 18,000 cars on site. In addition, the circuit's main entrance on to the Dadford Road would be widened to four lanes. As a result, when the World Council of the FIA met on 14 December it gave the go-ahead for the event.

After the announcement, Rob Bain said that the plans for the new pit and paddock complex after Club Corner were being abandoned, and that a new facility would instead be built on the site of the existing pits, which would be demolished. The first phase of improvements to the circuit, though, would involve building new roads and creating better access. A £10.6 million project to achieve this would include an extra lane being added to the Dadford Road from where it left the A43 Silverstone by-pass when it was built, a new main entrance to the circuit and new hardstanding car parks with capacity for 15,000 cars.

Responsibility for construction of the link road between the by-pass and the circuit rested with Octagon, but rain over the winter and the knock-on effect of the foot and mouth epidemic of 2001 meant that by February 2002 the by-pass was behind schedule. The by-pass was only part of a £56.6 million project to build a dual carriageway from the M40 to Towcester. The Highways Agency said that while it didn't anticipate the new road being fully open to the public by July, it did anticipate being able to open significant parts for race fans heading to Silverstone.

This was only after some serious lobbying by Sir Jackie Stewart, who had taken over as BRDC president after Ken Tyrrell, who had succeeded Lord Hesketh the previous year, died from cancer on 25 August 2001. Stewart persuaded then Prime Minister Tony Blair to fast-track the scheme with a grant to ensure it was completed in time. "Tony Blair got us £8 million to finish one side of the by-pass for the British Grand Prix of 2002," he explained. "There were 13 weeks of foot and mouth disease where cattle and sheep could not be moved, and therefore they couldn't continue the construction work. I went to see Tony Blair and said: 'Without this being finished we're going to have the biggest traffic problem you've ever seen in any British motor sporting event. And there's 700 journalists coming to the Grand Prix and UK plc is going to get hugely embarrassed.'

"I met with the Under Secretary of State for Transport and put a very strong case up for it. In the end they refused it, but Tony Blair overrode it and committed eight million. And that's the only time the government has ever contributed anything to the British Grand Prix." Blair was subsequently criticised for having given a personal commitment for the by-pass to be finished in time for the Grand Prix, apparently against the advice of Cabinet colleagues.

Despite a sell-out for race day, attendance on Friday and Saturday at the 2002 Grand Prix appeared to be low, with empty grandstands. Even so, the event was a success, and by and large the new road and traffic arrangements worked as planned. Bain was delighted at the way the traffic had been managed and said they had already decided that ticket sales could be increased to 90,000 for 2003. But he wouldn't be around to see whether this was realised or not. The morning after the Grand Prix he resigned, incensed at comments made by Bernie Ecclestone, who had been unable to land his helicopter because of poor visibility. The F1 boss had instead arrived by car via a back entrance, and it had taken him over an hour to circumnavigate the circuit's internal road system to get to the paddock.

"The people here are paying a lot of money to be looked after and it's not happening," he said. "They don't deserve to have a Grand Prix because these people are not capable of organising a big event. It's a country fair masquerading as a world championship event. If our contract with them was up next year I wouldn't be too excited about keeping it."

Bain issued a statement saying: "It is disheartening still to hear gratuitous comments about the event and I do not wish them to overshadow what the team has achieved." Perhaps the last straw was the fact that he was also sanctioned by FIA officials for talking to the media about Ecclestone's comments, it being deemed an unauthorised press conference. The FIA banned him from the paddock at the following year's Grand Prix, but Bain decided to walk instead. His place as managing director of Octagon was taken by Michael Browning.

The continually varying on-off plans for a new pits and paddock complex continued when Octagon announced in August 2002 that it had decided to postpone the building of a new complex until 2004, in favour of bringing forward plans to improve the public viewing areas at the circuit in time for the 2003 Grand Prix. The move was in answer to Bernie Ecclestone's earlier criticisms of facilities at the track. At the end of September, with the completion of the Dadford Road link from the A43, Silverstone's new main entrance was opened.

Things were still in a state of flux, though. By early 2003 it was clear that Octagon's parent company, Interpublic wanted to get out of its motorsport deals. Octagon had lost £37 million in the first nine months of 2002 and Interpublic stated that it wanted to find "a resolution of the Octagon Motorsports situation". A large element of its outgoings was the sanctioning fee paid to Bernie Ecclestone's FOM company for the rights to host the British Grand Prix, as well as the rent for Silverstone paid to the BRDC, and in January 2003 the company held high-level talks with Ecclestone about reducing costs.

Even against this background, Octagon was still investing heavily in the circuit. The network of internal roads was being improved, including a new route from the main entrance to the paddock. An extra bridge was to be built over Club Straight and new toilet blocks constructed, while the gravel trap run-off area at Stowe was covered in asphalt and new marshals' posts, barriers and debris fencing installed.

In March 2003, Interpublic announced that it had "retained independent advisors to evaluate exit strategies relative to its motorsports assets".

Bernie Ecclestone blamed the amount that the company had to pay the BRDC for leasing Silverstone as the reason, but club chairman Martin Brundle disagreed, saying it was the sanctioning fee that forced Octagon out. "It is clear for anyone to see that Bernie seems to have been trying hard to destabilise the British Grand Prix, Silverstone and the BRDC," he said.

In June, Ecclestone stepped up his pressure on the circuit, claiming that the money that had been put in by FOM, Octagon and the BRDC had been wasted. "We put in £20 million each," he said, "but the silly Octagon people let the BRDC manage the money. The BRDC spent two-thirds of it on doing things for them and their members, and nothing for Octagon and us." Meanwhile, Octagon had said that it would stand by its Silverstone lease and Grand Prix contracts despite Ecclestone stating that he felt the BRDC should be running and promoting the event.

It is noticeable that the number of significant meetings at the circuit had dropped under Octagon's stewardship throughout 2002–03, although the traditional club meetings continued to be held and the company carried on investing in the infrastructure.

After the 2003 Grand Prix, Ecclestone again reiterated that he would be willing to guarantee the future of the event until 2015 provided the government and the BRDC committed to upgrading the circuit's facilities. "The BRDC cannot say that they can't afford to borrow money," he said. "They get £5 million a year in rent from Octagon and they don't spend anything. I have never seen any money come out of the BRDC. What really gets up my nose is that we have had all these bloody lousy facilities, but they managed to spend three million on their own clubhouse."

The BRDC defended its position, stating that all the decisions about development had been made in conjunction with Formula One Management, and disputing that it would be solely to blame if the British Grand Prix were removed from the calendar. Meanwhile, the 2003 event was hailed as a huge success. An innovation had been a post-race concert, which took place on the infield by Becketts, featuring Status Quo, Eddie Jordan and Damon Hill with their bands, to encourage spectators to stay behind and therefore stagger the flow of traffic leaving the circuit.

In January 2004, the Interpublic Group sold Brands Hatch, Snetterton, Oulton Park and Cadwell Park to MotorSport Vision, a company set up by former Grand Prix driver Jonathan Palmer. The deal would not affect Interpublic's contract to run the British Grand Prix at Silverstone but its

David Coulthard

"Historically, if you look at Silverstone's role, not only in British motor racing but in Grand Prix motor racing, it's played a large part. And if you look at where it sits in the UK and where a lot of the motorsports suppliers and teams are, a lot of them branch out within an hour or two hours of Silverstone. So I think Britain has a lot of great tracks, a lot of great history, but Silverstone has to be the number one.

"My father used to sponsor long circuit karting, so I would have gone there maybe as a ten- or eleven-year-old watching the long circuit racing. The first time I tested there myself was 1989 in a Formula Ford, and my first race would have been 1989 in Formula Ford on the National circuit.

"One of my outstanding memories is standing down at Stowe Corner in 1990, and the V12 Ferrari coming out of the morning mist and coming down Hangar Straight. You could obviously hear it long before you could see it. That was a pretty special sounding engine.

ABOVE *David Coulthard scored his second consecutive British Grand Prix victory in 2000, driving his West McLaren-Mercedes MP4/15 to victory ahead of team-mate Mika Häkkinen. (LAT)*

"My first British Grand Prix win in 1999 was where Mika had a problem with a wheel at the stop, so it was slightly fortunate, but I think the following year was a more complete victory in many ways. Obviously I'm happy to have had the chance to stand on the top spot of my home Grand Prix, and to do back-to-back British Grand Prix victories is a fantastic feeling.

"It's such a high-speed circuit that you've got to be very precise. You've got to have total confidence in your car and your ability to hold on. So it's a very different challenge from somewhere like Monaco, for instance, which is all 90–98 per cent entry speed because you can't afford to over-speed on entry, whereas at Silverstone you can't afford not to be 100 per cent on entry, apex and exit.

"I'd definitely say it's one of my top three or four Grand Prix tracks – Monaco, Spa, Silverstone, Suzuka."

motor sport arm, Brands Hatch Circuits Limited, was renamed Silverstone Motorsports Limited. Interpublic then decided to buy itself out of the contract to lease Silverstone, and three months later, in April 2004, it pulled the plug on its contract to host the British Grand Prix as well, agreeing to pay Ecclestone £55 million over five years to buy its way out. Effectively it was paying him for the privilege of not running the race, and in July it negotiated a settlement with the BRDC whereby the club was paid £27 million in instalments to terminate the lease on the circuit.

This left Silverstone back under the control of the BRDC, but with the task of rebuilding a business that had been damaged by uncertainty and still had a British Grand Prix contract to negotiate with Ecclestone. According to F1 journalist and then BRDC board member Alan Henry, writing in his book *The Battle for the British Grand Prix*, the BRDC initially proposed a three-year deal for 2005–2007, starting at $10.8 million and rising by the annual rate of inflation. The thing about Ecclestone's Grand Prix contracts is that they always have an escalator built into them, so that the cost of hosting each race increases over the life of the contract.

Despite the fact that he had effectively already been paid for these races, given that Interpublic had bought its way out of the contract, Ecclestone still insisted on playing tough. He wanted $15.9 million for 2005 and $17.3 million for 2006. He then proposed a seven-year deal starting at $13.5 million and rising by 10 per cent each year. He then revised this to remove the escalator, but with the proviso that his companies take over the lease and promotion of the event, rent-free, with the BRDC building a new pit and paddock complex but not receiving any income.

The good news for the circuit was that, for the first time since 1999, the 2004 British Grand Prix was set to be a sell-out. That year, 100,000 people had come through the gates over the weekend, with 90,000 the following year. In 2001 and 2002, sales had been restricted to just 60,000 to alleviate traffic problems, but in 2003 had gone up to 70,000. Despite some fans being unhappy that only three-day tickets could be bought for the event, a record 60,000 turned up for qualifying in 2004 and a capacity crowd of 100,000 on race day itself.

A major change as far as fans were concerned, though, was that ordinary spectators were no longer able to purchase Centre Transfer tickets, ending a long-standing tradition that had enabled access to the infield. The decision was based on poor sales of the tickets the previous year, but it meant that fans would have no opportunity to get close to the paddock or get autographs and photographs of drivers over the Grand Prix weekend. The viewing areas on the inside of Copse and Vale were also no longer available, but fans were allowed access to the infield for the popular post-race party, which this year featured the Beach Boys.

The race may have been a success, but the BRDC continued to argue with Ecclestone over the fee to stage the following year's race, and in July he said he would give the circuit until 30 September or it would be removed from the 2005 calendar. Sir Jackie Stewart said: "It is perfectly conceivable we will not have a British Grand Prix. We can't allow our club or our company to go bankrupt just because the BRDC is blamed because it can't find money for an uneconomical project. If Bernie likes to give a bit back, then we can run a joint venture."

The club offered to pay £6 million a year for three years for the right to promote the event, but Ecclestone said this was significantly less than other European circuits were paying. He wanted around £1.5–£2 million a year more in a seven-year deal. The BRDC, however, was unwilling to commit beyond 2007 as that was when the Concorde Agreement, which covers the terms under which the F1 teams compete, was up for renewal. It also claimed that it couldn't risk paying any more without endangering the future of the circuit and the club. Part of the problem stemmed from the fact that a circuit hosting a Grand Prix only gained income from ticket sales. The money from trackside advertising, hospitality, television rights and title sponsorship went elsewhere.

In October, when the FIA issued its draft calendar of Grand Prix races for 2005, the British event had been omitted.

With the deadline of 13 October for the final F1 calendar to be announced, the BRDC finally made an offer of £9 million per race for two years, to cover 2005 and 2006, with a five-year option. The club was able to increase its offer because of a rearrangement of its tax liabilities, thereby releasing extra cash. Ecclestone, however, was now proposing only a one-year deal at £7.4 million with a six-year option. The BRDC would also have to redevelop the pits and paddock complex prior to the following year's race for the option to be taken up, a task which it said was not possible within the timescale. Alex Hooton, then chief executive of the BRDC, said: "As much as we want to keep the race, we cannot tie ourselves to a six-year deal which has a 10 per cent year-on-year accumulator attached to it. That would not be the proper thing to do."

While Ecclestone was publicly stating that the British event should not be a 'special case', it is interesting that he was still willing to try to negotiate a settlement instead of just walking away, but by now his patience was running out. "I'm tired of the whole thing," he said. "The deal on the table to the BRDC is a one-year one with a six-year option. I spoke to the government minister and he urged me to meet them on price – I've met them 50-50 on price, even though that's put me in an awkward position with other events. They were supposed to sign a contract by the end of September and that hasn't happened."

When the final calendar for 2005 was published, Silverstone had been allocated a provisional date of 3 July, the same day as the Wimbledon men's tennis final, which it was felt would impact on attendance. Ecclestone was understandably unsympathetic. In a letter to BRDC chairman Ray Bellm, part of which was published in *Autosport*, he said: "I allocated the British Grand Prix a provisional date, exactly as you asked, since when the BRDC have lost no time complaining in the media about the July date, because of a possibility that a British tennis player may reach the finals of Wimbledon on the same day. A British man has not reached the Wimbledon singles final since 1938."

The BRDC need not have worried. When the FIA World Council finally ratified the F1 calendar in December, the French race, which had initially been omitted, had been reinstated and allocated the 3 July date. Silverstone was scheduled for the following week, 10 July.

Finally, on 3 December 2004, it was announced that the BRDC had reached a five-year agreement with Ecclestone, securing the future of the race at Silverstone until 2009. This was achieved because the F1 teams agreed to an extra two races on the calendar (French and British) above the number they had originally agreed to under the Concorde Agreement, and Ecclestone brokered a deal between Silverstone and the teams for them to race. He had wanted a longer contract than just one or two years in order to tie circuits into F1 and head off a possible challenge from the rival Grand Prix World Championship (GPWC) series, which was being proposed by Ferrari, Renault, Mercedes and BMW.

Instead of solving the problems, the Grand Prix deal to host the race until 2009, which had been agreed between Bellm and Ecclestone, proved to be a source of further internal fighting within the BRDC. Bellm had been appointed chairman in 2004 and clashed frequently with Sir Jackie Stewart over the British Grand Prix contract and the long-term future of the circuit. He felt that negotiations should have been left to the chairman or chief executive and not be undertaken by the president.

Bellm and Stewart fell out. Stewart had wanted a three-year Grand Prix contract which would end coincident with the end of the current Concorde Agreement, but instead a five-year deal had been signed. On 11 January 2005, Bellm was ousted as chairman, and he was replaced by Stuart Rolt. Afterwards, Bellm was critical of the club, saying that it had got rid of the person who had delivered the Grand Prix.

The move split the BRDC board into pro-Stewart and pro-Bellm factions, causing much unrest within the club and calls for Stewart to resign as president. A motion of no confidence in both Stewart and the board was defeated at an EGM in May 2005, resulting in Bellm resigning as a director. Stewart nonetheless stepped down as president at the 2006 AGM.

Despite all the political wrangling and internal fighting, Silverstone as a circuit was still hugely popular with spectators and enthusiasts. In 2005, an FIA survey of F1 fans listed Silverstone as the third favourite circuit, behind only Monaco and Spa. The result was borne out by the sell-out attendance at that year's Grand Prix, with 100,000 on race day and 200,000 over the event's three days.

In October 2005, the circuit unveiled a £600 million plan for a racing, leisure and business complex – and commissioned financial services firm KPMG to look for an investor to join the project. The scheme would involve leasing the 800-acre site for 125 years to a consortium willing to invest. Rather than submit a proposal itself, the BRDC was looking for potential investors to propose their own plans. BRDC chief executive Alex Hooton said that the club had come to the conclusion that it would never be able to make enough money out of motor sport alone to pay for the most basic upgrades required to make the circuit a 21st-century facility. More basic improvements continued, though, as work started the following year on a second grandstand at Club and an expansion of the seating at Copse, Stowe and Luffield.

As a result of the search for a partner, Sir Jackie Stewart wrote to all BRDC members in early 2006 asking that they back the board's recommendation to appoint property development company St Modwen to undertake redevelopment of the circuit. Another proposal was that horse-racing promoter Northern Racing should take over the running of the British Grand Prix for the next 25 years. These two were the BRDC board's preferred bidders. Under the deal, the club would remain owners of the track but it would be leased to St Modwen on a 125-year lease for around £1 million a year, during which time the company would redevelop the circuit and construct retail, hotel and leisure facilities.

An EGM was called for 22 February to allow members to vote on the idea, but the meeting was described by one member as "five hours of confrontation", and the investors from St Modwen and Northern Racing who were present were heckled and jeered. There was concern from some quarters about proposals for residential properties to be built close to the circuit, but the opposition was seen by others as placing the future of the Grand Prix in jeopardy, since the circuit needed upgrades before it would be granted a contract beyond 2009. A vote on the proposal was postponed.

In March, the BRDC admitted that it would have to rethink its plan as it became obvious that there was no chance of the deal being agreed, and Alex Hooton resigned as chief executive at the end of June.

It was clear that something needed to be done to stop the infighting at the BRDC, and this finally happened at the 2006 AGM on 28 April. A proposal to remove the existing board and replace it with a caretaker board was defeated and, with Sir Jackie Stewart standing down as president, Damon Hill was elected in his place. It marked the start of a period of reason within the club.

BRDC chairman Stuart Rolt explained: "Damon has no political internal club agendas and, of course, he has a very high profile. Above all, this marks a shift in generation. He is a young man by BRDC standards. This is a tremendous change. There is a perception that BRDC members are out of touch with the modern world, and that is something we have to dispose of."

After being elected, Hill asked members, "Do you want a Grand Prix or not?" He said the club's future was in its own hands and it had to decide whether it wished to redevelop the circuit to remain as host to the Grand Prix or lose its F1 heritage. Hill also believed that it was unlikely that the government would put any money into the track, since F1 was perceived as being awash with money, even though Silverstone was run on a very tight budget.

As F1's popularity had increased over the years, so the governments of countries such as Turkey, China, India and Bahrain were happy to fund magnificent new tracks in order to make a statement about their country. And they were willing to pay Ecclestone's premium rates of around $50 million to host a Grand Prix, but with government backing.

Meanwhile, the facilities at Silverstone had fallen behind those of other circuits, particularly new ones being built. There was also the perennial problem of a non-profit making members' club running a world-class facility, and whereas elsewhere Ecclestone would be dealing with the head of a motorsport organisation or a government, he baulked at what he felt was the BRDC members' apparent attitude that it was their God-given right to have a Grand Prix.

But many people within the sport also felt that there had to be a British Grand Prix. Sir Frank Williams said: "Most F1 teams believe there really has to be a British Grand Prix because it's one of the core races in the world championship and has been for more than 50 years, but also nearly all the teams are based in Great Britain. Most of F1's suppliers are based in Great Britain. It would be a setback for Williams for several reasons, one of which is morale and teambuilding – our staff need a weekend with their wives, to see their product racing. It would destabilise the home industry far too much to remove the Grand Prix."

In early 2007, Richard Phillips, who had taken over as managing director of Silverstone Circuits in November 2004, told *Autosport* that he had already met with Ecclestone on a couple of occasions during the previous six months and was optimistic about a deal beyond 2009 being agreed.

At this time, Silverstone, which was valued at £61 million according to the accounts of the BRDC, paid around £7 million a year to host the Grand Prix, with a 10 per cent escalator increasing that cost year-on-year. But in order for it to continue to hold the event, Ecclestone not only wanted more money but better facilities, including a new pits and paddock complex and a new media centre.

On 30 July 2007, at an EGM, the BRDC voted to go ahead with a £25 million project for a new pit and paddock complex to be located between Club and Abbey, new grandstands, hotel and conference centre and a science park. Work on a driver-training centre for Porsche Cars GB, located on the outside of Hangar Straight, was already underway.

The Grand Prix that year had been a huge success, with ticket sales boosted by the arrival in F1 of British driver Lewis Hamilton, who helped attract record crowds of 42,000 on the Friday, 80,000 on Saturday and a capacity 85,000 on Sunday. Before that, though, Ecclestone had upped the ante in May when he said that he was not interested in negotiating a new Grand Prix contract with the BRDC any longer, and would only strike a deal if the club gave up responsibility for running the event. "I want to deal with a promoter rather than the BRDC," he told *Autosport*. "It is too difficult with the BRDC because you get no guarantees with them."

In response to this, the BRDC appointed an independent specialist team, headed by Neil England, to negotiate a new post-2009 contract. England was a member of the FIA Commission and had previously been involved with sponsorship of F1 by Gallaher's tobacco. The idea was to bring in someone who was not "sullied or tainted", as Damon Hill put it, by any previous connection to the BRDC. "There have been many problems with this relationship historically, and I think we've solved all those by acting as trustees and guardians rather than being directly involved in the business decisions," Hill said at the time.

Ahead of the 2008 Grand Prix, Silverstone announced an additional 2,200 grandstand seats would be available, but the future of the race was still in doubt beyond 2009. How serious the situation had become was highlighted prior to the event when Hill said he thought the circuit's chances of retaining the race were only 50-50.

Then, on Thursday 3 July 2008, on the eve of the British Grand Prix, Bernie Ecclestone signed a ten-year deal for Donington Park in Leicestershire to host the British Grand Prix from 2010 onwards. The announcement was made the following morning, despite a request from the BRDC to delay it, and the bombshell totally overshadowed the rest of the weekend's proceedings.

Ecclestone had got fed up with waiting. He'd offered the BRDC a contract in May of £11 million a race, with a 5 per cent escalator and a deadline of the Grand Prix weekend to sign it. He insisted he could have signed the Donington deal a lot sooner but had set a deadline of the British Grand Prix weekend. "Obviously these people [Donington] wanted to get it done quickly, because they've got to get cracking," he said. "They would have signed three months ago if they could have done.

"I said to them wait until we've got a 'no go', and if we haven't got a definite answer by Silverstone, we're in business with you. So that's what's happened. Silverstone arrived, we didn't have an answer, so that was it."

"Nothing had particularly gone wrong with the negotiations," explained Silverstone's managing director Richard Phillips. "What had happened is that we hadn't got the planning through. Bernie had basically said, 'Here's the contract, sign the damn thing and you can have the Grand Prix.' And if we had signed at that time, we'd have probably bankrupted the club. So that's the reality of where we were. We had no means to build the pits at the time, even though we were going for planning for it, no money in order to be able to do that, and no means to be able to guarantee that we'd be able to pay the fee level that he was putting on the table.

"So he said, 'All right, well if you don't sign I'm going off to Donington.' He made that threat and he carried it through, basically. And that's what we were faced with on that Friday, which was a life-changing time to be honest, and we thought the whole thing had gone to pants, and we then, over a period of time, sort of worked our way back into it behind the scenes."

Ecclestone denied personal issues had come into play over his dealings with the BRDC. "They'd had a contract on their desks for a few months and they haven't signed. The important thing really and truly is that we have got a British Grand Prix still, whereas we would have lost it 100 per cent."

The lease to Donington had been sold by circuit owner Tom Wheatcroft to Donington Ventures Leisure (DVL), a company set up by software entrepreneur Simon Gillet and property developer Paul White, but questions remained as to how DVL was going to be able to raise the necessary funds to bring the circuit up to the required standard. Gillet, however, kept stating that details of the funding would be made public in due course.

The deal DVL had struck with Ecclestone to host the Grand Prix was for $25 million a year, more than that paid by Silverstone. On 9 January 2009, planning permission for the work was granted and the bulldozers moved into action. Some still remained sceptical, though. McLaren team principal Ron Dennis stated: "I really do struggle to understand how the economics of Donington will work. The contract will be a dollar-based contract and they have had a 25 per cent swing in the dollar. It has also got a massive investment into infrastructure."

Silverstone hadn't given up hope by any means. Despite what Ecclestone had said about the race being at Donington or not being held at all, Richard Phillips insisted that the circuit must be ready to step into the breach if plans to develop Donington were delayed. This would mean the circuit pushing ahead with plans for its new pits and paddock complex between Club and Abbey.

But that wasn't all. In February 2009, plans were announced for the biggest changes to the layout of the Silverstone track itself in 20 years. The circuit was to be reprofiled at Abbey, with the corner becoming a right-hander sending cars the wrong way up the International circuit to a new left-hander, the 'Arrowhead', which took them on to Club Straight and back down towards Brooklands. The new configuration would be 3.52 miles in length, and new banking and grandstands would be built at the Arrowhead.

"There were two reasons really to change the circuit," Phillips explained. "One was because it just wasn't safe for motorcycle racing, so although we had grandfather rights for World Superbikes and things, the old Bridge section there wasn't right, so it needed changing if we really wanted to bring something like MotoGP back here.

"And the other thing was it was actually value inside the circuit in terms of development. So if we could indent the circuit and pull some of that land out into the general public areas in the future, that would be an added value."

Meanwhile, things weren't progressing well at Donington. In April, the Wheatcroft family sued DVL for £2.47 million in unpaid rent on the circuit. Gillet still stated that he was "100 per cent certain" that the 2010 Grand Prix would take place, despite the fact that Wheatcroft's signature was needed to obtain one of the crucial planning documents. Meanwhile, Bernie Ecclestone stated: "There is no question of us going back to Silverstone." However, he added later: "If they were to do what they should have done, and what we've been asking them to do for five years, we'd have a look at it."

The mood at the 2009 British Grand Prix meeting over the weekend of 19–21 June was certainly very different from a year previously, and there was almost a party atmosphere – if this was going to be the last Grand Prix for a while, then let's at least make it a good one. And that's exactly what did happen. For a start, Donington's plight seemed to indicate that it was unlikely the race would take place there in 2010, and anyway Silverstone had secured the prestigious MotoGP

– stolen from under Donington's nose – and was pressing ahead with plans for that.

"We were, to be fair, running two business plans," explained Phillips. "One with a Grand Prix and one without. MotoGP was strategic. Donington was focusing on the Grand Prix and we knew their business plan would have to be more than just one event, so they were thinking they'd got MotoGP and World Superbikes and all these different events. Put the jewel in the crown – the Grand Prix – go out to investors and they'll invest in it.

"So, during that period we pinched MotoGP and World Superbikes and left them with the Grand Prix contract, which they then couldn't fulfil and that all fell over. So to an extent it was strategic, bringing MotoGP here. We wanted to have it back actually, it was on our list of target events and we're very pleased to have it, but we might have taken a bit longer over those negotiations had the Donington issue not been there."

And despite having previously stated that the race would not return to Silverstone, even if Donington was not ready in time for the 2010 event, Ecclestone backtracked, saying: "We've got an agreement and I'm hoping they can complete the agreement and do all the things they are supposed to do. And if they can't, for sure we will come back to Silverstone."

Silverstone's position was also strengthened by the contrast between its event and the previous Grand Prix held just a fortnight before in Turkey. Attendance there was pitifully low, whereas at Silverstone around 83,000 fans turned out for the Friday practice sessions alone, with a record figure for the weekend as a whole. If ever the powers that be needed reminding of where the heart of F1 lay, it was demonstrated amply over that June weekend.

As the year went on, it became increasingly apparent that the Donington Grand Prix was never going to happen. In June, Ecclestone extended the contract with the circuit to 17 years in order to help hospitality sales, but in August he gave a deadline of the end of September for DVL to produce a bank guarantee for the £80 million it needed to upgrade the track. This was extended to 9 October, and when that passed he said that they were in breach of contract and had just two weeks to remedy the situation.

By the end of October, Silverstone was in negotiations with Ecclestone to secure a new deal to host the Grand Prix.

"If you're in the industry, you know what it takes to put on a Grand Prix, how much effort it takes to build the facilities that are required and so on," said Phillips. "If you're not in the business and looking from the outside, you'd probably be under the impression somebody else has signed the contract, that's fine, things will happen. So we had to sit there, rather than shaking our fists and saying bah, hoo, we said well good luck to them but if they can't succeed, which we knew they wouldn't be able to, then we were here. And that continued for another 12 months until the 2009 Grand Prix. Bernie was then getting a bit less dogged in his 'I'm going off to Donington, well maybe Silverstone', but it still took until November or December that year to actually do the deal."

As part of its development programme, the circuit announced that it was to host club racing on the Stowe circuit, which had traditionally been used for driver training and track experience days, from 2010. The circuit was to be extended from 0.795 miles to 1.15 miles and new pit garages and hospitality units built. The move meant that, together with the National and Southern circuits, it would be possible to hold three separate licensed events at once.

Finally, on 7 December 2009, Silverstone signed a 17-year deal to host the British Grand Prix from 2010 onwards. By the end of the day tickets, which would normally have been available the previous summer, were at a record level of advanced sales.

The unprecedented term of the contract meant the circuit could finally make long-term investments into developing the track and upgrading the infrastructure. Richard Phillips explained: "In the past we've always had five-year deals and we've never been able to make the investment required to bring the circuit forward. The 17-year deal gives us that ability now to invest."

The plan was for the new layout to be ready towards March and in use in time for the 2010 Grand Prix. The new pit and paddock complex would be built between Club and Abbey corners, allowing the existing pits to be used while the new build was in progress. In this way, racing could continue at the circuit uninterrupted.

What had seemed like a disaster had finally worked in Silverstone's favour, and even Simon Gillet had joked that he had "done what no one else has managed to do and united the BRDC".

It is certainly true that, had Silverstone agreed to the original five-year contract that Ecclestone was demanding, it would not have been able to invest in the same way, and the future would have remained uncertain. As it was, a tempestuous decade had come to a close with the circuit's future, together with that of its blue riband event (the British Grand Prix), finally secured.

Martin Whitmarsh

"Silverstone is important because I think a lot of us still feel that it's the home of Grand Prix racing, and for teams in the UK it's an opportunity for lots of our staff who don't get to see the cars running to go and see them. It's the home of some great races. The drivers have loved the circuit, we've all got memories of triumphs and disasters that have happened there, so I think it's important in that respect. I think for this country not to have a Grand Prix would be pretty awful.

ABOVE McLaren team principal Martin Whitmarsh feels that it is the fans who make Silverstone so special. (LAT)

"One of the things about Silverstone is that it's one of the last camping venues. We used to go to a lot of Grands Prix, and we had a lot of fans who were real advocates of racing, camping around the circuits, but increasingly that's not the case. You turn up at circuits with people who have gone to perhaps watch a Grand Prix but aren't the fanatics that you get there. One of the magical things about Silverstone actually is the crowd that surrounds it, the campsites and the sense that you get of people who are just real enthusiasts for the sport. And so it's really the people, more than the physical entity, which makes it for me.

"You're aware of the atmosphere and the spectators because they bump into you in the morning, they talk to you about it and you can see, feel and sense the passion. However you go in, whether you go in by helicopter, whether you drive in, or whatever, you see them all. It has an atmosphere that has seemed to become unique. There's not really another Grand Prix with such a contingent of people who are living under canvas for the three days of the event.

"We've had a few wins, so certainly for me – winning with Mika, winning with Lewis – there were some great moments. Winning with Juan Pablo was a funny moment for various reasons, and there were also some sad ones. Running Ayrton out of fuel in '91 on the last lap was a bit grim. Like any venue you have a mixture of memories from it, and I've been going there for over 20 years.

"I think it was '91, we were having an interesting season and things weren't going terribly well in the race and, about the only time in my memory, I left the garage with a few laps to go, got on my bicycle and rode down to the bottom end of the circuit and got to around Club where Ayrton came round on the last lap and to my horror stopped in front of me, run out of fuel, climbed out of the car, and I was literally stood by the side of the track as he was walking towards me. I remember the horror of it."

2000

■ The Foster's British Grand Prix was held over the Easter weekend of 21–23 April, prompting the circuit to promote it with the slogan "Good Friday, Great Saturday, Grand Prix Sunday", but torrential rain in the weeks beforehand meant that the car parks were waterlogged, and 18-mile traffic jams built up as spectators struggled to get into the circuit. Race day itself was dry, though, and David Coulthard in his West McLaren-Mercedes MP4/15 scored his second home victory after making a bold move around the outside at Stowe on lap 31 to take the lead from pole-sitter Rubens Barrichello's Ferrari F1-2000. The Brazilian retired later, leaving Coulthard's team-mate Mika Häkkinen to make it a McLaren one-two, with Michael Schumacher's Ferrari in third.

■ Mark Webber splashed his way to victory in Saturday's wet F3000 encounter in his European Arrows-run Lola-Zytek B99/50. Conditions were so bad that the race was started behind the safety car, with Darren Manning's Arden Lola the initial leader before Webber forced his way past. Justin Wilson took third for the Nordic team. In the supporting Porsche Supercup event, rally ace Richard Burns, competing as a guest driver, barrel-rolled at Club after being hit by another car. Burns was unhurt in the incident.

ABOVE *The F3000 race at the 2000 Foster's British Grand Prix meeting had to be started behind the safety car due to the soaked track. (LAT)*

RIGHT *David Coulthard chases pole-sitter Rubens Barrichello for the lead of the 2000 Foster's British Grand Prix. Soon after, Coulthard took his West McLaren-Mercedes MP4/15 past the Ferrari F1-2000 in a bold move at Stowe. (LAT)*

■ The circuit hosted two 500km races (one for the European Le Mans Series (ELMS) and the other for FIA GT cars) over the weekend of 13–14 May at its 'Days of Thunder' meeting. The ELMS event started at 6pm on Saturday evening and ran into the dusk in front of 11,000 spectators. The pole-sitter and early leader was the Rafanelli Lola-Judd B2K/10 of Mimmo Schiattarella and Didier de Radigues, until this was delayed by a broken throttle cable, leaving the BMW V12 LMR pairing of JJ Lehto and Jörg Müller the unexpected victors after an enthralling race-long battle with the two works Panoz cars and the sole Audi R8R. David Brabham and Jan Magnussen took the runner-up spot in their Panoz LMP-1 Roadster S after team-mates Hiroki Katoh and Johnny O'Connell, who were running second, stopped on the circuit with transmission failure on the last lap, leaving the Audi R8R of Allan McNish and Rinaldo Capello to take third.

■ The following day, 14 May, Julian Bailey and Jamie Campbell-Walter gave Lister its first British Empire Trophy victory since 1957, in their Lister Storm GT2. The pair finished a full minute ahead of the Chrysler-Viper GTS-R of Mike Hezemans and David Hart.

■ Takuma Sato scored his maiden British F3 victory at the PowerTour meeting on 21 May in his Carlin Motorsport Dallara-Mugen Honda F300, beating the similar Manor Motorsport car of Antonio Pizzonia.

BELOW *The rear of the field for the 2000 European Le Mans Series 500km race lines up in echelon formation prior to the Saturday evening start. (Author)*

■ James Thompson won the sprint race at the 11 June round of the *Auto Trader* British Touring Car Championship in his Honda Accord, while Yvan Muller took the honours in the feature race for Vauxhall in his Vectra.

■ The Coys International Historic Festival on 21–23 July celebrated 50 years of F1 and attracted 90,000 visitors over the three days. Nigel Mansell delighted the crowd with a series of donuts in front of the packed grandstands in a Lotus 79, while other stars in attendance included Tony Brooks, Jackie Stewart, Sir Stirling Moss and John Watson.

BELOW *The Rafanelli Lola-Judd B2K/10 of Mimmo Schiattarella and the Panoz LMP-1 Roadster S of David Brabham lead the ELMS field around Luffield for the rolling start of the 500km event in May 2000. (Author)*

■ Takuma Sato dominated the round of the Green Flag British F3 Championship at the PowerTour meeting on 20 August, in his Dallara-Mugen Honda F300, again beating Antonio Pizzonia's similar car.

■ The final round of the *Auto Trader* British Touring Car Championship was run on the evening of 16 September, with racing starting at 4.30pm. Tom Kristensen took his Honda Accord to victory in both the sprint and feature races. Third place in the feature race was enough for Alain Menu to secure the title in his Ford Mondeo.

■ Takuma Sato took his third Silverstone F3 victory of the year at the PowerTour meeting on 8 October in his Dallara-Mugen Honda F300, ahead of Andy Priaulx's Renault-powered Dallara F300.

2001

There were fears that the outbreak of foot and mouth disease in the UK might cause the cancellation of some race meetings, but the PowerTour meeting on 1 April went ahead as planned. Newcomer James Courtney emerged the winner of round one of the Green Flag British F3 Championship in his Jaguar Racing Dallara-Mugen Honda F300, while Matt Davies in his Avanti-run Dallara-Opel Spiess F301 just held off the Fortec Renault-powered F301 of Gianmaria Bruni to win round two.

There was heartbreak for Jamie Campbell-Walter and Tom Coronel in the three-hour FIA GT Championship round on 13 May, as their Lister Storm, which had dominated the race, suffered steering failure just five laps from the end. This left Christophe Bouchut and Jean-Philippe Belloc to inherit the victory in their Labre Competition-run Chrysler Viper GTS-R, ahead of the Team Carsport Holland Viper of Michael and Sebastiaan Bleekemolen.

Vauxhall Astra driver Jason Plato took a brace of wins at the www.theAA.com British Touring Car Championship round run on the evening of 2 June, winning both the sprint and feature races.

Mika Häkkinen was the winner of the Foster's British Grand Prix on 15 July in his West McLaren-Mercedes MP4-16. The Finn took the lead from the pole-sitting Ferrari F2001 of Michael Schumacher on lap five, and a two-stop strategy by the McLaren team proved to be the correct one, allowing Häkkinen to take victory by 34sec. Schumacher was second, ahead of his team-mate Rubens Barrichello.

BELOW *McLaren scored a hat-trick of British Grand Prix victories when Mika Häkkinen took his Mercedes-powered MP4-16 to victory in the 2001 event ahead of the Ferrari F2001s of Michael Schumacher and Rubens Barrichello. (LAT)*

■ Sébastien Bourdais scored his maiden F3000 victory in Saturday's supporting race in his DAMS-run Lola-Zytek B99/50 ahead of Justin Wilson's Nordic entry, while the F3 International Invitation Challenge race on Sunday provided yet another Silverstone victory for Takuma Sato in his Carlin Motorsport Dallara-Mugen Honda F301, ahead of team-mate Anthony Davidson.

■ The 50th anniversary of Ferrari's first-ever Grand Prix victory by Froilán González in 1951 was marked by Michael Schumacher driving demonstration laps in the sister car to González's winning Ferrari 375 prior to Sunday's Grand Prix.

■ Ken Tyrrell, who had succeeded Lord Hesketh as president of the BRDC in 2000, died of cancer on 25 August.

■ The Silverstone Historic Festival moved from its usual late-July/early-August date to the Bank Holiday weekend of 25–27 August. The three-day event included a two-hour race on Saturday evening for Group C sports cars, run for the British Empire Trophy and won by the Jaguar XJR-11 of Graham Hathaway and Gary Pearson.

■ Phil Bennett won the sprint race at the 9 September round of the www.theAA.com British Touring Car Championship in his Egg Sport Vauxhall Astra. The works Astras of Yvan Muller and Jason Plato were leading the feature race when Plato tried to force his way past on the last lap as Muller's car suffered a misfire. The pair clashed, and Muller dropped to third. When Plato was handed a 30sec penalty for the incident, this left the other Egg Sport car of James Thompson the victor.

■ The PowerTour series came to a finale with night races on Friday 28 September and more events the following day. The final rounds of the Green Flag British F3 Championship were run on Saturday 29 September, Andy Priaulx winning a wet first race in his Alan Docking-run Dallara-Mugen Honda F399, after Takuma Sato spun out of the lead in his Carlin Motorsport Dallara F301 while behind the safety car. The Japanese driver made up for his indiscretion by taking victory in the second race.

ABOVE *The Carlin Dallara-Mugen Honda F301 of Anthony Davidson passes the Alan Docking Racing Dallara F301 of Andy Priaulx at the Abbey chicane during the supporting F3 race at the 2001 Foster's British Grand Prix. (Author)*

BELOW *Michael Schumacher demonstrated a Ferrari 375 at the 2001 Foster's British Grand Prix to mark the 50th anniversary of Ferrari's first-ever Grand Prix victory by Froilán González at the 1951 British event. (LAT)*

2002

■ There was a full programme at the Eurosport Super Racing weekend over 4–5 May at the circuit, with rounds of the FIA GT Championship, FIA European Touring Cars and British F3. The three-hour FIA GT encounter, held on the Saturday evening and running into dusk, was won by the Belmondo Chrysler Viper GTS-R of Fabio Babini and Marc Duez, ahead of the Lister Storm of Bobby Verdon-Roe and Paul Knapfield.

■ The following day, it was the turn of the FIA European Touring Car Championship contenders to take the spotlight with two closely-fought races, producing victories for Alfa Romeo as Nicola Larini in his Nordauto 156 GTa led home team-mate Fabrizio Giovanardi in race one, with the positions reversed in race two.

■ The Green Flag British F3 Championship supporting rounds produced victories for Mark Taylor, in a Manor Motosport Dallara-Mugen Honda F302, and Robbie Kerr, in his Alan Docking-run similar car.

■ The Green Flag MSA British F3 and Touring Car championships shared the bill over the Bank Holiday weekend of 1–3 June. Mark Taylor inherited the race one victory in his Manor Dallara-Mugen Honda F302 on Sunday after on-the-road winner Robbie Kerr was penalised for clashing with series-leader James Courtney. The following day, Courtney took his Carlin-run Dallara-Mugen Honda F302 to victory. In the British Touring Car encounters on Sunday, Warren Hughes scored his maiden BTCC win in an MG ZS in the sprint race, while the feature race provided a victory for James Thompson in his Triple Eight Astra Coupé.

■ Juan Pablo Montoya started from pole and was the early leader of the Foster's British Grand Prix on 7 July in his Compaq Williams-BMW FW24. After just 12 laps it began to rain, though, and once everyone had pitted, the Bridgestone wet tyres on the Ferrari F2002 of Michael Schumacher proved better suited to the conditions than Montoya's Michelins. The German was soon past and into the lead, which he held to the flag. His team-mate, Rubens Barrichello, had started from the back of the grid but worked his way up to second by lap 19. Despite a battle towards the end with Montoya, he held on to make it a Ferrari one-two.

■ Tomas Enge won the International F3000 Championship round on Saturday 6 July in his Arden Lola-Zytek B2/50, finishing 13sec ahead of the Super Nova-run Lola of Sébastien Bourdais. In Sunday's F3 International Challenge race, Heikki Kovalainen and Fabio Carbone made it a one-two for Fortec in their Dallara-Renault FR302s.

■ The club season continued throughout the remainder of the year with meetings organised by the MG Car Club, the 750 Motor Club, BARC, Bentley Drivers' Club, BRSCC, the VSCC, the Historic Sports Car Club and the Eight Clubs. The final meeting of the year was the BRDC's own Winter Warmer Raceday on Saturday 9 November.

ABOVE *Michael Schumacher took his Ferrari F2002 to victory at the 2002 Foster's British Grand Prix, leading home team-mate Rubens Barrichello, who had started from the back of the grid. (LAT)*

2003

■ Williams F1 driver Juan Pablo Montoya escaped uninjured from a 180mph crash while testing at the end of April. The Colombian lost control of his Williams-BMW FW25 at the Becketts complex and went across the gravel trap, the car becoming embedded underneath the tyre barrier, leaving Montoya trapped in the car. Concerns were expressed by the FIA about why the car became lodged under the barrier.

■ The Green Flag MSA British F3 Championship paid its only visit of the year to the circuit over the Bank Holiday weekend of 24–26 May. Nelson Piquet Jr took victory in Sunday's race in his Piquet Sports Dallara-Mugen Honda F303, but it was Alan van der Merwe who dominated the following day in his Carlin Motorsport Dallara-Mugen Honda F302.

BELOW *The 2003 Foster's British Grand Prix was interrupted on lap 12 when a religious activist invaded the track on Hangar Straight, causing the safety car to be deployed. (LAT)*

■ James Thompson, driving a Vauxhall Astra Coupé, inherited the race one win at the British Touring Car Championship meeting on 8 June after Matt Neal retired his Honda Civic from the lead with engine problems. Thompson's team-mate Yvan Muller came home in second. The top two positions were reversed in race two.

■ Rubens Barrichello, driving a Ferrari F2003-GA, emerged the victor of an absorbing and somewhat bizarre Foster's British Grand Prix on 20 July. Renault R23 driver Jarno Trulli took the lead at the start, with McLaren's Kimi Räikkönen in his Mercedes-powered MP4-17 slotting into second ahead of pole-sitter Barrichello. The first interruption came when David Coulthard's McLaren shed a piece of its head restraint, causing the safety car to be deployed while the debris was cleared up. The biggest disruption, however, occurred on lap 12 when Neil Horan, an ex-priest and religious activist, invaded the track on Hangar Straight, before being tackled to

the ground by marshal Stephen Green, the safety car having again been deployed. With some drivers stopping while the safety car was out, at the restart the Toyota TF103s of Cristiano da Matta and Olivier Panis were in the lead. Once they had stopped, the order became Räikkönen, Barrichello and the Williams-BMW FW25 of Juan Pablo Montoya. On lap 41 out of 60, Barrichello took the lead with a move that started at Stowe and ended at Bridge, where the Brazilian swept past to a lead he was to hold to the finish. Eight laps later Montoya took second, leaving Räikkönen to finish third.

■ Björn Wirdheim took his Arden International Lola-Zytek B2/50 to victory in the supporting F3000 event on the Saturday, ahead of the Durango car of Giorgio Pantano and Vitantonio Liuzzi's Red Bull entry.

■ The meeting was marred by the death of David Heynes in the supporting Historic Sportscar Challenge Race, the final event of the weekend. The 58-year-old crashed his Lotus 15 at Becketts on the tenth lap of the 12-lap event after suffering a heart attack.

■ A post-race concert took place on the infield at Becketts at the end of the afternoon, featuring Status Quo, Damon Hill and the Six Pistons, and Eddie Jordan's V10.

■ Towards the end of the year it was announced that prices for the 2004 British Grand Prix would be reduced. Fans could buy a three-day ticket for just £90 – £100 less than a weekend ticket for the 2003 event.

■ Joey Foster swept to victory in the final of the Walter Hayes Trophy for Formula Ford 1600 cars on 9 November in his Reynard 92FF.

2004

RIGHT *Michael Schumacher dominated the 2004 Foster's British Grand Prix in his Ferrari F2004. (LAT)*

■ James Rossiter won a wet British F3 Championship round on 18 April in his Fortec Motorsport Dallara-Opel F302, but because of the torrential rain the meeting was abandoned before the second race could be run.

■ Matt Neal, James Thompson and Tom Chilton were the three winners at the Green Flag MSA British Touring Car Championship rounds held on the International circuit on 9 May. Neal took his Honda Civic Type-R to victory in race one, while the Vauxhall Astra Coupé of Thompson won race two. In race three, Chilton, driving another Honda Civic Type-R, finished first having taken advantage of a clash between Neal and the MG ZS of Anthony Reid while the pair were disputing the lead.

■ Silverstone's new Historic Tribute meeting, co-promoted by the VSCC and the HSCC, took place on 5–6 June and attracted 550 entries. Frank Sytner was the most successful driver over the weekend, taking four victories.

BELOW *Winner Matt Neal leads away in his Honda Civic Type-R at the start of race one at the Green Flag MSA British Touring Car Championship meeting on 9 May. (LAT)*

■ Michael Schumacher, in his Ferrari F2004, was unstoppable at the Foster's British Grand Prix over the weekend of 9–11 July, despite having a 20sec lead wiped out by a safety car intervention with just 19 laps left to run. Jarno Trulli's Renault R24 had crashed heavily and rolled on the exit of Bridge Corner, though thankfully the Italian was unhurt. This allowed pole-sitter and early leader Kimi Räikkönen in his McLaren-Mercedes MP4-19B, whom Schumacher had leapfrogged at the first pit stops, to close up but the German was still able to ease away at the restart to take his 80th Grand Prix victory. Rubens Barrichello's Ferrari was third.

■ After the race, fans were treated to the Beach Boys headlining the Grand Prix Party on a massive stage on the infield at Becketts. At the end, Jenson Button, David Coulthard, Eddie Jordan, Jackie Stewart and Adrian Newey were dancing on stage with them.

■ Vitantonio Liuzzi won the supporting F3000 event on Saturday in his Arden International Lola-Zytek B2/50, but was pressured all the way by the BCN Competition entry of Enrico Toccacelo.

SILVERSTONE

■ The BRSCC meeting on 8 August was marred by the death of Mini Cooper S racer Darren Needham, who crashed at Becketts during the John Cooper Challenge race.

■ Allan McNish and Pierre Kaffer took a dominant victory in the Silverstone 1000km Le Mans Endurance Series round on 14 August in their Veloqx Audi R8. Audis took the top three places, with the Team Goh entry of Rinaldo Capello and Seiji Ara in the runner-up spot and the other Veloqx entry of Johnny Herbert and Jamie Davies in third. The pole-sitting Zytek 04S of Robbie Kerr and Chris Dyson had built up a comfortable lead until it was delayed following a clash with a back-marker, eventually finishing fourth.

■ The first of two rounds of the British F3 Championship run on 15 August produced a win for Nelson Piquet Jr in his Piquet Sports Dallara-Mugen Honda F303. A gamble on slick tyres meant an unexpected victory in the second race for the other Fortec F302 of Marcus Marshall from 14th on the grid.

■ Driving a Reynard 89FF, Joey Foster again took victory in the Walter Hayes Trophy on 7 November.

ABOVE *As his team celebrates, Allan McNish crosses the line to win the Silverstone 1000km Le Mans Endurance Series round on 14 August, co-driving with Pierre Kaffer in their Veloqx Audi R8. (LAT)*

ABOVE *Vitantonio Liuzzi leads the field away in his Lola-Zytek B2/50 at the start of the 2004 Foster's British Grand Prix F3000 supporting race. (LAT)*

2005

■ Saloon car legend Gerry Marshall died of a heart attack while testing an ex-IROC Chevrolet Camaro at the circuit on 21 April, during the Historic Grand Prix Cars Association test day. He pulled up at Luffield Corner in front of the BRDC Clubhouse, but marshals and medics were unable to resuscitate him.

■ The circuit hosted rounds of both the World Touring Car Championship and the FIA GT Championship over the weekend of 13–15 May. The Autodelta Alfa Romeo 156s dominated the first WTCC race, with Gabriele Tarquini leading team-mates James Thompson, Fabrizio Giovanardi and Augusto Farfus Jr. to a one-two-three-four finish. The BMW 320i of Andy Priaulx was leading race two before it retired with a puncture, leaving Rickard Rydell to take victory in his SEAT Toledo Cupra, ahead of team-mate Jason Plato.

■ The RAC decided to resurrect the historic Tourist Trophy for Britain's round of the FIA GT Championship, and the three-hour race produced a one-two for the Prodrive-run Aston Martin DBR9s. Peter Kox and Pedro Lamy led home team-mates David Brabham and Darren Turner, the latter pair leading for most of the race before a close battle to the flag at the end. The Vitaphone Racing Maserati MC12 of Fabio Babini and Thomas Biagi finished third.

■ The Foster's British Grand Prix on 8–10 July produced a victory for Juan Pablo Montoya in his West McLaren-Mercedes MP4-20. The Colombian took the lead on the first lap from the Renault R25 of pole-sitter Fernando Alonso and then controlled the race carefully, taking the flag ahead of the Spaniard 60 laps later. Montoya's team-mate, Kimi Räikkönen, was third. Jenson Button, in a BAR-Honda 007, started from the front row but finished fifth, behind the other Renault of Giancarlo Fisichella.

■ Twenty years after Keke Rosberg set a stunning 160mph lap to take pole for the 1985 British Grand Prix, his son Nico produced an equally superb lap to grab pole for the first of the two supporting GP2 races in his ART Grand Prix-entered Dallara-Mader. Rosberg went on to take victory, while Olivier Pla won race two for Dave Price Racing.

■ A minute's silence was observed just before the Grand Prix in memory of those killed in the terrorist bombings in London on the Thursday prior to the event. Around 18,000 fans stayed for the post-Grand Prix party, which this year featured Jools Holland.

■ The MG Car Club's 75th birthday, along with 50 years of the BMC Competition Department, was celebrated on 22–25 July.

■ The inaugural Silverstone Classic, held over 30–31 July, attracted bumper grids and a crowd of 30,000. Races included Grand Prix Masters, FIA Thoroughbred Grand Prix, Group C/GTP, F5000 and World Sportscar Masters. The event was held on the 3.144-mile historic GP circuit.

■ The final 50 minutes of a very wet Silverstone 1000km, Britain's round of the Le Mans Endurance Series, on 13 August, produced a race to the flag on a drying track between the pole-sitting Creation Automotive DBA4-Judd 03S of Nicolas Minassian and Jamie Campbell-Walter and the Oreca Audi R8 of Stéphane Ortelli and Allan McNish. The race ran into the dark on Saturday evening after seven safety car periods had interrupted the event, with the Audi emerging victorious.

■ Saturday's supporting round of the British F3 Championship produced a victory for Charlie Kimball's Carlin Motorsport Dallara-Mugen Honda F305, ahead of his team-mate and points-leader Alvaro Parente. The following day, 14 August, races two and three were won by Parente, with Kimball second each time.

■ The Dunlop MSA British Touring Car Championship paid its only visit of the year to the circuit on 17–18 August, running on the 1.6-mile National layout. Tom Chilton, in his Arena Honda Civic, took victory in race one, but Jason Plato was excluded from first place in race two after clashing with Chilton, leaving his SEAT Toledo team-mate Luke Hines to inherit the victory. Race three produced a maiden BTCC victory for Gareth Howell in his Team Dynamics Honda Integra.

■ Carlin Motorsport's Charlie Kimball took both victories at the final rounds of the British F3 Championship on 9 October in his Dallara-Mugen Honda F305.

■ A record field of over 150 cars lined up for the Walter Hayes Formula Ford Trophy meeting on 5–6 November, but the meeting was blighted by bad weather, almost forcing it to be cancelled. The event was won for the third time in a row by Joey Foster in a Reynard 89FF.

BELOW *Juan Pablo Montoya scored his maiden F1 victory at the 2005 Foster's British Grand Prix in his West McLaren-Mercedes MP4-20, ahead of Fernando Alsonso's pole-sitting Renault R25. (Author)*

2006

■ The Vitaphone Maserati MC12 of Michael Bartels and Andrea Bertolini took victory in the RAC Tourist Trophy, Britain's round of the FIA GT Championship, on 7 May, ahead of the Zakspeed Saleen S7R of Jarek Janis and Sascha Bert after a race-long battle. Fabio Babini and Fabrizio Gollin took their Aston Martin DBR9 to third in the 300-mile event.

■ The Foster's British Grand Prix took place over the weekend of 9–11 June to avoid a clash with the football World Cup final on its traditional July date. Fernando Alonso took the honours in his Renault R26, converting his pole position into an emphatic victory, initially fighting off the attentions of Kimi Räikkönen's McLaren-Mercedes MP4-21 and the Ferrari 248 F1 of Michael Schumacher. Alonso eased away at the front to take victory, while Schumacher leapfrogged Räikkönen at the second round of pit stops to grab the runner-up spot.

■ Star of the meeting was Lewis Hamilton, who won both supporting GP2 races in his ART Grand Prix Dallara-Renault. It was in the second race that Hamilton really made his mark, with a stunning three-abreast overtaking manoeuvre through the Becketts complex, which took him past both Clivio Piccione and Nelson Piquet Jr. to take second place. He soon caught and passed the Campos Racing car of Felix Porteiro, which was later disqualified from second place, to take the victory.

■ After F1 qualifying on the Saturday, the England–Paraguay World Cup encounter was shown live on giant screens around the circuit. Qualifying was moved to 12.30pm to avoid a clash with the match, which kicked off at 2pm. Status Quo once again headlined the post-race party, hosted by Tony Jardine, with a number of Grand Prix drivers putting in an appearance.

■ The famous name of the *Daily Express* International Trophy race was revived at the second Silverstone Classic on 28–30 July, 28 years after the event was last run. The title was used for the second race of the Grand Prix Masters double-header at the meeting and was won by Count Manfredo Rossi de Montelera in his Brabham-Ford BT42/44. The meeting attracted a crowd of 38,000.

■ Grand Prix Masters of a different sort were at the circuit on 12–13 August for the British round of the GP Masters series,

featuring veteran F1 drivers. Eddie Cheever took victory in a rain-affected event, ahead of Eric van de Poele and Christian Danner. Crowd favourite Nigel Mansell spun three times on his warm-up lap, joined the race on the second lap, then retired after repeatedly spinning because of problems with the car. The supporting rounds of the Lloyds TSB Insurance British F3 Championship produced double wins for Mike Conway in his Double R Racing Dallara-Mercedes Benz F306.

■ Just over a month later, on 24 September, Conway again dominated the meeting, taking a brace of wins to clinch the British F3 title.

■ The final round of the Dunlop MSA British Touring Car Championship took place on 14–15 October, with Team Dynamics driver Matt Neal winning race two and clinching the title in his Honda Integra-R. Neal's team-mate Gareth Howell took victory in races one and three.

■ Peter Dempsey won the sixth Walter Hayes Trophy in his Ray GR06 ahead of Neville Smyth's Ray GRS05.

■ Peter Scott-Russell, long-time commentator at Silverstone and the person who coined the phrase 'a Silverstone-type finish', passed away in the last week of December.

ABOVE *Lewis Hamilton won both GP2 support races at the 2006 Foster's British Grand Prix meeting in his ART Grand Prix Dallara-Renault, including passing both Clivio Piccione and Nelson Piquet Jr. in a stunning three-abreast manoeuvre at Becketts during Sunday's race. (LAT)*

RIGHT *Fernando Alonso took pole position and an emphatic victory in his Renault R26 at the 2006 Foster's British Grand Prix, with Michael Schumacher in his Ferrari 248 F1 beating Kimi Räikkönen's McLaren-Mercedes MP4-21 to the runner-up spot. (LAT)*

2007

■ Formula Palmer Audi driver Matt Hamilton broke his leg in a start-line shunt at the 7 April BARC meeting. Hamilton had won the first race earlier in the day and had taken pole for both. After the 5sec board had been shown, the starting lights flicked on and off so quickly that confusion was caused among the runners, and Hamilton was struck from behind.

■ The RAC Tourist Trophy, Britain's round of the FIA GT Championship, was held on 5–6 May and provided a win for the Vitaphone Maserati MC12 of Thomas Biagi and Mika Salo. The early leader was the Jetalliance Aston Martin DBR9 of Karl Wendlinger and Ryan Sharp before the Phoenix Racing Chevrolet Corvette C6.R of Mike Hezemans and Jean-Denis Delatraz took over at the front. The Maserati was on the move, though, and took the lead after the first round of pit stops. At the flag, after two hours of racing, it was just 37sec ahead of the Corvette.

■ Guest driver Bruno Senna won both Ferrari Challenge Europe Trofeo races at the Ferrari Racing Days meeting over the weekend of 9–10 June.

■ Crowd favourite Lewis Hamilton grabbed pole position for the Santander British Grand Prix on 6–8 July in his Vodafone McLaren-Mercedes MP4-22, yet could only manage a third-place finish in the race. Hamilton led away at the start but was pressured by the Ferrari F2007 of Kimi Räikkönen and the other McLaren of Fernando Alonso – these three quickly pulling away from the rest of the field. With his rear tyres graining, Hamilton was the first to pit, and Räikkönen (who pitted two laps later) jumped into the lead. When Alonso stopped, he managed to leapfrog both the other cars to take first place, which he held until the second round of stops when Räikkönen, whose Ferrari was much faster than the McLarens on the day, retook the position which he held to the flag.

■ Adam Carroll took a popular victory in Sunday's supporting GP2 sprint race in his FMS International Dallara-Renault. The previous day's feature race had been won by Andi Zuber's iSport entry.

RIGHT *Dusk falls at the start of the final of the 2007 Walter Hayes Trophy for Formula Ford cars. The event was won for the second year running by Peter Dempsey in a Ray GR05. (LAT)*

■ The Silverstone Classic on 27–29 July celebrated the 25th anniversary of Group C with the largest-ever gathering of Group C and GTP cars. The two events for Group C cars were won by Gary Pearson's Jaguar XJR-11 and the Porsche 962C of Andy Purdie. Peter Dunn won both Grand Prix Masters events in his March 761.

■ A new initiative was tried on 2 August with the first Powernights meeting, attracting 2,000 people to the Thursday evening event, which featured eight races run between 6pm and 8.30pm. The idea was to attract a new audience to motor sport, and the races featured Classic Saloons, Toyota MR2s, Formula Fords and a Sports/Saloon handicap.

■ Marko Asmer dominated the Lloyds TSB Insurance British F3 round on 11–12 August, winning both races in his Hitech Racing Dallara-Mercedes Benz F307.

■ Marc Gene and Nicolas Minassian were the comfortable winners of the Silverstone 1000km round of the Le Mans Series on 14–16 September in their Peugeot 908 HDi. The pair took pole by half a second and raced away at the front of the field as their team-mates Stéphane Sarrazin and Pedro Lamy followed cautiously, wanting to wrap up the title rather than go for an outright win. By the three-hour point, the lead Peugeot was a lap ahead of its sister car in second place. In the fourth hour, Lamy suffered a puncture, damaging the bodywork, which ultimately resulted in a black flag and the car's retirement. This left the Pescarolo-Judd 01 of Emmanuel Collard and Jean-Christophe Boullion to take second, ahead of the Rollcentre-entered Pescarolo of Stuart Hall and João Barbosa.

■ Peter Dempsey made it two Walter Hayes Trophy wins in a row by taking victory on 3–4 November in his Ray GR05 ahead of the Van Diemen RF92 of James Nash in the final.

RIGHT *Fireworks over the BRDC clubhouse at the 2007 Walter Hayes Trophy meeting. (LAT)*

2008

■ Silverstone hosted the opening round of the FIA GT Championship with the RAC Tourist Trophy on 19–20 April. The two-hour race ended in a thrilling finish as a safety car period closed up the field with just 15 minutes left to run. The Gigawave-run Aston Martin DBR9 of Allan Simonsen and Phillip Peter had built up a 40sec lead at this point, but in the final run to the flag it lost out to both the Jetalliance-entered DBR9 of Karl Wendlinger and Ryan Sharp and the Vitaphone Maserati MC12 of Andrea Bertolini and Michael Bartels. Wendlinger and Sharp took the victory by just 3.807sec, with Simonsen and Peter having to settle for third.

■ Safety concerns over running meetings on two circuit layouts at the same time were raised when a car competing on the National circuit on 31 May ended up on the South circuit, narrowly missing two school cars. The throttle on Neil Cunningham's Ford Mustang stuck open at Maggots and he went off the track at high speed, glancing off a tyre barrier and eventually coming to a halt on the South circuit.

BELOW *A Ferrari enters the pit lane during qualifying for the 2008 Santander British Grand Prix. (Author)*

■ The first of the Formula Renault 3.5 World Series races on 6–8 June resulted in a win for Salvador Duran in his Interwetten.com Dallara-Renault. Rob Wickens took victory in race two for the Carlin Motorsport team, while the final event produced a win for P1 Motorsport's Giedo van der Garde.

■ Lewis Hamilton produced a stunning wet-weather drive to take victory at the Santander British Grand Prix on 4–6 July in his Vodafone McLaren-Mercedes MP4-23. His performance caused him to be hailed as "the best wet-weather driver of this generation" by three-time world champion Sir Jackie Stewart. Hamilton took the lead from his team-mate and pole-sitter Heikki Kovalainen at Stowe on lap five and immediately began to pull away, but it was his pace on intermediate tyres later in the race, while others were on full wets, which won him the race. Nick Heidfeld brought his BMW-Sauber F1.08 home in second ahead of the Honda RA108 of Rubens Barrichello.

■ Giorgio Pantano won the GP2 feature race on Saturday in his Racing Engineering Dallara-Renault, and in Sunday's wet sprint race, Bruno Senna took the honours for iSport.

ABOVE *Marshals at the pit lane entrance during the 2008 Santander British Grand Prix. (Author)*

■ The grid for the first RAC Grand Prix held in 1948 was recreated at the Silverstone Classic over the weekend of 25–27 July. Organisation and promotion of the event had been subcontracted to Roger Etcell's Motion Works company, and initiatives included a greater marketing effort and improved paddock access for fans.

■ Five times Le Mans winner Derek Bell demonstrated the 2003 24-Hours-winning Bentley Speed 8 at the Bentley Drivers' Club meeting on 2 August.

■ Oliver Turvey proved unbeatable at the British F3 round on 16 August, winning both races in his Carlin Motorsport Dallara-Mercedes Benz F308.

■ Heavy rain greeted the HiQ MSA British Touring Car Championship when it returned to the circuit on 30–31 August after a year's absence. Jason Plato took victory in race one in his SEAT Leon TDI, and Fabrizio Giovanardi emerged the winner of race two in his Vauxhall Vectra. Mat Jackson drove his Dealer Team BMW 320i to a win in race three. The event celebrated three anniversaries – 50 years of the BTCC, 60 years of Silverstone and 80 years of the BRDC. Touring car stars of the past, including Sir Jack Sears, Sir John Whitmore, Roy Pierpoint, Alec Poole, Bill McGovern, Richard Longman, Andy Rouse and Chris Hodgetts, took part in a demonstration run to mark the occasion.

■ The *Autosport* 1000km race on 12–14 September, Britain's round of the Le Mans Series, produced a win for the Audi R10 TDI of Allan McNish and Rinaldo Capello after accidents eliminated the Peugeot 908 HDi of Nicolas Minassian/Marc Gene and delayed team-mates Pedro Lamy/Stéphane Sarrazin. Minassian hit a back-marker after 1¼hr, and 30 minutes later Sarazzin collided with Capello. Despite being delayed by the clash, McNish and Capello fought back to take victory ahead of the Lola-Aston Martin B08/60 of Stefan Mucke and Jan Charouz, with Jean-Christophe Boullion and Romain Dumas's Pescarolo-Judd 01 in third. Fourth went to the other Audi of Alexandre Prémat and Mike Rockenfeller, which secured them the drivers' championship.

■ Conor Daly won the Walter Hayes Formula Ford Trophy on 1–2 November in his Ray GRS08, beating the Mygale SJ01 of Josh Fisher in the final.

ABOVE *Guests in the hospitality suites overlooking the inside of Woodcote enjoy a superb view of the action during the 2008 Santander British Grand Prix. (Author)*

ABOVE *Spectators had to brave the elements during a cold, wet and windy 2008 Santander British Grand Prix. (Author)*

2009

RIGHT *The Red Bull-Renault RB5 of Sebastian Vettel drives slowly down the pit lane past guests in the hospitality units at the 2009 Santander British Grand Prix. (Author)*

■ The FIA GT Championship kicked off on 3 May at the Tourist Trophy meeting and produced a dominant victory for Karl Wendlinger and Ryan Sharp, driving a Saleen S7R, their second TT win in a row. The Vitaphone Maserati MC12 of Andrea Bertolini and Michael Bartels took second ahead of the Chevrolet Corvette C6.R driven by Guillaume Moreau and Xavier Maassen. The two supporting Cooper Tires British F3 Championship rounds produced wins for Renger van der Zande in his Hitech Dallara-Mercedes-Benz F308 and Daniel Ricciardo in the Carlin-run Dallara-VW 308.

■ What was feared would be the last British Grand Prix at Silverstone took place on 19–21 June, a month earlier than usual, and produced a dominant one-two for Red Bull as Sebastian Vettel led his team-mate Mark Webber to victory in their Renault-powered RB5s. Rubens Barrichello brought his Brawn-Mercedes 001 home in third, while his team-mate and championship leader, Jenson Button, could only manage sixth.

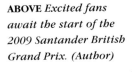

ABOVE *Excited fans await the start of the 2009 Santander British Grand Prix. (Author)*

LEFT *Sebastian Vettel, flanked by his team-mate Mark Webber and Rubens Barrichello, holds aloft the trophy for winning the 2009 Santander British Grand Prix. Red Bull chief designer Adrian Newey can be seen on the extreme left of the podium. (Author)*

■ Alberto Valerio and Pastor Maldonado were the stars of the two supporting GP2 events over the Grand Prix weekend. Valerio brought his Piquet GP-run car home first in the feature race, and Maldonado, driving for ART, won the sprint event.

■ The Formula Renault 3.5 meeting on 4–5 July produced wins for Marcos Martinez and Charles Pic in front of a crowd of 80,000. Martinez, driving for Pons Racing, took victory in the first event, and Pic utterly dominated the second race in his Tech 1 Racing entry.

■ The Silverstone Classic took place over the weekend of 24–26 July and included 21 races for 14 different groups of cars spanning nine decades. Two rock concerts on the Friday and Saturday evenings, featuring Carlos Santana, the Pussycat Dolls, Toploader and Blue, helped produce a festival atmosphere for the large crowd.

RIGHT *The Arden International Dallara-Renault of Edoardo Mortara is craned away after going off on the first lap of Saturday's GP2 race at the 2009 Santander British Grand Prix meeting. (Author)*

■ The British F3 and GT contingents visited the circuit over the weekend of 15–16 August, with Daniel Ricciardo scoring another victory in the first F3 encounter in his Carlin-run Dallara-VW F308, and Renger van der Zande winning race two in his Hitech Racing Dallara-Mercedes-Benz F308. The GT race produced a victory for the Ferrari 430 of Duncan Cameron and Matt Griffin.

■ The HiQ MSA British Touring Car Championship paid its annual visit to the circuit on 29–30 August, with RML-run Chevrolet Lacettis taking all three wins. Mat Jackson was victorious in race one, and team-mate Jason Plato took the race two win. The reversed-grid final race produced another win for Jackson.

■ The Oreca-AIM 01 pairing of Nicolas Lapierre and Olivier Panis scored a first victory for the team at the *Autosport* 1000km, the final round of the 2009 Le Mans Series, on 13 September in front of a crowd of 25,000. The pair crossed the line 50sec ahead of the Speedy Racing-run Lola-Aston Martin B08/60 of Andrea Belicchi, Marcel Fässler and Nicolas Prost after 5½hr of racing. Third place for the works Lola-Aston Martin of Stefan Mücke, Tomáš Enge and Jan Charouz was enough to give them the drivers' title.

■ Californian racer Connor de Phillippi emerged as the winner of the Walter Hayes Formula Ford Trophy on 1 November, driving exactly the same Ray GRS08 that his compatriot, Conor Daly, had used to win the event the previous year.

ABOVE *The Oreca-AIM 01 of Nicolas Lapierre and Olivier Panis is pushed on to the grid prior to the start of the 2009 Autosport 1000km, Britain's round of the Le Mans Series. (Author)*

TOP RIGHT *The pole-sitting Oreca-AIM 01 of Nicolas Lapierre and Olivier Panis, and the Gulf Lola-Aston Martin B09/60 of Stefan Mücke, Tomáš Enge and Jan Charouz, head the pack round for the rolling start of the 2009* Autosport 1000km. *(Author)*

RIGHT *Jason Plato leads the pack in his Chevrolet Lacetti during race two of the HiQ MSA British Touring Car Championship meeting on 30 August. (LAT)*

2010 onwards

"Over the last 60 years... Silverstone has grown beyond all recognition."

Damon Hill

The new 3.67-mile Silverstone Grand Prix circuit was officially opened on 29 April 2010 by the Duke of York, and the names of the new corners revealed for the first time. Abbey, which would become the first corner when the new pits and paddock complex was completed the following year, was now a fast seventh-gear right-hander leading through a fast left-hand kink named Farm to a sharp second-gear right at Village. The track then swung through a long first-gear left-hander named the Loop and along a short straight to a fourth-gear left-hander, Aintree, where it joined the old Club Straight, which was now renamed the Wellington Straight after the bombers which had been stationed at the old airfield during the war. This led down to the third-gear Brooklands Corner, rejoining the old Grand Prix circuit.

As part of the modifications to make the track suitable for MotoGP riders, the grandstands around Woodcote and along the old main straight were moved back considerably and the run-off area extended to 30 metres. This changed forever what had been a familiar vista at the circuit, the old Dunlop/Shell Oils/*Autosport* Tower at Woodcote having long gone as well.

The 2010 British Grand Prix on 9–11 July used the new configuration, but with the start-finish line in its traditional place. At the southern end of the circuit, work was progressing on the state-

RIGHT *A new view of Silverstone for the 21st century with the start for the Grand Prix circuit now relocated to the new pit complex at the Wing. Here, the grid is formed up prior to the start of the 2012 Santander British Grand Prix. (LAT)*

ABOVE *Mark Webber drove his Red Bull-Renault from the pit lane into the auditorium at the opening of the Silverstone Wing pit and paddock complex on 17 May 2011. (LAT)*

TOP RIGHT *The Duke of Kent officially opened the Wing on 17 May 2011. (Author)*

RIGHT *The Silverstone Wing overlooks the new pit lane at the 2011 Santander British Grand Prix. (Author)*

of-the-art pits and paddock complex, and by the following spring it was complete. On 17 May 2011, the new facility, christened the Silverstone Wing, was officially opened.

It's an impressive structure. Measuring 390 metres (almost ¼ mile) in length and 30 metres to the top of its distinctive 'blade', the facility comprises 41 pit garages, race control, a podium, media centre, hospitality and VIP spectator areas. The building also houses three large halls, conference facilities, a visitor centre and a 100-seat auditorium, making it suitable for accommodating product launches, conferences, even weddings and parties. It took 54 weeks to build, with up to 100 personnel on site at any one time, and the man hours spent on the project totalled around 260,000.

Five of Britain's six living F1 world champions – John Surtees OBE, Sir Jackie Stewart OBE, Nigel Mansell OBE, Damon Hill OBE and Jenson Button MBE – were among the 800 guests attending the launch, while others included Sir Stirling Moss, Sir Frank Williams, Christian Horner, Ross Brawn, David Coulthard and Murray Walker. From the world of bike racing, Cal Crutchlow, Jonathan Rea, James Toseland and nine-time world champion Valentino Rossi were in attendance.

The versatility of the new facility was demonstrated when Mark Webber drove his Red Bull Racing F1 car from the pit lane into the auditorium.

"Today was a very important day in the history of the British Racing Drivers' Club and Silverstone Circuit," said then BRDC president Damon Hill at the opening ceremony. "The official opening of the Silverstone Wing represents the culmination of many years' hard work and gives a clear statement of intent for the future. We are honoured that our president-in-chief, His Royal Highness The Duke of Kent, KG generously agreed to perform the opening ceremony.

"Over the last 60 years, under the stewardship of the BRDC, Silverstone has grown beyond all recognition. Silverstone has a significant historical legacy, but we maintain our place at the forefront of contemporary international motor sport, hosting an array of world-class events and activities. This is in no small measure because British competitors have consistently led the way at the highest level of global motor sport for over 80 years.

"The BRDC is extremely proud of this new building, but we acknowledge that none of it would have been possible without our superb and exceptional Silverstone team. Silverstone is a cornerstone of our industry and the BRDC will continue to develop the circuit to ensure that Britain has a world-class home for motor sport and related technology."

Even Bernie Ecclestone, president and CEO of Formula One Management, after all his scraps with the BRDC and Silverstone, sent his best wishes, albeit with a caveat. "I am very sorry that I am unable to be with you on this important occasion for F1 and the future of Silverstone," he said. "But rest assured I have followed all the progress from planning through to the current launch of the Silverstone Wing. The new pit and paddock complex is a state-of-the-art facility and will form the backbone of Silverstone's plans to be a world-class facility of its type. I am delighted with the progress and prospects for the future of Silverstone. It is a great shame that it could not have been completed ten years ago, but well done Silverstone."

The message, read out by the BBC's Jake Humphries, who was hosting the event, raised a laugh from the audience.

The first event to use the facility with the relocated start-finish line was the FIA GT1 World Championship event on 19–21 June, and it proved confusing for some, as John Watson who was commentating for television, explained. "To me, the whole dynamic of the circuit has changed, now that the Wing is in operation, because when you're down at the Wing, it doesn't feel like Silverstone. It feels you could be at any circuit, anywhere in the world.

ABOVE *The revised track layout opened up an extensive new spectator area around where Bridge Bend used to be, alongside Wellington Straight and around Brooklands and Luffield. (Author)*

RIGHT *Qualifying for the 2012 Santander British Grand Prix had to be suspended for 1½hr because of the appalling conditions. (Author)*

"Because for 60-odd years, what was the former pit complex was the face of Silverstone. And going in there for our event, you came over the bridge and you turned right and you went down towards where traditionally on the inside of the circuit there was nothing, no viewing, nothing at all.

"But also, when you're doing a broadcast on a race, you had to remember that turn one is now Abbey, not Copse, and to follow the lap commencing on the exit of Club as opposed to the exit of Woodcote. And there were many more people down at the new site, and looking at the camera shots of cars coming into Brooklands, Luffield and Woodcote it looked weird. It was not how I remember being at Silverstone or watching Silverstone on television. It was a strange experience, but it's one that no doubt with time we'll become used to."

A month later, at the Santander British Grand Prix on 8–10 July, the new complex drew mixed responses. While acknowledging that the facility took Silverstone into the 21st century, there were still minor niggles. One of the difficulties was that the track rises gently between Club and Abbey, but the pit lane has to be level, with cars climbing steeply as they exit to rejoin the track. This meant that, as viewed from the grandstands at the end of the main straight, the pits opposite were too low to be seen. This might not have been a problem had Bernie Ecclestone not requested that the allocation of the garages be swapped around. The complex had been designed with the idea of having the top teams, such as Red Bull and McLaren, at the Club end of the pit lane and highly visible from the stands opposite. But Ecclestone decided that he wanted the top teams directly beneath the F1 Paddock Club guests, who were housed at the far end of the pit lane. Hence the top teams being out of sight of the spectators in the stands.

"The pit lane has to be horizontal and the track obviously rises," explained Silverstone's managing director Richard Phillips. "If we'd cut into the track and made it more horizontal up to the Loop, we would have gone below the water table, so you would have had flooding.

"We did a 54-week build on the Wing," he continued. "Oddly, when you come to build facilities like that, there are no rules. There are guidelines and 'like-to-haves', but when it comes to, for instance, paddock power – all the things that the trucks plug into – you'd expect there would be a regulation that said you've got to have this power and that power, these sockets and those sockets, throughout the paddock, but you don't have any of it.

"There's no technical brief. So you go round the world looking at what everybody else does and you pick through what there is in terms of the media centre and numbers of commentary boxes and offices, and draw on your own experiences and so on. So there's a bit of guesswork in it, and when you actually open it, bits of it aren't right. And that happens all round the world."

In the media centre, journalists were disappointed to discover that they had no view of the track, the windows on that side of the room being taken up by television commentary booths, which will eventually be housed in a permanent grandstand opposite.

"There's a lot more to do here at Silverstone," said Phillips. "Everything at the Wing had to be self-contained because there's no way to get to it. There's no bridge over the top, there's no tunnel underneath. All of those things are planned for the future. So the commentary boxes should really be on the other side of the track, and the ultimate plan is that they'll be incorporated into a building over on the other side. But then you'll need a bridge across because the media like to do interviews in the pit lane and get on to the grid. So we had to keep them

on the inside, and consequently our media and commentary positions at the moment are a bit of a compromise."

There were more serious problems to contend with 12 months later, however. You can have the best facilities in the world, but the one thing that it is hard to plan for is the weather. Following the wettest June on record in the UK, the 2012 Santander British Grand Prix on 6–8 July provided a challenge for both drivers and spectators alike.

"It was the biggest crowd we've ever had over the three days – our Friday and Saturday are pretty much as big as the Sunday now," explained

ABOVE *Spectators, turned away from waterlogged campsites at the 2012 Santander British Grand Prix, used their ingenuity to find alternative places to pitch their tents. This is the roundabout on the Dadford Road. (Author)*

ABOVE *The Red Arrows fly over the start-finish straight as the cars line up on the grid for the 2012 Santander British Grand Prix. (Author)*

Phillips. "And the weather was unprecedented. We put in place contingency measures to cope with the car parks, but on the Thursday the campsites started to pack up because they couldn't get the people in at the same density they had previously, so they were rather more spread out. It was taking them longer to get people on to pitches and they were having to park them away from their tents.

"We gave up part of our parking to extra camping to try to facilitate that, but it just didn't stop raining. More campers arrived on the Friday morning and were turned away from some of the campsites here. We were trying to take them into our campsites as quickly as we could, but unfortunately the entrance to our campsite and the hard-standing car park were off the same roundabout, so you had one blocking the other.

Then we had to start pushing people on to grass car parks that we were trying to save for the weekend. That compounded during the day, and so we ended up late on Friday with a log jam on the A43, and some people didn't get in."

It was this that forced the circuit to take the same measures it had in 2000 – telling some spectators to stay away on the Saturday.

"Eventually we decided that the public coming into car parks here, not park-and-ride or hospitality or teams or anybody else, but people with car park tickets for Silverstone itself, would be best advised not to come," said Phillips.

"It was hard, and I certainly wouldn't want to do it again, but we made the right decisions. Had we tried to carry on blindly, those people that would have come on the Saturday would have gone into car parks which would have been

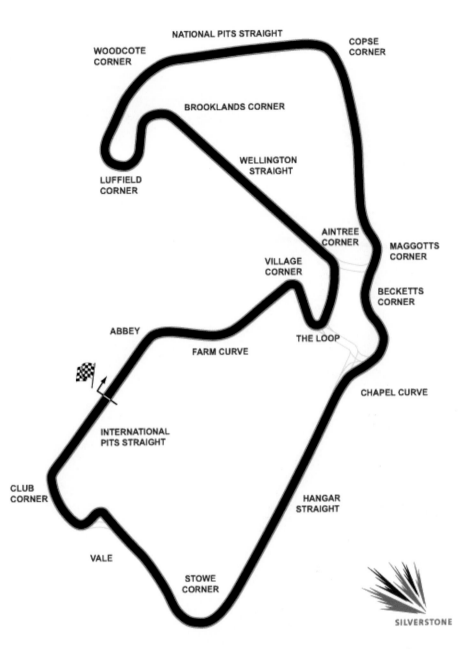

NATIONAL PITS STRAIGHT

WOODCOTE
CORNER

COPSE
CORNER

BROOKLANDS CORNER

WELLINGTON
STRAIGHT

LUFFIELD
CORNER

AINTREE
CORNER

MAGGOTTS
CORNER

VILLAGE
CORNER

BECKETTS
CORNER

ABBEY

THE LOOP

FARM CURVE

CHAPEL CURVE

INTERNATIONAL
PITS STRAIGHT

CLUB
CORNER

HANGAR
STRAIGHT

VALE

STOWE
CORNER

SILVERSTONE

ABOVE *The modern-day track layout.* *(Silverstone Circuits)*

ruined for Sunday, and we may have still had a problem on Saturday. Then Sunday could have been an absolute unmitigated disaster, so it was the best of a bad job, I think."

The strategy worked, and on race day 127,000 fans managed to get into the circuit on what turned out, against predictions, to be a dry and sunny day.

Silverstone came in for criticism, but there were a lot of factors – the weather and the inability of independent campsites to cope – that were out of its control, and everyone who had bought a ticket for Saturday and who couldn't get in was refunded. "It was less than 10,000 people altogether, out of a public crowd of well over 90,000," said Phillips. "So you're talking about 80,000 people who were here. The reality was that even though we said 'don't come on the

Saturday', quite a few people still tried to come and most of them actually got in.

"We've had people say, 'Well why don't you put a roof over the whole thing?' or 'You must have known it was going to be wet' – all these things. It's just not practical, you can't just tarmac the whole of Silverstone. It would be an ecological nightmare."

And Silverstone fans are nothing if not resourceful. Those who could not get on to the campsites or into the circuit on the Friday parked and pitched their tents by the roadside – even the roundabout on the Dadford Road was utilised – and Phillips praised their resilience. "It was a Dunkirk spirit and the British at their best, and I take my hat off to them," he said. "They made the most of it and they enjoyed themselves."

Lap of Silverstone with 2012 British Grand Prix winner Mark Webber

"The new layout of the track at Silverstone is still overall a very fast lap and the car needs to be very strong in fast corners.

"Turn one [Abbey] is a seventh-gear corner in a Formula 1 car, the entry is very tricky to get right, the turning point needs to be very accurate. It's also a little bit of a bumpy corner, so you need to make sure the car is settled into the apex over the bumps.

"Then you have a fast left-hander, braking for turn three [Village]. You need to be very strong on the brakes here because of the short acceleration from there into turn four [The Loop], which is a very tight corner that comes back on itself.

"You need to get a very good exit out of there because it's a very long straight down towards Brooklands. There you rejoin the old circuit with a very fast entry past the BRDC where you get a little bit of atmosphere because there is always a big crowd. Then you go into a very slow, long right-hander, Luffield. Exiting there is very important.

"After that you're on the old start-finish straight. You pass the old pits and get ready for one of the best sectors in Formula 1, which begins with Copse. That's a very fast corner, which you can take in sixth or seventh gear and you need to be very brave here. There is not much run-off on the exit, so you need to make sure you're very accurate on the exit.

"Then you're going into Maggots and Becketts, which is an extremely fast left-right, left-right combination of corners. There are two kinks at the start, into the first left and the first right, and it's very important to get those right because the further you get into Becketts the slower it is, relatively speaking. It's still fast, but it just gets slower the further you get into it, and you need a very good exit at the last right-hander on to Hangar Straight.

"This is a long straight down towards Stowe. You're not braking that heavily for Stowe because it's just rolling in and getting the car as fast as you can into the apex, in fourth or fifth gear, using the kerb a bit on the exit and then braking for the last sector into Vale and Club. It's quite a tricky section, the rhythm of the lap is broken down a little bit here, and then after a little kink you cross the start-finish line."

RIGHT *Mark Webber on the way to winning the 2012 Santander British Grand Prix in his Red Bull RB8, his second Silverstone grand prix win. (sutton-images.com)*

2010

■ The re-profiled Club Corner, which had been tightened to a sharper bend from its previous sweeping profile, was unpopular with some of the drivers at the opening Superleague Formula meeting on 4 April, which was won by Craig Dolby in the Tottenham Hotspur car. Sébastien Bourdais won the second encounter in the Olympique Lyonnais car, and in the €100,000 Super Final, Dolby triumphed again.

■ Work on the new 3.67-mile Grand Prix circuit was completed in April. The first cars to try the new configuration were the Formula BMW Europe series, which held an official test ahead of their Grand Prix support race.

■ Jolyon Palmer, in his Williams-Audi JPH1, scored a win and a second place at the opening round of the FIA F2 Championship on 17–18 April. Palmer won race one, with Philipp Eng victorious in race two.

■ The new Silverstone Grand Prix circuit was officially opened on 29 April by HRH the Duke of York, who was then driven around the track in the Santander two-seat Grand Prix car by BRDC president Damon Hill. On track at the same time were F1 driver-turned broadcaster David Coulthard, driving a Red Bull F1 car, and the motorcycling father-and-son combination of Ron and Leon Haslam, representing the worlds of MotoGP and World Superbikes.

BELOW The F1 drivers' parade prior to the 2010 Santander British Grand Prix. (Author)

ABOVE *Sebastian Vettel tries his hand on the guitar at the 2010 Santander British Grand Prix post-race party, open to all on the infield. (LAT)*

■ The Sumo Power Nissan GT-R of Warren Hughes and Jamie Campbell-Walter was declared the winner of the RAC Tourist Trophy, despite only finishing third on the road at the second round of the FIA GT Championship on 1–2 May. The Aston Martin DBR9 of Darren Turner and Tomáš Enge, which had taken the flag, was disqualified as its skid plank had worn beyond the allowed limits, while the other Aston of Frederic Makowiecki and Thomas Accary, which had finished second, was given a 15 sec penalty for waiting too long to take a drive-through penalty during the race. This, therefore, remained second, while the Nissan was awarded the win. Inheriting third was the Lamborghini Murcielago R-SV of Jos Menten and Frank Kechele.

■ James Calado scored two lights-to-flag victories in races one and three of the supporting Cooper Tires British F3 round in his Carlin-run Dallara-VW F308. The second encounter was won by Alexander Sims in his ART Grand Prix Dallara-VW F310.

■ The Santander British Grand Prix on 9–11 July was the first to use the new track layout, albeit with the start line in its traditional position for the last time. Mark Webber, in his

ABOVE *The GP2 field negotiates the tight Village Corner at the 2010 Santander British Grand Prix meeting. (Author)*

Red Bull-Renault RB6, became the eighth different winner in eight years, beating the McLaren-Mercedes MP4-25 of Lewis Hamilton into second, with Nico Rosberg third in his Mercedes MGP W01. Webber's team-mate Sebastian Vettel had been on pole but was forced wide at the first corner by Webber and touched Hamilton's McLaren, picking up a puncture, which forced an early pit stop. He eventually finished seventh.

■ The two supporting GP2 races were won by Pastor Maldonado, driving for Rapax, and Sergio Perez in the Barwa Addax car.

■ Competitors at the Silverstone Classic on 23–25 July used the old 'Bridge' circuit rather than the new layout.

■ James Calado, Adriano Buzaid and Jean-Eric Vergne, all driving Carlin Dallara-VW F308s, each took a win at the Cooper Tires British F3 round on 14–15 August. The two-hour British GT encounter was won by the Porsche 997 GT3R of David Ashburn and Glynn Geddie.

■ Ford dominated the Dunlop MSA BTCC rounds on 22 August, with Tom Chilton taking his Focus ST to victory in races one and two, but only after team-mate Tom Onslow-Cole, who was leading both races, was instructed to move over and let him by. Onslow-Cole took victory in the third event.

■ It was a Peugeot one-two at the *Autosport* 1000km on 12 September, as the works 908 HDi of Anthony Davidson and Nicolas Minassian led home the Oreca 908 HDi of Nicolas Lapierre and Stéphane Sarrazin. The pole position works Audi R15-plus TDI of Allan McNish and Tom Kristensen had led initially, but retired after just 15 laps with a differential failure. The sister Audi of Timo Bernhard and Rinaldo Capello came in third.

■ The 750 Motor Club's Birkett 6-Hour Relay race attracted a record entry of 60 teams for its 60th anniversary, as it was run for the first time on the 'Bridge' Grand Prix circuit on 30 October. Scratch winners were the Nearly Six Sevens team, but on handicap, victory went to event newcomers OX4R, with their combination of Minis and Mitsubishi Evos.

■ The Walter Hayes Formula Ford Trophy final was won by Peter Dempsey in his Ray GRS05 from the Van Diemen RF00 of Ivor McCollough. It was Dempsey's third victory in the event, having won in 2006 and 2007 as well.

■ Former BRDC chairman Tom Walkinshaw died on 12 December.

2011

■ Mirko Bortolotti took a dominant 6sec victory in race one at the opening round of the FIA F2 Championship on 16–17 April, and Miki Monras took victory in race two.

■ On 18 April, Silverstone launched a 24-hour, seven-days-a-week radio station broadcast on its website, www.silverstone.co.uk, as well as on 87.7MHz at all of the circuit's events. Radio Silverstone was based at the circuit and headed up by motor sport presenters Gary Champion and Alan Hyde.

■ Silverstone's new Wing pits and paddock complex was officially opened by HRH the Duke of Kent, president-in-chief of the BRDC, on 17 May.

■ The round of the FIA GT1 World Championship on 5 June for the RAC Tourist Trophy was the first meeting to use the new complex and the relocated start-finish line between Club and Abbey. It produced a thrilling finish, with the Nissan GT-R of Michael Krumm and Lucas Lohr crossing the line just 0.220sec ahead of the Aston Martin DBR9 of Tomáš Enge and Alex Müller. The latter pairing would have won had it not been for a controversial clash on Hangar Straight between both teams' other entries. The resulting safety car period allowed Krumm to close right up on Lohr and leapfrog him during the pit stops. The Chevrolet Corvette C6.R of Mike Hezemans and Andreas Zuber was third.

■ The 2011 Santander British Grand Prix on 8–10 July was the first GP to use the new Wing pit complex, together with the relocated start-finish line. A heavy rain shower, which soaked half the circuit an hour before the start but left the rest comparatively dry, meant that the whole field started on intermediate tyres. Sebastian Vettel took an early lead in his Red Bull-Renault RB7 from his team-mate and pole-sitter Mark Webber, chased by the Ferrari F150 of Fernando Alonso. The man on the move, though, was Lewis Hamilton in his Vodafone McLaren-Mercedes MP4-26, who started from tenth but was soon up to fourth and then passed Alonso for third. His progress was halted by the need to conserve fuel, allowing Alonso back in front. The Ferrari driver was on a mission and, aided by costly pit-stop errors for the two Red Bull drivers, assumed the lead, which he held to the flag to record Ferrari's first victory of the year, 60 years after it had scored its first Grand Prix win at the same track.

RIGHT *Cars accelerate past the new Wing pits and paddock complex during practice for the 2011 Santander British Grand Prix. (Author)*

BELOW *The Toro Rosso-Ferrari of Jaime Alguersuari negotiates the streaming wet track during practice for the 2011 Santander British Grand Prix. (Author)*

ABOVE *Shortly before the start of the 2011 Santander British Grand Prix, Fernando Alonso marked the 60th anniversary of Ferrari's first-ever Grand Prix victory by completing a few demonstration laps in the sister car to the 375 that Froilán González drove to a win in the 1951 event at Silverstone. (Author)*

BELOW *A few hours later, Alonso completed the celebrations in style by winning the 2011 Santander British Grand Prix in his Ferrari F150. (Author)*

RIGHT *Traffic jam in village centre – the Renault R31s of Nick Heidfeld and Vitaly Petrov, the Sauber-Ferrari C30 of Sergio Perez, the Lotus-Renault T128s of Heikki Kovalainen and Jarno Trulli, and the Toro Rosso-Ferrari STR6s of Jaime Alguersuari and Sébastien Buemi fight their way around Village Corner on the opening lap of the 2011 Santander British Grand Prix. (Author)*

LEFT *Crowds flocked to the traditional post-race concert at the 2011 Santander British Grand Prix. (Author)*

■ That 60th anniversary was marked two hours before the start of the race by Alonso driving a 1951 V12 Ferrari 375, a sister car to the one which Froilán González had taken to victory on 14 July 1951, around the circuit. Alonso revelled in the opportunity, sliding the priceless, scarlet machine – part of Bernie Ecclestone's private collection – around the track.

■ The supporting GP2 races produced wins for Jules Bianchi and Romain Grosjean. Race one was run in changing conditions, and Bianchi, driving for ART Grand Prix, battled furiously with Racing Engineering's Christian Vietoris, the lead changing four times in a single lap at one point. Grosjean took a dominant win in race two in his DAMS-run car, moving up from fifth on the grid to take victory ahead of Racing Engineering's Dani Clos. The two GP3 encounters produced wins for Nico Müller and Lewis Williamson.

■ The Silverstone Classic meeting over the weekend of 22–24 July produced one of the best races seen at the circuit for many years. In Saturday's Historic Formula Junior race, Sam Wilson and Jon Milicevic, in their Cooper T59s, had battled hard, with Wilson just taking the flag by 0.236sec. The following day the pair scrapped throughout the race, continually swapping the lead, with Wilson again the victor. At the end, the pair were all smiles, having thoroughly enjoyed the race every bit as much as the spectators. Stuart Graham,

ABOVE *The safety car leads the GP2 field around a streaming wet track for Saturday's race at the 2011 Santander British Grand Prix meeting. (Author)*

ABOVE *Romain Grosjean, seen here ahead of Sam Bird, won Sunday's GP2 encounter in his DAMS-run car at the 2011 Santander British Grand Prix. (LAT)*

already the only man to have won the Tourist Trophy on two wheels and on four, added to his tally by taking victory in the historic TT event, sharing an Aston Martin DB4GT lightweight with Richard Attwood.

ABOVE *Around 1,000 E-type Jaguars gathered at the 2011 Silverstone Classic to mark the 50th anniversary of the iconic British sports car. (Author)*

■ The Bentley Drivers' Club celebrated its 75th anniversary at the track over the weekend of 13–14 August.

■ The British round of the Formula Renault 3.5 Championship on 20–21 August drew a crowd of 120,000, thanks to free ticket offers and a packed programme of entertainment. It produced a brace of victories for Robert Wickens, with Daniel Ricciardo taking the runner-up spot in both races.

■ The *Autosport* Silverstone 6-Hours on 9–11 September, a round of both the International Le Mans Cup and the Le Mans Series, was won by the Peugeot 908 of Sébastien Bourdais and Simon Pagenaud after a close fight in the

opening stages with the Audi Sport Team Joest R18 TDI of Allan McNish and Tom Kristensen. A clash with a slower car cost the Audi time, allowing team-mates Timo Bernhard and Marcel Fassler to eventually take the runner-up spot. Third place went to the OAK Racing Pescarolo-Judd 01 of Jean-Christophe Boullion and Andrea Belicchi. Gianmaria Bruni and Giancarlo Fisichella won the GT category in their AF Corse Ferrari 458 Italia.

■ The supporting F3 Euroseries races produced wins for the Dallara-Mercedes F308s of Roberto Merhi and Marco Sorensen in races one and two, and the Dallara-VW F308 of Marco Wittman in race three.

■ Kevin Magnussen won race one at the Cooper Tires British F3 Championship finale on 8–9 October in his Carlin Dallara-VW F308. Alexander Sims was the victor in race two in his Motopark VW-powered Dallara, and the final race produced a one-two-three for Carlin, with Carlos Huertas beating Magnussen by just 0.510sec, and Rupert Svenden-Cook following up.

■ Matt Neal clinched the Dunlop MSA British Touring Car Championship title on 15–16 October with a win and a second place in his Team Dynamics Honda Civic. Neal led home team-mate Gordon Sheddon in race one, and the top two positions were reversed in race two. Race three was won by Tom Chilton's Arena Ford Focus.

■ On 22 October, the BRSCC ran a nine-race meeting on the new International layout, which incorporated the new GP start-finish straight, Abbey and Village, and then a right-hander which took cars on to Hangar Straight. At the same time, the Historic Sports Car Club ran its traditional season finale on the National layout.

■ There were 101 entries for the 11th Walter Hayes Formula Ford Trophy on 6 November, with victory going to Adrian Campfield in his Spectrum 011C ahead of Wayne Boyd's Van Diemen JL012K.

ABOVE *Allan McNish gets it all wrong on the parade lap of the 2011 Autosport 6-Hours, spinning his Audi R18 TDI at Abbey Corner as the field sets off. (Author)*

ABOVE *Sébastien Bourdais and Simon Pagenaud won a closely fought 2011 Autosport 6-Hours, a round of both the International Le Mans Cup and the Le Mans Series, in their Peugeot 908, beating the Audi R18 TDI of Timo Bernhard and Marcel Fassler. (Author)*

LEFT *The Lola-Aston Martin B09/60 of Christian Klien, Adrian Fernandez and Harold Primat, rounds Club Corner during the 2011 Autosport 6-Hours. (Author)*

ABOVE *Cars head down Hangar Straight during the 2011 Autosport 6-Hours. (Author)*

2012

■ Silverstone hosted the opening round of the FIA F2 Championship on 14–15 April. Luciano Bacheta was victorious in both races in his Williams-Audi JPH1B, the British driver assuming the lead on the penultimate lap in each case.

■ The MG Live! meeting on 23–24 June attracted over 600 entries, including 55 MGBs for a race to mark the 50th anniversary of the car entering production.

■ Torrential rain affected practice and qualifying for the 2012 Santander British Grand Prix on 6–8 July, the latter being suspended for 1½hr on Saturday because of the conditions. Race day was dry, though, and for a while it looked as if Fernando Alonso would take his second Silverstone victory in a row in his Ferrari F2012. The Spaniard had started from pole position and slowly edged away from the Red Bull-Renault RB8 of Mark Webber. Alonso briefly lost the lead around the time of the first pit stops to Lewis Hamilton's Vodafone McLaren-Mercedes MP4-27 which stayed out longer than others before pitting, but built up enough of a gap to make his second stop without losing a place. Webber, though, was on a different tyre strategy, and towards the end began to close on the Ferrari, driving around the outside of Alonso at Brooklands on lap 48 out of 52. Sebastian Vettel in the other Red Bull completed the podium.

■ Esteban Gutierrez, in a Lotus GP-run Dallara-Mecachrome GP2/11, won Saturday's supporting GP2 race, which had to be started behind the safety car because of a soaking wet track. Sunday's dry race provided a victory for Luiz Razia in his Arden-run car.

■ Antonio Felix da Costa gave Carlin its first GP3 victory in his Dallara-Renault GP3/10 in Saturday's race, but the drive of the entire weekend came from his team-mate Will Buller who started from the back of the grid with slick tyres on a wet track on Sunday to drive through the field and take victory.

■ Mixed fields of F5000 and F2 cars provided close racing at the Silverstone Classic on 21–22 July, with both races for the Peter Gethin Memorial Trophy being won by just over a tenth of a second. Michael Lyons took his Lola-Chevrolet T400 to victory in the first, and it was the Trojan-Chevrolet T101 of Simon Hadfield that triumphed in the second. Other races for Group C sports cars, Grand Prix Masters and Super Touring cars were among a packed programme of events.

■ The Silverstone 6-Hours on 25–26 August provided a win for the Audi R18 e-tron Quattro of Andre Lotterer, Marcel Fassler and Benoit Treluyer, but not before a close fight with the Toyota TS030 HYBRID of Alex Wurz, Nicolas Lapierre and

LEFT *Wet weather badly affected practice and qualifying for the 2012 Santander British Grand Prix. Race-winner Mark Webber in his Red Bull-Renault RB8 is seen during Friday practice. (Author)*

Kazuki Nakajima. The Toyota took an early lead and pulled away but wasn't as fuel-efficient as the Audi, and the extra pit stop required over the course of six hours meant that it finished second, despite a stop-go penalty incurred by the winning Audi for contact with a back-marker. Tom Kristensen and Allan McNish took their Audi R18 ultra into third.

■ Two Formula Renault 3.5 Series events supported the 6-Hours and resulted in wins for Tech 1 Racing's Jules Bianchi in a rain-affected Saturday race, and ISR's Sam Bird on Sunday.

■ Alex Lynn won on the road in the first of the Cooper Tires British F3 races over the weekend of 8–9 September in his Fortec Dallara-Mercedes-Benz F312, but a penalty for a jumped start dropped him to fourth, handing victory to Jazeman Jaafar's Carlin-run Dallara-VW F312. Lynn's team-mate Felix Serralles took the win in race two, but it finally came good for Lynn in race three when he took his maiden F3 victory after a close battle with Jaafar.

■ Jason Plato could have won all three races when the Dunlop MSA British Touring Car Championship made its annual visit on 6–7 October, but he had to settle for a brace of wins instead. The Triple Eight MG KX driver took victory in race one after Mat Jackson's leading Ford Focus retired with electronics problems, but the situation was reversed in race two when Plato retired from the lead, handing the win to Jackson. In the third encounter he stormed through the field from 20th on the grid to beat Jackson to the flag.

■ Tristan Nunez emerged the victor in his Ray GR08 at a rain-affected Walter Hayes Trophy meeting on 3–4 November. The 12th running of the event attracted an entry of 116 cars, but was only able to go ahead after large quantities of standing water were pumped and swept away from parts of the National circuit.

ABOVE *Fernando Alonso leads the field in his Ferrari F2012 at the start of the 2012 Santander British Grand Prix. The Spaniard looked on course to take his second consecutive Silverstone victory, but had to settle for second place behind the Red Bull-Renault RB8 of Mark Webber. (Author)*

BELOW *The Lotus GP/ART-entered Dallara-Mecachrome GP2/11 of James Calado is craned away during Saturday's GP2 encounter at the 2012 Santander British Grand Prix weekend after it suffered gearbox problems, while the safety car leads the rest of the field around the circuit. (Author)*

Personalities

JIMMY BROWN

One thing that consistently emerges from a look through the archives of the BRDC, in particular the board meetings of the fifties and sixties, is the praise heaped upon track manager Jimmy Brown.

In September 1958, the secretary was instructed "to inform Mr Brown of the committee's appreciation of his loyal and enthusiastic service". In March the following year, "the secretary reminded the committee that excellent financial results at Silverstone during 1958 could not have been achieved without the help of the invaluable track manager, Jimmy Brown". It went on: "Members who only see Silverstone at a major meeting can hardly appreciate the amount of constant and enthusiastic work needed to obtain a figure of £4,728 for hire of track." And in 1961, the secretary's report drew attention to "the unselfish service of our track manager, Mr Jimmy Brown, which in my opinion goes far beyond the line of duty".

James Wilson (Jimmy) Brown was 'Mr Silverstone'. Like his counterpart John Webb at Brands Hatch, he lived and breathed the life of the circuit for 40 years.

The RAF had vacated the site just a year before Brown arrived at Silverstone in August 1948, and he was faced with a disused airfield with five aircraft hangars, various run-down buildings and odd bits of military equipment lying around – and just eight weeks in which to organise that first Grand Prix.

He was employed by the RAC for a three-month trial period and used to joke that "they never told me to go away". When the BRDC took over the lease of the circuit at the beginning of 1952, Brown continued in his post as track manager, and proceeded to transform the temporary track into something more permanent. And when the club took over the agricultural land on the inside of the circuit in 1961, he had to become a farmer as well, moving his family into the farmhouse on the inside of the circuit "for the better performance of his supervisory duties on behalf of the company". Needless to say, he made a success of both roles,

and at the club's AGM in 1963 it was pointed out that he had been doing two men's jobs.

He later became a director of Silverstone Circuits Ltd when it was formed in 1966, and managing director in 1974. On top of that, he had already been made managing director of Silverstone Leisure Ltd on its formation in 1971 to develop land not required for racing.

Brown was also a great supporter of initiatives to encourage young drivers, such as the BRDC club championships, which he instigated, and the Silverstone Racing School. He would often spend time at a major race meeting walking among the crowd, buying a hot dog, and chatting to spectators, thereby keeping in touch with his audience.

Speaking to *Motor Sport* in 1992, outgoing BRDC president Gerald Lascelles said: "Getting Jimmy Brown to come out of his farming shell and really become a moving force in the circuit world was quite an achievement, because he was a very shy, retiring person. He did a lot of background work at a time when perhaps other people took all the kudos, but he was a major force towards the end of his career and he knew a hell of a lot about the business – probably more than anybody."

This is a point echoed today by Sir Jackie Stewart. "Jimmy really was the boss," he said. "Because you had a board of directors, and you had presidents and you had chairmen, but Jimmy more or less told them what to do and made it happen. Silverstone and the BRDC has a lot to thank Jimmy for."

Jack Sears was chairman of Silverstone Circuits at a time when Brown was managing director. "Jimmy was an incredibly sound man," he recalled. "Whenever he spoke it was worth listening to. He was a no bullshit man. Facts were facts, and if he thought the facts weren't correct he'd soon get them corrected. He was a pilot in the last war and he was indeed a character because he was incredibly far-sighted and he was incredibly adaptable.

RIGHT *For 40 years, Jimmy Brown – the man who had been track manager at the very first Grand Prix in 1948 and who went on to become chairman of Silverstone Circuits – was 'Mr Silverstone'. (BRDC Archive)*

"He had no knowledge of farming whatsoever, but he very quickly made pigs pay, and his wife Kay was the secretary of the farm office. It was a little chalet-type building close to the farmhouse. Nothing to do with the circuit at all, the circuit office was another building altogether. And he suddenly became a farmer, and it's quite difficult to do that without proper training, but he'd got such an insight into business and costs, and that sort of thing, that he made it pay.

"And he made the circuit pay as well, because he was a very astute businessman – Scottish to his fingertips, and with a gentle Scottish brogue."

And it wasn't just the circuit and the farm that Jimmy Brown looked after – he made sure that the inhabitants of nearby Silverstone village were kept happy as well.

"Jimmy Brown was incredibly clever at looking after the village," explained Sears. "He and Kay were well known and well liked by the parishioners of Silverstone, and if there were any difficulties they might have had, following a race meeting – damage to their property or whatever – he would arrange for it to be repaired immediately. And if somebody came to live in the village and started making a fuss about the noise levels, he'd go down and have a chat to them and give them some tickets to the next race meeting, to come and see what it's all about and understand it better. Very diplomatic, very clever, and it always worked like a charm. He was very clever, Jimmy, and he made that one of his responsibilities."

Indeed, speaking in 1977 on the subject of relations with the local community, Brown himself said: "On the whole we have very good relations. After all, we've been running nearly 30 years and we couldn't have done it without the cooperation and blessing of the locals. We get the odd grouse, but we take notice and if we can put right the grouse, we do so. The most vulnerable areas for noise are Whittlebury, on high ground to the right of Copse Corner, and Silverstone village. There are two churches involved, which is why we don't allow engines to be started before 11.30 to 11.45am on Sundays."

Sears recalled the human side of Jimmy Brown as well. "If a driver was injured at the circuit and taken into Northampton General Hospital, he would always go and visit them to see how they were," he said. "If they were in there for several weeks, he would come regularly. I was one who did have a bad accident at Silverstone and I spent six weeks in Northampton General Hospital, and he came and saw me every week. I wasn't even a director of BRDC in those days, I was just a driver."

Jimmy Brown organised the very first Grand Prix at the circuit in 1948, and all the succeeding ones until his death on 19 April 1988 at the age of 67. It was particularly poignant that he should pass away in the year of the circuit's 40th anniversary, and the subsequent programmes for the major events that year carried an appreciation written by Ray Hutton. He described Brown as being "prickly, but with twinkling eyes", and the stereotypical 'canny' Scot, but also a "kind, thoughtful man of good judgement".

On Friday 8 July that year, at the British Grand Prix meeting, the new press centre was officially opened jointly by Jimmy's widow Kay and Bernie Ecclestone. It was named the Jimmy Brown Centre.

COMMENTATORS

The commentators at any circuit are the first point of contact for the spectator. Particularly in the days before huge television screens could relay all the action at the major meetings, they were the ones tasked with keeping the crowd informed and entertained. The voices of Peter Scott-Russell, Neville Hay, Keith Douglas, Ian Titchmarsh and, at major meetings, Anthony Marsh, were familiar to racegoers throughout the seventies and eighties. They were joined in later years by names such as Russell Douglas (Keith's son), Paul Truswell, Martin Haven and David Addison.

The principal commentator in the early days at Silverstone was Rodney Walkerley of *The Motor,* and the commentary point for the 1950 British Grand Prix was a small box slung underneath the outer pier of the footbridge over the circuit at the start line. The lap scorers occupied a similar box on the opposite pier. Walkerley later related that: "For some reason there was no second commentator at Stowe that day, nor a relief for me. I was in that box from about 9.30am until after 6pm and the RAC forgot to send me even a sandwich or drink all day."

But perhaps the man whose voice became synonymous with Silverstone for many years was Peter Scott-Russell, himself a BRDC member who had competed twice in the Mille Miglia. It was he who coined the phrase 'a Silverstone-type finish'.

"Peter wasn't really a race commentator, he was a presenter," explained Ian Titchmarsh, who has been principal commentator at the circuit since 1985. "He was a star, a fantastic presenter. A lot of the phrases that I've carried on come from Peter. He was great at coming out with them. 'Silverstone-type finish' was absolutely Peter; 'eyes right under the *Daily Express* bridge' was another one he used to come out with – referring to the old road bridge that went over the track between Abbey and Woodcote. There'd come a point in qualifying for a Grand Prix when Ronnie Peterson, or someone, was on a really hot lap and Peter would say, 'eyes right under the *Daily Express* bridge', and Peterson or whoever it was would burst into view and fling the car through Woodcote.

"'The home of British Motor Racing', a strapline used to this day – that was Peter as well. And 'a future world champion if ever I saw one' was another famous Peter expression. He was such a huge character, Peter Scott-Russell, he was a great bloke."

Neville Hay was a regular commentator at the circuit between 1960 and 1975, and he also recalled him fondly. "He was the most amazing man, a larger-than-life character, but his great talent was that he could make you laugh as well as inform you. And so you felt very much part of the whole thing. He could be, for those days, a little bit risqué and say a few things that you couldn't get away with today, though.

"At one *Daily Express* Trophy meeting there was a really fierce battle going on for the lead, and poor old Peter was

getting really excited. He said: 'And they're coming down towards you for the last time. Everyone's on their feet, I am speechless, I can't hear what's happening, I can't see what's happening, what a commentator – f***ing deaf and dumb!' This was Peter at his absolute best."

Ian Titchmarsh, who began reporting on meetings before taking up commentating, recalled the primitive press facilities in those days. "The very first press box I remember, and this is going to be mid-sixties, I think was on the inside of the circuit on the top of the pits at the Woodcote Corner end. I can remember sitting in the press room and the thing waving in the breeze. It was certainly a fairly frail structure if the wind was at all strong. It just had a few desks. You had a reasonably good view because it was a very good place to watch from, looking over Woodcote Corner. You didn't worry about facilities, because in those days you used a typewriter and sent your report by Red Star on the train that evening, so you didn't have any instant communications.

"The commentators' facilities were pretty good. Silverstone had one of the best. There was the main commentary box in the Dunlop Tower, which was fine. There was a box at Becketts, which was OK, and which doubled up for the Club circuit, so there were two commentators for the Club circuit, and there was the box at Stowe. And then, for major meetings in the days before electronic timekeeping and sophisticated screens all over the place, I used to go into the timekeepers' box, which stuck out by the starting grid at Woodcote. That was a fairly small room, and at each Grand Prix, as each year went by, it used to get more and more full of equipment of one sort or another.

LEFT *Peter Scott-Russell in the commentary booth of the Dunlop Tower at Woodcote in 1976. (BRDC Archive)*

RIGHT *Principal commentator Ian Titchmarsh in the new commentary box overlooking Abbey Corner in 2011. (Author)*

"In the days when I started, you used to have a team of timekeepers led by a chap called Roy Oates, who was the chief BRDC timekeeper, with their chronographs, timing and doing the mental arithmetic and writing the times down. I'd just look over their shoulders and see who'd done the quickest time.

"Other commentators in those days included Keith Douglas, Neville Hay, and in the early days there was a chap called Peter Hamilton-Smith. At the early meetings I did, he was at Becketts, Neville or Anthony Marsh would be in the pits – Anthony used to be imported because he was the country's number one commentator – and Keith was at Stowe. Peter Scott-Russell was the presenter, he was the main commentator and did all the podium stuff. Then Peter Hamilton-Smith stopped commentating in the late seventies and Russell Douglas, Keith's son, came on the scene."

Keith Douglas commentated on 20 British Grands Prix, starting in the pits at Silverstone in 1959, and was a regular incumbent of the Stowe Corner commentary box from the early sixties until the late eighties.

"There'd be Peter or Keith in the main box and I'd be in the timekeepers' box relaying the times as they were worked out on a piece of paper," continued Titchmarsh. I was there when Keke Rosberg did his 160mph lap in 1985. That was certainly given out by me when I saw it in the timekeepers' box. There was no electronic timekeeping then, so you used to have to wait while they checked the figures. It never came up on a screen anywhere.

"For the early long-distance races, I wouldn't be in the timekeepers' box, so you had to do a manual lap chart. In the early days there were two people. The first six-hour race was 1976 and I had Jeremy Shaw, who was writing in those days for *Autosport*, and he was the most amazing lap-charter. It ended up with what Peter Scott-Russell would call a 'Silverstone-type finish'. And Jeremy with his one stopwatch and his lap chart was able to predict when the pit stops would come, and we were able to build it up into a fantastic finish. And that was before any kind of electronic timekeeping."

Titchmarsh recalled another occasion that wouldn't happen in today's world of instant electronic timing. "It was the last round of the BRDC Brush Fusegear Formula Ford Championship in 1977, and Nigel Mansell needed to win and take fastest lap to beat Trevor van Rooyen to the title. Well he won the race but we were waiting to hear from the timekeepers who had got fastest lap. At the end of the race there was this trolley that was wheeled out at the foot of the Dunlop Tower for the podium presentations – that went on for years and years and years; even happened when John Watson won the Grand Prix in '81.

"So this little trolley trundled out, and PSR was down there, and it was the last race of the day because the Formula Ford final was always the last race at National meetings because it was always dramatic. So this was the last race of the championship, last race of the year, and I remember Nigel standing on the podium waiting to hear whether or not he'd got the fastest lap, because the timekeepers were still doing the sums. Peter was down there, but didn't have any radio communication so he was waiting for me to say who had got it, then the call came through and Nigel had got fastest lap, and it was the first car racing championship he ever won."

SILVERSTONE SYD

One of the most familiar images of Silverstone is of a red Jaguar fire tender, lined up at the back of the grid and chasing the pack around on the first lap of every race. And the man behind the wheel of that Jaguar, 'Silverstone Syd' Herbert, has probably driven more laps of the circuit than anyone else.

"We've always tried to work out how many laps I've done, but we can never do it," Syd laughs. "It goes into too many. There's at least 30 race meetings I've done this year [2011] and if you say you do four laps for every race and you've got nine or ten races, when you multiply it up it comes to thousands."

In fact, on this basis and allowing for other outings, Syd must have completed around 50,000 laps of Silverstone over the last 40 years.

Syd Herbert spent 15 years working for the London Ambulance Service and briefly raced a 500cc Kieft in the mid-fifties before starting to marshal at Silverstone. In 1968 he became part of the British Motor Racing Marshals' Club emergency services team when it was formed at the request of the track's managing director Jimmy Brown.

"I joined the British Motor Racing Marshals' Club and a few of us started the emergency services up here, because I had a friend who was going to get us an ambulance," he explained. "They didn't have ambulances here as such. Well they had an ambulance – they called it the horse box. No windows in the side, but it had windows in the roof. The marshals' club got together and through the circuit we bought two ambulances, and then we decided we were going to start this emergency services team, and we kitted out a van with cutting equipment."

Syd was taken on in a permanent role at the circuit following an incident in June 1969 during testing for the British Grand Prix.

"Jack Brabham had a big off at Club and was trapped in the car," he explained. "It took them ages to get him out, and he was sitting in fuel, and you know how that burns you, so he wasn't very pleased about it. And they had to wait to get his mechanic down there, and his mechanic in those days was Ron Dennis, and they got him out." Brabham was taken to hospital where it was discovered that he had broken his ankle.

"Jimmy Brown said, 'We're not having that again, we want somebody here who knows what they're doing on the medical side, but also knows how to cut people out.' Anyway, they had

BELOW *Some of Silverstone's rescue vehicles: a 1960s FG Ambulance, the Patrick Motors Incident Vehicle, Land Rover Fire Tender No.3 and the V12 Jaguar Fire Tender No.7. (Syd Herbert collection/Harold Barker)*

a meeting and decided to ask me to come to work here. So I
came up here, and that was in September '69.

Prior to this, testing at the circuit had been very informal.
Drivers just turned up, paid Jimmy Brown the fee and parked
their vehicles on the outside of the track between Abbey and
Woodcote corners, opposite where the first pits had been
located. There were no marshals and the whole exercise was
completely unsupervised, with cars of all varieties taking to
the track at the same time.

"My responsibilities were medical aid and getting people
out, and running the testing," explained Syd. "I ran all the
testing that was on here. In those days there was only me on
the *Daily Express* bridge. There was a little sentry box and I
used to sit in there and I had a phone. And I used to stand up
there looking out and watching them going round, and I used
to go to the paddock in the morning and see the drivers, so
that if anybody saw anything or heard anything they gave me
a wave. So then I jumped in the ambulance, and in there I had
a pair of bolt croppers and spanners and bits of rope, and that
was how it all started.

"At the main entrance, where the visitor centre is now,
that's where the office used to be. It was in an old Nissen hut,
which was the original guardroom of the camp years ago, and
on the end of it there was a garage, and in that garage they
used to keep the first ambulance we had. All the rest of the
kit was down this back road with the pigs, and if you came
testing on a Friday it was very smelly because they always used
to pump the effluent out on a Friday. Then they used to take
it down to Dadford and spray it on those fields.

"You came in the gate, and Jimmy Brown's wife Kay had
this big board behind her, and it had all these big keys
hanging on it for all these different huts that were on the site.
You had to sign on and pay your money – it was about ten
shillings I think – and then you had a day's testing.

"When you were marshalling you'd start off with the lowest
job, and that was running messages. You used to get the
results, run across the track between races, climb up the top
of the ladder and give it to the commentator and then climb
all the way down again.

"The original pedestrian bridge was taken down and a
bigger one put up. They stood the old one on end on the
Copse runway and that was a tower, fire tower we called it.
And you had a ladder to climb up, and you stood at the top of
this tower looking round, and if you saw something happen,
like a fire or something, you had a load of stones up there,
and you threw them down on the hut below and that used to
turn them out, and you'd say 'over there'. That was about '66
or '67.

"Land Rover used to loan them a Series One that had
places in the back for fire extinguishers, and we used to put
air tools in so we could use rip chisels, and things like that,
to get bodywork away. Rover decided that if Jimmy Brown or

the BRDC would allow them to put a Rover sign at the end of Woodcote, they could have the Land Rover.

"So we'd got this Land Rover, which was number one fire tender. Then, after a few accidents we had with a couple of fires, they decided to buy six second-hand Land Rovers. Then we got Pyrene, as it was in those days, which then became Chubb, and they put these cylinders in there. You had two vessels, one was full of water and the other was full of mixed concentrate, so you could either put the fire out with just water or put it out with the concentrate.

"Northants Fire Brigade used to come up here at the big meetings and they used to bring two big fire tenders. One used to park with us at the fire tower and the other used to park at the outside by the *Motor* bridge, where the gap was.

"We had long talks about these fires and decided it would be a good idea to have people up here during the week when testing was on. So we got in touch with Brackley and Daventry Fire Stations, and so we used to get off-duty firemen who were willing to come and man the fire tenders on the corners.

In the aftermath of the major accident at the 1973 British Grand Prix, 'Lofty' England, chief executive of Jaguar, suggested that Silverstone use an XJ12 as a fire tender, and this turned out to be the catalyst for Syd's nickname being bestowed upon him.

"I don't know who first called me Silverstone Syd," he said. "Some commentator, but I don't remember who it was. There used to be two blokes and they were like the two old boys in the *Muppet Show*, just talking to themselves, not telling you what's going on on the track. And one of them called me Pyrene Percy, then it suddenly became Silverstone Syd.

"After the '73 accident, that's when we first got hold of the Jaguar. Jimmy Brown and Lofty England were great mates, and Lofty said, 'If I give you a car and we get it converted by Pyrene into a fire tender, could you use it as a chase car?' Jimmy said 'yes', so they got the car and it came down here, and I had to look after it and make sure it was fuelled up and everything.

"We used to park it up on the ramp outside what used to be the drivers' wives' Doghouse Club, so there were always all these females to chat to. The first time I drove it, it was an historic sports car race. I was sitting there, and Jimmy came up and said, 'What are you doing there?' I said, 'You told me no one else was to drive it', and he said, 'You'd better follow them then, hadn't you.' So I go off the ramp, round behind them and off we go. And I hadn't driven it quick – ever. So I arrived at Becketts, turned in and I lost the back end. It had power steering and I lost where the wheels were going. There was a load of blue smoke. Anyway, I suppose I did nearly a 360, as it didn't go all the way round. I got it straight and carried on. And, of course, by then the observer had reported it, the commentator had mentioned it, and I think that might have been when I was first called Silverstone Syd.

"On the Monday, Lofty England came down and said, 'You've been mucking my car around,' because it was originally his company car and it was the only one with a six-litre engine. And I said, 'Well, all I can tell you is the back end went out and there was no way I could get it back.' He said, 'Let me drive it.' So he drove it and promptly nearly spun at Becketts. He said, 'I know what's wrong, there'll be some blokes down tomorrow to fix it.' And they came down the next day and put an anti-roll bar on the rear, and it was like driving a lovely little saloon car after that."

The red Jaguar with Syd at the wheel soon became a familiar sight at every meeting, including the Grands Prix, where the FIA's medical delegate Professor Sid Watkins would be in another chase car.

"We used to chase every Grand Prix with the Jag before anybody else chased it," explained Syd. "And then we got a car for Sid Watkins, and at one Grand Prix I nearly ran into his car. He used to agree with me that it's better that I went first and they went second, because if there's a fire, he can't do anything until you've put the fire out. But then the people in charge decided that it should be the FIA bloke first.

"So we go into Copse, it was in the turbo era and Derek Warwick and Stefan Johansson had a coming together. Johansson's in the Ferrari, Warwick's in the Renault. Warwick was punted off but Stefan carried on. But he'd pulled the oil cooler out of the sidepod, so there's oil all the way round the circuit. We didn't notice it to start with, turned into Becketts and Sid's driver has got it real sideways and I'm steaming straight for the side of the car. But he managed to catch it and he went out wide, and I went inside him and then down Hangar Straight I let him go by again."

In recognition of his skills, in 1988 Syd was presented with the 1987 International Jaguar Driver of the Year Award at a ceremony in front of the Shell Oils Tower at the *Autosport* 1000km meeting in May. He is also one of the 'Guardians' of the BRDC, charged with protecting the interests of the club.

And, as many drivers found out over the years, Syd's word was the law. "During testing I used to tell people, no matter who they were, you either worked to the rules that we had here, or you didn't bother," he said. "There have been drivers I used to send home – told them that they couldn't go out any more and had better go to the office and get their money back. If people don't obey the rules there's going to be an accident."

And even the greatest racing drivers in the world respected and sometimes feared him. "When we ran on the South circuit, you came up to Abbey and then you went through this slot to get to Becketts. The first time that Ayrton Senna ran on it, he went out and he turned right instead of left. He got down to Club, and by then I've got on the radio saying, 'stop him, whatever you do, turn him round and tell him to come back'. So the bloke stopped him down there and said to him, 'They want you back there.' And he said, 'I don't want to go back because Syd's waiting for me and he'll give me a bollocking.'

"I think that I was here at the right time to really have had an enjoyable umpteen years."

Bikes, karts and trucks

"I well remember some great dices on my 500cc Matchless, with five or six of us going at it for the whole race, with the usual do or die 'suicide run' through the old flat-out Woodcote on the last lap trying to beat each other across the line. Crazy stuff, but good fun."

Stuart Graham

The first motorbike event at Silverstone was on 8 October 1949 when the British Motorcycle Racing Club (BMCRC) held its prestigious Hutchinson 100 meeting at the circuit, which became home to the event until 1965. The winner that day was Les Graham, who set a lap record of 90.05mph on an AJS 'porcupine'. The following year, the Motor Cycle Club (MCC) held the first of what was to become an annual meeting at the circuit, and during the fifties the BMCRC organised a 'Silverstone Saturday' each April, with a dozen or so scratch races.

All the top riders of the day competed at the circuit, and in 1951 Geoff Duke won three major races and set a new lap record of 92.92mph. At the same meeting, Eric Oliver won the first sidecar event held at the circuit on his Norton-Watsonian.

On 4 July 1959, the first Clubman's Trophy meeting was organised at the circuit by the BMCRC, with the two main races, at 116.8 miles over 40 laps of the circuit, being the longest to have been held on the mainland of Great Britain since the war. This was surpassed on 20 May 1961,

RIGHT *Leon Haslam leads the field on his BMW at the start of the World Superbike Championship round on 4–5 August 2012. (LAT)*

though, when the club held the Silverstone 1000, a 1,000km (620 mile) race for production touring machines, with two riders per bike. It was won by Bruce Daniels and Peter Darvill on a BMW.

By 1962, the circuit was hosting the Hutchinson 100, the Silverstone 1000, and the Baragwanath Trophy meeting for novices on the club circuit, in addition to the annual MCC meeting. Over the years, top names who raced and won at Silverstone included John Surtees, Mike Hailwood, Derek Minter, Giacomo Agostini, Phil Read and Barry Sheene.

LEFT *Mrs Bluebell Gibbs pictured at Becketts Corner on a Norton during the Motor Cycle Club's meeting of September 1952. (BRDC Archive/Harold Barker)*

BELOW *The start of the fifth event of the day at the 1953 Hutchinson 100 meeting. (Mortons Archive)*

ABOVE *Norton's Eric Oliver, twice a winner on the day, leads double runner-up Cyril Smith at the 1953 Hutchinson 100 meeting. (Mortons Archive)*

John Surtees

"I first went to Silverstone with my father, who raced there with his motorcycle and sidecar just after the war. When I first raced there I saw the circuit very closely, and particularly Abbey Curve. I had a little 1938 250cc Triumph Tiger 70, which I modified for racing as a number of other people did, and I'd tried to improve performance – all my own work as a lad tinkering in the shed, and as an apprentice down at Vincents. And I thought I'd increased its performance. Perhaps I had, because the con-rod broke in the middle of Abbey Curve and sent me sliding down the road – so that was my first insight into Silverstone.

"After that, I went there and rode on Nortons, MV Augusta, and I won on each of the motor cycles I ever raced there. After having tried for two years as a privateer to beat Geoff Duke – who was a world champion on a Gilera, while I was on my private Norton – in 1954 I nearly did it. But one of the most momentous races for me was a ride when I beat Geoff Duke fair and square riding a Norton, and him on a Gilera, at the end-of-season race in 1955. And what was nice about it, it was the last race for the renowned head of Norton, Joe Craig, who had been the chief engineer and architect of much of Norton's success over the years.

"Silverstone was a wide circuit, but remember there is a line and a lot of space which is never used. There's a section of a racetrack that has all the activity, and so vast spaces of concrete don't make much difference. What the difficulty is on airfield circuits is there are no features to be able to judge, so you couldn't rely on features round the circuit, you had to work purely on distances.

"Silverstone's a good circuit, but you wouldn't have put it along with the old Nürburgring, the old Spa or the old Monza. I would put Silverstone in the second tier."

Another regular competitor was Stuart Graham, son of Les Graham, and he went on to enjoy success on four wheels at the circuit as well. "I well remember some great dices on my 500cc Matchless, with five or six of us going at it for the whole race, with the usual do or die 'suicide run' through the old flat-out Woodcote on the last lap trying to beat each other across the line," he recalled. "Crazy stuff, but good fun."

On 22 August 1971, the Auto Cycle Union (ACU) organised the John Player Silverstone Trophy International, which provided wins for Giacomo Agostini on his three-cylinder MV Agusta in both the 350cc and 500cc, and Barry Sheene won the 125cc event on a Suzuki and the 250cc on a Yamaha. Every lap record was broken that weekend, witnessed by a crowd of 27,000, up to then a record for a Silverstone bike meeting.

In 1975, the British round of the new Formula 750 Championship was held at the John Player Grand Prix meeting on 10 August, providing a popular home win for Sheene on his Suzuki in front of a crowd of 30,000. But it wasn't until 14 August 1977 that an actual British Motorcycle Grand Prix was held at the track, with victory going to Pat Hennen on a Suzuki. Prior to this the British round of the world championships had always been held on the Isle of Man. The riders used the old Woodcote Corner, bypassing the chicane, which had been built in 1975.

Kenny Roberts

"Silverstone was one of my favourites for sure, and was one of the racetracks that I excelled at.

"At the 1979 British Grand Prix I was leading in the world championship and I knew Barry [Sheene] was going to be tough – it's in Britain. And I really had to beat a guy named Eugenio Ferrari. I had a great qualifying; I was on pole. So I started the warm-up lap, did a huge wheelie and it plugged the airbox up – the vent in the transmission – and it blew the clutch seal out. And I realised that it was all oily, so I came back to the start line, and in those days you came back to the start, shut the bike off, and you got ready to push it.

"But they're like – 'Shit, the clutch seal's out!' So they pushed the clutch seal back in and they cleaned it off. Even Giacomo Agostini was cleaning it because the wheel had oil over it. And I was very lucky, they came over and said, 'We can't wait any longer', and we were cleaning it as we were going to pole position.

"So, for me the whole thing was very lucky. Now, Sheene was another thing. When I caught Sheene I got in the duel with him. I tried to outrun him, but I couldn't. I couldn't outrun him; he couldn't outrun me. So I knew it was going to come down to the last lap, and so we spent the whole race me sizing him up, him sizing me up, and where we were going to make the pass, because we knew it was going to come down to the last lap. 'Cos if you did it as long as we've done it, you know what's going to come up.

"And the corner coming on to the short back straight [Abbey], I could take that left-hander flat out. I couldn't do it every lap, but if everything was right I could do it, and that's what won the race. The Yamaha did accelerate. Sometimes it didn't accelerate as good as the Suzuki, but at Silverstone it was all high-speed and I was a lot better at high-speed stuff than I was at low-speed stuff. So Silverstone was right up my alley.

"So the advantage I felt to me was that corner, and the advantage to him he felt was the straightaway coming on to that, but I got such a gap on him, he couldn't make it up. I could go through Abbey flat, but he couldn't, he had to shut off, and when he'd shut off – too late, you know, I'm already gone. So it really capped him right there. That's what won the race, because he would have beat me had I not been able to do that, because if he'd just come into that corner beside me there was no way I could have beaten him, no way.

"We came into the last corner with me leading. And he tried to pass me on the outside, 'cos he knew he wasn't going to get me on the inside. So I knew where he was at, and I knew where I had to be. I was going to make it tough for him. I could see the start-finish line. I knew where that was, and the thing about racing with Barry, I knew he would give me room and he knew I would give him room. We weren't going to kill each other. We didn't like each other, but we weren't going to kill each other.

"Obviously we both won, but I got the money and the trophy and that's what everybody talks about. There's a couple of races in my career that everybody talks about, and that's one of them."

ABOVE *Kenny Roberts and Barry Sheene battle it out during the 1979 Marlboro British Motorcycle Grand Prix. Roberts just beat Sheene to the line by three-hundredths of a second. (Mortons Archive)*

The circuit continued to host the Grand Prix for the next ten years. Kenny Roberts was the most successful 500cc rider, winning on his Yamaha in 1978, '79 and '83, though the latter race was marred by the deaths of Peter Huber and Norman Brown in an accident on the fifth lap. The South African rider Kork Ballington won more Grand Prix races than any other rider at the circuit over those ten years, winning both 250cc and 350cc events, riding for Yamaha and then Kawasaki.

But it is perhaps the 1979 Marlboro British Motorcycle Grand Prix that has gone down in history for producing one of the greatest duels ever fought over the circuit between Kenny Roberts on a Yamaha and Barry Sheene on a Suzuki, with Roberts just pipping Sheene to the line by three hundredths of a second (see sidebar).

In 1982, Sheene was seriously injured at the track during testing. It was an incident that Syd Herbert, who ran all the test sessions at the track, remembers well. "That was partly my fault," he said. "I was putting the chequered flag out and I saw him and Jack Middelburg coming round, and I thought, they'll catch the slow ones up, so they can have another lap. So I let them go by, and some bloke had dropped his bike and the blokes on the bridge had run down and got hold of the rider and pulled him on the grass, but they had left the bike out on the track. Barry came round and, he always did it if he was having a bit of a go with someone as he was with Jack Middelburg, he was looking under his arm, looking back. By the time he looked up it was too late. He hit it hard. The fuel tank of the Suzuki hit the bridge on fire and left a burn mark on there for ages until I told them it should be rubbed off."

Wayne Gardner

"I used to like Silverstone. I not only won a Grand Prix around there but I also won many four-stroke races when I was racing for Honda Britain. I'd won in the dry, I'd won in the wet, so I had a little bit of a history on the track and understood it. But I used to love riding Silverstone, and I always looked forward to riding there. That was the old circuit; now it's changed since then. But I used to like the big long Hangar Straight, and the fast left coming up the hill towards Woodcote, the last corner.

"It was a great layout and unique in its way. I regard two tracks in the world as the best, and that's Brno in Czechoslovakia [now the Czech Republic] and Phillip Island in Australia. But I regard Silverstone up there near them, because I like fast, flowing corners. I don't like start-stop type second-gear corners or first-gear corners. I never did like that, and I like a more ballsy style track and that is what Silverstone was – fast and sweeping and high-speed, where you've got to have a big set of goolies to make the most out of your lap time.

"My recollection of the '86 British Grand Prix was that it was heavy rain. I've always been well known for being fast in the wet, so I realised that obviously we had a chance of winning. I remember it being freezing cold – very, very cold that day,

and there was a lot of rain. It was really hard to see and I know it was really slippery because I had a couple of near crashes during the race – like big slides.

"It was my first year as a works Honda rider and I went into the race knowing that I had a chance of possibly winning it, but I didn't know the potential of some of the other riders. I had really, really cold hands and I could hardly feel the controls, but I was working my way through the field and I remember passing Didier de Radigues, who's a really good friend and who was leading the race, and unfortunately he never won a 500cc Grand Prix, so I probably took it off him that day.

"But I remember coming round Woodcote, and sliding and slipping, spinning the wheel, and I remember looking up, trying to see the team with their pit board, and then the first corner – that's where I had a couple of big slides, I'd turn in and the rear would let go.

"So, yeah, I rode really, really hard that day, but again I had a history of doing very well in the wet conditions, so obviously I used that opportunity and it gave me confidence. But I can tell you, I didn't win without having some big moments. It was f***ing slippery, but a great memory for sure."

The last 500cc British Motorcycle Grand Prix to be held at the track was in 1986 and was won by Wayne Gardner, riding a Rothmans Honda. The event moved to Donington in 1987, and bike racing all but disappeared from the Silverstone calendar until the Superbike Challenge meetings of 1992 and April '93, followed by a Classic Motorcycle Festival, which started in 1995. The British Superbikes were back in September 1998 and became a regular fixture on the calendar. World Superbikes appeared for the first time in May 2002 and produced an epic battle between Troy Bayliss and Colin Edwards, while other meetings organised by MCRCB and the MCC made a reappearance.

When it was announced in 2008 that Silverstone was to lose the F1 British Grand Prix to Donington, the circuit responded swiftly by negotiating for the British round of MotoGP to head in the opposite direction from 2010 onwards, and initial plans for changes to the layout of the circuit were made with the bike riders specifically in mind. And so, with the existing British and World Superbike meetings well established on the calendar, when Jorge Lorenzo, on a Yamaha, won the 2010 Air Asia British Grand Prix on 20 June it completed the hat-trick of top-line bike racing at Silverstone.

BELOW *Reigning world champion Anton Mang leads the 350cc field on his Kawasaki at the 1982 British Motorcycle Grand Prix. (Mortons Archive)*

Karts and trucks

In 1978, Jimmy Brown, together with Dean Delamont of the RAC, instigated the first-ever British Kart Grand Prix. The event, which was supported by the *Daily Express* and Hermetite, was held over six laps of the Grand Prix circuit on 30 July. A total of 328 entries were received from eight countries, with the Hermetite Zip-Yamaha works team taking a one-two victory in the hands of Paul Elmore and Martin Hines.

During the eighties the British Kart Grand Prix became a major event, and although it declined in importance, it remained a regular event at the circuit for 20 years before moving to Pembrey in 1998.

The other on-track phenomenon of the eighties was the Multipart British Truck Grand Prix, first held on 18 August 1985, which used to draw up to 50,000 spectators and included star names such as Barry Sheene and Barry Lee. The trucks raced on the Grand Prix circuit, but with a special tight chicane inserted on the exit of Woodcote, and were separated into three different categories with differing horsepower and weight to achieve a degree of equivalency. Each category had its own race, and then the three combined for a grand final.

That first event, held in appalling conditions, was won by Gaudenzio Mantova in his orange-coloured Scania, who then stopped on Hangar Straight, tipped up the cab, and was seen fiddling with the seals of the fuel pumps. When challenged after the presentation, he ran off with the trophy and wasn't seen again. The Italian was subsequently excluded from the results, handing the victory to Richard Walker's Leyland Roadtrain, ahead of the Mercedes-Benz duo of Steve Parrish and Barry Lee.

Willie Green stormed through the field in the following year's event after having to pit after the engine cover of his ERF flew up and hit the windscreen while he was lying third. Green dropped to tenth but fought back to regain third place at the finish, just behind winner Curt Goransson's Volvo N12 and the Iveco of Angelo Rangoni.

Former ATS and Tyrrell Grand Prix driver Slim Borgudd, driving a Volvo White Boss II, won the 1987 event, which was broadcast live by the BBC, with Goransson's Volvo N12 in second ahead of the Mercedes-Benz of Heinz Dehnhardt. The event was interrupted by a big accident at Abbey when two trucks collided with such force that a rear axle was broken off and gouged lumps out of the track as it bounced along. In subsequent years a truck event was held at the track, but not a race on the scale of the three Grands Prix.

The future

The building of the Wing in 2011 completed phase two of Silverstone's plans. Phase one had been the opening of the new track layout the year before, but there was still much to be done. In December 2011, both Aylesbury Vale District Council and South Northamptonshire Council approved the circuit's outline planning application for its 20-year Masterplan – the next big step towards securing the long-term future of the circuit.

The term 'Masterplan' is appropriate, since the development is both ambitious and extensive, including permanent cantilevered grandstands, three hotels, a new visitor and heritage centre, a kart track and business and technology parks.

"There's a number of different initiatives in there, but which ones will come first will depend," explained Richard Phillips. "One that we're looking at is an international kart circuit. That will be on the inside of the National circuit, over near the Copse runway. We have a business plan for that, we know how much it's going to cost, we know who our partners are going to be and we have planning permission for that to develop. So that's one, which will stand up on its own two feet.

"We have a plan for a corporate, debenture grandstand and integrated hotel the other side of the track from the Wing, with a bridge across to the commentary boxes, but that's a massive project. There will be a bridge that will take pedestrians, and the Wing is actually engineered to take it, so it's not a brand new thing, it's something that's already been designed in. It comes into the building at high level.

"We also have plans for a tunnel near the Wing, though that will be quite expensive, but that's how we'll get vehicles in and out in the future. Then there's the visitor centre, or Silverstone Square. We're putting a lottery bid together for that, and there'll be an archive, museum, and 3D cinema, lots for kids, and other things in there as well including a big superstore, but obviously that's further in the future."

It's one thing planning development, of course, it's another funding it, and Silverstone has been actively seeking an investment partner.

"Where we've got to now," said Phillips, "is we've stabilised the business, we've doubled the turnover, we've made it profitable, we've diversified it and we're further diversifying it. But there comes a point where you've got to say, this is about as far as we can go. We've got the ability to go further but we haven't got the cash in order to be able to do it. So that's why we've been looking for a potential partner in terms of an investor who will come in and start to do these other big projects, and that includes developing the estate."

One development already in place is the Silverstone University Technical College (UTC), due to open at the circuit in autumn 2013. The college is located on the outside of the circuit between Woodcote and Copse corners, directly opposite the old pits and paddock complex.

University Technical Colleges offer 14–19-year-olds the opportunity to learn in a very practical way, integrating national curriculum requirements with technical and vocational elements. The Silverstone UTC is an educational partnership between Tresham College of Further and Higher Education, University of Northampton and Silverstone Circuit. It will specialise in technical and academic learning in high-performance engineering and motor sport, as well as technical events management. "That's the sort of project that we love," said Phillips. "It's really giving opportunities to kids who don't get opportunities in the normal educational system. That's a government flagship project."

One of the ways in which Silverstone has diversified is by selling its expertise. "We've got two attitudes to the way we're building the business here," explained Phillips. "A few years ago we introduced something called Silverstone International, which organises car launches. We did the Nissan GTR launch, we handle the Bentley account, the Audi account and various other accounts, including Sony Playstation. And we do them all over the world, so we've worked in the Middle East, the Far East, America and Russia, and we've got pretty good people here running that side of it. So we've got capital projects, but also other projects that don't need capital expenditure but that will diversify the business and increase our revenues."

The work with car manufacturers will eventually evolve into what Phillips describes as 'Motor City'. "We've brought in Mercedes this year [2012] and there's a lot of these programmes we run now. The whole concept eventually comes round more or less to what Porsche have here, which is a brand centre with facilities where you can demonstrate the cars and compare cars to each other. It's the buying experience for the top end of the market.

"It's not easy, but I think people are beginning to see the brand is building, and they can see that Silverstone is something to be proud of, and it's got a great future for the nation really.

"Whatever happens, Silverstone will be here. We've brought it a long way now and it's on the verge of doing great things, and it needs the right partners to do that. A lot of people have got a lot of faith in it now and it's getting that sort of recognition."

The hunt for the right partner has not been an easy task. Towards the end of 2011, negotiations were well advanced with one group, but by May the following year no deal had been reached and the exclusivity on the agreement ran out. The BRDC said at the time that if a suitable partner could not be found, the club would still continue with developments, albeit at a slower pace.

In early 2013, the BRDC seemed to be close to concluding a deal with an external investor which would further secure the circuit's long-term future.

Squint at a map of the new track layout and you can just about recognise that it's Silverstone. On the ground, though, there are few familiar landmarks anymore. The bridge over the old main straight between Woodcote and Copse has gone, and the spectator banking that used to run down to Copse, affording views of the pits to the general spectator, has been replaced by a faceless gravel run-off area.

Copse is still there, with the raised concrete terracing, and the walk down to Becketts is the same as it used to be. Around the Becketts esses sits a high viewing bank, leading down to Hangar Straight and Stowe Corner. Here

a grassy bank affords good views of the cars as they head through Vale towards what is now the last corner of the lap – Club. And beyond that sits the somewhat incongruous edifice that is the Wing. With the building of this new complex, Silverstone finally stopped being a part of rural Northamptonshire and Buckinghamshire and took on the appearance of a state-of-the-art facility comparable to any of the new tracks that have sprung up in remote parts of the world.

Abbey is now the first corner, and the cars sweep round, flat out, until they brake heavily for Village and the Loop. Grandstands along this section afford good views before the cars power down Wellington Straight to the Brooklands and Luffield area.

The area around Luffield is vastly improved now the infield has been opened up, increasing the number of ordinary spectators the circuit can accommodate. And then there's Woodcote – such an evocative name to any motor racing enthusiast.

When the start line was moved Woodcote lost some of its significance, but the spirit of that corner still survives: standing on the inside of the track at the Silverstone Classic, as F1 cars of the seventies and eighties powered on the edge of adhesion out of Club, it was easy to imagine you were watching Woodcote in the old days.

With all the changes of recent years, and those still planned to be phased in over the next 20 years or so, the Silverstone of today is a far, far cry from the circuit of the fifties. But look at a schedule of events there today and you will see that many of the clubs which started organising races in the early days, such as the Vintage Sports Car Club, the MG Car Club, the Bentley Drivers' Club, the Aston Martin Owners' Club, the 750 Motor Club, with its annual six-hour event, and the British Motorcycle Racing Club, still run meetings at the circuit today, demonstrating a continuity of over 60 years of club racing at Silverstone.

So perhaps it is fair to say that, despite all the changes since its inception, Silverstone is still very much the home of British motor racing.

Appendix

Many of the names of corners and features on the Silverstone Grand Prix circuit date back to 1948 and/or derive from local history.

International Pits Straight (2010)
The straight between Club and Abbey, a named feature since 2010.

Abbey Curve (1948)
Luffield Abbey Farm is what the existing farm used to be called. It was the farm serving the Abbey or Priory, which seems to have its origins in the 12th century. A chicane was introduced in 1994, although the old Abbey Curve, the last corner of the 1948 track still in use, was preserved for the Historic Festival until 2007. Since 2010, Abbey has been a right-hander and, since 2011, the first corner after the start when the full Grand Prix circuit and international pits are in use.

Farm Curve (2010)
This is the long left-hander after Abbey and passes close to the farm and the BRDC campsite.

Farm Straight (1991)
This was the relatively short straight between Abbey and Bridge and is a name that has rarely been used over the years. Originally it would have been part of the Pits Straight, since from 1948 until 1951 the pits were located between Abbey and Woodcote.

Bridge Bend (1991)
This corner did not exist before 1991 and was named after the vehicle bridge that crosses over the track just before the corner. It ceased to be used after the track changes in 2010.

Village Corner (2010)
This is the right-hander after Farm Curve and is named after Silverstone village.

The Loop (2010)
The long left-hand corner following Village, so called because of its configuration and because it loops back towards the original circuit.

Aintree (2010)
The gradual left-hander following the Loop. It is named after the circuit where the British Grand Prix took place in 1955, 1957, 1959, 1961 and 1962.

Wellington Straight (2010)
This used to be known as the National Straight and was renamed in 2010 as a tribute to the aircraft which were based at Silverstone during the Second World War. The straight follows the line of one of the old runways.

Priory Corner (1991)
Named after Luffield Priory (see Abbey). This ceased to be used after the track changes in 2010.

Brooklands Corner (1991)
Named after the UK's original racetrack.

Luffield Corner (1991)
Named after the old Priory (see Abbey and Priory). Originally two separate corners, Luffield One and Luffield Two, joined by a short straight, but revised to one continuous corner in 1997.

Woodcote (Corner) (1948)
For some reason the word 'Corner' is not shown on the circuit map in the 1948 race programme. It was named after the RAC's Country Club in Surrey as was the last corner at Goodwood, also opened in 1948. In 1975, the famous and spectacular Woodcote Chicane was introduced for that year's Grand Prix. It was replaced in 1987 by a 90° left on the approach from Abbey, followed by a right-hand curve leading into the original Woodcote. This lasted until the major revamp in 1991 and was simply known as 'New Woodcote'.

National Pits Straight (2010)
The straight between Woodcote and Copse. A named feature since 2010.

Copse Corner (1948)
Adjacent to Chapel Copse wood and Foxhole Copse.

Maggots Corner (1948)
Adjacent to Maggot (sic) Moor.

Becketts Corner (1948)
Adjacent to the ancient (1174) Chapel of St Thomas the Martyr, named after Thomas Becket, Archbishop of Canterbury, who had been murdered by knights of the court of King Henry II in December 1170.

Chapel Curve (1948)
As Becketts above.

Hangar Straight (1948)
Alongside this straight there used to be two hangars, a legacy of the Second World War.

Stowe Corner (1948)
Located just north of Stowe School.

Vale (1991)
This feature was introduced in 1991 when both the exit of Stowe and the entry to Club Corner were reprofiled. The link between the two corners bypassed the old circuit and was set at a lower level to provide some undulation in an otherwise rather flat circuit. It was thus a kind of vale and was also located in the area of Aylesbury Vale District Council. Circuit maps issued in 1991 refer to the straight between Stowe and Club as 'Vale' not 'The Vale'. 'The Vale' is common usage but not what was originally intended.

Club Corner (1948)
The RAC organised the first Grand Prix and was instrumental in the naming of the corners, so that this name was chosen to reflect the RAC's clubhouse in Pall Mall. When the entry to Club was substantially modified in 1991 with a 90-degree left before the long right-hander, the whole sequence was still called Club. The tight left-hander is *not* 'Vale', or 'The Vale', but the first part of Club Corner.

Ian Titchmarsh

Bibliography

British Grand Prix: A History,
by Richard Hough, published by Hutchinson, 1958

The Silverstone Story,
by Philip Turner, supplement to the *Motor*, week ending
14 July 1973

Silverstone: The Story of Britain's Fastest Circuit,
by Peter Carrick, published by Pelham Books, 1974

Autocourse 1985–86,
edited by Maurice Hamilton, published by Hazleton Publishing, 1985

40 Silverstone Years,
edited by Ray Hutton, published by Motor Racing Publications Ltd, 1988

British Grand Prix,
by Maurice Hamilton, published by The Crowood Press, 1989

Silverstone: Fifty Golden Years,
edited by Ray Hutton, published by the BRDC and Motor Racing
Publications Ltd, 1998

Frank Williams,
by Maurice Hamilton, published by Macmillan, 1998

Silverstone: An Historical Mosaic,
compiled by Elaine Lovell, published by Silverstone Appraisal Group,
2001

Maserati: A Racing History,
by Anthony Pritchard, published by Haynes, 2003

Lotus 72: Formula One Icon,
by Michael Oliver, published by Coterie Press, 2003

Grand Prix Data Book,
by David Hayhoe and David Holland,
published by Haynes, 2006.

Sports Car Racing in Camera, 1960–69,
by Paul Parker, published by Haynes, 2007

Winning is Not Enough,
by Jackie Stewart, published by Headline, 2007

**Endurance Racing at Silverstone in the
1970s & 1980s**,
by Chas Parker, published by Veloce, 2010

The Battle for the British Grand Prix,
by Alan Henry, published by Haynes, 2010

Bernie: The Biography of Bernie Ecclestone,
by Susan Watkins, published by Haynes, 2010

Sports Car Racing in Camera, 1950–59,
by Paul Parker, published by Haynes, 2010

www.wartimememories.co.uk
www.silverstonevillage.org
www.silverstone.org
www.forix.com
www.oldracingcars.com
www.500race.org
www.silhouet.com/motorsport
www.formula2.net

Sundry copies of **Autocar**, 1948.
Every issue of **Autosport**, 1950–2012.

Motor Sport Digital Archive 1924–1949; 1950–59; 1960–69; 1970–79;
1980–89; 1990–99.

Silverstone Dream 1979,
a Castrol Classic, published by Duke Video, 2006

The Birth of Formula One,
BP Video Library, published by Duke Video, 2010

Index

GENERAL INDEX

INDEX OF PEOPLE

INDEX OF CARS, CLUBS, RACES AND EVENTS

Please note that sponsors' names have been omitted from race titles.
Cars are only indexed if photographed – references to cars in the main text are not included.